NO GROWTH WITHOUT EQUITY?
INEQUALITY, INTERESTS, AND
COMPETITION IN MEXICO

NO GROWTH WITHOUT EQUITY?
INEQUALITY, INTERESTS, AND
COMPETITION IN MEXICO

Santiago Levy and Michael Walton

Editors

A copublication of Palgrave Macmillan and the World Bank

A copublication of The World Bank and Palgrave Macmillan.

Palgrave Macmillan
Houndmills, Basingstoke, Hampshire RG21 6XS and
175 Fifth Avenue, New York, N. Y. 10010
Companies and representatives throughout the world

Palgrave Macmillan is the global academic imprint of the Palgrave Macmillan division of St. Martin's Press, LLC and of Palgrave Macmillan Ltd.

Macmillan® is a registered trademark in the United States, United Kingdom and other countries. Palgrave® is a registered trademark in the European Union and other countries.

This volume is a product of the staff of the International Bank for Reconstruction and Development / The World Bank. The findings, interpretations, and conclusions expressed in this volume do not necessarily reflect the views of the Executive Directors of The World Bank or the governments they represent.

The World Bank does not guarantee the accuracy of the data included in this work. The boundaries, colors, denominations, and other information shown on any map in this work do not imply any judgement on the part of The World Bank concerning the legal status of any territory or the endorsement or acceptance of such boundaries.

Softcover
ISBN: 978-0-8213-7767-3
eISBN: 978-0-8213-7768-0
DOI: 10.1596/978-0-8213-7767-3

Hardcover
ISBN: 978-0-8213-7769-7
DOI: 10.1596/978-0-8213-7769-7

Library of Congress Cataloging-in-Publication Data
No growth without equity? : inequality, interests and competition in Mexico / editors Santiago Levy and Michael Walton.
    p. cm.
  Includes bibliographical references and index.
  ISBN 978-0-8213-7767-3 (pbk.) — ISBN 978-0-8213-7769-7 (hardback) — ISBN 978-0-8213-7768-0 (electronic)
  1. Income distribution—Mexico. 2. Economic development—Mexico. I. Levy, Santiago. II. Walton, Michael.
  HC140.I5N6 2009
  330.972—dc22
                        2008044234

Other Titles in the Equity and Development Series

Contents

Part III: Equity and Core Institutions in Mexico: Social Security, the Labor Market, and Banking

Part IV: How Unequal Structures Hurt Competition in Major Sectors

Figures

Tables

Contributors

François Bourguignon is Director of the Paris School of Economics. At the time of writing he was Senior Vice President for Development Economics and Chief Economist at the World Bank.

Rafael del Villar is Subsecretary (Vice Minister) for Communications in Mexico's Ministry for Communications and Transport. At the time of writing he was an Economic Researcher at the Bank of Mexico.

Sébastien Dessus is a Senior Economist in the Development Economics Vice Presidency of the World Bank.

Carlos Elizondo Mayer-Serra is a Professor and Researcher at the Centro de Investigación y Docencia Económicas, Mexico.

Isabel Guerrero is the Vice President for South Asia at the World Bank. At the time of writing, she was Country Director for Colombia and Mexico.

Stephen Haber is the A. A. and Jeanne Welch Milligan Professor of Humanities and Sciences at Stanford University and the Peter and Helen Bing Senior Fellow at Stanford University's Hoover Institution.

Adrián Lajous is Chairman of the Oxford Institute for Energy Studies and President of Petrométrica. He was Director General of Petróleos Mexicanos (PEMEX) from 1994 to 1999.

Santiago Levy is Vice President for Sectors and Chief Economist for the Inter-American Development Bank. He was General Director of the Instituto Mexicano del Seguro Social from 2000 to 2005.

Luis Felipe López-Calva is Chief Economist for Latin America and the Caribbean at the United Nations Development Programme.

William F. Maloney is Lead Economist in the Latin America Vice Presidency of the World Bank.

Roger G. Noll is Professor of Economics Emeritus at Stanford University and a Senior Fellow Emeritus at the Stanford Institute for Economic Policy Research.

Raghuram G. Rajan is the Eric J. Gleacher Distinguished Service Professor of Finance at the University of Chicago's Graduate School of Business. At the time of writing, he was Chief Economist at the International Monetary Fund.

James A. Robinson is Professor of Government at Harvard University.

Michael Walton is Visiting Senior Fellow, Centre for Policy Research, Delhi, and a Lecturer in International Development at Harvard University's Kennedy School of Government.

Acknowledgments

This book is based on papers originally presented at a conference held in Mexico City on November 27–28, 2006, and sponsored by the David Rockefeller Center for Latin American Studies at Harvard University and the World Bank. Particular thanks to Isabel Guerrero for conceiving of and organizing the conference, to François Bourguignon for his advice and support, and to Roby Senderowitsch for his management of the overall process and event.

In addition to the paper authors, many conference participants contributed to the substantive ideas developed there, including Pamela Cox, Augusto de la Torre, José Francisco Gil Díaz, José Antonio González Anaya, Rashad Kaldany, Danny Leipziger, Guillermo Ortiz, Eduardo Pérez Mota, Guillermo Perry, and Yeidckol Polevnsky. Thanks also to Gabriela Águilar, Fabiola Longgi, Carolina Monsalve, and Alexandra Zenzes for their excellent support during the conference.

Abbreviations

AFORES	administradoras de fondos para el retiro
Banxico	Bank of Mexico
CFC	Comisión Federal de Competencia (Federal Competition Commission)
CFE	Comisión Federal de Electricidad (Federal Electricity Commission)
CNA	Comisión Nacional del Agua (National Water Commission)
CNBV	Comisión Nacional Bancaria y de Valores (National Securities and Exchange Commission)
CTM	Confederación de Trabajadores de México (Confederation of Mexican Workers)
COFETEL	Comisión Federal de Telecomunicaciones (Federal Telecommunications Commission)
CONSAR	Comisión Nacional del Sistema del Ahorro para el Retiro (National Commission for the Pension System)
CPP	calling party pays
CRE	Comisión Reguladora de Energía (Energy Regulatory Commission)
EBITDA	earnings before interest, taxes, depreciation, and amortization
ENESTYC	Encuesta Nacional de Empleo, Salarios, Tecnología y Capacitación (National Survey of Employment, Salaries, Technology, and Training)
ENIGH	Encuesta Nacional de Ingresos y Gastos de los Hogares (National Survey of Household Income and Expenditures)

FDI	foreign direct investment
FOBAPROA	Fondo Bancario de Protección al Ahorro (Banking Fund for the Protection of Savings)
FSTSE	Federación de Sindicates y Trabajadores al Servicis del Estado
GDP	gross domestic product
ICT	information and communication technology
IMCO	Instituto Mexicano para la Competitividad (Mexican Competitiveness Institute)
IMSS	Instituto Mexicano del Seguro Social (Mexican Social Security Institute)
INEGI	Instituto Nacional de Estadística y Geografía
INFONAVIT	Instituto del Fondo Nacional para la Vivienda de los Trabajadores (Institute of the National Fund for Housing for Workers)
IPAB	Instituto para la Protección al Ahorro Bancario (Bank Savings Protection Institute)
ISSSTE	Instituto de Seguridad Social y Servicios para los Trabajadores del Estado (State Employees' Social Security and Social Services Institute)
NAFTA	North American Free Trade Agreement
OECD	Organisation for Economic Co-operation and Development
PAN	Partido Acción Nacional (National Action Party)
PEMEX	Petróleos Mexicanos
PISA	Programme for International Student Assessment
PRI	Partido Revolucionario Institucional (Institutional Revolutionary Party)
PRD	Partido de la Revolución Democrática (Party of the Democratic Revolution)
PROGRESA	Programa de Educación, Salud y Alimentación (Education, Health, and Nutrition Program)
RJP	régimen de jubilaciones y pensiones (pension and retirement system)

RPP	receiving party pays
SCT	Secretaría de Comunicaciones y Transportes (Secretary of Communications and Transportation)
SME	Sindicato Mexicano de Electricistas (Mexican Trade Union of Electrical Workers)
SNTE	Sindicato Nacional de Trabajadores de la Educación Nacional (National Union of Education Workers
SNTSS	Sindicato Nacional de Trabajadores del Seguro Social (Union of Social Security Workers)
STRM	Sindicato de Telefonistas de la República Mexicana (Telephone Workers' Union of the Republic of Mexico)
TELCEL	Radiomóvil Dipsa
TELMEX	Teléfonos de Mexico
VoIP	voice over Internet protocol

Equity, Competition, and Growth in Mexico: An Overview

Santiago Levy and Michael Walton

This volume is concerned with explaining an important puzzle: why has Mexico's development performance been disappointing with respect to growth and equity despite an array of economic reforms and the transition to democracy? This issue is intensely contested in contemporary debates, both in Mexico and beyond.

Introduction

In this introduction, we do three things. We first introduce the puzzle and relate it to existing interpretations from market reformists and their critics, arguing that both sets of views are inadequate. We then offer an alternative interpretation: that entrenched inequities sustained by a rent-sharing political equilibrium are a primary source of inefficiencies and weak growth. Moreover, this equilibrium has been resilient to democratization in ways that can be explained by the nature of the underlying forces. Finally, we draw some tentative implications for the future, suggesting how public action could potentially support a shift to a more equitable and more efficient equilibrium. The volume's chapters are introduced within the structure of this argument.

Mexico as a Growth and Development Puzzle

Over the past three decades, Mexico's growth performance has been unsatisfactory. Figure 0.1 plots the country's gross domestic product (GDP) per capita since 1950 and compares it with that of Ireland, the Republic of Korea, Malaysia, and the United States. Relative to other middle-income and high-income countries, Mexico's performance can at best be classified as lackluster. These results hold even if we concentrate on the period 1994–2006. After a sharp drop in 1995 because of that year's macroeconomic crisis, a period of recovery follows, but growth tapers off in 2001 and rebounds only mildly thereafter.

Aside from being disappointing, these results are puzzling, particularly since 1996. This is so for three reasons. First, starting in 1985 with Mexico's accession to the World Trade Organization (then the General Agreement on Tariffs and Trade), the country has undergone significant economic reforms designed to make the economy more efficient and competitive and has backed these reforms with various macroeconomic adjustment programs. Second, because Mexico is located next to the United States, the largest economy in the world, which, as depicted in figure 0.1, has actually grown faster than Mexico. Third, because some of the reforms effected in the mid-1990s—particularly, the North American Free Trade Agreement (NAFTA) and a newly autonomous central bank—were meant to provide domestic and foreign investors with credible commitments

Figure 0.1 GDP Per Capita, Mexico and Selected Comparators, 1950–2004

(US$ at purchasing power parity)

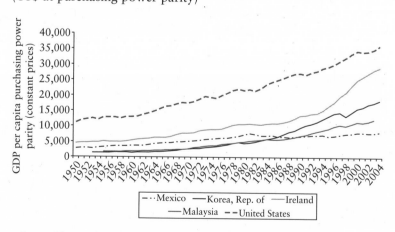

Source: Heston, Summers, and Aten 2006.

to sound money and to integrate Mexico into the world economy; as a result, most observers expected that larger flows of foreign and domestic private investment would follow. It was believed that these reforms, together with persistent efforts to reduce fiscal deficits, would produce higher and sustained growth rates of output and productivity. Yet productivity has also grown slowly: estimates indicate that during 1995–2004, average product per worker grew at an annual average rate of 1.4 percent (Bassi and others 2006).

Reforms were expected to provide Mexico with both faster growth and more equity, at least in the minds of advocates. A reduced inflation tax, increased real wages as a result of higher labor productivity, and reduced protection-induced rents because of NAFTA, along with a new competition law and a revamped regulatory framework, were all expected to lead to a more equitable development process than the process in effect during Mexico's previous sustained growth period that ended in the 1970s.[1] However, more equity has not been forthcoming either. Extreme poverty is less prevalent because of a shift from generalized food subsidies to targeted income transfers and increased remittances from Mexican workers abroad. This has been associated with a mild reduction in income inequality as measured by household surveys, but the high degree of concentration of income observed before the reforms has persisted and, perhaps, even increased at the very top of the distribution. When broader measures of inequality are used, such as access to secondary and higher education, justice, information, and finance, the picture that emerges is that of a country characterized by large inequalities. Furthermore, levels of private wealth are closely associated with sectors of the economy in which competition is absent (Guerrero, López–Calva, and Walton, chapter 4 in this volume).

A troubling picture also emerges in relation to access to pensions, health, and housing. Mexico has a dualistic system of social provisioning, whereby workers in formal jobs have access to better statutory nonsalary benefits than informal workers. However, the number of social programs for informal workers has increased over the past 10 years. Although this increase may have reduced the gap in access to some social benefits, workers with similar characteristics and abilities performing similar jobs still have unequal access and unequal rights: some workers with formal contracts in the private sector are entitled to health insurance, housing loans, and various pension programs; others, particularly in the public sector, are entitled to substantially better benefits. However the majority have erratic access to various dispersed social programs (Levy, chapter 6).

Overall, despite the reduction in extreme poverty and the modest decline in income inequality, what stands out are the persistent high levels of income inequality; the unequal social entitlements; and the division of firms and workers into formal and informal sectors with different rights, diverse degrees of compliance with the law, and varying productivity. One indicator of the combined effects of high inequality and low growth is that approximately three-fourths of 1 percent of the total labor force migrates abroad every year.

Mexico's growth and inequality outcomes over the past decade are doubly puzzling because, in addition to the economic reforms, the country has witnessed a notable transition toward democracy. Constitutional reforms in 1996 and observed practice since that time have given credibility to the Federal Electoral Institute and the Electoral Tribunal that were made autonomous in that year. The long-standing dominance of the main political party, the Institutional Revolutionary Party (Partido Revolucionario Institucional, or PRI), came to an end in 1997 in the lower house of Congress and in 2000 in the upper house and the presidency. Rotation between political parties at the state and municipal levels of government has accompanied these changes.

A strengthened democracy has ambiguous effects on short-run growth, because the links between democracy and growth are complex. Although the policies implemented are the result of broad consensus, efficiency considerations may give way to more redistributive efforts. This result can increase uncertainty or increase the distortions associated with taxation and translate into lower private and public investment, resulting in a negative impact on growth. In fact, growth accelerated modestly in the late 1990s, but this was at least partly due to the recovery from the 1994–95 decline and the rapid expansion of output in the United States. With respect to taxes, Mexico's tax effort is almost certainly too low rather than too high relative to the need for public goods. An alternative view is that strengthened democracy would shift political power toward the majority, which should result in measures to correct the root causes of inequality. Yet, this shift has not occurred. Although the effectiveness of poverty programs has increased and each year's federal budget has approved more resources for social programs (notably for workers in the informal sector), few legal changes have been approved that would eliminate the conditions that create and sustain special privileges for business or labor, whether in the private or public sector. Some changes have actually enhanced these privileges, and the few approved to reduce them have either not been implemented or faced major difficulties (Elizondo, chapter 5).

In sum, Mexico seems to be caught in a high-inequality, low-growth state. Before turning to our argument that this situation is a product of a self-sustaining equilibrium, let us look at alternative interpretations in the policy discourse on Mexico.

Interpretations of Market Reformers and Their Critics

These puzzling and troubling results have generated a search for explanations by economists, political scientists, policy makers, and the general public. A rich and growing number of analyses contain hypotheses and interpretations to this effect. A useful distinction among these hypotheses is to split them into the market reform view and the critics of this view.

THE MARKET REFORM VIEW

Advocates of reform as a central route to faster growth and reduced inequalities have played a central role in policy design and debates in Mexico since the late 1980s. The starting point of this view is the emphasis on sound macroeconomic management as a precondition for growth given the negative effects of uncertainty, the crowding out of private investment by large public deficits, the pernicious effects of overvalued exchange rates on competitiveness, and the high burden on the country's finances of a large external debt. Advocates also argue that prudent macroeconomic management has positive distributional effects, because of both the regressive nature of the inflation tax and the regressive features of economic crises.

Macroeconomic stability is a necessary, but insufficient, condition for growth. Measures to increase efficiency and productivity are also essential. In this context, proponents of the market reform view argue that the incompleteness of economic reforms is the major explanation for Mexico's continued low growth. More precisely, they argue that NAFTA provided the incentives to increase efficiency in the tradable sectors of the economy, but that further reforms are necessary to increase efficiency in sectors producing nontraded inputs (nontraded either because of their nature or because of government regulation) that are widely used throughout the economy, principally in energy, transport, telecommunications, financial services, and labor.

The dominance of public enterprises in oil, natural gas, petrochemicals, and electricity is a major source of inefficiencies for three reasons. First, the enterprises themselves have high-cost production structures given their large labor costs, slow execution of investments, and absence of incentives to reduce costs and provide quality services. Second, private investment in many energy-related fields is restricted, including exploration for natural gas and crude oil, distribution of gasoline and liquefied petroleum gas, and production and distribution of basic petrochemicals.[2] Third, high costs and low-quality energy lowers the competitiveness of all tradable production (see Lajous, chapter 11, for the case of Petróleos Mexicanos [PEMEX]).

From the market reform point of view, weak performance incentives in public enterprises and the cumbersome regulations governing their planning, investment, and procurement practices (which are at times also subject to political interference and the vagaries of the public budget), are substantial impediments to increased efficiency and investment. Proponents of this view argue for increased private participation in energy and a progressive reduction in current areas of state dominance, or at least for greater flexibility for public enterprises to engage in joint ventures with private firms. This argument does not imply that natural monopolies should not be regulated. On the contrary, those who hold the market reform viewpoint argue that the state is better at regulating than producing efficiently. The state does not need to own firms to regulate natural monopolies. Indeed, regulation through ownership is more costly precisely because of monopoly features, weak internal incentives, and susceptibility to interest group pressures.

A similar situation occurs in transport, particularly in railroads and ports. Mexico privatized these in the mid-1990s, but many years of public management meant that these two sectors inherited sparse and aging networks that are increasingly inadequate for supporting the integration of Mexico's producers into the world economy at low cost. Imported intermediate inputs take too long to come in and export products take too long to go out, imposing high costs of trading relative to competitors such as China. The situation in telecommunications is much the same. Many years of public ownership and operation of Teléfonos de Mexico (TELMEX) resulted in a low level of telephone penetration and the underdevelopment of new services and technologies (del Villar, chapter 9; Noll, chapter 10). TELMEX's privatization in the early 1990s was essential to increase competitiveness. Similarly in the banking sector, the period of public ownership and operation of banks after their 1982 expropriation hindered the vigorous competition that could have offered firms access to the financial products they needed to be competitive (Haber, chapter 8).

In all these areas, proponents of the market reform view recognize issues of natural monopoly and the need for efficiency-promoting regulations. They see the creation of the Comisión Federal de Competencia (CFC) and of regulatory bodies for specific sectors, including telecommunications and banking, as an essential element for reducing monopoly rents and supporting growth.

The market reform view also emphasizes labor market distortions, which are especially important because the price of labor strongly influences income distribution and because labor is a key nontraded input. The absence of reforms in this area is particularly costly for two reasons. First, obsolete and costly regulations in the Federal Labor Law are equivalent to a tax on this primary factor of production, further lowering competitiveness and limiting the growth of formal employment to the detriment of firms and workers. Second, the existence of large and powerful unions of public workers reduce the quality of key social services that are indispensable to increasing workers' productivity and welfare (see Elizondo, chapter 5, on education; Levy, chapter 6, on social security; and Maloney, chapter 7, for a general discussion of labor markets).

An important issue associated with labor is pensions. Proponents of the market reform view argue that the 1997 reform of the pension system for private sector workers was necessary on both efficiency and fiscal grounds. However, in the short to medium term, it worsened Mexico's fiscal constraints because of the costs of the transition from a bankrupt pay-as-you-go pension system to a defined-contribution system and because of the inability to reform the even more bankrupt pension system of public workers.[3] Resources channeled into subsidies for pensions are resources not channeled into investments in education and infrastructure that are necessary for growth and competitiveness.

The proponents of the market reform view thus argue that privatization of banks, telecommunications, railroads, ports, secondary petrochemicals, airlines, and sugar mills in a competitive framework generates efficiency gains that public firms are inherently unable to deliver. In other words, a "regulating state" is much better for productivity growth than a "producing state." They do not advocate the complete withdrawal of the state, nor do they believe that markets will solve all problems, but they do believe that the state's role needs to change and that market failures need to be addressed by means of more effective interventions. Without well-functioning markets, Mexico is extremely unlikely to achieve the efficiency required to compete globally.

At the same time, proponents of the market reform view emphasize the need for two other areas of state action. The first area is vigorous and effective social programs as the main instrument to increase the welfare and human capital of the poor and reduce inequality. The second area is provision of public goods that are essential for growth and competitiveness, including public investment in infrastructure activities where private investment would not occur and in the provision of the rule of law and protection of private property rights through well-designed judicial institutions and laws.

Social programs progressively extended to informal workers play the leading role in reducing poverty and improving distribution. Proponents of the market reform view argue that such programs are transitory and should gradually be phased out as faster economic growth allows more workers to find jobs in the formal sector. They also argue for efficient targeting of benefits directly to needy beneficiaries. They draw a distinction between the financing and regulation of social programs, on the one hand, and the actual provision of the goods and services, on the other. For example, financing housing may involve government subsidies for the poor, but housing construction is best done by private firms. Similarly, financing pensions or health care needs government interventions to solve contracting problems in insurance markets, but the management of pension funds and the delivery of health services are best done by private firms.

Because of the importance of sound public finances, proponents of the market reform view also emphasize the need for tax reform for growth. Higher taxes are a necessity, but they must be obtained at the least cost possible in terms of efficiency. A distorted tax system is one more source of lower growth, because the tax burden falls mainly on firms and workers in the formal sector. A misguided attempt to pursue redistributive goals through the revenue side of the budget has led to many exemptions and distortions related to specific sectors or consumption goods that lower the tax take. The redistributive agenda can be efficiently pursued only through social programs, and it is hindered by complex tax laws that punish investment and foster evasion. This is why a broadly based value-added tax with few or no exemptions is often a preferred tax instrument.

The market reform group, therefore, argues that an incomplete transformation of the state is the main impediment to growth and equity. The state should do more of some things and less of others. The elements associated with macroeconomic stability are generally present, although at a suboptimal level of expenditure on public goods and social programs. The change from a producing state to a regulating state is incomplete, and the use of more effective instruments by the regulating state is very much a work in progress. Furthermore, while China was joining the World Trade Organization in 2000 and other middle-income countries in Asia and elsewhere were accelerating their reforms to increase their competitiveness, Mexico's reform process—which had already slowed since 1998— came to a stop and, in some regards, went into reverse.

CRITICS OF THE MARKET REFORM VIEW

A diverse group of analysts criticize the market reform view. Their common denominator is the view that Mexico's low growth is not the product of an incomplete reform process and that the issue is, instead, the need for a reassessment of this process. In particular, these analysts emphasize that large and systemic errors in the sequencing and implementation of reforms are the outcome of a conceptually flawed reform agenda rather than of failures in implementation. They argue that reforms have increased the concentration of wealth, weakened the state, and generated large fiscal costs and new obstacles to economic growth.

Most critics agree that sound macroeconomic management is necessary for growth, but point out that the events leading to the 1994–95 crisis were the result of unsound exchange-rate management and an imprudent issuance of domestic debt indexed to foreign currency. They may also agree that private banks are, in principle, better at financial intermediation and risk assessment than public banks, but ask why banks were privatized before the regulatory framework was put in place and why they were allowed to be bought with borrowed resources often from the same banks. Not only were the fiscal resources channeled to the subsequent banking rescue regressive and fiscally costly, but also they have not even been reflected in more lending by banks to the private sector, which remains extraordinarily low, especially to small and medium firms (Haber, chapter 8). This is surely partly responsible for low growth.

Most critics also agree that private telecommunications firms innovate more rapidly than public ones and have more incentives to expand coverage and introduce new products, but ask why the telephone company was privatized as a single unit (including fixed and wireless communications), and again why this was done prior to the creation of a regulatory commission (del Villar, chapter 9). They may agree that private–public partnerships are required for infrastructure development, but they may ask why private investors in highway construction were given government guarantees against what should have been private risks. This also resulted in fiscal subsidies to private firms. More generally, critics ask if the objective of transferring assets from the public to the private sector was efficiency, then why were privatizations designed to maximize revenues instead?

Some critics might also agree that a defined-contribution system of portable individual accounts for retirement pensions is better than a pay-as-you-go system, given the large mobility of workers in the labor market and the demographic transition, and that it may even increase domestic savings. However, they ask why these accounts should be administered by a private oligopoly whose commissions have so far resulted in low real rates of return on workers' savings while absorbing all of the government's subsidies meant to increase retirement pensions (Levy, chapter 6).

Critics agree with proponents of the market reform view on the importance of competition, but point to the ineffectiveness of the CFC in eliminating anticompetitive practices in many sectors, highlighting cement, airlines, television, telecommunications, and banking. They also argue that regulatory bodies in various sectors, notably telecommunications and finance, fail to ensure that the efficiency gains of TELMEX and private banks translate into more, better, and cheaper services for firms and households as opposed to high commissions and monopoly rents for a few large firms (Guerrero, López–Calva, and Walton, chapter 4).

Critics also agree on the need to increase taxes to strengthen public spending in infrastructure, education, and general public goods, but they point to the inequality of the tax burden, because various loopholes and legal maneuvers allow wealthier individuals and large corporations to lower their effective tax rates (Elizondo, chapter 5). It is in this context that they question, for instance, why the sale of one of the two largest banks in the country to a foreign bank implied no tax payments.

More important, critics point out that these problems are systemic, that is, they are the rule and not the exception. The privatization and deregulation process has not been a transition from an inefficient producing state to an efficient regulating state. Rather, it has been a progressive dismantling of a state that has been unable, and perhaps unwilling, to defend small and medium-sized firms and consumers from rent-seeking activities by a few, increasingly wealthy private groups, and also unable to protect workers and agricultural producers from external shocks. One manifestation of the ineffectiveness of the new institutions of the regulating state is the increase in the number of Mexican billionaires over the past decade. Critics of the market reform view are often not criticizing markets, but the concrete circumstances in which markets in Mexico operate.

Critics further argue that NAFTA should have been more than a commitment device for international integration and protection of the property rights of foreign investors. To the extent that the efficiency gains of trade are associated with employment reallocation, the social protection system should have been strengthened before, or at least in parallel with, the agreement. At the same time, critics point out that the social protection system cannot be substituted with ad hoc and discretionary social programs that are susceptible to political influence, especially near elections. They also note that the investments required to offset a NAFTA-induced deepening of regional disparities between the north and the south of Mexico have yet to be carried out, nor have those needed to increase the competitiveness of agriculture. In other words, in the view of critics, the government has been willing to make binding commitments to open the economy to international markets, but unwilling to make equally binding commitments to compensate those affected by these changes and equip all Mexicans with the productive capabilities to participate on equal terms in the market.

It is from this perspective that critics interpret the slowdown of the reform process in the late 1990s. In their view, Congress's refusal to approve further reforms when a single party no longer controlled it was not the product of some parties' nostalgia for Mexico's state-led development. Rather, a more democratic Congress was now able to exercise its legitimate veto power on a sequence of reform proposals whose only effects so far had been to concentrate income and leave the state without the fiscal resources and intervention mechanisms required to promote development, let alone equity.

Tax reform provides an example. Congress rejected proposals to increase revenues and the efficiency of tax collections by switching to a uniform value-added tax, because the proposals were not accompanied by commitments of equal legal weight to compensate low-income households for the negative distributional effects of those proposals. Another example is labor reform. Congress rejected proposals to modify the labor law to make labor regulations more flexible because the proposals were not accompanied by measures of equal legal weight to strengthen social security institutions. Indeed, the government was channeling increasing resources to new social programs for informal workers, effectively undercutting the social security system. Energy reform offers a third example. Experience had shown that the newly created or revamped commissions to promote competition in general and to regulate telecommunications, banking, and pensions were failing to produce the expected efficiency results. So why should proposals to allow for "appropriately regulated" private investments in oil and natural gas exploration and production be approved?

In sum, critics of the market reform view argue that rapid growth cannot occur in the context of a state that lacks credibility in delivering the institutional mechanisms for efficient and equitable social provisioning and the effective regulation of oligopolists in an economy integrating into global markets. Further privatization or deregulation would simply repeat in other sectors the efficiency-reducing and income-concentrating effects observed in telecommunications, finance, cement, and other sectors. They also argue that although workers' welfare can be increased in the short term by channeling oil rents to an ad hoc set of social programs, the underlying conditions that generate inequity will continue as long as current economic policy persists. Critics understand that efficiency is necessary to compete globally, but they are convinced that many Mexican markets do not generate efficient outcomes. They understand that labor flexibility is needed for competitiveness, but they believe this cannot be done without unemployment insurance and properly legislated universal social entitlements. They also recognize that public unions need to be made more efficient and accountable, but not before the development of the state's regulatory functions with respect to large corporate interests. Critics understand that tax reform is needed, but they consider that it should not accentuate income inequalities. Finally, they understand the importance of NAFTA and globalization, but they argue that this should not occur at the costs of enhanced regional inequalities and, according to some, the unilateral dismantling of Mexican agriculture.

The various critics of the market-reform point of view do not agree unanimously on a constructive agenda. Some believe that growth could be enhanced with sector-specific interventions akin to Korean or Japanese industrial policy, while others argue that the same forces that have led to the capture of other government policies would be repeated in this case as well. All probably agree that the large fiscal and current account deficits witnessed in the 1970s and early 1980s were counterproductive. However, some would consider the government overly zealous if it aimed for an exactly balanced budget, and that moderate deficits, as in other countries of the Organisation for Economic Co-operation and Development, could be useful if resources were channeled to infrastructure investments. Others would worry about the credibility of such policies and the risks involved in a context of oil-dependent fiscal revenues. Regardless of individual differences about the specific contents of an alternative package of policies to promote growth and equity, all would agree that pursuing further reforms along the lines witnessed in the past two decades would do more harm than good.

COMMONALITIES AND CONTRASTS

Few, if any, analysts of Mexico unequivocally hold either the market reform view or the views of what we have referred to as critics of the market. The point of the previous discussion is not to identify individual positions or specific schools of thought, but rather to clarify the broad lines of reasoning behind the main explanations for Mexico's growth and equity puzzle. Most analysts would hold a more nuanced and richer view than the ones sketched here. Some would hold more extreme views for or against markets.

At the same time, proponents of the market reform view and their critics agree on some central matters, namely: the importance of channeling oil rents to productive investments in infrastructure and other areas, and not toward current spending; the essential role education plays; the importance of productivity growth; and the centrality of equity in its own right and as an important element of a solid democracy. Many of the differences relate to the weights attached to different objectives and to the sequencing of policy. All would perhaps agree that more tax revenues are needed, but the balance between consumption and income taxes is a common point of disagreement. All would agree that more oil and natural gas exploration is required, but hold different views on the combination of PEMEX and other agents to do so. All would also agree that reducing inequality is essential for the health of the social fabric and that this is different from eradicating extreme poverty, but many would disagree on the factors that produce inequality and the measures to reduce it.

Another aspect of broad agreement is the need for a "distributing state." Whether to improve workers' human capital to enhance productivity and accelerate growth, to simply increase the welfare of those in need, or both, all emphasize the importance of social programs to redistribute income and create opportunities. For some, these programs are the tools to correct for inequality. For others, these programs are the palliatives that make inequality politically tolerable and do not substitute for measures to correct for the forces that generate inequality.

Regardless of the interpretation, an important point for the purposes of this volume is the continuance of an old practice of using social programs, particularly those benefiting informal workers and poor households, to bolster the government's political legitimacy. With few exceptions, this practice has been invariant to the political party in power. In the exercise of this practice, the programs' negative impact on workers' and firms' incentives to increase productivity has been largely ignored, and the government has not been unduly concerned with financing sources. Abundant oil rents have facilitated this practice, because program costs are not directly internalized by anybody.

The Perspective of This Volume

This book brings a new perspective to the debate on growth and equity in Mexico. We argue that economic and social institutions and policies are developed within the context of a political equilibrium shaped by the interests and power of many actors—political parties, business and labor interests, and organizations—and by legal and paralegal arrangements and understandings that are a product of history and that mold history. For reasons that are explored later, this political equilibrium is characterized by a high degree of rent seeking that, in a context of inherited high inequality, translates into behaviors that are both efficiency reducing and wealth concentrating. The issue is not so much whether the producer is private or public, in energy or in telecommunications, say, as it concerns the incentives to be efficient and to pass efficiency gains on to consumers and firms in the form of lower prices and better services. The issue is also not whether unions exist or not, but the role they play in a political context that allows them to extract rents and engage in socially harmful behavior. In other words, the problem is not with the adjective placed before the state (producing, regulating, or distributing), but with the institutions that shape the behavior of the state—that is, their incentives, the rules that govern their day-to-day functioning, and their accountability.

In a maturing democracy such as Mexico's, the institutions that matter are no longer only in the executive branch of government, but are also in Congress, the judiciary, and subnational governments. Rapid growth and increased equity do not occur in a vacuum, but result from an institutional environment that aligns everybody's incentives in the direction of productivity and efficiency and that expands social entitlements to all workers without discriminating on the basis of labor status. Few institutions of the Mexican state face these incentives. On the contrary, they operate mainly in a context of lack of transparency (which has only recently begun to be corrected) and little accountability. The same is true with respect to the substantial public resources channeled to political parties that may develop a dynamic of their own that can diverge, at times significantly, from the interests of those whom they claim to represent. Regulatory capture, rent seeking, special privileges (de facto, if not de jure), and discretionary applications of the law are a way of operating that benefits a few powerful business and trade union interests. In this context, a nomenklatura from all political parties shuffles and balances the interests of those in business and labor who are able to exercise voice and power as often as needed to maintain and reproduce their hold on power, while the population at large is able only to exercise its vote when scheduled in formal elections. This arrangement is far removed from a world of well-defined property rights, systemic rule of law, and transparency and accountability, which is where sound money and free trade translate into equity and growth.

We argue that Mexico is characterized by a self-sustaining, rent-sharing equilibrium, and that this is the main obstacle to faster growth and reduced inequality. This equilibrium evolves and changes in form, but its inherent properties are persistent and resilient. Understanding the nature of this rent-sharing equilibrium is necessary before attempts are made to change it, but changing this political equilibrium is essential for faster growth and reduced inequalities.

This book brings together 11 essays that attempt to shed light on Mexico's growth-equity puzzle and to contribute to the debate on the alternatives for breaking away from the current high-inequality, low-growth equilibrium. The essays are written by a mix of Mexican and non-Mexican authors and focus on the relationship between growth and equity from two perspectives: through an analytical exploration of the links between growth and equity; and through case studies that try to identify these links in the areas of energy, telecommunications, finance, labor, and social security. The book does not deal with taxation, education, agriculture, and decentralization, all of which are important for shaping productivity and equity dynamics and are areas where the volume's argument applies with force. Although some chapters discuss taxation and education, they are not dealt with comprehensively, and agriculture and decentralization are not discussed at all. If the approach taken here is judged to be fruitful, the hope is that it will lead to further work in these areas.

In the remainder of this overview chapter, we seek to expand on the core concept of the rent-sharing equilibrium and how this is linked to the high-inequality, low-growth "trap," drawing on the main views contained in the essays.

Interpreting Mexico's Development Puzzle

Equity, Efficiency, and Inequality Traps

How are inequality and growth processes linked? The interactions are multiple and flow in both directions, from growth to patterns of inequalities and from patterns of inequalities to growth. This volume's approach draws on work in theoretical and empirical economics, political science, and sociology. This work is summarized in Bourguignon and Dessus (chapter 1) and synthesized in World Bank (2005).[4]

The approach involves shifting attention away from ex post inequality of incomes, which has dominated empirical work in economics, to an ex ante concept of inequality of opportunity, or inequity. In most philosophical traditions and societal perspectives, equity, understood as equality of opportunity, is a fundamental ethical concept that has intrinsic value. Nevertheless, important as such an intrinsic concern with equity is, our focus in this volume is on exploring the instrumental or causal influence of equity on processes affecting growth. Inequality of incomes is then an outcome that is a product of interactions between these more fundamental dimensions of inequity and economic, political, and social processes.

It is useful to think about two categories of instrumental influences from equity to economic processes (World Bank 2005):

- *Interactions between market imperfections (for example, in credit, insurance, and education markets) and the distribution of wealth, power, or status.* When markets are incomplete or imperfect, for example, because of information asymmetries and failures in contracting, resources are allocated by means of other criteria. These typically favor individuals or households with greater assets and influence: credit is allocated to people with collateral or connections, wealthy individuals can better manage uninsured risks, and those with greater resources and social connections are more likely to send their children to better schools. These allocations may be inefficient because they can lead to both underinvestment by groups with lower wealth or influence and overinvestment by relatively advantaged groups with less-efficient investment opportunities.
- *Effects of unequal power and influence on the choice of policies and the design of institutions.* The economic institutions that shape the structure of opportunities influence the pattern of market imperfections. In turn, responses to these imperfections are themselves reflections of underlying patterns of power and struggle, and can be shaped in ways that further the interests of the powerful. These include the whole range of financial, educational, insurance, infrastructure, social service, and regulatory institutions that determine economic interactions in a society.

The second category of influence is related to the growing emphasis on the influence of institutions on development in general, and on growth in particular (see, for example, Acemoglu, Johnson, and Robinson 2002; Acemoglu and Robinson 2006; Easterly and Levine 2003; North 1990; Rodrik, Subramanian, and Trebbi 2002; for contrasting views, see Glaeser and others 2004; Rajan 2006, chapter 2 in this volume). The focus here is on links with inequity: market failures hurt those with lower incomes more, and institutions and policies dominated by the rich will not correct market failures because they have no incentives to do so. For example, the wealthy and powerful may have an interest in a weak justice system because they can buy or otherwise influence judicial decisions (Glaeser, Sheinkman, and Shleifer 2003).

The primary concern of this volume is how unequal power and influence shape economic institutions in ways that lead to outcomes that are both inequitable and a source of slow growth. To explore these influences, it is necessary to elaborate on how economic and social policies and institutions are formed, how they function, and how they relate to political processes. In this context, Bourguignon and Dessus (chapter 1) present a political economy perspective in which elite and non-elite groups face different payoffs from reforms: when those in power stand to lose from a reform, they will resist change in the absence of credible mechanisms for compensation. Bourguignon and Dessus illustrate this for several areas of policy relevant to Mexico. Many of the sectoral chapters take up the subject in more depth.

An important question for Mexico concerns the role of political institutions, especially as Mexico's transition to democracy has so far not led to radical changes in this sphere. Rajan (chapter 2) argues that focusing on the pattern of economic interests of different groups (or constituencies in his terminology) is essential. In this context, in a complementary perspective to that of Bourguignon and Dessus, he suggests that interaction between different groups can be one source of resistance to efficiency- and equity-increasing reforms. If each group in a society gets some rents from the existing system and fundamental change to increase competition might lead to the loss of these rents, a form of collective action failure can occur whereby each group seeks to resist changes that threaten its own rents, even if it has a long-term interest in reform. This behavior can leave a society stuck in an equilibrium characterized by inequality and low growth.

With respect to political institutions, Elizondo (chapter 5) discusses both the transitions and the continuing areas in which they are likely to create distortions in the aggregation of preferences. He also suggests that the transition to a more democratic political system from the executive-dominated system under the PRI may have led to perverse outcomes in the political decision-making process.

The mechanisms that shape institutions (economic, social, and political) and policy choices can be sources of the persistence of inequalities, creating what has been termed an inequality trap—that is, mechanisms that lead to individuals or groups maintaining their relative position in the distribution of income, wealth, status, or power over time (see Bourguignon, Ferreira, and Walton 2007 for a formal treatment; Rao 2006 for an informal statement; and World Bank 2005 for a discussion). This trap is central to connections with growth, for if the institutions that lower efficiency were not persistent, growth costs would be transitory. Drawing on the approaches discussed in Bourguignon and Dessus (chapter 1) and Rajan (chapter 2), we characterize Mexico as exemplifying a rent-sharing equilibrium that is a form of inequality trap, albeit one whose particular features may slowly shift over time.

To make the rent-sharing equilibrium concept useful, two things are needed. First, we need a richer account of how economic and political institutions are formed and sustained. Big business, unionized workers, and other interests do not exercise their influence in a vacuum. Policies and institutions are products of a political equilibrium that reflects the strategic interactions between different groups. We argue that in Mexico, rent creation and rent sharing are central to this equilibrium, but that belief systems also play a significant role.[5] This is important for Mexico, because it can make efficiency- and equity-increasing reforms more difficult. Second, the particular mechanisms whereby unequal structures hurt efficiency and growth need to be explored in detail, because the specifics matter. A major objective of this volume is to work through these interactions and explore these mechanisms in a number of sectors that are central to Mexico's growth problem.

To give more context to these general concepts, the remainder of this section sketches the nature and evolution of Mexico's rent-sharing equilibrium. After reviewing the historical formation of the core institutional structures, we focus on the past three six-year presidential terms, which include both a major economic liberalization and the transition to democracy.

The Evolution of Mexico's Rent-Sharing Equilibrium in the Transition to Democracy

Mexico's political equilibrium and associated economic institutions and policies are a product of the interaction between the various groups within a complex and changing landscape. This interaction can be thought of in terms of two fundamental challenges that political elites face: (a) provide sufficient security of property rights for private investors to invest, despite the weakness of checks and balances on a powerful state; and (b) provide sufficient social and economic benefits to non-elite groups to offset the risk of expropriation of elites, whether through revolution or other means.

These challenges are classic dilemmas in the development process. Historically, Mexico resolved these through a rent-sharing system in which the state mediated two implicit pacts: between the state and the private sector and between the state and subordinate groups (see Haber, Razo, and Maurer 2003 for an account of the historical formation of the rent-sharing system; Elizondo, chapter 5 in this volume, for a description of rent-sharing pacts; Bazdresch and Levy 1991 on the state's protagonist role). These pacts were institutionalized structures that effectively preserved an inequality trap, albeit one that was restructured after the 1910–17 revolution.

THE HISTORICAL FORMATION OF CREDIBLE PACTS

The first challenge concerns how to deal with the risk of expropriation by the state (this section draws on Haber, Razo, and Maurer 2003). Investment is essential to growth and requires protection of investors' property rights. If investors believe that the profits from their investments may be expropriated, they will not invest or will demand a high risk premium.[6] The dilemma is that a state that is strong enough to protect property rights is also strong enough to take them away. Investment is irreversible, and once it is in place, the state has incentives to expropriate it. The long-term historical solution in countries that are now rich is that of limited government—that is, the development of institutionalized checks and balances that place limits on the opportunistic behavior of governments by means of independent judiciaries, autonomous bureaucracies, parliaments, strong regulatory agencies, and civil society institutions. However, such a system is the product of long-term historical evolution, and transplants of formal institutional structures from one country to another typically fail.

In Mexico, the threat of expropriation was genuine. The country experienced periods of severe political instability during much of the 19th century and in the two decades following the 1910 revolution. Even during relatively stable political periods, the state has at times expropriated private investors. The most dramatic examples are the nationalization of the petroleum industry by President Lázaro Cárdenas in 1938 and the expropriation of the banks by President José López Portillo in 1982.

As Haber, Razo, and Maurer (2003) argue, during both the late 19th century administration of Porfirio Díaz and the postrevolutionary period, this dilemma was resolved through two inter-related mechanisms. The first was the creation of rents for the economic elite through various forms of protection, especially in industry and finance. The second was through the sharing of rents with groups who had the power to impose costs on the government if it expropriated investors. The latter were often third parties with de facto enforcement powers, including governors and, from the 1920s, organized workers. This arrangement was also supported by rent sharing with the political elite through both economic and social ties, thereby giving them a stake in sustaining the rent-creating structures. The combination of these types of mechanisms increased expected rents and provided sufficient incentives for investment. This was central to the accumulation of capital during the administration of Porfirio Díaz and in the 20th century under the PRI.

With respect to the second challenge, the threat that subordinate groups could take power and expropriate economic elites has been credible in Mexico, as dramatically illustrated by the revolution. Even if full expropriation of the elites is not the objective, these groups could still pose difficult political problems, as was the case with railroad workers in the late 1950s. This dilemma was managed by two categories of mechanisms. First, organized workers were incorporated into the rent-sharing system: some sharing of the rents was associated with monopoly rights to workers' organizations affiliated with the PRI and its precursors in return for support for the governing party. Second, poorer "outsider" households—initially dominated by the peasantry—achieved (to some degree) their principal demand for land, but were then incorporated into a form of submissive dependency with the state that involved modest benefits, including some basic services (even if of low quality), in exchange for political support. These arrangements were formalized in the corporatist structures developed under President Cárdenas in the 1930s. For all groups, mechanisms were in place, both clientelistic exchanges of jobs and limited services for political support and repressive action when needed, that assured that the ruling party maintained support in the formal electoral process. These mechanisms were at times backed by direct manipulation of the vote. However, repression and manipulation were used only occasionally and would not have been sustainable were it not for the broader context of the underlying social pacts.

Both pacts were effected and implemented within the context of a dominant state, with the presidency as the central protagonist. Presidential dominance was not, however, a product of formal institutions; the constitution actually grants significant powers to the legislature and judiciary to balance the executive branch. Rather, it was an outcome of the development of the pervasive influence of the PRI over all societal structures, combined with the PRI's own internal presidential bias.

Complementing these arrangements was the evolution of belief systems that pragmatically blended nationalist revolutionary ideology with the expectations of economic elites that they would not be expropriated. These belief systems were not based on pure rhetoric: the introduction of progressive labor laws, the extension of social security, the development of the *ejido* system of communal land for peasants, and the nationalization of oil and gas in the 1930s and of electricity in the 1960s could be interpreted as evidence of a state-led socialist, or at least social democratic, system. Critically, however, these actions were accompanied by credible mechanisms to support the rents of the economic elite and high levels of overall economic inequality (for example, incumbent bankers wrote the banking laws in ways that protected their own interests). These belief systems were—and, in some cases, still are—an important part of understanding both the change that has occurred and the perpetuation of an inequitable and inefficient system.

The outcome was sufficient investment to support decades of growth, but with major inefficiencies, accompanied by steady expansion of social services with a strong bias toward organized urban workers. Protected or monopolistic structures for business and workers were essential features of both the strengths and the weaknesses of the system. Economic inefficiencies would eventually come home to roost, but these were initially hidden by the expansion of oil output and revenues in the late 1970s that provided not only a source of growth, but also an abundant (if volatile) additional source of rents.

EXECUTIVE-LED MODERNIZATION AND PARTIAL LIBERALIZATION UNDER PRESIDENT CARLOS SALINAS (1988–94)

Mexico's economic and political equilibrium was shaken by the crisis and stagnation of the 1980s (see Haber and others 2007 for a discussion of the period since 1980). The crisis resulted from external price and interest rate shocks, internal inefficiencies, and macroeconomic mismanagement, and the fallout from the crisis constituted a major threat to a political equilibrium that had been sustained for more than five decades. What we termed the first pact with investors was threatened by the 1982 bank expropriation (rhetorically termed a nationalization). A decline in profits and asset values ensued as a result of the protracted economic recession that followed. The second pact with social groups was hurt by the major decline in real wages and the fiscal constraints on public services in the 1980s. Traditional mechanisms for shoring up formal support were increasingly ineffective, and the PRI may have won the 1988 presidential election only by a last minute "adjustment" of the vote count.

The threats to the system created both opportunities and constraints, and President Salinas responded to these by effecting a major shift in economic institutions and policies. Also relevant to the reforms promoted at that time were changes in the belief systems of intellectual and political elites worldwide, and especially in Latin America, in response to the global and regional shift to favoring market-led over state-led development solutions (see Murillo 2002 for a discussion of the widespread shift to privatization in different political regimes across Latin America in the 1990s). The main elements of change relevant to the discussion in this book were the following:

- restructuring the pact with investors through a combination of liberalization, NAFTA's credibility-enhancing effects, and central bank independence (which effectively substituted for the earlier mechanisms for providing credibility) together with the design of privatization in ways that furthered the interests of important segments of the domestic economic elite—more important, non-oil taxes remained low;
- designing educational and energy reforms in a way that did not compromise the interests of organized worker groups, especially teachers, PEMEX workers, and electricity unions; leaving restrictive labor legislation intact; and maintaining the social security system together with the privileged position of workers in key unions like that of the Mexican Social Security Institute (Instituto Mexicano del Seguro Social, or IMSS) staff and those of public sector workers;
- developing a large-scale, clientelistic program of basic service delivery (the Programa Nacional de Solidaridad) for outsider groups that was closely identified with the presidency.

This implied that under President Salinas, economic modernization would occur under PRI hegemony, with more democracy nominally on the list of reforms, but implicitly with lower priority than economic change. The power of the presidency was, if anything, strengthened during this time: reforms were the product of the executive branch, with the legislature following closely behind. A number of "modern" regulatory agencies were created, including the CFC and the Energy Regulatory Commission (Comisión Reguladora de Energía, or CRE), but these were, and are, formally subservient to the executive branch (Guerrero, López-Calva, and Walton, chapter 4; Elizondo, chapter 5). A partial shift from a producing state to a regulating state occurred, but regulators lacked the political and institutional basis for real independence, and in any case, the absence of changes in the judiciary would limit the effectiveness of regulators because of the intensive use (or abuse) of the *amparo*.[7]

Thus, Mexico's modernization and liberalization were constrained by the underlying political equilibrium, and constrained in ways that meant that the necessary complementarities for efficient and rapid growth were missing. Some restructuring of the institutionalized pacts that sustained the inequality trap did occur, but these were limited. Manufacturing lost protection, but gained from a reduced threat of expropriation (Tornell and Esquivel 1995). Elements of the economic elite gained substantially from the privatizations, as illustrated by the rise in the number of billionaires (Guerrero, López-Calva, and Walton, chapter 4). Organized industrial workers in the private sector lost some product market protection, but they kept their job security, and their bargaining position had in any case been reduced by the years of stagnant economic growth. Organized workers in the public sector had also suffered wage declines, but their contractual position was unaffected by changes. The *ejido* system was partially reformed in 1992, but in ways that let communities decide on land titling. Farmers received transitional protection and compensatory programs, in particular, the Programa de Apoyos Directos al Campo, a program that was designed to provide grants to maize growers and that was intended in principle to compensate them for the loss of land rents associated with future product market liberalization, but that was rapidly extended to other crops not facing the same problems as maize.

PARTIAL INSTITUTIONAL CHANGE UNDER PRESIDENT ERNESTO ZEDILLO (1994–2000)

The administration of President Zedillo involved some consolidation of economic reforms, but the more fundamental institutional shifts involved laying the basis for the transition to democracy and, at least in principle, creating more effective checks and balances. In Mexico in the mid-1990s, almost by definition more democracy involved a reduction in the power of the presidency. Major reforms were undertaken to strengthen the independence of the judiciary, but these changes would inevitably take time. The mirror image of reduced executive power was increased influence of Congress and, in practice equally important, increased influence of subnational governments, principally governors.[8] The Zedillo democratization could be interpreted as recognition that a Salinas-type combination of economic modernization with preservation of old political structures was unsustainable at this stage of Mexico's development.

Democratization started with a major electoral reform and, gradually, devolution of power to Congress and to subnational governments. Budgetary resources were rebalanced as part of the rebalancing of political power. Critically, however, power was deposited in agents that did not have the right incentives to always use it in a socially desirable way and that had low levels of accountability (Elizondo, chapter 5). Not surprisingly, big business, organized labor, and corporatist interests in agriculture and other sectors soon realized that now they had to work with the legislature as well as with the executive branch to preserve their interests, and increased their influence in Congress. This was facilitated by the lack of transparency in Congress and the lack of experience of members of Congress.

Policy design under Zedillo involved formally sound reforms, but ones that failed to change deeply ingrained underlying power structures. The executive branch undertook reforms to telecommunications in 1995, but the result was a weak regulatory agency easily captured by private monopolies in a context of low transparency (del Villar, chapter 9; Noll, chapter 10). Pension reform was undertaken, but, in the initial years, the financial sector captured some of the benefits of the change from the pay-as-you-go system to the defined-contribution individual account system in a context of little competition. Furthermore, the special pension regime of IMSS workers remained in place (Levy, chapter 6).[9] Reforms opened up access to transportation of natural gas, but without touching PEMEX's commanding role or the special privileges of its workers (Lajous, chapter 11). An important reform of poverty policy occurred with the creation of the Programa de Educación, Salud y Alimentación (better known as PROGRESA and renamed Oportunidades by the next administration), but the dualistic structure of social programs for formal and informal workers remained intact. Resources for health and education were decentralized to the states, but without affecting the interests of the national unions of public health and education workers, both key supporters of the PRI (Elizondo, chapter 5; Maloney, chapter 7). The labor legislation that, by international standards, provides unusually high levels of job protection for formal sector workers did not undergo significant changes (Maloney, chapter 7).

Overall, President Zedillo undertook reforms that supported the transition to democracy and increased efficiency, but that were insufficient to structurally weaken the underlying powers that influenced policy making in ways detrimental to growth and equity. The major interests of big business and unionized workers in protected sectors learned that they could directly exert their influence in new fields of action, particularly Congress, and governors learned the same. What the presidency could no longer deliver or guarantee could now be obtained from the legislature. Indeed, the countervailing power on these interests provided by a strong presidency had been reduced before alternative institutions had been consolidated.

DEMOCRACY WITH WEAK INSTITUTIONS UNDER PRESIDENT VICENTE FOX (2000–06)

The administration of President Fox is generally characterized as having failed in relation to economic reforms. This failure is often attributed to the lack of experience of the first non-PRI government in 70 years and to insufficient decisiveness in both policy design and weakness of political resolve. The list of failures is long. President Fox attempted tax reform in 2001 and 2003 and failed twice, the administration attempted energy reform that stalled, it tried labor reform that stalled, and it attempted reform of public sector pensions that failed. The administration did not even attempt some potentially endowment-enhancing reforms, notably, fundamental changes in incentives for quality in education.

Other reforms did take place, but they were either not enforced, such as those affecting IMSS workers (Levy, chapter 6), or involved retrogression, such as those aimed at telecommunications (del Villar, chapter 9). On a more positive note, pro-efficiency reforms in relation to competition policy were undertaken, although their relevance in the face of cumbersome judicial procedures has yet to be demonstrated (Guerrero, López-Calva, and Walton, chapter 4; Elizondo, chapter 5). In parallel, weak regulatory structures allowed continued rent extraction to the detriment of efficiency and equity. A relevant example is agriculture, where the rising number of clientelistic programs reversed many of the advances in the direction of efficiency observed during the administrations of presidents Salinas and Zedillo (Rodríguez 2006). Yet another example is the petroleum and gas sector, where the CRE manipulated input prices to the benefit of a few large industrialists (Lajous, chapter 11). Not only did the executive branch obtain or regain special privileges, but also Congress did as various laws were passed to target benefits to teachers (cast as support for education because of its importance for development); medium-sized and large agricultural producers (cast as support for rural areas because that was where the poor were); and incumbents in telecommunications (passed in less than an hour in the lower house of Congress without attempts to cast a broader justification). The result was that, with the partial exception of finance (Haber, chapter 8), the substantive reforms needed to increase productivity and sustain long-term growth did not occur.

As a simple listing of reform failures, this is accurate, but the causal explanation of weakness may be incomplete. Another interpretation is that a pure efficiency-seeking reform agenda would not have worked even with a more decisive and stronger president. As opposed to the full term of President Salinas and the first half of President Zedillo's term, President Fox lacked a majority in both houses of Congress from the beginning, and Congress objectively lacked the incentives to support such a reform agenda (Elizondo, chapter 5). Equally, governors also lacked incentives to pursue an efficiency- and growth-oriented reform agenda: they were getting more of the fruits of the rent-sharing equilibrium than before and obtaining greater resources from the federal budget at no political cost to themselves, and their enhanced presence in Congress became essential to the approval of many laws. Disparate belief systems among central political actors also played a role in the erratic interplay between the presidency and Congress. Some interpreted the stagnation in growth as a failure of the president's reform agenda, while others saw it as a result of the failure to implement the president's reform agenda.

However, the absence of agreement on growth- and efficiency-inducing reforms was accompanied by a de facto, if not de jure, agreement on another front: expanding social benefits. Indeed, this may reflect what was the most significant structural shift in the political equilibrium effected by the transition to democracy. With the increased political salience of "outsider" groups of informal and rural households—now that votes counted more—both the presidency and Congress had incentives to support the expansion of popular social programs. Crucially, the availability of oil rents provided sufficient funding for expanded government-financed social provisioning that was concentrated mostly among workers in the informal sector. Given the absence of tax reform, this choice implicitly led to strong intertemporal effects, because few of the increased oil rents were channeled to growth-promoting infrastructure investments. Thus, redistribution occurred from the future to the present without growth. The more things change, the more they stay the same. Social programs sustained a political equilibrium that generated the policies and institutions resulting in high inequality and little growth, with external rents facilitating this outcome. A change in the political party in power might by itself do little to change this political equilibrium. Differently put, power might have changed from the PRI to the National Action Party, but the distributing state persisted, indeed, increased in scope, regardless of the shortcomings of the producing state or the regulating state.

More generally, the point is that the results of the Fox presidency must be looked at in the context of a rent-driven political equilibrium and the institutions and policies that emerge from such an equilibrium. There is a role for leadership, but the more important outcomes are a question not only of the individual personalities in the presidency, Congress, subnational governments, and the rest of the structures of formal power, but also of the large business, labor, agriculture, and other corporatist interests that have been much more resilient and persistent in the face of changing personalities and political parties. There is a difference between a weakened presidency and a weak president. Getting the right interpretation is of more than historical interest; it is critical for the future.

Implications for Equity and Growth

The interpretation of the past implies that Mexico's problem of low growth is inextricably linked to high levels of inequity. Mexico is not moving along the upward segment of a Kuznets-style inverted U-shaped relationship between inequality and growth, in which high levels of inequality are a necessary and transitional concomitant of the development process.[10] Rather, high levels of inequality are sources of a range of inefficiencies that lie at the core of the growth problem. Equity is a growth issue.

More precisely, the argument is that the presence of powerful and entrenched interests, especially of big business and protected unions, have led to a self-sustaining political equilibrium that supports a range of inequitable and inefficient economic institutions in finance, petroleum and gas, electricity, education, social security and social protection, telecommunications, agriculture, and other sectors. We have characterized this as a rent-sharing equilibrium, because the creation of economic rents through restrictions on competition in product, labor, and capital markets has been intrinsic to its design. Economic interests get shares of the rents in return for political support for the government and the continuation of the established institutions. Although this equilibrium has been modified by the economic liberalization and the advent of democracy, it has not fundamentally changed. In some respects, greater democratization may have been associated with worse economic policies and institutions, in part because of the decline in the power of the presidency that acted as a countervailing force against entrenched economic interests.

Both Bourguignon and Dessus (chapter 1) and Rajan (chapter 2) present their analyses using highly aggregated social groups. Bourguignon and Dessus use three groups: the elite, the middle class, and the poor. Rajan also has three groups: existing oligopolists, the skilled, and the unskilled. Table 0.1 takes the spirit of these approaches in providing a stylized representation of the various actors. We aggregate these into five categories. First are the various actors that form part of the state and the formal political process. Second are the major interest groups, or constituencies using Rajan's terminology, that are organized into insiders and outsiders among both firms and workers (and their households), where insider and outsider refers to both their economic position and the extent of their institutionalized political influence. Insiders are current incumbents, with entrenched economic positions among firms and households. The powerful farmers' lobby, which largely represents the interests of large farmers, falls somewhere in between the firm and the worker and household sectors. Outsiders are other firms, including potential new entrants and small informal firms, and informal workers and peasants. Future cohorts constitute a final and important outsider group, with the exception of those who expect to inherit insider status, a common feature not only of monopolistic business families, but also of protected unions.

Under our interpretation, the current rent-sharing equilibrium is

- *inequitable* in the sense that opportunities for outsiders, both firms and workers, are substantially restricted relative to those for insiders;
- *inefficient* because of the range of policies and institutional mechanisms whereby restriction of competition in or access to

Table 0.1 Major Actors in Mexico's Rent-Sharing Equilibrium

| Political actors and state institutions | Interest groups and constituencies | | | |
| | Firms | | Workers and households | |
	Insiders	Outsiders	Insiders	Outsiders
The presidency, the executive branch, Congress, political parties, the judiciary, state governors, regulatory authorities	Big business incumbents, state-owned companies (PEMEX, electricity utility, etc.)	Other firms, especially small and medium-sized firms, potential new entrants	Workers in protected unions (petroleum, electricity, teachers, IMSS, etc.), other workers in formal jobs, organized farmers	Informal workers, peasants, future cohorts of workers and unborn generations

Source: Authors.

> product, labor, education, and capital markets is leading to
> forgone economic opportunities for outsiders and inefficient
> production and investment choices by insiders; and
> - *self-sustaining* in the sense that its internal dynamics tend to
> reinforce existing structures and, in particular, to sustain the
> position of insiders.

Given our focus on the possibility of policy and institutional
change, the self-sustaining character of the existing equilibrium is of
special interest. In abstract terms, its character implies that it is in
the interests of current insiders to "pay" the political actors (whether
financially or in terms of political support) to sustain the existing
structures rather than to support a shift to more efficient and equitable policies and that this "payment" exceeds what outsiders are
willing to pay for such a change. Bourguignon and Dessus emphasize
that incumbents often have the power to block change. Rajan suggests that the equilibrium of the strategic interaction is often no
reform, because beneficiaries are unwilling to risk losing their rents.
Both chapters emphasize that compensation of losers from efficiency
gains is likely to face credibility problems.

This gives rise to numerous implications for policy design. As
summarized earlier, there are alternative, seemingly coherent views
on this. However, the main contribution of this volume is not
intended to be a list of desirable policy changes. Rather, its aim is
to shift the way policy change in Mexico is conceptualized in two
ways. First, as a direct corollary of the diagnosis, policies aimed
at promoting efficiency and growth cannot be separated from
policies aimed at fostering equity.[11] In particular, policy and institutional changes that tackle the existing inequities between
entrenched insiders and outsiders are likely to be essential to get
Mexico onto a dynamic, efficient growth path, and this applies to
reducing the power of both big business and protected unions, as
well as changing the behavior of state actors (table 0.1). This does
not mean that all pro-equity policies are desirable. Indeed, some
policies aimed at increasing equity can have adverse efficiency
effects as, for example, in the case of expansion of social protection to informal households (Levy, chapter 6). Second, policy
design should be assessed in terms of the interactions between the
various constituencies and political actors shown in table 0.1 that
are sustaining the current political equilibrium. Otherwise, well-
intentioned policy efforts will never get through the institutions of
the state into policy action. Alternatively, the implementation of
seemingly well-designed policies will be distorted or neutralized
by the behaviors of existing actors.

Analyses of policy design that recognize political economy influences often assume that all policy is effectively endogenous, in the sense that it represents the underlying structure of power and institutions of coordination in a society. Bourguignon and Dessus start from this perspective. As already noted, Rajan further argues that where major groups share rents, competitive rent preservation can lead to a form of gridlock. The comprehensive reforms needed for efficient and equitable growth (in relation to education and increased competition in his example) do not occur because no group is willing to give up its rents, absent credible mechanisms to compensate losers out of an expanded pie.

These perspectives leave those interested in changing policy, whether in the executive branch, Congress, or civil society, in a somewhat depressing position of impotence. Little can be done except wait for the underlying structures to change, whether through internal processes of economic and social transformation or through exogenous shocks. A more subtle view is that of Greif (2006), who distinguishes between whether institutions and policies are self-enforcing or self-undermining. Self-undermining means that internal, endogenous processes change the parameters of behavior over time, in ways that lead to eventual institutional transition. This is an important perspective that is undoubtedly relevant to contemporary Mexico, but it still does not help proactive policy makers. Neither are such policy makers helped by waiting for a large exogenous shock such as the exhaustion of oil resources.

Although recognition of the power of entrenched interests and institutional structures is at the center of the argument of this book, we adopt a cautiously optimistic view on the potential for change: different actors in the system summarized in table 0.1 do have some room for maneuver, and this maneuver has potentially been enhanced by the increase in democracy and the associated expansion in access to information. At the broadest level, this view is supported by two considerations that are related to the earlier comment on existing payoffs. First, as well-designed change will expand the pie over the medium term, there is at least the potential for most groups to gain (in principle, all will gain, although compensating all losers may not be desirable). Second, outsiders stand to gain substantially from policy change, and their failure to have successfully provided political support for such change reflects failures in collective action and distorted belief systems, in addition to the entrenched influence of insiders.

The cross-cutting essays in the volume help us organize thinking about possible change in Mexico, and the following subsections highlight some of the lessons.

Democratic Transition and Collective Action

Can democratization lead to the reduced influence of entrenched interests and more efficient economic outcomes? Robinson (chapter 3) discusses two major episodes in U.S. history that followed democratization. In the first case, that of the South after the Civil War, entrenched interests reconstructed unequal social and economic institutions despite democratization, effectively preserving the power of oligarchic white groups and the subjugated economic, social, and political position of blacks. Many blacks chose the exit option, migrating to the industrial cities of the North. Substantive internal change within the South had to wait until the civil rights movement, almost a century later. In the second case, the antitrust movement from the late 19th century to the 1920s effectively mobilized to break the power of the major economic monopolies. In this case, democracy provided a political framework for fundamental change, but this was contingent on a set of other factors, especially the capacity of outsider groups to solve their collective action problems to effect change. This episode also illustrates that change can take decades rather than a few years.

The U.S. experience has salutary lessons for Mexico. It illustrates how entrenched interests can reshape institutions to further their position under new economic and political conditions. This lesson is consistent with our interpretation of Mexico's experience in the past 15 to 20 years, but it also provides an optimistic note, showing that the political equilibrium can shift, even when entrenched economic interests appear to be extraordinarily powerful. Although the comparison with the United States is only indicative, it appears to have at least three features relevant to Mexico (beyond the existence of a functioning, if imperfect, democracy): coordination and effective action among constituencies interested in change; leadership, including from the presidency; and high levels of information and debate.

Information and Debate

The contributions by Bourguignon and Dessus (chapter 1) and by Elizondo (chapter 5) emphasize the role of information. Both chapters argue that part of the reason that the inefficient and inequitable equilibrium is sustained is that actors have incomplete information. This affects both the motives and the organizational capacity of outsiders, although it may also lead to insider groups underestimating the aggregate efficiency losses of the existing position. Better information can potentially lead to a change in the equilibrium. Information has many elements: transparency, the media, and the capacity of sophisticated independent groups (commentators, academics, party intellectuals, and think-tanks) to interpret complex developments. Bourguignon and Dessus argue for independent analyses of the distributional effects of current institutional arrangements and of alternative reforms to inform public debate.

Action to improve information is highly desirable. This is particularly salient for Mexico given the prevalence of belief systems that form part of the self-sustaining institutional structures. For example, the belief that public ownership of PEMEX and electricity production is good for the country probably extends to outsider groups who are almost certainly being hurt by the current highly inefficient production. Similarly, pro-agriculture policies are often framed as being pro-poor, when the substantial subsidies channeled to the sector go disproportionately to relatively better-off farmers. Increased transparency at the federal level was a notable achievement of the Fox administration in relation to access to information and the introduction of legal requirements on the evaluation of social programs.[12] There is at least anecdotal evidence that this is having specific positive effects, though whether access to information is having an influence on public debate is unclear.

Better-Functioning Political Institutions

Another view is that the real problems concern how political actors and associated institutions of the state aggregate preferences, mobilize support, and countervail arbitrary action by the executive branch and powerful interest groups. As Elizondo discusses (chapter 5), members of the legislature are often inexperienced in policy formation, poorly informed, and aligned with specific sectoral interests. This is, in part, a function of structural features such as the no re-election rule. This rule makes members of Congress more dependent on their party than on their electoral constituency and provides weak incentives to invest in understanding policy. These structural distortions to effective decision making in Congress (effective in the sense that it makes efficient choices that represent the interests of the electorate) have become more important in view of the rising relative power of Congress in relation to the presidency. Of at least equal importance is the weakness of the judiciary, particularly at the state level, and especially in the potential for powerful interests to use the *amparo* to hold legal decisions at bay for years pending appeal. Guerrero, López-Calva, and Walton (chapter 4) provide empirical information on the use of the *amparo* by big business to render anticompetitiveness decisions by the CFC ineffective.

Better information and structural changes in the functioning of the various organs of the state are highly desirable and complement each other. They are likely to form an essential part of a successful long-term transition and should be pursued. However, whether rapid transition toward effective political mechanisms would lead automatically to efficient and equitable outcomes is unclear in both cases. As Rajan (chapter 2) highlights, a substantial risk exists that the different groups that succeed in extracting some rents from the existing system will resist the more fundamental changes needed to shift to a better equilibrium for all, even if they are better informed.

Also required is longer-term development of capacity in government and civil society and changes in political culture. For this reason, we see a role for proactive policy design by actors that have some degree of autonomy inside the political system, perhaps especially, but by no means exclusively, in the executive branch. This is a complement, not a substitute, for action on information and political reform.

Sequencing

The contributions in this volume have a variety of perspectives on what sequencing is likely to be feasible given the initial political equilibrium. Rajan argues that a shift to a more efficient and equitable equilibrium may require changes in endowments, because the endowments of the different constituencies are what shapes their interests and strategies. In particular, he suggests that expanding access to human capital-creating institutions is needed to change the interests of (payoffs to) different constituencies and make a new equilibrium possible. This is an important insight, but an account of how to tackle the political economy of access expansion is still needed, especially when problems of low-quality education and health services flow at least in part from protected unions.

A modification of this view is to focus on what is both strategically effective (by changing structures that shape the overall equilibrium, as with Rajan's argument about endowments) and practically feasible in terms of political support.

Specific Coalitions and the Modification of Payoffs

We group two distinct ideas here. The first idea is that specific, sectoral opportunities for action will often arise, drawing on commonalities of interest, and with the potential to mobilize public support by exerting genuine leadership to solve collective action problems. The second idea is that a fundamental change is needed in relation to the perceived payoffs between protecting the status quo and more equitable and efficient outcomes. In particular, this means two things: (a) changing the net benefits for insiders in favor of pro-equity, pro-growth changes; and (b) increasing the willingness of outsider groups to support change. The complementarity with the earlier areas of action is immediately clear: better information is important so that different groups are aware of the potential gains from change and a more effective political process can help ensure that the functioning of Congress, the judiciary, or regulatory authorities does not subvert policy design or implementation.

Concluding Comments

This overview is not the place to propose a specific agenda for policy change. Rather, its objective is to suggest ways of thinking about policy design and implementation and to provide some suggestive illustrations. For example, a more dynamic growth path will require action to reduce the power of the private monopolies or, more accurately, the large-scale business interests that are organized in pyramidal corporate structures (Guerrero, López-Calva, and Walton, chapter 4). These groups are beneficiaries of rents in the current equilibrium. Although losing rents imposes a cost, they will plausibly also prosper under a more competitive environment, especially one with better provision of tax-financed public goods. Indeed, many of the big businesses are already expanding into foreign markets, demonstrating their capacity to earn profits under competitive conditions. The state has, in principle, instruments to reduce their economic power through existing regulatory authorities, but the effectiveness of these instruments is currently being reduced either by the judicial system (for the CFC) or by regulatory weakness or apparent capture (for instance, for the telecommunications authority [del Villar, chapter 9; Noll, chapter 10]). What is required is a coalition to support both better regulatory design and implementation, effectively increasing the costs to big business of sustaining the existing system. In principle, a relatively pro-business executive branch is well-placed to do this, given the heightened awareness of the power of these interests and the concern among business groups that the tight 2006 election outcome could presage a more radical, and hence more costly (to them), political resolution in a future election. Concerted action under President Felipe Calderón, supported by better information, could lead to a more efficient outcome for business functioning and a less polarized political situation.[13]

Both del Villar and Noll argue that reducing TELMEX's market dominance is indispensable for a faster process in relation to technology adoption and innovation by firms. They also indicate feasible ways in which regulatory behavior and specific policy decisions could lead to a pattern of provision of telecommunications services that is both cheaper and more broadly based. Noll also argues that TELMEX is a relatively efficient company by global standards: it effected major efficiency improvements in the wake of privatization, but the gains led disproportionately to higher profits rather than lower prices and better services. From a broader context, action to improve competitiveness in telecommunications would provide a signal that the government is serious about tackling anticompetitive structures. This also applies to competition in the provision of television and radio services, which now also face restricted competition. This is critical, because these are important means of providing better information and bringing more informed debate into the public realm.

A small number of private business interests have traditionally dominated the financial system. According to Haber (chapter 8) and Haber and others (2007), this is one sector where the explicit hold of domestic big business was effectively broken: in the aftermath of the 1994–95 crisis, the subsequent regulatory and supervisory reforms, and the sell-off to foreign banks that now own some 80 percent of the sector. The sector, nevertheless, remains both highly concentrated and remarkably averse to lending to private firms by international standards. Haber argues that one of the main underlying causes is the continued weak property rights system, which increases the risks of lending to firms. Tackling this will require concerted effort, especially at the state level, backed by substantial expenditure, and thus, it is also entwined with tax reforms and incentives to subnational governments. As an interim measure, Haber recommends working to liberalize entry into the sector while maintaining strong prudential standards—in this case, building on the achievements of the Fox administration.

Many other areas within the existing, self-sustaining, rent-sharing equilibrium involve corporatist unions in protected sectors. Because of existing protections in the labor market, benefits are substantially higher for insiders than for outsiders (Guerrero, López-Calva, and Walton, chapter 4), incentives for greater effort are weak (Elizondo, chapter 5; Maloney, chapter 7), and these highly organized groups can be effective lobbies against broader reform in their respective sectors. At first sight, change may seem particularly hard to achieve in these areas, because pro-efficiency and pro-equity reform would likely reduce benefits for these insider groups, and many years of growth may be required before positive net gains are apparent. Yet change did occur for the manufacturing sector in the wake of the major crisis of the 1980s and, as Maloney argues, in the 1990s, unions in manufacturing appeared to negotiate for employment rather than wages.[14]

The case of the IMSS (Levy, chapter 6) illustrates both the potential of and the obstacles to reform. On the negative side, a legal reform promoted by President Fox in 2001 to increase transparency and accountability helped expose the risks to the long-term viability of the IMSS as a result of the special pension regime of its own workers and highlighted that workers affiliated with the IMSS were the main losers. That reform led to a further legal reform in 2004, this time promoted by Congress, that took the classic political economy approach of grandfathering existing employees in return for creating a level playing field for new employees. So far, this could be interpreted as a specific application of the arguments about the importance of information and collective action problems emphasized by Bourguignon and Dessus and by Elizondo. The IMSS union, which operates a closed shop in line with Mexican labor law, stood to lose its rents and its leverage over future workers, but the vast majority of affiliated workers would gain in the form of better services. In this context and even though the reform was legally binding, the union was effective in pressurizing the executive branch to shelve it.[15] Instead, the IMSS and its union agreed to a "reverse" pay-as-you-go pension scheme, perhaps the only one of its kind in the world, thwarting the reform and creating even larger legal and financial problems for the future. The case of the IMSS illustrates the important difference between transparency and access to information, on the one hand, and accountability of public officials, on the other. Reforms to increase access to information are essential. In this case, they translated into legal changes to gradually correct the problem, but at least in some cases, legal reforms need to be accompanied by measures to promote compliance though effective accountability mechanisms. Reforms in a context of weak rule of law can produce the same or a potentially worse outcome as no reform.

An example of a positive change concerns reforms that reduced rents held by private retirement funds. After the pension reform of 1997, a new source of inefficiency and rent was introduced through the excessive profits of the retirement fund administrators (administradoras de fondos para el retiro, or AFORES). A concentrated market structure has been associated with unusually high profits by Mexican and industry standards, lasting for almost a decade (Levy, chapter 6). In this case, both pro-competitive measures promoted by the regulators and information provided to Congress and the public at large by the CFC led to a debate about the behavior of the AFORES. As a result, the level of their commissions has fallen significantly since 2005, and in early 2007, legislation was passed to increase transparency and simplify the complex structure of commissions that was one of the factors that created difficulties for competition in this industry. Despite the long transition and the substantial monopoly rents already extracted at the cost of reduced workers' pensions in the future, these measures are welcome. More important in the context of the foregoing discussion, this is a good example of how concerted action by regulators and the competition authorities, together with increased information and debate, can achieve results that are both equity and efficiency enhancing. An interesting hypothesis for future research is whether these changes were facilitated by the change in ownership of banks, because banks were the owners of the major AFORES.

The case of PEMEX, discussed by Lajous (chapter 11), illustrates several themes. Lajous argues that rent extraction by the federal government, large business, and PEMEX's own union have placed PEMEX in a position where it not only fails to contribute to growth and productivity, but also results in the loss of economic value, because the country's hydrocarbon resources are inefficiently exploited. Effective reform of the sector would require both changing the market environment and tackling the internal incentives for inefficiencies, overstaffing, and low effort. Given the strength of belief systems about public ownership and the need to build regulatory capacity over time, Lajous argues for a gradual process of opening up the sector to competition. He also sees reform as inextricably linked to tax reform, because otherwise the Ministry of Finance would be unwilling to let go of its excessive and inefficient controls over the company, and to union reform, given the power PEMEX's union to hold up change.

With respect to general issues of labor market reform, Maloney (chapter 7) argues that change is needed, but notes the political economy of sequencing. He suggests that introducing more competition into labor market institutions is likely to be easier after reforms to tackle the rents of the truly rich, entrenched business interests in the country and, more broadly, greater confidence that the state is representing a reasonably equitable social compact. The government may then have more credibility in trying to obtain support both from outsider groups and, in some areas, from insider workers.

As noted, this volume contains specialized chapters on selected areas of the Mexican economy. As already mentioned, other sectors that are central to the existing rent-sharing equilibrium include agriculture, education, taxation, and the behavior of subnational governments, and reform in each area will be important to move the country toward a more efficient and equitable equilibrium. We believe that the general approach outlined in this overview chapter applies to thinking about change in these areas as well as those covered in more detail in this volume.

More generally, however, we believe that what is most important at this juncture is to change the terms of the debate and to increase awareness of the interactions between equity, institutions, and growth, both for economic dynamics and for the political equilibrium. The central issues for development in Mexico are not between private versus public, between business versus labor, between neoliberalism versus structuralism, or between technocrats versus state-promoters. The central issue is rather how reforms can occur in an evolving democracy that are in the direction of both more equity and more productivity. This implies preventing such reforms from being captured and distorted or diluted by those affected. This can have implications for the specific content and sequence of reforms. More broadly, it concerns the nature of a state that in all three of its roles—producer, regulator, and distributor—has yet to achieve growth and equity outcomes in accordance with the country's underlying possibilities, and that is by-and-large a spectator in the face of massive outmigration of its labor force.

After reading this book, outside observers unfamiliar with Mexico would perhaps ask themselves whether it points to anything new. Are not the issues and problems described here the ones we would expect in any society experiencing democratic change? Are not rent seeking, inequity, and privilege characteristics of many societies whose extent and perniciousness diminishes with deepening democracy? Are not all these essays, in the end, a reflection of unjustified impatience given that history shows that democratic transformations take decades and that ups and downs during the process are inevitable? Such outside observers are indeed almost certainly correct in seeing Mexico as an example of a much more general condition of developing countries, and will, we hope, be proven right with regard to change. However, we would point to the urgency of accelerating the process, because Mexico is not experiencing its pains and pangs of change in a vacuum. It is experiencing them in the context of an increasingly competitive and dynamic international environment, and time lost is welfare foregone for most of Mexico's citizens. Mexico has made major advances in macroeconomic management and is not in a crisis now. High oil prices may further reduce the pressure to undertake change (except, perhaps, for changes necessary to keep the quantity of oil flowing). Nevertheless, undertaking serious change is urgent if the majority of Mexico's citizens are not to remain long-term victims of a slow-growth, inequitable society.

Notes

1. The previous period occurred from the late 1950s to the early 1970s when GDP grew at around 6 percent per year. We ignore here the 1978–81 growth spurt associated with the high oil prices in effect at that time (Bazdresch and Levy 1991).

2. Mexican legislation makes a unique distinction between basic petrochemicals (for example, ethane), which are within the monopoly domain of Petróleos Mexicanos (PEMEX), and secondary petrochemicals (for instance, ethylene), which are open to private investors. In many cases, the production technology does not allow for such a distinction, and private investors in ethylene must build their plants next to PEMEX's ethane facilities and depend on PEMEX's pricing and supply strategies for their medium-term plans. This generates substantial uncertainties that deter investment unless the pricing rules are clear and long-term contracts can be signed and enforced, which PEMEX has few incentives to do.

3. The Instituto Mexicano del Seguro Social is responsible for providing social security benefits to formal workers in the private sector, and their pension system changed from a pay-as-you-go to a defined-contribution scheme in 1997. Public sector workers are covered by their own social security institute and were under a pay-as-you-go pension scheme until 2007, when a change to a defined-contribution scheme was finally legislated.

4. There is an immense amount of literature in this area. For surveys of the economics literature, see Aghion, Caroli, and García-Peñalosa (1999) and Bénabou (1996).

5. We use the term "belief system" rather than "ideology," because the latter has potentially misleading associations. See Greif (2006) for a discussion of the role of belief systems in supporting self-sustaining equilibriums in a game theoretic sense.

6. More precisely, they will invest until the expected returns (net of expected expropriation) equal their cost of capital, so investment will be reduced in line with increases in the risk of expropriation.

7. The *amparo* is a mechanism whereby private parties can defer the effects of an act of authority by a regulator until the merits of the case are thrashed out in the courts (Elizondo, chapter 5). As an example, del Villar (chapter 9) points out that the courts took eight years to render their final judgment on a ruling by the CFC that TELMEX had "substantial power" in the telephone market. The CFC lost the case, because the courts argued that the evidence on which the case was based was obsolete.

8. As the presidency-dominated PRI disappeared in 2001 with the election of President Fox, part of the vacuum was filled by PRI governors (still the majority) who, given the system for nominating, electing, and rewarding members of Congress, now acquired—indirectly, but nonetheless effectively—an important role in Congress.

9. The IMSS provides social security benefits for private sector workers in formal jobs, but it also provides social security benefits for its own approximately 360,000 workers, who, through their labor contract, have additional, much more favorable benefits, particularly with regard to pensions. The same is true for public workers in the two public electricity companies and in PEMEX.

10. Kuznets famously argued that inequality in the distribution of income would rise and fall in the long-run development process, because of labor shifts from low- to high-productivity sectors and the dynamics of human capital accumulation. In this interpretation, however, high inequality is not only transitional, it is also essentially benign, because it does not itself shape institutions and policy choices. This is in sharp contrast to the perspective of this volume, where inequality is harmful because it helps shape institutions and policies that perpetuate inequality and create inefficiencies.

11. For students of economics, this is equivalent to the statement that the Fisher Separation Theorem does not hold. Intuitively, this theory states that where complete, perfect markets exist, separating decisions about efficiency from decisions about distribution is efficient. The theorem does not hold when markets are imperfect, but this seems to be frequently forgotten in policy practice.

12. Some of the changes enhancing transparency and access to information, particularly with regard to budgetary allocations and evaluation of social programs, were initiated during the administration of President Zedillo in the context resulting from the PRI's loss of control of the lower house of Congress in 1997 (Levy 2004). However, these changes were given broader scope and a more solid institutional basis with new legislation proposed by President Fox.

13. The extent of both polarization and radicalization of the left also depends, of course, on a whole range of other factors, including social service provision and employment outcomes.

14. Excess employment still has efficiency costs, but in the context of competitive product markets, industries have strong incentives for efficiency and the external costs of labor rationing are less.

15. In this case, the *amparo* was not the reason for bypassing application of the reform. Various judges and magistrates denied the union all the *amparos* solicited after President Fox promulgated the reform, so the reform was legally binding all along. In early 2007, the Supreme Court rejected the last *amparo* by the union.

References

Acemoglu, D., S. Johnson, and J. A. Robinson. 2002. "Reversal of Fortune: Geography and Institutions in the Making of the Modern World Income Distribution." *Quarterly Journal of Economics* 117 (4): 1231–94.

Acemoglu, D., and J. A. Robinson. 2006. *Economic Origins of Dictatorship and Democracy*. New York: Cambridge University Press.

Aghion, P., E. Caroli, and C. García-Peñalosa. 1999. "Inequality and Economic Growth: The Perspective of New Growth Theory." *Journal of Economic Literature* 37 (4): 1615–60.

Bassi, M., C. Fox, G. Márquez, J. Mazza, and C. Ricart. 2006. "Creando Buenos Empleos: Políticas Públicas y Mercado de Trabajo." Documento de Trabajo. Departmento de Investigación, Inter-American Development Bank, Washington, DC.

Bazdresch, C., and S. Levy. 2004. "Populism and Economic Policy in Mexico, 1970–82." In *The Macroeconomics of Populism in Latin America*, ed. R. Dornbusch and S. Edwards, 627–71. Chicago: University of Chicago Press.

Bénabou, R. 1996. "Inequality and Growth." In *National Bureau of Economic Research Macroeconomics Annual 1996*, ed. Ben Bernanke and Julio J. Rotemberg, 11–74. Cambridge, MA: Massachusetts Institute of Technology Press.

Bourguignon, F., F. H. G. Ferreira, and M. Walton. 2007. "Equity, Efficiency and Inequality Traps: A Research Agenda." *Journal of Economic Inequality* 5 (2): 235–56.

Easterly, W., and R. Levine. 2003. "Tropics, Germs, and Crops: How Endowments Influence Economic Development." *Journal of Monetary Economics* 50 (1): 3–39.

Glaeser E., R. La Porta, F. Lopez-de-Silanes, and A. Shleifer. 2004. "Do Institutions Cause Growth?" *Journal of Economic Growth* 9 (3): 271–303.

Glaeser, E., J. Scheinkman, and A. Shleifer. 2003. "The Injustice of Inequality." *Journal of Monetary Economics* 50 (1): 199–222.

Greif, A. 2006. *Institutions and the Path to the Modern Economy: Lessons from Medieval Trade*. New York: Cambridge University Press.

Haber, S. H., H. S. Klein, N. Maurer, and K. J. Middlebrook. 2007. *The Second Mexican Revolution: Economic, Political and Social Change since 1980*. New York: Cambridge University Press.

Haber, S. H., A. Razo, and N. Maurer. 2003. *The Politics of Property Rights: Political Instability, Credible Commitments and Economic Growth in Mexico, 1876–1929*. New York: Cambridge University Press.

Heston, A., R. Summers, and B. Aten. 2006. *Penn World Table Version 6.2*. Philadelphia: University of Pennsylvania, Center for International Comparisons of Production, Income, and Prices.

Levy, S. 2004. "Transparencia, discrecionalidad y eficiencia en el presupuesto de egresos de la Federación." In *Ensayos sobre el desarrollo económico y social de México*. Mexico City: Fondo de Cultura Económica.

Murillo, M. V. 2002. "Political Bias in Policy Convergence: Privatization Choices in Latin America." *World Politics* 54 (4): 462–93.

North, D. C. 1990. *Institutions, Institutional Change, and Economic Performance*. Cambridge, U.K.: Cambridge University Press.

Rajan, R. 2006. "The Persistence of Underdevelopment: Constituencies and Competitive Rent Preservation." Working paper, University of Chicago, Chicago.

Rao, V. 2006. "On 'Inequality Traps' and Development Policy." *Development Outreach* (February): 10–13.

Rodríguez, E. 2006. "Progresa-Oportunidades y la Política de Desarrollo Rural en México: ¿Estrategias Complementarias?" Documento de Trabajo, Departamento Regional Dos, Mimeo. Inter-American Development Bank, Washington, DC.

Rodrik, D., A. Subramanian, and F. Trebbi. 2002. "Institutions Rule: The Primacy of Institutions over Geography and Integration in Economic Development." Working Paper Series 9305, National Bureau of Economic Research, Cambridge, MA.

Tornell, A., and G. Esquivel. 1995. "The Political Economy of Mexico's Entry to NAFTA." Working Paper 5322, National Bureau of Economic Research, Cambridge, MA.

World Bank. 2005. *World Development Report 2006: Equity and Development*. New York: Oxford University Press.

PART I

Concepts and International Experience

1

Equity and Development: Political Economy Considerations

François Bourguignon and Sébastien Dessus

Observers frequently explain the lack of dynamism of Latin American countries by pointing to their excessive income inequality. This is indeed a characteristic common to these countries—and increasingly to Sub-Saharan African countries—in comparison with the rapidly growing countries in Asia and in Eastern and Central Europe. Yet these same observers do not always clearly explain the actual channels through which inequality acts as a brake on growth. The 2006 *World Development Report* (World Bank 2006) explains the relationship. It emphasizes the logical link between inequality of opportunities (including access to education, credit, infrastructure, and public decision making) and economic growth. Inequality of opportunities prevents some economic agents—whether individuals, households, or firms—from fully expressing their economic potential, thereby reducing economic efficiency and slowing growth. At the same time, and along with other factors, the inequality of opportunities feeds into inequality of outcomes. In Latin America, inequality of opportunities appears to be responsible for both slow growth and high income inequality.[1]

If inequality of opportunities, henceforth referred to as inequity, is responsible for slower growth, what can be done to redress this situation? The basic problem with promoting equality of opportunities is that this is likely to directly harm the interests of some privileged groups. Either the government will levy more taxes to fund equity-promoting programs and such taxes might affect such groups

proportionately more, or some economic advantages accruing to
such groups and the corresponding rents they derive from them will
be reduced. Whether a country undertakes such policies depends on
(a) the overall efficiency gains of such policies and how they are
distributed among the entire population, and (b) the way in which
policy decisions are taken. If everybody is likely to gain more or less
proportionally to his or her initial level of welfare, everyone benefits
from the envisaged reforms and they should eventually be implemented. If this is not the case, policy implementation will depend on
the relative weights of the groups of winners and losers in the political decision process. Even though equity may be beneficial to
growth, the likelihood of undertaking equity-enhancing policies
depends on political economy factors.

Ultimately, political economy factors may be the main reason that
some countries grow at a slower pace than others. These countries are
inequitable to start with and, therefore, are inefficient, and this situation is perpetuated because elites have captured both economic and
political power and naturally have no interest in relinquishing either.
Such a setting is behind many cases of slow or stagnating development. Historically in most such cases, exogenous shocks have been at
the origin of the weakening of elite capture. Hence, economists and
other analysts can do little except maybe widen public knowledge of
the opportunity costs of elite capture. Although not a sufficient condition, improved transparency in this area is nonetheless vital to
enlighten the various actors in the political economy game about
reforms that might go against the elites' interests. We argue that more
empirical work needs to be undertaken in this domain and identify
some difficulties that economic analysis confronts in this regard.

This chapter, which elaborates on the 2006 *World Development
Report*, provides a conceptual background for the other chapters in
this volume.

The Complementarity between Equity and Development

Latin American countries, including Mexico, record extremely high
levels of income inequality or, more generally, of economic welfare
inequality. Whereas the Gini coefficient, a common measure of
income inequality, is around 0.35 in developed countries and around
0.40 or slightly higher in Asian countries, it is closer to 0.5—and
often more, in most Latin American countries. Given the sharp contrast with rapidly growing Asian countries, attributing Latin American
countries' disappointing growth performance to this specific feature
of their economies is tempting.[2]

Confirming statistically whether this has actually been the case would require measuring the influence of inequality on growth rates across countries while controlling for all other factors likely to affect growth. Unfortunately, the number of such factors is too large, the interactions among them are too complex, and the number of statistical observations is too limited for such an exercise to deliver reliable conclusions. The ambiguous results cited in recent cross-country literature are, therefore, not surprising (for a short survey of the cross-country literature on the relationship between inequality and growth and a candid view of the available evidence, see Banerjee and Duflo 2003). Of greater interest is that some of the recent economic literature focuses on the theoretical mechanisms that could explain why inequality may be an obstacle to growth. This literature is essentially from the early 1990s, and the pioneering work in this area includes Aghion and Bolton (1992), Alesina and Rodrik (1994), Banerjee and Newman (1991), Bertola (1993), Galor and Zeira (1993), and Persson and Tabellini (1994). This literature concludes that the inequality of income (or of consumption) is less responsible for slow growth than for the inequality of endowments—wealth in particular—and of access to particular markets, income-generating facilities, and public decision making. In other words, both income inequality and slow or stagnating growth are consequences of more fundamental inequalities in individuals' opportunities to generate income and influence policy.

Following the social justice literature, referring to these inequalities as inequality of opportunities is logical. Individuals with limited access to education, credit, and various types of infrastructure; those who are discriminated against in the labor market; or those who have little influence in local or national political debates have limited opportunities to realize their economic potential. We will refer to this particular type of inequality as inequity to distinguish it more clearly from the concept of inequality that implicitly tends to refer to outcomes of economic activity, including incomes, rather than to the determinants of those outcomes. Poverty can be seen through this lens, because poor people tend to lack opportunities; at the same time, their welfare level is below some threshold, but the concept of inequity cannot be restricted solely to the analysis of poverty. Inequity is also apparent elsewhere in society. Elite capture of economic or political power is a case in point. It may occur at the expense of the opportunities of the poor and of other groups in society. For instance, barriers to entry into a specific area of economic activity restrict the opportunities available to potential entrepreneurs or investors in comparison with those available to incumbents. Another example is a group of people who control, even if only partially, the political decision-making process or who influence the justice system, which prevents others, both poor and nonpoor, from expressing their views about the provision of certain public goods or from defending their property rights. The concept of economic inequity is thus much broader than is the distinction between the poor and the nonpoor. It encompasses all situations where some opportunities, especially income generation, are open to some but not to others.

The idea of capture is central to the definition of inequity. Inequality of access to some economic facilities is unavoidable in any society whose level of affluence does not permit making these facilities available to all. However, such a situation would not give rise to inequity if access were completely independent of individual characteristics such as social or parental background, ethnicity, gender, or age—in other words, if access to limited facilities were purely random. The capture of limited facilities by some specific groups and, therefore, the exclusion of other groups are what constitute the source of inequity. The barriers to entry to the financial sector raised by a powerful economic elite, the impossibility of getting a job without joining a union, the restriction of access to the best schools to children of economic or cultural elites, or the control of local public decision making by politicians acting in their own personal interests are all examples of opportunities being denied to part of the population and, therefore, of inequity.

Inequity negatively affects economic efficiency and growth through three basic channels. The first channel has to do with the realization of individual economic potential and the misallocation of talent and resources. Lack of access to income-generation opportunities such as education or credit prevents talented people from realizing their economic potential and reduces their incentives for effort, saving, and innovation. It also results in a misallocation of existing resources and lowers their average rate of return. Good investment projects are not undertaken for lack of credit, whereas mediocre projects are launched because their promoters could rely on personal wealth or credit. This mechanism applies at all levels, from the talented child of a poor family unable to attend school; to a dynamic, innovative entrepreneur unable to enter a sector controlled by a monopoly; to the public goods that an elite group rather than the majority of citizens will consume.

The second channel is through the persistence of inefficient institutions for public decision making, for the regulation of the economy, and for justice. Unequal political rights or the capture of political power by a group of citizens prevents the reform of inefficient institutions. In turn, deficient institutions—in particular, imperfect protection of property rights because of unequal access to justice—generate disincentives to effort, saving, and entrepreneurship in that part of the population that is discriminated against.

Economic efficiency and growth are then lower than what they could be given adequate institutions.

The third channel is through political tension and conflict. The permanent exclusion of part of the population from income-generation facilities and that same group's lack of voice in public decision making inevitably lead to social and political tensions. Those who have political and economic power may contain these tensions, but this containment comes implicitly or explicitly at a cost that reduces the amount of resources that can be invested in productive activities. From an economic point of view, investing in the production of goods and services rather than in security and political repression is certainly preferable. Open conflicts may also result from such a situation, with even bigger costs in terms of development.

Through all these channels, inequity makes the economy less efficient and slows growth. It also tends to perpetuate itself over time through its impact on the inequality of outcomes. Unequal opportunities feed into inequality of outcomes and low economic efficiency, which, in turn, are likely to generate inequality of opportunities through intergenerational transmission mechanisms. The generation born in the poorest group will have limited access to income-generation facilities, whereas their high incomes permit elites to pay the bribes necessary to maintain their monopoly power over part of the economy or the policy-making system and to protect their children's position. In that sense, one can refer to inequality traps, where initial inequity generates slow economic development and high inequality of outcomes, both of which contribute, in turn, to the persistence of inequity (for a more formal definition of inequality traps, see Bourguignon, Ferreira, and Walton 2006).

Evidence for inequality traps and the various channels through which inequity affects development are found at the microeconomic rather than at the macroeconomic level. Indeed, summarizing the impact of inequity on economic efficiency into a single coefficient that could then be related to the pace of economic growth across countries or time periods is difficult given the multiple dimensions of inequity. In other words, the standard cross-country approach is unlikely to provide reliable evidence of the relationship between inequity and growth. In contrast, ample microeconomic evidence is available about how limited access to income-generation facilities such as credit, land, or education negatively affects individual economic outcomes and potentially reduces economic efficiency and growth at the aggregate level. The 2006 *World Development Report* reviews this evidence in detail (World Bank 2006, in particular, chapters 5 and 6). Cross-country evidence about the negative impact of weak governance and institutions on economic growth is probably more reliable than other macroeconomic evidence, given the macro-economic nature of the institutions examined (see, in particular, Knack 2006). To the extent that this weakness is most often the result of the capture of institutions by an elite, this literature provides another confirmation that inequity has a negative impact on development. Finally, analyses of the causes of recent conflicts in several countries show how inequity across ethnic groups, along with a low level of development, generates fights for the appropriation of existing rents, which, in turn, are responsible for weak development and persistent inequity (see, for instance, Bannon and Collier 2003; Collier and Hoeffler 2004; Otsby 2006).

While the recent history of some conflict-ridden countries pro-vides a good illustration of the negative development impact of inequity, the experience of other countries demonstrates the positive role that equity can play in development. Note, in particular, that several of the fastest-growing Asian countries started with an extremely equitable distribution of opportunities because of major land reforms as in the Republic of Korea and Taiwan (China), or because of the legacy of communist regimes as in China and Vietnam. At the same time, however, equity is clearly not the only factor responsible for growth. Some relatively equitable countries or regions have not have always exhibited the best growth performance while other more inequitable ones have witnessed periods of accel-erated growth. The Indian state of West Bengal is an example of the former, whereas the so-called Brazilian miracle of the 1960s and early 1970s is an example of the latter.

The Political Economy of Equity-Enhancing Reforms

If equity is conducive to growth and inequity hinders it, then the means to promote equity or, in other words, to equalize opportunities among citizens is an important policy issue. Identifying reforms to make progress in that direction is not difficult, from equalizing access to education, credit, infrastructure, and justice to regulating competi-tion and fighting corruption. The difficulty lies in convincing the heterogeneous groups that form a society to adopt such policies and to free the resources needed to implement them. If most of the ineq-uities in a society are a result of the capture of economic and political power by a specific group, correcting the situation implies going against the interests of that group. This is clearly impossible if the group has the political clout to oppose the reform that is being con-sidered and if its short-run losses are not compensated for by the overall efficiency gains of the economy in the long run.

As mentioned earlier, this is one of the important explanations for the existence of inequality traps that lock some countries in a vicious circle of inequity and low development. An important cause for slow growth in a country is the existence of elites with a limited appetite for development because of their own wealth and ability to resist at a low cost the pressures for reforms that would reduce the control they have on society and that threaten the source of their income.

A Simple Analytical Framework for Elite Capture

The schematic representation of the costs and benefits accruing to stylized, aggregate actors of a potential reform shown in table 1.1 helps examine the conditions for getting out of this kind of trap and promoting reforms that will enhance both equity and development. The table shows the choice a society faces between (a) the status quo, where three groups of citizens, ranked by decreasing order of affluence, keep the same level of income over time, and (b) a reform whereby each group registers changes in current and future incomes. The policy reform implies an immediate loss for the richest group $(-T_1)$, the middle class $(-T_2)$, and the poorest group $(-T_3)$. In the future, all groups benefit from the reform, with the net difference between their gains and the status quo being, respectively, g_1, g_2, and g_3.[3]

This simple representation permits an interesting review of the political economy issues that arise when trying to implement equity-enhancing reforms. Suppose that the three groups have different levels of income because they face unequal opportunities, with group 1 being the most advantaged and group 3 being the most disadvantaged.

Table 1.1 Schematic Representation of the Distributional Impact of an Equity-Enhancing Reform

(income under status quo or reforms)

Condition	Group 1 (richest group)	Group 2 (middle class)	Group 3 (poorest group)
Status quo			
Current period	Y_1	Y_2	Y_3
Future	Y_1	Y_2	Y_3
Reform			
Current period	$Y_1 - T_1$	$Y_2 - T_2$	$Y_3 - T_3$
Future	$Y_1 + g_1$	$Y_2 + g_2$	$Y_3 + g_3$
Net Gain			
Current Period	$-T_1$	$-T_2$	$-T_3$
Future	g_1	g_2	g_3
Total	$g_1 - T_1$	$g_2 - T_2$	$g_3 - T_3$

Source: Authors.

Suppose also that enhancing equity by improving some specific opportunities available to group 3—say access to education—may be achieved by raising taxes that all three groups will pay, but will be borne proportionally more by the richer groups. For instance, group 3's access to secondary or tertiary education may be improved by raising taxes in some progressive way so that groups 1 and 2 end up being the main contributors to the expansion of access to the education system. In the second period, all three groups enjoy some returns from the reform either directly, such as group 3 benefiting from easier access to secondary or tertiary education, or indirectly, for instance, because a more skilled labor force contributes to higher profits in the businesses run by people in groups 1 and 2 or accelerates overall growth.

The preceding reform can also be interpreted in terms of privileges rather than in terms of additional spending on education. For instance, the reform may consist of making recruitment into secondary and tertiary education more merit based, thereby reducing the privileges that groups 1 and 2 had enjoyed. The losses T_1 and T_2 would then be interpreted as the monetary equivalent of the loss of privileged access to secondary school and university, whereas the loss T_3 could reasonably be assumed to be nil.

Still another reading of the reform is the partial or complete abolition of some economic capture by groups 1 or 2 or both. Say that group 1 enjoys some monopoly power in a specific sector of the economy such as finance. The reform then consists of opening up that sector to competition. Group 1 will lose the monopoly rent it was enjoying before, the amount of that rent being T_1, whereas T_2 and T_3 are nil, or possibly are negative if groups 2 and 3 directly benefit from cheaper financial services. The result of this reform is to increase the efficiency of the economy so that the income of all groups increases by different amounts depending on how they are directly or indirectly affected by the expansion of the sector opened up to competition, that is, through lower prices and higher employment not just in that sector, but also in other upstream and downstream sectors.

Many of the monopoly situations in Mexico that are analyzed in this volume resemble the latter case. Making the telecommunications sector more competitive would reduce the rents of the owners of that sector, who presumably belong to group 1, and would generate immediate gains among users in groups 2 and 3 (T_2 and T_3 thus being negative). Second period gains, g, would then be the long-run efficiency gains resulting from the expanded use of all services emanating from the telecommunications sector (see chapter 9 in this volume for an assessment of the extent of competition in Mexico's telecommunications sector). In the case of the pension system managed by the Instituto Mexicano del Seguro Social (IMSS), monopoly power is located in the union of IMSS employees (see chapter 6 in this volume). Bypassing this power and reforming the pension system would correspond to a loss for part of the middle class (T_2), to a gain for another part of the same class in the form of better social services, and potentially a gain for business owners because of reduced social security contributions resulting from a lower effective cost of IMSS employees. In the long run, group 3 would also gain because of the lower degree of informality of the economy, and all groups would enjoy faster economic growth.

Various other situations lead to the same simplified representation of the costs and benefits of an equity-enhancing reform. The rent T_1 or T_2 may come from sources other than monopoly power. It may arise through the sheer appropriation by some groups of some resources available in the economy, public or private. It may also come from corruption. The size of losses T_1, T_2, and T_3 and benefits g_1, g_2, and g_3 will depend on the kinds of privileges being lost and the reform's effects on overall efficiency. In the case of corruption, for instance, T_2 and T_3 are the payments that groups 2 and 3 cease to make to group 1 and are thus negative, whereas the gains g_1, g_2, and g_3 reflect how the efficiency gains brought about by the disappearance of corrupt practices are distributed in the economy.

The argument made in the previous section about a complementarity between equity and economic efficiency is equivalent to assuming that the sum of benefits derived from the reform $(g_1 + g_2 + g_3)$ is greater than the costs $(T_1 + T_2 + T_3)$. In other words, the reform is more than a mere zero sum game redistribution across groups. The reduction of the privileges of the elite—group 1, group 2, or both—increases the total income of the community. If B is the overall increase in income, then[4]

$$B = (g_1 + g_2 + g_3) - (T_1 + T_2 + T_3) > 0.$$

All groups would, therefore, find the equity-enhancing reform being considered acceptable if the total gain could be redistributed among all the groups in a lump sum fashion, that is, in a way that would be independent of economic activity, so that no one would lose. From a simple accounting point of view, this approach is possible because the overall surplus, B, is taken to be positive.[5]

In practice, things are much more complicated than this simple arithmetic suggests. Practically, redistribution of the overall benefit B may be difficult to achieve for economic or political economy reasons. On the one hand, lump sum redistribution is never easy. Groups directly benefiting from the reform might oppose lump sum redistribution because they may consider it unfair and possibly "inequitable." In the case where T_1 corresponds, for instance, to the elite losing some privilege, fully compensating the elite for that loss may not be socially or politically acceptable, yet at least full compensation is required for the elite not to oppose the reform. On the other hand, time consistency is an issue. If compensation or redistribution is to take place in the future, and if group 1 will be the main or only loser, it would not accept losing its privileges for an amount equal to T_1 without a commitment by the two other groups to compensate it for that loss in the future, but strong political institutions need to be in place for such a commitment to be credible. In the absence of such institutions, which is often the case, beneficiary groups cannot offer a guarantee that they will not renege on their commitment in the future. For these two sets of reasons, just because the reform being considered yields a positive overall net gain is no guarantee that it will be accepted unanimously.

Economic analysis often overlooks the basic fact that a positive overall surplus is a necessary but insufficient condition for a reform to be unanimously accepted. Appropriate redistribution or compensation mechanisms must also be in place for the reform to be adopted and to succeed. Trade liberalization is one of the most obvious examples. In accordance with economic theory, advocacy in favor of trade liberalization emphasizes that, together with an improvement in the functioning of domestic factor markets, it will produce an overall gain in efficiency that could benefit all groups. At the same time, economic theory also suggests that some people will lose as a result of the reform. If the appropriate channels for redistributing income and compensating the losers will not be available at the time the overall gains to the economy will turn positive or will be costly,[6] the reform may not be adopted.

Of course, these distribution issues should not arise in the case of a reform from which all groups actually benefit ($g_i - T_i > 0$ for $i = 1$, 2, and 3). Even in this case, however, some groups might try to block the reform if they feel that their gain is proportionally much lower than that of other groups. In matters of policy reform, the issue of interest is that of the trade-off that arises when some groups gain while others lose (whether in absolute or relative terms). If the possibility of compensation is ruled out, either for economic reasons or because of the difficulty of finding time-consistent arrangements, then whether the reform takes place depends essentially on how public decisions are made—and ultimately on political influences.

We consider various ways that decisions are made according to the political institutions in place. To simplify the discussion, consider the case where only elite group 1 loses from the reform, so that $g_1 < T_1$, whereas $g_2 > T_2$ and $g_3 > T_3$. A first case is when group 1 has captured political power. Within such an autocratic state, the reform will clearly not be undertaken, thereby reducing the economy's efficiency and pace of growth. Development-enhancing reforms that harm the ruling elite are simply ignored. In such a society, development takes place only if it benefits the elite. Examples of such inequality traps abound, such as Joseph Mobutu's Zaire.

Of course, such a situation may seem rather obvious. Clearly, the elite will not adopt a reform that benefits other groups in society but is against its own interests. More fundamentally, if the elite has all the power, why does it simply not expropriate other groups? The answer is that such predatory behavior has a rational limit. Where the elite lives on rents levied on non-elites, that limit comes from the need to maintain sufficient incentives for non-elites to invest and produce. More generally, it also comes from the possibility of rebellion by other groups and the cost to the elite of repression, all of which increase with the degree of predation. However, because this case is somewhat extreme, we will not explore it further, even though it is clearly of historical relevance in many countries and is still relevant in some countries (see Acemoglu 2006; Acemoglu and Robinson 2000, 2006, 2008; Robinson 2001).

A second case is where the political decision process is under the joint control of groups 1 and 2, with some dominance by group 2. Several situations fit that case. An extreme situation is that of an autocratic regime controlled by group 2. Within such a setting, the society actually has two elites with divergent views. The economic elite, group 1, controls part of the economic power and draws rents from it. The political elite, group 2, controls the public decision-making process and can impose reforms on group 1. In other words, a potential conflict exists within the elite between those who control the economy and those who control the politics. Conflict can be avoided by collusion among the two elites, in which case group 1 is likely to bribe group 2 so as to block the reform. The outcome is the same as with an autocratic regime controlled by group 1 and development is slowed. However, collusive arrangements are unstable. Group 1 will always have an interest in minimizing the bribe given to group 2 and in hiding income from it, whereas group 2 will always have an interest in passing the reform. The conflict between the two elites may thus reappear at some stage, and the reform may eventually pass.

The outcome would be the same if public decisions were taken according to an imperfect democratic process whereby only elite groups 1 and 2 have effective influence, under the assumption that group 2 has a majority and, indeed, has political power. Within such a limited democratic regime, an equitable reform would be adopted because group 2 gains from the reform along with group 3.

Of course, this would not be the case if the interests of group 2 did not coincide with those of the majority of group 3.

Numerous examples are available of this type of two-group situation where one group controls the natural resources or is the wealthiest segment of an economy and another group controls the political power. The latter may hold its power from a legacy of some form of autocratic regime, but it may also have acquired power through apparently democratic processes dominated by patronage and corruption. The two-group structure may also come from the splitting of a single elite group following a fight for power, with one side having been able to mobilize the rest of the population in its favor. The *perestroika* that Mikhail Gorbachev undertook in the Soviet Union in the mid-1980s and the ensuing confrontation with the *nomenklatura* may be interpreted as such a split of initially homogeneous elites.

The third case is that of a fully democratic regime where group 3 has a majority. Because its gain is positive, the reform will be adopted, thereby boosting economic efficiency and growth. Note, however, that this outcome does not necessarily follow directly from the numerical dominance of group 3 over the other groups. In democratic regimes, decisions also depend on political participation and activism, which may be weaker among poorer and less educated groups. Thus, for group 3 to be able to actually express its views and be decisive in the adoption of the reform, previous steps may have to be taken, such as mass education, which may themselves form part of an equity-enhancing package. In this perspective, separating the adoption of equity-enhancing reforms and the structure of political decision making may be somewhat artificial.[7]

Given some trade-off in the gains from reform across population groups, the preceding simple analysis suggests that the final decision will essentially depend on the nature of the joint structure of political and economic power. Who controls the rents or the economic privileges that the reform intends to abolish and who controls the decision-making process in relation to the reform are the key parameters that determine whether equity-enhancing policies with positive effects on the economy's long-run growth will be adopted. Although autocratic regimes are unlikely to adopt such policies except in the case of conflicting interests within the elite, a democratic regime—even one with some limitations to the democratic process—might move ahead with equity- and development-enhancing reforms.

The Importance of Information

The preceding schematic presentation of the political economy of equity-enhancing reforms relies on an important assumption: perfect information. For political decision-making mechanisms to potentially lead to the desired reform, all actors must be able to identify with some precision the losers and the winners of the reform and must know how much they stand to lose or gain. Practically, this is not always the case. Group 3 may be aware of the gains that it would get from having better access to secondary and tertiary education and that this improvement must somehow be paid for by the upper classes in society. Those in group 3 may, therefore, be in favor of a more merit-based system of recruitment for higher education or of a heavier and more progressive tax system or both. At the same time, they may be unaware that they could stand to gain possibly much more from the abolition of some of the rents and privileges of the elite through overall efficiency gains and that these efficiency gains might partly compensate for the loss incurred by other groups. Elite groups who stand to lose may have better information about the extent of their rents or privileges. The absence of such information about the full distributional effects of a reform (for example, one that reduces elite capture of part of the economy) can lead to biases in the exercise of political power across groups, thereby weakening democratic mechanisms and leading to a failure to achieve equity and efficiency reforms of the type discussed here.

This lack of information may be why democratic mechanisms that could lead to equity- and development-enhancing reforms are not triggered. At the same time, it is clearly in the interest of losing groups to retain the information or to disguise the truth so as to avoid the adoption of specific reforms. At the borderline between democratic and nondemocratic decision systems, public information about all the implications of equity-oriented reforms may itself be the object of a complex political game. This area is where third parties, think tanks, nongovernmental organizations, and international agencies can play an important role by disclosing information that highlights the opportunity costs of the status quo, by having a strong reputation for objectivity, and by building and promoting independent analytical capacities and a free press.

Several chapters in this volume provide good illustrations of (a) the potential power of information in promoting equity-enhancing reforms and (b) the incentives for rent-extracting agents to curb it. In his analysis of the way regulation works in the Mexican telecommunications sector, del Villar (chapter 9 in this volume) emphasizes the secret nature of the productivity gain factor entering the determination of price caps for telecommunications services. The figures he quotes suggest that the productivity gain taken into account in the negotiations with the regulatory authority is much below what has been observed in other countries. Levy (chapter 6 in this volume) provides another example, namely, the reform of Mexico's pension system and the apparently oligopolistic power of pension funds, which leads to a rate of return on pensions that is below market rates. Information now seems to have begun to spread, because workers appear to be gravitating toward the pension funds that are offering the highest returns. Studies like these and, in effect, most chapters in this book are essential for the diffusion of information and the promotion of equity-enhancing reforms.

Information may be an important factor in change and is one that tends to be neglected. The arguments developed earlier in this section lie behind the rapidly growing economic literature on the relationship between institutions and development (see, for instance, Acemoglu and Robinson 2006). However, this literature is essentially descriptive, not prescriptive. It tells us about the consequences of inequity or discusses the structure of political power in relation to development. It does not tell us what to do about it.

In effect, economists and analysts equipped with this knowledge but confronted with apparently stable institutions against which they are powerless seem to be heading down a cul de sac. However, this is true only as long as one assumes that (a) all actors in society have perfect information about the implications of reforms that promote equity and, indirectly, development; and (b) political equilibria are everlasting.

If information is imperfect, considerable scope exists for all parties to interact in a public debate on the impact of a particular reform so as to try to learn from each other about its distributional effects and for credible and neutral third parties to influence reforms. Casual observation suggests that this debate does not always take place, for instance, in strongly autocratic societies, or that it is not as transparent and informed as it should be, sometimes because the information is not available and sometimes because the information made public is biased in the interests of some parties.

Better information might be insufficient to unlock political equilibria, which are often persistent given the inequitable initial distribution of power and the ability of elites to maintain their dominance over non-elites. Historically, elite capture weakens mostly as a result of exogenous shocks, but highlighting the evolution of parameters underpinning the equilibrium might be instrumental in further unlocking it.

Take the example of a society in which a political elite has captured rents stemming from the exploitation of a natural resource and in which it redistributes only part of those rents in the form of social services provided to the population. As the resource begins to become depleted (that is, depletion is a form of exogenous shock), the elite might progressively look for alternative means of rent extraction from the population, most likely through increased taxes or the creation of monopoly situations. During the transition, however, the elite group might find itself particularly vulnerable to the disclosure of information revealing the distributional effects of the reforms envisaged to protect its privileges. The disclosure of that information may be necessary for the exogenous shock pertaining to natural resources to actually trigger institutional changes.

Identifying all the distributional effects of a reform is not a simple matter. This may be why much of the economic literature and political debate about reforms that promote competition and weaken rent-seeking behavior in an economy focus on the aggregate benefits rather than on the disaggregated benefits of doing so. This section has shown that it is not only the overall benefit, B, of an equity-enhancing reform that matters, but also the entire distribution of the individual or group net gains, $g_i - T_i$.

The Distributional Effects of Reforms

A cursory examination of the literature reveals many attempts at determining the full distributional impact of unequal opportunities in fields such as access to education, health care, and specific infrastructure (see, for instance, van de Walle 1998; World Bank 2005).[8] The literature on the distributional impact of obvious cases of elite capture is much more limited. It tends to be restricted to analyses of monopoly situations without consideration of general equilibrium and dynamic effects, yet this is precisely where the arguments presented earlier suggest that many of the problems arise.

The difficulties of identifying the distributional effects of monopoly situations within a dynamic general equilibrium framework are easily understood. Such identification cannot rely on ex post observations of an economy with and without a monopoly in some specific area. Rather, it must rely on ex ante counterfactual analysis based on some kind of economic modeling approach.[9] Because a systematic review of those few studies that have tried this approach is beyond the scope of this chapter, this section focuses on the main mechanisms that such studies should take into account and the existing general evidence. Three situations are analyzed: (a) standard monopoly situations with non-negligible general equilibrium effects, (b) oligopolistic behavior in the financial sector, and (c) corporatist monopoly power exerted by trade unions.

Monopoly Power in Markets for Goods and Services

The direct effects of monopoly power are well known. Those enjoying such power receive extra income on top of the normal profit rate in the economy, whereas their customers pay a higher price, have less to buy, and possibly obtain goods and services of lower quality than under conditions of perfect competition. The size of these distortions essentially depends on the elasticity of demand. For instance, an elasticity of demand equal to 1.5 leads to a price margin of 3.0 with respect to marginal cost. In other words, consumers pay triple the price they would pay under perfect competition. At the same time, they reduce their demand by two-thirds, which weakens the effect of the monopoly on their overall welfare.

Some of the distributional effects can be easily quantified when monopoly situations are well identified, but as Creedy and Dixon (1999) note, few studies of the distributional effects of monopoly situations are available, even though the identification of direct effects does not seem to be conceptually difficult. Analyzing the distributional impact of a change in price of specific services resulting from monopoly power can be done in a simple way using household surveys with information about expenditures on the service supplied by a monopoly. Figuring out the markup of the monopoly with respect to the competitive price is sufficient, and the distributional effect of the monopoly can be evaluated in the same way as the incidence of indirect taxes. A good example of this approach is the analysis by Waddams, Price, and Hancock (1998) of the introduction of more competition in the United Kingdom's utility sector. However, this kind of analysis ignores the possible difference in the quantity or quality of the service that the monopoly delivers in comparison with delivery in a more competitive market (see chapters 4, 9, and 10 in this volume with regard to monopoly effects on Mexico's electricity and telecommunications sectors). Furthermore, in the field of infrastructure, the issue is not so much the quantity being consumed and the corresponding cost but the unequal access.

Work on the effects of privatization tries to take access into account as well as household consumption and expenditures before and after privatization (see, for instance, the various studies in McKenzie and Mookherjee 2002 and Nellis and Birdsall 2005), but this approach has some drawbacks. First, it is ex post, whereas decision making in the field of competitive regulation calls for an ex ante perspective. Second, the before and after comparison does not always correct for the effects of other phenomena that are contemporaneous with but independent of the reform being analyzed. An analysis of the distributional impact of a reform that changes a sector's competitive structure must rely on some kind of counterfactual, but defining such a counterfactual is not always a simple matter.

Complete identification of the distributional effects would require going beyond price and quantity effects. It should also take into account the impact of the monopoly situation on sectors upstream and downstream of the firm, as well as the overall impact on factor markets and on employment in particular. When dealing with a major infrastructure sector such as transport or with any sector that has tight links with the rest of the economy (for instance, cement or steel) ignoring general equilibrium effects may lead to severe underestimation of the impact of monopolistic situations.

Many applied general equilibrium models now include imperfect competition features and can be used to determine the impact of introducing more competition in specific sectors, but fewer models explicitly take into account the heterogeneity of the household population and permit a distributional analysis of monopoly power. A good example of such a model is Chisari, Estache, and Romero's (1999) analysis of the effects of privatization and regulation in Argentina. In addition to taking distributional factors explicitly into account, the general equilibrium model should also be dynamic to account for the possible effect of monopolies on labor participation, investment, innovation, and growth.[10] Conventional static and partial equilibrium analyses using Harberger triangles suggest that the aggregate welfare loss of a single representative agent caused by monopolies is small. The outcomes may be quite different when considering heterogeneous population groups, linkages of the sector under monopoly with the rest of the economy, and dynamic effects of monopoly; however, models combining all these features are rare. Thus, the availability in the literature of only a few estimates of the distributional and development effects of monopolies is not surprising.

Barriers to Entry in the Financial Sector

General equilibrium and dynamic effects are likely to be especially important when monopoly or oligopoly power is exerted in the financial sector, because of the sector's impact on practically all productive sectors and on their development. The economic literature provides some aggregate evidence of the effect of the lack of competition in the banking sector on access to financial services and on economic growth. It also provides evidence of the impact of the underdevelopment of credit on the degree of income inequality, other things being equal.

Using firm-level survey data for 74 countries, Beck, Demirguc-Kunt, and Maksimovic (2004) study the impact of bank regulations, concentration, and ownership and of other institutions on access to external finance. They find that bank regulations that impede competition, such as entry and activity restrictions, result in higher financing obstacles for firms and decrease the likelihood that they will obtain bank finance, with this effect being exacerbated for small firms. A case study confirms these findings. Cetorelli (2004) presents evidence on the effects of changes in banking structure on average firm size in 27 manufacturing sectors in 29 Organisation for Economic Co-operation and Development countries over time. The results show that in sectors where incumbent firms have more need for external finance, these firms are also of disproportionately larger size if they are in countries whose banking sector is more concentrated. The results also show that this effect of bank concentration is substantially weakened in European Union countries, where the banking system is much more competitive because of the implementation of pro-competition deregulation.

Empirical evidence also suggests that financial development, as measured by access to the banking system or the ratio of credit to gross domestic product (GDP), is associated with higher growth, lower levels of poverty, and reduced income inequality. Beck, Demirguc-Kunt, and Levine (2004) find that higher financial depth leads to the incomes of the poorest 20 percent of the population growing more rapidly than average GDP per capita and, therefore, to declining income inequality. Honohan (2004) finds that a 10 percentage point change in private credit over GDP is associated with a 3 percentage point drop in the headcount poverty index. Burgess and Pande (2005) find that a 1.0 percent increase in the number of rural banking locations in India reduces rural poverty by 0.3 percent. Finally, the success of microcredit institutions demonstrates the effectiveness of credit for poverty reduction, even if the emergence of such institutions is not necessarily linked to lower levels of financial repression.

A substantial body of literature also looks at the political economy of financial development. For instance, using panel data for 26 countries over the period 1973–99, Girma and Shortland (2005) find that it is predominantly fully democratic regimes that have liberalized their financial systems. Using a panel of 24 countries over the period 1913–99, Rajan and Zingales (2003) suggest that financial systems become liberalized as they become ineffective in shielding elite-controlled industries from competition after trade and capital account liberalization. Haber (chapter 8 in this volume) defends the view that high barriers to entry to Mexico's banking sector were erected to compensate for the high risk of expropriation by authoritarian political institutions, thereby reflecting collusion between the business and political elites.

All this evidence is consistent with the theoretical considerations that some kind of elite capture prevents access to the financial sector by small and medium enterprises, microfirms, and households, thereby slowing the pace of growth and contributing to a higher level of income inequality. The problem is that most of this evidence is based on cross-country comparisons and might be difficult to use at the country level to feed the debate on reforms aimed at making the financial sector more competitive. More work is needed at the microeconomic level to identify those agents that are rationed on the credit market because of the barriers to entry to the financial market, the losses they incur because of this, and the resulting lack of efficiency and economic growth for the entire economy.

Restrictive Corporatist Unions

Capture does not necessarily result from the power of the elite. It may also occur in some sectors or professions dominated by groups belonging to the middle class that have been able to erect barriers to entry or to regulate part of the labor market in their favor. Trade unions may play a positive role for equity by preventing some workers in a given profession from being exploited by employers because of their lack of bargaining power. In some cases, however, their equity impact is debatable, because their primary effect is to protect incumbents from outside competition, thereby harming potential outsiders and contributing to a loss of efficiency in some part of the economy.

This is particularly the case in monopolistic or oligopolistic sectors where trade unions can capture a significant share of the rents arising from imperfect competition (see, for instance, Blanchflower, Oswald, and Sanfey 1996; Borjas and Ramey 1995).[11] In this case, unions will obtain above market wages, extending the inequity originating with the product market to the labor market (see Spector 2004 for a theoretical discussion).[12] However, by doing so they also tend to reduce the advantages granted to firm owners who benefit from monopolistic positions, and the net effect in terms of equity is, hence, generally more difficult to establish. On the one hand, unions reduce the rent accruing to monopolists and oligopolists in the sectors they control, but on the other hand, they contribute to a worsening of the labor market for non-union workers outside these sectors.

The public sector is a special case in this respect. It enjoys a monopoly position for most of its activities, and the implicit rent it generates—the difference between the monetary equivalent of its impact on social welfare and the wages paid to civil servants—accrues to the general public if wages reflect rates in competitive markets in the economy. However, in this setting, powerful trade unions can enjoy sizable monopolistic advantages and may have substantial effects on the rest of the economy. By setting a wage higher than the market wage, they reduce the implicit rent accruing to the population from the activities of the government sector and contribute to a low-ering of workers' wages in the private sector. In the case of Mexico, Levy's analysis of the IMSS pension system (chapter 6) provides a good illustration of how a union in the public sector can indirectly reduce the welfare of IMSS affiliates in the private sector and, more gener-ally, the size of GDP. The negative impact of this lack of competition on both equity and efficiency may be due less to the higher wages that union members are able to secure in comparison with the com-petitive segments of the labor market than to the lower work efforts and lower quality of the services delivered (Freeman and Medoff 1984; Johnson and Mieszkowski 1970; Rees 1963).

Although difficult to measure formally, considerable anecdotal evidence points to the inefficiency of social service delivery in many countries where such services are managed by the central govern-ment, which implicitly or explicitly must deal with organized civil servants. Absenteeism or weak performance by teachers and health care workers when they are employed directly by a central, or even regional, government is well documented in a number of countries (World Bank 2004). Whether in education or in health care, the con-sequences of such a situation for equity and efficiency are sizable. Whereas the elite can substitute public schooling and health care with private services, less well-off members of society suffer from the low quality of the public services, and human capital does not accumulate in the economy proportionately to the money that is spent on these public services. An illustration of this phenomenon is given in chapter 6 of this volume, which notes that workers in formal sectors who consider that the value for money of the services they receive is not worth their implicit price (in the form of social security contributions, for instance) might prefer to move to informal sectors to improve their welfare. In turn, growth will suffer if informality is associated with lower productivity or slower human and physical capital forma-tion. Numerous experiments show that these problems tend to disap-pear when users directly supervise service delivery (for instance, local governments and parent associations in the case of teachers).

Conclusion

Inequity—inequality of opportunities—is a severe deterrent to eco-nomic development. In many instances, it mirrors the capture of economic opportunities by some powerful groups or elites because of their ability to control the public decision-making process, whether directly or indirectly, and to shape institutions to their advantage. In turn, the elites' interests in not relinquishing their economic or political advantages and their lack of interest in overall development can often explain the persistence of inequity and slow development.

Historically, external or technological shocks have often given rise to shifts in relative power across groups, which have weakened elites and encouraged the development of institutions preventing future elite capture. Rarely were such shifts the result of an endogenous process, and in many countries the persistence of inequity and slow development can be seen as a low, but stable, equilibrium.

Improved transparency and widespread economic information are probably the best vehicles for fostering equity and development-enhancing reforms. A better understanding by the population and competing elites of the welfare and distributional impacts of the status quo versus reform is an indispensable instrument for creating the space for reform. Although probably insufficient, public awareness is a necessary condition for forging coalitions for change, especially in vertical political structures where programmatic parties are absent.

This calls for greater efforts in this domain. Little has been done so far and the analytical difficulties are obvious. Even though precise quantification of the distributional effects of selected reforms is difficult to obtain, obtaining rough orders of magnitude should be possible in a number of cases. Because only those reforms with a large potential impact matter, working with schematic counterfactuals that yield plausible orders of magnitude of gains and losses of relevant population groups may be sufficient. At a minimum, some consensus on the basic economic mechanisms at work, who the losers and the winners are, and whether their losses or gains are large or not should be possible in many instances. This should be enough to improve the transparency of the public debate and, depending on the initial political institutions, to lead to more effective decision making for development.

Notes

1. Exceptions such as Chile, which exhibits both satisfactory growth and relatively high income inequality, would have to be explained by a lower level of inequality of opportunities. Testing this hypothesis opens up an interesting field of research.

2. The early literature on the relationship between inequality and growth emphasized this stylized fact (see, in particular, Alesina and Rodrik

1994; Persson and Tabellini 1994). Interestingly, unlike in other East Asian countries, inequality in China has increased substantially over the past two decades, with the Gini coefficient now standing at around 0.45, but without any apparent negative effect on growth as yet.

3. Note that the short-run costs of an equity-enhancing reform may actually be nil—or even negative—for some groups, such as, for instance, when abolishing privileges accruing to the richest group or equalizing access to some facility initially restricted to the richest group. Note also that the net gains, g, in the second (future) period are net of the losses that the reform may entail in the first (current) period.

4. Logically, one should introduce a time discount factor to compare the costs and the benefits. This discount factor may be implicit in the benefits. Taking it into account explicitly would not modify the argument.

5. The case where B is negative but the reform is, nevertheless, imposed by one of the political actors, either within an autocratic regime or even through democratic processes, is also important but of no direct interest for the issues discussed in this chapter.

6. The cost of redistribution may even exceed the overall gain of the reform, therefore making it impossible that it could benefit everyone. See Guesnerie (2001) and Spector (2001), which extend earlier treatment of this issue by Dixit and Norman (1986).

7. For clarity of the argument, this simultaneity between equity-enhancing reforms and changes in the structure of political decision making will not be discussed here. For a discussion see, for instance, Bourguignon and Verdier (2000).

8. Note that such analyses are often incomplete because they are essentially static and are based on debatable assumptions. See Bourguignon and Rogers (2007) for the case of education.

9. However, most general equilibrium analyses of monopoly power in key sectors are based on a single representative consumer and do not permit assessments of distributional effects.

10. In relation to innovation, the conventional Schumpeterian view defends the idea that some market power (either on product markets or in the form of intellectual property rights) is necessary for enterprises to innovate and that social welfare unambiguously increases as a result. Yet this proposition also necessitates assuming that monopolies gain a transitory competitive edge only from innovating and not from continued market dominance. In relation to growth, Dessus and Ghaleb's (2008) paper on the effects of monopoly power in the Lebanese economy is based on a dynamic applied general equilibrium model. It does not incorporate household distributional effects, but it does analyze changes in factor incomes between labor and capital.

11. Tzannatos and Aidt (2006) conclude that the resources and efforts unions will eventually devote to rent seeking depend on the legal environment

(nature of collective bargaining, cost of militant actions) and the economic environment (degree of product market competition) in which they operate.

12. Spector suggests that the general equilibrium effects of product market deregulation on consumers' welfare might be insufficient to compensate for the elimination of rents accruing to workers in protected sectors.

References

Acemoglu, D. 2006. "A Simple Model of Inefficient Institutions." *Scandinavian Journal of Economics* 108 (4): 515–46.

Acemoglu, D., and J. Robinson. 2000. "Why Did the West Extend the Franchise? Democracy, Inequality and Growth in Historical Perspective." *Quarterly Journal of Economics* 115 (4): 1167–99.

———. 2006. *Economic Origins of Dictatorship and Democracy.* Cambridge, U.K.: Cambridge University Press.

———. 2008. "Persistence of Power, Elites and Institutions." *American Economic Review* 98 (1): 267–93.

Aghion, P., and P. Bolton. 1992. "Distribution and Growth in Models of Imperfect Capital Markets." *European Economic Review* 36 (2–3): 603–11.

Alesina, A., and D. Rodrik. 1994. "Distributive Politics and Economic Growth." *Quarterly Journal of Economics* 109 (2): 465–90.

Banerjee, A., and E. Duflo. 2003. "Inequality and Growth: What Can the Data Say?" *Journal of Economic Growth* 8 (3): 267–99.

Banerjee, A., and A. Newman. 1991. "Risk-Bearing and the Theory of Income Distribution." *Review of Economic Studies* 58 (2): 211–35.

Bannon, I., and P. Collier. 2003. *Natural Resources and Violent Conflict: Options and Actions.* Washington, DC: World Bank.

Beck, T., A. Demirguc-Kunt, and R. Levine. 2004. "Finance, Inequality and Poverty: Cross-Country Evidence." Policy Research Paper 3338, World Bank, Washington, DC.

Beck, T., A. Demirguc-Kunt, and V. Maksimovic. 2004. "Bank Competition and Access to Finance: International Evidence." *Journal of Money, Credit and Banking* 36 (3): 627–48.

Bertola, G. 1993. "Factor Shares and Savings in Endogenous Growth." *American Economic Review* 83 (5): 1184–98.

Blanchflower, D., A. Oswald, and P. Sanfey. 1996. "Wages, Profits and Rent-Sharing." *Quarterly Journal of Economics* 111 (1): 227–51.

Borjas, G., and V. Ramey. 1995. "Foreign Competition, Market Power and Wage Inequality: Theory and Evidence." *Quarterly Journal of Economics* 110 (4): 1075–110.

Bourguignon, F., F. Ferreira, and M. Walton. 2006. "Equity, Efficiency and Inequality Traps: A Research Agenda." Faculty Research Working Papers

Series 25, J. F. Kennedy School of Government, Harvard University, Cambridge, MA.

Bourguignon, F., and H. Rogers. 2007. "Distributional Effects of Educational Improvements: Are We Using the Wrong Model?" *Economics of Education Review* 26 (6): 735–46.

Bourguignon, F., and T. Verdier. 2000. "Oligarchy, Democracy, Inequality and Growth." *Journal of Development Economics* 62 (2): 285–313.

Burgess, R., and R. Pande. 2005. "Do Rural Banks Matter? Evidence from the Indian Social Banking Experiment." *American Economic Review* 95 (3): 780–95.

Cetorelli, N. 2004. "Real Effects of Bank Competition." *Journal of Money, Credit, and Banking* 36 (3): 543–58.

Chisari, O., A. Estache, and C. Romero. 1999. "Winners and Losers from Privatization and Regulation in Argentina." *World Bank Economic Review* 13 (2): 357–78.

Collier, P., and A. Hoeffler. 2004. "Greed and Grievance in Civil War." *Oxford Economic Papers* 56 (4): 563–95.

Creedy, J., and R. Dixon. 1999. "The Distributional Effect of Monopoly." *Australian Economic Papers* 38 (3): 223–37.

Dessus, S., and J. Ghaleb. 2008. "Trade and Competition Policies for Growth in Lebanon: A General Equilibrium Analysis." *Review of Middle East Economics and Finance* 4 (1): Article 4.

Dixit, A., and V. Norman. 1986. "Gains from Trade without Lump-Sum Compensation." *Journal of International Economics* 21 (1): 111–22.

Freeman, R. B., and J. L. Medoff. 1984. *What Do Unions Do?* New York: Basic Books.

Galor, O., and J. Zeira. 1993. "Income Distribution and Macroeconomics." *Review of Economic Studies* 60 (1): 35–52.

Girma, S., and A. Shortland. 2005. "The Political Economy of Financial Liberalisation." Working Paper 05/12, University of Leicester, Department of Economics, Leicester, U.K.

Guesnerie, R. 2001. "Second Best Redistributive Policies: The Case of International Trade." *Journal of Public Economic Theory* 3 (1): 15–25.

Honohan, P. 2004. "Financial Development, Growth and Poverty: How Close Are the Links?" Policy Research Working Paper 3203, World Bank, Washington, DC.

Johnson, H. G., and P. Mieszkowski. 1970. "The Effects of Unionisation on the Distribution of Income: A General Equilibrium Approach." *Quarterly Journal of Economics* 84 (4): 539–61.

Knack, S. 2006. "Governance and Growth." Paper presented at the Workshop on Governance and Development, Dhaka, November 11–12.

McKenzie, D., and D. Mookherjee. 2002. "Distributive Impact of Privatization in Latin America: An Overview of Evidence from Four Countries."

Working Paper 2003-01, Institute of Public Policy and Development Studies, Universidad de las Américas, Puebla, Mexico.

Nellis, J., and N. Birdsall, eds. 2005. *Reality Check: The Distributional Impact of Privatization in Developing Countries.* Washington, DC: Center for Global Development.

Otsby, G. 2006. "Horizontal Inequalities, Political Environment, and Civil Conflict." Paper presented at the National Conference on Political Science, Bergen, Norway, January 4–6.

Persson, T., and G. Tabellini. 1994. "Is Inequality Harmful for Growth?" *American Economic Review* 84 (3): 600–21.

Rajan, R., and L. Zingales. 2003. "The Great Reversals: The Politics of Financial Development in the 20th Century." *Journal of Financial Economics* 69 (1): 5–50.

Rees, A. 1963. "The Effects of Unions on Resource Allocation." *Journal of Law and Economics* 6 (1): 69–78.

Robinson, J. 2001. "Social Identity, Inequality and Conflict." *Economics of Governance* 2 (1): 85–99.

Spector, D. 2001. "Is It Possible to Redistribute the Gains from Trade Using Income Taxation?" *Journal of International Economics* 55 (2): 441–60.

———. 2004. "Competition and the Capital-Labor Conflict." *European Economic Review* 48 (1): 25–38.

Tzannatos, Z., and T. Aidt. 2006. "Unions and Microeconomic Performance: A Look at What Matters for Hard Core Economists (and Employers)." *International Labor Review* 145 (4): 257–78.

van de Walle, D. 1998. "Assessing the Welfare Impacts of Public Spending." *World Development* 26 (3): 365–79.

Waddams Price, C., and R. Hancock. 1998. "Distributional Effects of Liberalising UK Residential Utility Markets." *Fiscal Studies* 19 (3): 295–319.

World Bank. 2004. *World Development Report: Making Services Work for Poor People.* New York: Oxford University Press.

———. 2005. *World Development Report: A Better Investment Climate for Everyone.* New York: Oxford University Press.

———. 2006. *World Development Report: Equity and Development.* New York: Oxford University Press.

2

Saving Growth from Unequal Influence

Raghuram G. Rajan

The relationship between inequality and prosperity is a longstanding concern of social scientists and citizens alike. Recent years have seen a resurgence of interest in this topic, including among economists.

An important strand in recent work is that the poverty of nations is related to economic inequality because a common causal factor, poor political and economic institutions inherited from the past, is responsible for both. I will argue for an alternative explanation: that when endowments and opportunities are unequally distributed in a poor society, disagreements about the most appropriate reform path are harder to resolve (see Rajan forthcoming for a model and the analysis underlying this chapter). Each subgroup's desire to preserve its economic rents against all others—what I term competitive rent preservation—tends to ensure that moving away from the status quo is extremely difficult.

This can be seen as complementary to Bourguignon and Dessus's (chapter 1) more classical political economy explanations. As with the latter approach, I focus on interactions between distinct groups in a society, each concerned with using its influence to shape or resist policy changes so as to preserve its economic interests. This chapter offers an analysis of how these interactions can lead to the avoidance of reforms that would raise aggregate welfare. My analysis supports the view that inequalities between different groups can lead to the persistence of both inequality and suboptimal economic policies, despite substantial improvements in political institutions. Mexico's transition to democracy may be just such a case, with political reform not leading to dramatic economic reforms, despite the undoubted desire of the country's presidents for economic progress.

The policy implications are quite different depending on whether underdevelopment in a country is seen as primarily flowing from persistent political institutions or from the types of rent-preserving equilibria proposed here. This is why this debate is not simply an academic one. However, before turning to policy implications, let us consider the different views.

Coercive Political Institutions and Underdevelopment

The political institutions' view of development (see Hoff 2003 for an excellent survey) suggests that persistent, coercive political institutions, typically set up in the past to assert the power of a ruling elite, serve to entrench the elite and their suboptimal self-interested policies today, even after they have lost their initial sources of power. Thus, many former colonies, where the initial colonizers set up coercive political structures to entrench their military power and economic rents, are still mired in poverty because of the weight of history.

A theory of underdevelopment that relies primarily on inherited, coercive political institutions does, however, give rise to several questions. For one, underdevelopment has persisted despite a dramatic increase in inclusiveness and decrease in coerciveness of the political institutions in poor countries, including independence from colonial status, emancipation of slaves, democratization, and new constitutions. One explanation is the existence of deep, hard-to-observe, micro political institutions that completely offset any effects resulting from democratization or the rewriting of constitutions and that continue to entrench the coercive power of the elite. This is possible, though it seems implausible. It would imply that micro political institutions do shape economic behavior, but that the most important macro political institutions we know of do not.

Indeed, if persistent, coercive political institutions were so easy to put in place, the reasons why the elite would have to follow suboptimal economic policies are not clear. Instead, it would be better for the elite to follow the best economic policies they could, and then to use their political power to tax some of the resulting higher income. For instance, instead of allowing suboptimal economic monopolies to limit national income, the elite should allow competition and maximize national income. Of course, the elite's power to tax arbitrarily could reduce incentives to invest (and the elite themselves may be the only ones to invest in full confidence), but this is still no reason to limit competition.

A second problem with the argument that political institutions can be used to project power forward is that there is not strong evidence that regimes that see their current power waning can create institutions to preserve that power. Consider, for example, Zimbabwe. As Acemoglu, Johnson, and Robinson (2005: 41) write, "The white negotiators at the Lancaster House talks in 1979 that produced these agreements understood that any promises made by the black majority negotiators about what would happen after independence could not be believed. They sought, therefore, to find a set of rules [political institutions] that would get around this problem." However, the political institutions that preserved white interests were quickly overridden. In 1990, the Senate was abolished and the constitution was amended by the Mugabe government to allow for redistribution of land, leading Acemoglu, Johnson, and Robinson (2005) to conclude that "these guarantees were not enough to protect the property rights (and rents) of the whites in anything other than the short run."

Consider Chile next. Augusto Pinochet had a strong incentive to put in place constitutional features that protected him from prosecution after he relinquished power. Indeed, he was willing to abide by the results of the 1989 plebiscite that he lost, in part because, as a senator, the constitution protected him from prosecution. Clearly, this faith in political institutions was misplaced, because Pinochet only escaped impending prosecution by dying.

Indeed, coming up with examples of unpopular political institutions that endured without support from those rendered powerful by other means is difficult. Most examples of persistence are either inclusive institutions, such as the U.S. constitution, that commanded popular support or exclusionary institutions, such as literacy requirements for voting in Latin America or Jim Crow laws in the U.S. South, that were supported by a powerful elite.[1]

If political institutions cannot project the power of an elite even just a few years into the future, imagining them conferring power on an elite centuries after the elite have lost their noninstitutional sources of power is difficult. Coercive political institutions seem unlikely to be the primary source of persistence of bad policies. More generally, political institutions are not free-floating entities, but they need to be understood in terms of how they reflect and mediate the interests of different groups in a society.

Economic Power as the Source of Persistence

Perhaps the elite have economic power and simply use that power to implement preferred policies (see, for example, Engerman and Sokoloff 2003; Przeworski 2004). For instance, suppose that the elite control economic monopolies. They would then have enough money power to buy off legislatures and preserve their monopolies.

The problem with this view is that economic power that is based on rents, purchased from the public using that same economic power, is likely to be unstable. At the very least, some dissipation of those rents should become apparent when political institutions become more inclusive unless we espouse the extreme view that political institutions are totally ineffective. If this is the case, then why does democratization not lead to a dissipation of those rents, a breakup of monopolies, and much stronger economic growth? Put another way, why—even in an imperfect democracy—does the larger public accept limited opportunities and high costs for itself, while the elite enjoy a privileged existence? As many chapters in this volume discuss, this is a central question for Mexico. Although the process of democratization has indeed led to some shifts (for example, in social spending), it has not led to fundamental changes in the structure of economic privilege and, in particular, has been consistent with the persistence of major domains of monopoly power that protect the interests of entrenched groups in both business and labor.

In my view, the answer lies in doing away with the implicit assumption in the preceding question that the wider public is united in its interests and in opposing the elite. Let us consider a constituency to be a group in which each member has the same factor endowments and, therefore, similar preferences about policies, whether or not the members are organized.[2] In a developing country, the status quo constrains the opportunities of all constituencies except the elite. If we assume the constrained are one uniform constituency, they would be unified in their desire for reform. In that case, why reforms do not take place is puzzling. An immediate diagnosis is the overwhelming power, de facto or de jure, of the elite. The solution to the problem of underdevelopment then seems to be to destroy the power of the elite, often through reform of oppressive political institutions. Yet, as observed earlier, political reform rarely seems to be the key to economic growth.

In reality, the constrained in a developing country consist of multiple, unequal constituencies, and therefore matters are no longer as simple as for a two-constituency economy. Each reform typically expands the opportunities of a hitherto constrained constituency and reduces the rents of the elite, but its effects on the other constituencies can be uncertain. Indeed, the disproportionate expansion of opportunities for one formerly constrained constituency can make other constrained constituencies worse off. As a result, the constrained may not act as a unified collective. Instead, they may act like crabs in a bucket—willing to pull down any crab that appears to be climbing out—with the active help of the elite, who prefer them all to stay in the bucket. The elite may even forego some reforms that could enhance their rents for fear that the reforms would unify the crabs in the bucket and help them climb out and overwhelm the elite. Competitive rent preservation ensures that the collective choice is indeed poverty.

Competitive Rent Preservation: A Stylized Account

Consider a stylized society with three constituencies: the monopolists, who own all the factories; the educated middle class, who are employed as factory managers and who hold professional jobs, such as architects and doctors; and the uneducated poor, who work in the factories. Suppose that any two groups who vote for a reform can push it through. As in all democracies, outcomes are a function of both money and numbers, with the rich having power because of their money, the poor having power because of their numbers, and the middle class having a bit of both.

Consider two reforms. First, pro-market reforms allow anyone to open a factory in competition with the monopolists. Only the educated, however, can draw up the business plans and get the finance to take advantage of this opportunity. Second, education reforms allow everyone to get an education of decent quality.

Clearly, the monopolists will oppose pro-market reforms because they will face competition that will reduce their profits and the educated will oppose education reforms because they will experience competition from the now educated masses for the lucrative jobs they currently occupy. The question is whether either group will obtain the support to vote down the reforms they dislike.

The answer could well be yes. The monopolists would prefer to educate the poor, because this training would give them a larger labor pool from which to pick managers and professional workers, thereby allowing them to lower salaries. However, the monopolists also know that if they vote to expand education, they will have a workforce consisting of the formerly uneducated and the formerly educated that is united in their interests. This enlarged constituency will then push for pro-market reforms that would reduce or eliminate the monopolists' rents. If the monopolists face a greater loss from pro-market reforms than gains from being able to reduce the salaries of educated workers, the monopolists will align themselves with the currently educated against expanding education.

However, if education reforms are unlikely to be enacted, the uneducated may reject pro-market reforms, preferring the status quo instead. Although pro-market reforms expand opportunities for the educated, they also have a dark side for the poor. Given that the educated have greater business opportunities, they may benefit disproportionately from pro-market reforms, leading to higher salaries for the educated and higher costs for a whole range of services involving inputs from the educated, including even basic services such as health care. The uneducated, whose job opportunities go up relatively little, may face a substantially higher cost of living because of the opportunities the educated now have. In addition, the effects of pro-market reform may be uncertain, especially if it leads to a (desirable) acceleration of the process of destruction of old unskilled jobs and the creation of new skilled jobs. In this situation, the uneducated may side with the monopolists in voting against pro-market reforms.

A fuller analysis would undoubtedly involve more constituencies interacting with each other. Indeed, many of the chapters in this book analyze Mexico's situation with respect to the three groups in this stylized account, but they also consider the role of organized labor in protected areas, of the agriculture lobby, and so on. The thesis that competitive rent preservation plays a central role could readily be extended to a more complex overall structure.

In sum, even in a society where political institutions ensure that citizens' preferences matter, initial inequalities in education and wealth may be self-perpetuating in the form of inequality traps. Fearing that the advantage gained by one group may come at the expense of their own meager rents, citizens may block reforms. Uncertainty about who will receive the benefits of reforms can further compound resistance. Underdevelopment can, therefore, persist with the full support of the exploited, even with reasonably well-functioning political institutions.

Although highly stylized, the example discussed here is consistent with the evidence that far too many poor economies, including India and most countries in Latin America, have underemphasized universal education of decent quality while overemphasizing higher education. Pro-market reforms have occurred, but they have typically occurred in response to economic crises. In terms of content, reforms have typically been partial in their scope and generally in areas such as liberalizing trade, opening up to foreign direct investment, and divesting bankrupt state enterprises that governments can undertake relatively easily when crisis conditions have weakened popular resistance. As many chapters in this volume illustrate for the case of Mexico, reforms have generally not tackled areas in which influential vested interests are important, especially with respect to powerful business elites or public sector unions. Some two decades of reform in Latin America have seen a combination of significant rises in returns to educated workers, alongside the persistence, or even extension, of the economic privileges of vested interests. Moreover, the poor and uneducated in a number of countries in the region have turned against economic liberalization because they see few of the new opportunities while bearing additional costs.

Competitive Rent Preservation in a Theory of Underdevelopment

Thus, inequalities in endowments and opportunities within a society might themselves cause adverse interactions between exploited constituencies, which might result in an underdevelopment trap. Appealing to the mediating role of coercive political institutions or some other source of power for the elite is unnecessary. This is not to say that such coercive, distorted, or weak institutions do not play a mediating role, but rather that if the structure of inequality itself is the root cause, simply changing political institutions may have little effect on economic outcomes.

In my view, therefore, the primary legacy of the early colonialists was the differential degrees of initial inequality in their colonies. In some settlements, they came upon existing, heavily populated, hierarchical societies following feudal modes of production and simply displaced the rulers. In others that were amenable to plantation modes of agriculture or mining, such as Bolivia and Haiti, they enslaved the local population or imported slaves (Engerman and Sokoloff 2005). In yet others where land was fertile and plentiful, the disease environment was not inhospitable, and the local population was scarce, (for example, Costa Rica), the colonists worked the land themselves in smallholdings, leading to a relatively equal underlying structure of endowments.

Initial inequality did lead to policies or economic institutions such as schooling (Engerman, Mariscal, and Sokoloff 2002) that reproduced the inequality. Indeed, my model results in persistence of inequality without the imposition of coercive political institutions. This result is consistent with the view that political liberalizations may have had little effect on economic outcomes if they left the underlying inequalities of opportunity and endowments untouched.

Once we accept that political institutions, especially bad ones, may not be able to project power very far on their own, it becomes easier to understand why—even though the years spent under communism affected peoples' attitudes (Alesina and Fuchs-Schundeln 2005)—market institutions replaced socialist institutions with remarkable speed. "Bad" socialist institutions were certainly not durable. Indeed, one of the virtues of communism is a strong emphasis on education. This emphasis created the broad constituencies that could press for market reforms once the power of the *nomenklatura* (which is based on control of the military and the secret services) was broken. Ironically, instead of capitalism containing the seeds of its own destruction, the seeds for flourishing capitalism may have been nurtured in the soil of communism.

Evidence

Selected further examples from the empirical literature illustrate the thesis of this chapter. Many observers increasingly believe that the problem in many poor countries is not so much that they do not have any periods of high growth, but that those that stay poor do not sustain growth. Berg, Ostry, and Zettelmeyer (2006) analyze the factors that lead to longer duration growth spells and find that one of the strongest explanatory variables is the degree of income inequality at the beginning of the spell. By contrast, they do not find that the quality of political institutions at the beginning of the spell has much explanatory power.

A study by Banerjee and Iyer (2005) is persuasive that inequality of endowments matters, because they examine its effects within a common political system, that of colonial and independent India. They find that districts in which the British gave proprietary rights to large landlords had much greater inequality in land and incomes than districts in which they gave rights directly to the cultivators, and this inequality persisted until India's independence. Although inequality diminished after independence as a result of land reforms, it lingered on because the reforms were incomplete, and sometimes ineffective. Banerjee and Iyer find that landlord-dominated areas could take much less advantage of the postindependence agricultural reforms, spending far less on development, even after correcting for differences in income. As a result, agricultural productivity was lower in landlord-dominated areas, despite some evidence that the nonlandlord-dominated areas were poorer at the outset in colonial times.

Particularly relevant to my model is the finding that in the period after independence, landlord-dominated areas had 21 percent fewer villages equipped with primary schools, while the gap in middle school and high school availability was 61 percent and 63 percent, respectively, relative to the more equally endowed nonlandlord-dominated areas. This occurred within a common national political system. The persistence of inequality, the difficulty of taking advantage of reforms including those funded by the central government, and the underemphasis on education in unequal areas are all consistent with my model.

In a similar vein, Erikson and Ramcharan (2006) examine the effects of inequality in landholdings on public expenditure—such as on education—in the United States. Unlike Banerjee and Iyer (2005), where the pattern of landholdings is likely to be exogenously determined because the colonial system of land tenure was exogenously imposed, the system of land tenure in the states Erikson and Ramcharan examine is likely to be endogenous. Using the volatility of weather as an instrument (more volatile weather patterns mean that larger farms emerge to diversify risk), they indeed find that higher inequality in landholdings around the beginning of the 20th century meant lower public expenditure on public goods such as education.

Thus, the evidence indicates that initial inequality results in poor public policies and investment and lower growth, even in systems that have broadly the same political institutions.

Glaeser and others (2004) go further and offer evidence questioning whether political institutions play even a contemporaneous role in economic growth. They argue that the best measure of institutions—a measure of constraints on the executive branch of government—does not predict economic growth, while other factors such as human capital do. Also, the historical instruments in the literature, specifically settler mortality and population density in 1500, are more highly correlated with contemporaneous measures of human capital than with contemporaneous measures of political institutions. Indeed, when Glaeser and others (2004) use instrumental variable estimation applying the historical instruments, they find that measures of human capital trump measures of political institutions in explaining growth.

Discussion and Implications for Development

When attempting to explain the slow economic growth in a country such as Mexico, which has been through independence, revolution, one-party rule, and democratization, far too many people continue to blame political institutions. When faced with a paralyzed economic and social reform process, those with presidential systems seek parliamentary systems and vice versa, those with proportional representation seek to change to a majoritarian system and vice versa, and some seek to decentralize while others seek to centralize decision making. Although economists have found some effects of these changes (for an excellent overview, see Persson and Tabellini 2002, 2005), they are subtle and far more limited than one might expect. Indeed, it is hard to rule out the possibility that the economic effects reflect the underlying changes in circumstances that prompt the changes in political structures, rather than the effects of changes in political structures themselves.

Thus, economic paralysis may well reflect the process whereby the preferences of the electorate and of other influential economic groups are aggregated. Even though everyone can see a better place for the economy to be in, each constituency's better place is not the same as every other constituency's better place, because each starts with different endowments and opportunities and, therefore, wants to protect different rents. The status quo may be the only common ground because it happens to be what everyone is standing on.

Sequencing

How does one jumpstart the economy in these circumstances? Doing what is possible may be tempting. For instance, some have argued that strengthening property rights and expanding competition and associated opportunities will help the very poor (see, for example, De Soto 1989, 2002). Such reforms could certainly create growth for a while, but the lack of endowments, especially of education, may leave the poor unprepared for the market economy, and possibly worse off. Reforms could grind to a halt. To the extent that a large constituency—the uneducated or, more generally, the poorly endowed—benefit little from these pro-market reforms, the outcome is general skepticism about reform. Furthermore, this converts a constituency—the educated or, more generally, the well-endowed— that is hungry for reforms into one that is unenthusiastic about further reforms. Thus in some situations of extreme inequality, focusing first on broadening access to endowments may be wiser. If market-oriented reforms follow soon after, they may fall on more fertile ground.

Therefore, sequencing matters. Broadening the ability to take advantage of opportunities first and then broadening opportunities will ensure widespread support for comprehensive and thorough reforms, while the reverse sequence, even though politically more feasible in the short term, will likely leave reforms stalled and incomplete. Unfortunately, reforms expanding access to endowments such as education or land are the hardest to effect, which is perhaps one reason why underdevelopment is so hard to cure.

Motivated Government

Leaving aside the possibility of a benevolent dictator, which would solve many political economy problems—but is an unrealistic and unhelpful approach—what if a government sought reform, but was in a situation where competitive rent preservation paralyzed polity? One common view is that the government's task is persuasion and that it needs only to lay out its long-term vision clearly for everyone to buy into the reform process. Information can make a difference where groups have inaccurate beliefs about the effects of reforms, as Bourguignon and Dessus (chapter 1) stress. Yet if the conditions in the model hold, the polity may not want comprehensive reforms, and too clear an articulation of the road to reform may mobilize the opposition.

Instead, the government may have to seize every opportunity it can, leaving its ultimate destination unclear. As we have seen, the right reforms can give political momentum to further reforms. If those initial reforms can be undertaken without much discussion of future steps—reform by stealth, so to speak—a government might have more success, especially if this builds sequences that can lead the society to a position in which the collective action issue is less problematic.

The right circumstances could also be a spur to reforms. Often, economic (especially fiscal) crises can break gridlock (Binswanger and Deininger 1997). In normal times, a constituency may be reluctant to place its rents on the negotiating table for fear that only its rents will be reformed away. A grave economic crisis may make it credible that one constituency's rents will be insufficient to remedy the situation, and it could create a more conducive environment for negotiation, in which all constituencies have to give up some of their rents. As Levy and Walton discuss in the introduction to this volume, this was clearly relevant to Mexico's opening to the World Trade Organization (WTO) and the North American Free Trade Agreement, with the private business elite preferring to lose some rents in return for greater certainty about respect for property rights in the economy. (However, as noted earlier, support for complementary reforms in areas where entrenched interests were strong was insufficient to support sustained growth.)

At the opposite extreme, rapid growth, especially through trade, could also create a conducive environment for reform by creating enough opportunities to go around.[3] In particular, the educated may be more willing to tolerate education for the uneducated when growth is rapid and more than enough new jobs are being created. Agglomeration economies would make them even more supportive. Similarly, oligopolists—seeing the larger world market they could have access to if they became globally competitive through reform—may welcome an educated workforce, even if it eventually means more domestic competition. For example, Galor and Moav (2006) document that English industrialists supported universal education at the end of the 19th century as a way to increase their ability to compete with French and German companies. The proposal to use a period of growth to undertake reforms that both expand endowments and undertake deeper market reforms is perhaps more realistic than may appear at first sight: many countries experience periods of several years of rapid growth, but only a few are able to sustain growth over long periods. Unfortunately, too often governments and their supporters enjoy the immediate pleasures of the growth period without undertaking the more difficult reforms.

Noneconomic Reasons for Promoting Mass Education

Forces outside economics have played an important part in helping some countries overcome the natural incentives of interest groups. With respect to expansion of education, perhaps the strongest force has been religion. For example, Protestant leaders believed strongly in the value of personal knowledge of the Scriptures unmediated by the church and, hence, emphasized education. As early as 1524, Martin Luther sent a letter to German municipalities insisting that it was their duty to provide schools and the parents' duty to educate their children. In 1647, Massachusetts passed the Old Deluder Satan Law, requiring local authorities to set up compulsory elementary schools. The law was so called because the preamble said the old deluder Satan kept men from knowledge of the Scriptures (Wiener 1991).

Nationalism seems to have been a second factor. After the revolution, the French government tried to break the hold of the Catholic Church on education by creating state-run primary schools, thereby forcing religious schools to follow an official curriculum and employing teachers as civil servants. It redoubled its efforts as a way to strengthen the army after being defeated by Germany in 1870. In Japan, the Tokugawa elite believed that education would make the masses more moral and more obedient (Dore 1965). Indeed, a high level of literacy on the eve of the Meiji Restoration facilitated the introduction of compulsory education by the state in 1872 (Wiener 1991). The Japanese concern for education also made its way into its colonies, Korea and Taiwan, although the Korean emphasis on mass education may have been spurred, in part, as a way of building national consciousness against Japanese influence (Wiener 1991).

Communism has also been a strong force. Weiner (1991) argues that although the rulers of imperial China regarded mass education as a political threat, the postimperial regimes saw it as a way to bridge the differences between the elite and the masses and to develop China as an industrial and military power (see also Easterlin 1981). The communists may also have been more confident of their hold on power. The Chinese were not uninfluenced by Japan, whose success they saw as resulting from its emphasis on education. Thus again, national rivalry can help break the hold of narrower domestic interest groups.

Finally, successful land reforms also appear to have been undertaken under circumstances of political change. The rise of the gentry in Britain, the force behind the growing power of parliament, accompanied the seizure of land from the great lords and the church by Henry VII and Henry VIII and the sale of their lands to the gentry (Rajan and Zingales 2003; Tawney 1949). Similarly, the desire of the Allied occupiers to reduce the power of the Japanese landlords who had backed the prior militaristic regime (see, for example, Nelson 1993), or of Koreans to cut down to size landlords who had been too cozy with Japanese occupiers (Jeon and Kim 2000), led to successful land reforms in these countries.

External Pressure

Regional organizations such as the European Union or organizations such as the World Trade Organization can promote reforms by offering the substantial benefits of membership to only those who reform enough to qualify. For instance, countries that desire membership in the European Union have to undertake a wide set of reforms to obtain the market access and transfers that accompany membership. Of course, to the extent that the underlying structure of a society is still fundamentally unequal upon access and replete with rents, the pace of reform could slow considerably after membership, as has often been the case for accession countries in practice. For the required reforms to not just mandate macroeconomic stability but also more egalitarian access to factor endowments might, therefore, be beneficial. In a similar vein, countries such as China have accepted tough conditions for accession to the WTO as much because they value the impetus this membership gives to the domestic reform process as well as the benefits of accession itself.

Finally, consider external advice. As international organizations have increasingly realized, the problem in many countries is not so much identifying necessary reforms, but instead obtaining political support for them. One extreme reaction is to throw up one's hands and to blame the historic weight of institutions, but that way lies paralysis. A second approach is to pressure a country into adopting reforms that do not have underlying consensus, perhaps through the threat of withdrawing foreign assistance. As the international organizations have learned, this approach will typically be met with subtle sabotage as domestic constituencies subvert the reforms. This is why international agencies' recent focus on requiring country authorities to demonstrate ownership of reform programs is so important. This is not to say that the international agencies are irrelevant. They can have some effect at the margin, especially if they can strengthen the hand of an emerging reformist constituency in the government.

Conclusion

What lessons does all this suggest for development? The answer "fix the institutions" is probably incomplete, and quite possibly is incorrect. "Fix the constituencies" is probably more on the mark. A number of development successes such as those in the Republic of Korea undertook serious land and education reforms before their takeoff, as have a number in the rapidly growing Indian states. Reforms that reduce inequalities in factor endowments such as land and that improve access to education and finance can apparently strengthen the constituencies for broader economic liberalization. That is, the free-access economy may be a necessary stepping stone to the free-enterprise economy. The difficulty of enacting such endowment-spreading reforms in highly unequal societies should not, however, be minimized. The bottom line is that development is likely to be a complex political process where the people themselves must do much of the heavy lifting. The outside world can help at the margin, but only if the people have ownership, and ownership—even of something as beneficial as development reforms—cannot be taken for granted.

Notes

1. Of course, good institutions, such as the U.S. constitution, can for all practical purposes become exogenous. Yet a constitution can also be simply a piece of paper, as suggested by the very different effects of much the same U.S. constitution when transplanted to Liberia. Similarly, the same institutional environment and leadership that gave rise to Chiang Kai-Shek, whom the United States deemed too corrupt to support against the communists, laid the foundations for the prosperity of Taiwan (China).

2. I prefer the term "constituency" rather than interest group or class. Interest groups (for example, textile workers) are typically much narrower

than my notion of constituency (for instance, the uneducated) and imply organization and thus, possibly, institutions, while the term "class" has prior associations (for example, links to the ownership of the means of production) that may confuse rather than enlighten.

3. Policies such as pro-market reforms should lead to improved institutional outcomes such as rule of law. Johnson, Ostry, and Subramanian (2005) document an improvement in institutional outcomes as a result of growth spurts in poor countries with high initial levels of education and a competitive external sector.

References

Acemoglu, D., S. Johnson, and J. A. Robinson. 2005. "Institutions as the Fundamental Determinants of Long-Run Growth." In *Handbook of Economic Growth*, ed. Philippe Aghion and Steven Durlauf, vol. 1A, 385–472. Amsterdam: North-Holland.

Alesina, A., and N. Fuchs-Schundeln. 2005. "Good Bye Lenin (or Not?): The Effect of Communism on People's Preferences." Unpublished manuscript, Harvard University, Cambridge, MA. http://post.economics.harvard.edu/faculty/alesina/papers/goodbyelenin.pdf.

Banerjee, A., and L. Iyer. 2005. "History, Institutions, and Economic Performance: The Legacy of Colonial Land Tenure Systems in India." *American Economic Review* 95 (4): 1190–213.

Berg, A., J. Ostry, and J. Zettelmeyer. 2006. "What Makes Growth Sustained?" Working Paper, International Monetary Fund, Washington, DC.

Binswanger, H., and K. Deininger. 1997. "Explaining Agricultural and Agrarian Policies in Developing Countries." *Journal of Economic Literature* 35 (4): 1958–2005.

De Soto, H. 1989. *The Other Path*. New York: Harper and Row.

———. 2002. *The Mystery of Capital: Why Capitalism Triumphs in the West and Fails Everywhere Else*. New York: Basic Books.

Dore, R. P. 1965. *Education in Togukawa Japan*. Berkeley, CA: University of California Press.

Easterlin, R. 1981. "Why Isn't the Whole World Developed?" *Journal of Economic History* 41 (1): 1–19.

Engerman, S., E. Mariscal, and K. Sokoloff. 2002. "The Evolution of Schooling Institutions in the Americas, 1800–1925." Working Paper, University of California, Los Angeles.

Engerman, S., and K. Sokoloff. 2003. "Institutional and Non-Institutional Explanations of Economic Differences." Working Paper 9989, National Bureau of Economic Research, Cambridge, MA.

———. 2005. "Colonialism, Inequality, and Long Run Paths of Development." Working Paper 11057, National Bureau of Economic Research, Cambridge, MA.

Erikson, L., and R. Ramcharan. 2006. "The Impact of Inequality on Redistribution: Evidence from U.S. Counties and States, 1890–1930." Unpublished report. International Monetary Fund, Washington, DC.

Galor, E., and O. Moav. 2006. "Das Human Capital: A Theory of the Demise of the Class Structure." *Review of Economic Studies* 73: 85–117.

Glaeser E. L., R. La Porta, F. Lopez-de-Silanes, and A. Shleifer. 2004. "Do Institutions Cause Growth?" *Journal of Economic Growth* 9 (3): 271–303.

Hoff, K. 2003. "Paths of Institutional Development: A View from Economic History." *World Bank Research Observer* 18 (2): 205–26.

Jeon, Y.-D., and Y.-Y. Kim. 2000. "Land Reform, Income Distribution, and Agricultural Production in Korea." *Economic Development and Cultural Change* 48 (2): 253–68.

Johnson, S., J. Ostry, and A. Subramanian. 2005. "Africa's Growth Prospects: Benchmarking the Constraints." Working Paper 07/52, International Monetary Fund, Washington, DC.

Nelson, G. 1993. "Agricultural Policy Reform in Eastern Europe: Discussion." *American Journal of Agricultural Economics* 75 (3): 857–59.

Persson, T., and G. Tabellini. 2002. *Political Economics: Explaining Economic Policy (Zeuthen Lectures)*. Cambridge, MA: Massachusetts Institute of Technology Press.

———. 2005. *The Economic Effects of Constitutions*. Cambridge, MA: Massachusetts Institute of Technology Press.

Przeworski, A. 2004. "The Last Instance: Are Institutions the Primary Cause of Economic Development?" *European Journal of Sociology* 45 (2): 165–88.

Rajan, R. G. Forthcoming. "Competitive Rent Preservation, Reform Paralysis, and the Persistence of Underdevelopment." *American Economic Journal: Macroeconomics.*

Rajan, R. G., and L. Zingales. 2003. *Saving Capitalism from the Capitalists.* New York: Crown Business.

Tawney, R. H. 1949. "The Rise of the Gentry, 1558–1640." *Economic History Review* 11 (1): 1–38.

Weiner, M. 1991. *The Child and the State in India: Child Labor and Education Policy in Comparative Perspective*. Princeton, NJ: Princeton University Press.

3

The Political Economy of Equality and Growth in Mexico: Lessons from the History of the United States

James A. Robinson

This chapter discusses what Mexico could learn from the economic and political history of the United States about how to facilitate the creation of a dynamic, innovative, industrial economy. The challenges facing Mexico are how to overcome the institutional and economic overhang resulting from the long period of one-party rule under the Institutional Revolutionary Party. Even though democracy has finally arrived, the form that this rule took has in many ways shaped the initial conditions in which the new democracy must function, chief of which is the extremely unequal distribution of power and wealth. These inequalities were not simply a coincidence. They were a natural outcome of the strategy that the Institutional Revolutionary Party used to consolidate and sustain its power (Haber and others 2008).

To illustrate why and how such inequalities matter for the future economic prospects of Mexico, this chapter analyzes two critical periods in the history of the United States. One is the period of failed reform in the U.S. South after the Civil War (1861–65). The other, the era of the Populist and Progressive movements from around 1880 to 1920, is an instance of successful reform. In both cases, the main issue was whether to tackle critical inequalities of power and influence. In the U.S. South, the victorious North abandoned the attempt to challenge the real power structures after 1877. In consequence, the Southern economy stagnated for the next 80 years and a highly unequal and divisive system perpetuated itself. During the Progressive era, by contrast, the federal state challenged the "robber barons," the monopolies, and the political bosses who engaged in endemic political fraud and corruption. These interventions helped sustain the dynamic nature of the Northern and Midwestern economy and facilitated rapidly falling inequality over the subsequent half century.

Failed Reform, Economic Stagnation, and Persistent Inequality in the Postbellum South

"De landlord is landlord, de politician is landlord, de judge is landlord, de shurf is landlord, ever'body is landlord, en we ain' got nothin." (Testimony of a Mississippi sharecropper to an official of the Agricultural Adjustment Administration in 1936, Schulman 1994: 16.)

The history of the U.S. South before and after the Civil War provides a cautionary tale of how great concentrations of power and assets can cause prolonged economic stagnation. Most striking about this experience was the continuation of the economic system based on labor repression and cheap, uneducated labor in the U.S. South after the significant changes in political and specific economic institutions brought about by the Civil War.

Before the Civil War, the South was significantly poorer than the U.S. average, with income being about 70 percent of national gross domestic product per capita (Easterlin 1960).[1] The South lacked industry (Bateman and Weiss 1981; Wright 1986), and in 1860, the total manufacturing output of the entire South was less than that of either Massachusetts, New York, or Pennsylvania (Cobb 1984). The South had low rates of urbanization, around 9 percent compared with 35 percent in the Northeast, and relatively little investment in infrastructure. For example, the density of railroads (miles of track divided by land area) was three times higher in the North than in the South. The situation with respect to canal mileage was similar (Wright 1986). Perhaps more important, especially in the context of the potential for future economic growth and industrialization, the South was not even innovative in the goods in which it specialized. For example, during 1837–59, the average numbers of patents issued per year relating to corn and to wheat were 12 and 10, respectively, but just 1 was issued for cotton (Schmookler 1972).

The backwardness of the South was clearly related to the plantation economy and slavery. Wright (1986) argues that because slaves were a mobile asset, planters had no incentive to support investment in public goods such as infrastructure, and thus manufacturing could not develop. Bateman and Weiss (1981) show that Southern planters did not invest in industry, even when the rate of return was superior to that in agriculture. A plausible explanation for the lack of innovation is that slavery limited the possibilities for productive investment. Slaves were forbidden to own property or to become educated in most Southern states, presumably because these restrictions made them easier to control, but this pattern of labor repression also condemned plantations to low-skilled labor forces and possibly removed planters' incentives to innovate.

In the aftermath of the Civil War, the per capita income of the South fell to about 50 percent of the U.S. average. If the slave economy had been the reason why the South had been relatively backward in 1865, one might have imagined that abolishing slavery in 1865 and granting freed slaves the right to vote would have removed this blockage to Southern prosperity. The evidence and historical interpretations show, however, that the abolition of slavery had a surprisingly small effect on the Southern economy.

Although planters initially tried and failed to reintroduce the gang labor system with freed slaves, a low-wage, labor-intensive economy based on labor repression emerged from the ashes of the Civil War. Cut off from the rest of the United States, per capita income remained at about half the U.S. average until the 1940s, when it finally began slowly to converge. As Wright (1986: 70) notes: "The isolation of the southern unskilled labor market was a basic background condition for virtually the whole epoch between the Civil War and World War II."

Just as before the Civil War, systematic underinvestment in education continued (Margo 1990). The main incentive for this seems to have been to impede migration (Wright 1986). By 1900, all but two of the non-Southern states had enacted compulsory schooling laws, while no Southern states had such laws except Kentucky (Woodward 1951). At the same time, industrial development did begin to take place more systematically after 1865. Cobb (1984: 17) notes: "The industries that grew most rapidly in the post-Reconstruction decades were typical of an underdeveloped economy in that they utilized both cheap labor and abundant raw materials.... [S]uch industries hardly promised to elevate the region to economic parity with the rest of the nation."

Thus, the issue is why the economic system of the South changed so little following the Civil War, especially given the significant changes in political and economic institutions. The continuity in the economic institutions of the South appears to be at odds with the significant changes that took place after the Civil War, for example, the enfranchisement of the freed slaves and the repeal of the Missouri Compromise, which had previously cemented the political power of the South in the federal government.

Yet despite these changes, the Southern landed elites persisted after the Civil War and were able to regain control of labor and the political system. As Wright (1986: 84) notes: "The plantations survived the Civil War, and their survival had little to do with their efficiency as producing units.... [C]otton and tobacco could be grown just as efficiently on family-sized farms. No, the key to the survival of the plantation was the ability of the former slave owners to hold on to their land in the midst of intense legal and political struggles after 1865. In national politics, the planters successfully blocked proposals for land confiscation and redistribution to the freedmen."

Wiener's (1978) study of the planter elites in four counties of the so-called Black Belt of western Alabama points to the considerable persistence in the identity and power of the political elites. Tracking families using the U.S. census and considering those with at least US$10,000 worth of real estate, he finds that "of the 236 members of the planter elite in 1850, 101 remained in the elite in 1870" (9). This rate of persistence was similar to that experienced in the antebellum period: "Of the 236 wealthiest planter families of 1850, only 110 remained in the elite a decade later" (9). Nevertheless, "Of the 25 planters with the largest landholdings in 1870, 18 (72%) had been in the elite families in 1860; 16 had been in the 1850 elite group (Wiener 1978: 18)." Death during the Civil War appears to have had little impact on the persistence of the planter elites, because the law exempted one slaveholder from military service for every 20 slaves held. Table 3.1 reproduces these data from Wiener (1978) and shows the high degree of persistence of the southern landed elites.

After the end of the Civil War, more or less the same group of planter elites controlled the land and used various instruments to re-exert their control over the labor force. Even though the specific economic institution of slavery did not persist, the economic system of the South, a system based on plantation-type agriculture with cheap labor, did persist.[2] The South, maintained this economic system through a variety of channels, including both control of local politics and exercise of potentially violent power. As Du Bois (1903: 88) famously puts it, the South became "simply an armed camp for intimidating black folk."

Table 3.1 The Persistence of the Landed Southern Elite in Four Black Belt Counties of Alabama, Selected Years

| | | Real estate holdings[a] | | |
| | | 1870 | 1860 | 1850 |
Name	County	(US$)	(US$)	(US$)
Minge, G.	Marengo	85,000	—	30,000
Lyon, F.	Marengo	75,000	115,000	35,000
Paulling, William	Marengo	72,000	150,000	29,000
Hatch, Alfred	Hale	70,000	120,000	40,000
Alexander, J.	Marengo	69,000	38,000	10,000[b]
Whitfield, B.	Marengo	65,000	200,000[b]	100,000
Terrill, J.	Marengo	62,000	93,000	—
Taylor, E.	Marengo	61,000	—	—
Robertson, R.	Marengo	60,000	—	—
Dew, Duncan	Greene	52,000	200,000[b]	41,000
Walton, John	Marengo	50,000	250,000	25,000
Collins, Charles	Hale	50,000	201,000[b]	30,000
Hays, Charles	Greene	50,000	113,000	—
Brown, John	Sumter	50,000	69,000	13,000
Pickering, Richard	Marengo	50,000	42,000	15,000
Withers, Mary	Hale	50,000	40,000	75,000[b]
Jones, Madison	Hale	50,000	36,000[b]	27,000
Nelson, A.	Hale	48,000	—	10,000[b]
Taylor, J.	Hale	48,000	—	—
Pickens, Wm.	Hale	45,000	210,000[b]	51,000
Reese, Henry	Marengo	45,000	52,000	24,000
Walker, R.	Hale	42,000	55,000	—
Smaw, W.	Greene	42,000	32,000	—
Blanks, E.	Marengo	41,000	—	—
Walker, Morns	Marengo	41,000	—	—
Number of planters	—	25	18	16
Percentage present in 1870	—	—	72	64

Source: Wiener (1978, table 2: 12).

Note: — = not available.

a. Rounded off to the nearest 1,000, as reported in the U.S. Census of Populations' manuscript schedules.

b. Wealth of father or husband.

The planter elites successfully staffed or co-opted the members of the Freedmen's Bureau, whose remit was to supervise the freed slaves. In 1865, Alabama's state legislature passed the Black Code, an important landmark in the repression of black labor. Wiener (1978: 58) describes this repression as follows: "The Black Code of Alabama included two key laws intended to assure the planters a reliable supply of labor—a vagrancy law, and a law against the 'enticement' of laborers." These laws were designed to impede labor mobility and reduce competition in the labor market. In addition to molding the legal system in their favor, the "planters used Klan terror to keep blacks from leaving the plantation regions, to get them to work, and keep them at work in the cotton field" (62).

In his seminal study of the politics of the South after World War II, Key (1949: 9) sums up the persistence of the institutions of the South both before and after the Civil War as the "extraordinary achievement of a relatively small minority—the whites of the areas of heavy Negro population."

A key to the persistence of the antebellum system after the Civil War was the elites' continued control over land. For example, in the debate about the redistribution of 40 acres of land to each freedman (which President Andrew Johnson vetoed in 1865), Congressman George Washington Julian argued: "Of what avail would be an act of congress totally abolishing slavery ... if the old agricultural basis of aristocratic power shall remain?" (quoted in Wiener, 1978: 6).

A complementary strategy was control of the local political system. Following the Civil War, the period known as Reconstruction lasted until 1877 (see Foner 1989 for a seminal history). During this period, Republican politicians contested power in the South and, with the help of the Union Army, engineered some social changes. However, this induced a systematic backlash in the form of support for the Democratic Party and the so-called Redeemers. In 1877, in the context of a logroll between President Rutherford B. Hayes and southern national politicians, Union soldiers were withdrawn from the South, and the region was left to its own devices. The period after 1877 marked the real renewal of the antebellum elite. The "redemption" of the South involved the systematic disenfranchisement of the black (and poor white) population through the use of poll taxes and literacy tests (Key 1949; Kousser 1974) and the creation of the one-party Democratic regime.[3]

Wright (1986: 78) confirms this picture: "Even in the 1930s, southern representatives in Washington did not use their powerful positions to push for new federal projects, hospitals, public works and so on. They didn't, that is, as long as the foundations of the low-wage regional economy persisted."

In addition to disenfranchisement, Southern states enacted a whole gamut of segregationist legislation, the so-called Jim Crow laws (see Woodward 1955 for the classic analysis). These laws effectively turned the postbellum South into an apartheid society where blacks and whites lived different lives. As in South Africa, these laws were aimed at controlling the black population and its labor supply.

Consequently, the South entered the 20th century as a primarily rural society. "It remained an agrarian society with a backward technology that still employed hand labor and mule power virtually unassisted by mechanical implements" (Ransom and Sutch 2001: 175–76). In 1900, the South's urbanization rate was 13.5 percent, compared with 60 percent in the Northeast (Cobb 1984: 25).

Ransom and Sutch's (2001: 177, 186) assessment of the implications for economic progress of this economic and political system in the South is representative of the consensus view:

> When whites used threats of violence to keep blacks from gaining an education, practicing a trade, or purchasing land, they systematically prevented blacks from following the three routes most commonly traveled by other Americans in their quest for self-advancement. With over half the population held in ignorance and forced to work as agricultural laborers, it is no wonder that the South was poor, underdeveloped, and without signs of economic progress....

> Southerners erected an economic system that failed to reward individual initiative on the part of blacks and was therefore ill-suited to their economic advancement. As a result, the inequities originally inherited from slavery persisted. But there was a by-product of this effort at racial repression, the system tended to cripple all economic growth.

The Southern equilibrium, based on the exercise of power by the landed elites, plantation agriculture, and cheap labor, persisted well into the 20th century and started to crumble only after World War II. It was only after the demise of this equilibrium that the South started its process of rapid convergence with the North.

Why did the reforms attempted in the South after 1865 not work? The main reason is that the victorious North did not change the underlying inequalities of asset holdings (no 40 acres and a mule as promised to the freed slaves). In consequence, the North also left the antebellum elites in power.

Successful Reform, Industrial Dynamism, and Falling Inequality in the Progressive Era

"What do I care about the Law? Hain't I got the power?" Cornelius Vanderbilt (quoted in Josephson 1934: 15)

The absence of reform in the U.S. South in the 1880s and later is in stark contrast to the situation in the North. The rapid economic growth that the North sustained after the Civil War led to the emergence of a class of highly unscrupulous robber barons, who began to consolidate large business empires and monopoly "trusts." Perhaps the most notorious of the robber barons was John D. Rockefeller, who started Standard Oil in 1870. He quickly eliminated his other rivals in Cleveland and attempted to monopolize the transportation and retailing of oil and oil products. In 1882, he created a massive trust consisting of all the different companies he owned. By 1890, Standard Oil controlled 88 percent of the refined oil flows in the United States, and by 1916, Rockefeller became the world's first billionaire. Figure 3.1 shows a contemporary cartoon depicting how Standard Oil wrapped itself around not just the oil industry, but also Capitol Hill.

Almost as famous was J. P. Morgan. In 1901, along with Andrew Carnegie, Morgan founded U.S. Steel, which became the first corporation with a capitalized value of more than US$1 billion and by far the largest steel corporation in the world. Table 3.2 shows the emergence of the great trusts in the 1890s. By the end of the 1890s, a large number of trusts had been created that accounted for more than 70 percent of the market in a number of industries. These trusts included many famous names, such as DuPont, Eastman Kodak, and International Harvester. Figure 3.2 shows one of the consequences of these trends in the economy: the rapid increase in wealth inequality.

Figure 3.1 The Standard Oil Company

Table 3.2 The Merger Boom, 1895–1904
(market shares of consolidation)

Consolidations with <40%	Consolidations with ≥40% but <70%	Consolidations with ≥70%
Amalgamated Copper	American Bicycle	American Brake Shoe & Foundry
American Cigar	American Brass	American Can
Cleveland & Sandusky Brewing Co.	American Car & Foundry	American Chicle
Dayton Breweries	American Felt	American Fork & Hoe
Empire Steel & Iron	American Fisheries	American Hide & Leather
Independent Glass	American Linseed	American Ice
Maryland Brewing	American Malting	American Locomotive
Massachusetts Breweries	American Sewer Pipe	American School Furniture
New Orleans Brewing	American Shipbuilding	American Seeding Machine
New York & Kentucky	American Smelting & Refining	American Snuff
Pacific Coast Biscuit	American Stove	American Stogie
Pennsylvania Central Brewing	American Thread	American Window Glass
Pittsburgh Brewing	American Woolen	American Writing Paper
Providence Ice	California Fruit Canners Assoc.	Casein Co. of America
Pure Oil	General Chemical	Central Foundry
Republic Iron & Steel	International Salt	Chicago Pneumatic Tool
Standard Shoe Machinery	International Silver	Contiental Tobacco
Susquehanna Iron & Steel	National Biscuit	Corn Products
United Breweries	National Candy	Crucible Steel
U.S. Flour Milling	National Enameling & Stamping	Distilling Co. of America
Virginia Iron, Coal & Coke	National Fireproofing	DuPont

(Continued on the following page)

Table 3.2 (*Continued*)

Consolidations with <40%	Consolidations with ≥40% but <70%	Consolidations with ≥70%
	National Glass	Eastman Kodak
	New England Cotton Yarn	General Aristo
	Royal Baking Powder	Harbison-Walker Refractories
	Rubber Goods Mfg. Co.	International Harvester
	Standard Table Oil Cloth	International Paper
	United States Cotton Duck	International Steam Pump
	United States Shipbuilding	Mississippi Wire Glass
	United States Steel	National Asphalt
	Virginia-Carolina Chemical	National Carbon
		National Novelty
		Otis Elevator
		Pittsburgh Plate Glass
		Railway Steel Spring
		Standard Sanity Mfg.
		Union Bag & Paper
		United Shoe Machinery
		United Box Board & Paper
		United States Bobbin & Shuttle
		United States Cast Iron Pipe & Foundry
		United States Envelope
		United States Gypsum

Source: Lamoreaux 1985: 3-4.

Figure 3.2 The Evolution of Wealth Inequality, 1780–1980

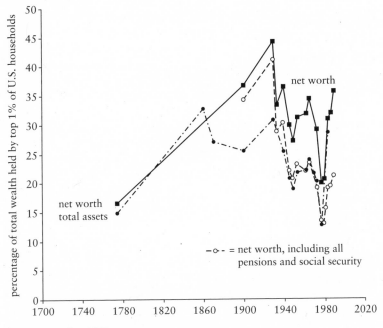

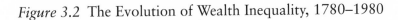

Source: Lindert 2000.

The political system in the North and the Midwest did not take these events lying down, however. The victims of monopolistic practices and other features of the institutional status quo began to organize against the monopolies, and this strategy led to a series of reforms to the role of the state. The opposition coalesced into two broad political movements, the Populists and, subsequently, the Progressives.

The Populist movement emerged out of the agrarian crisis that began to afflict the Midwest from the late 1860s onward (Sanders 1999). The National Grange of the Patrons of Husbandry, known as the Grangers, was founded in 1867 and began to mobilize farmers against what they saw as unfair and discriminatory business practices. In 1873 and 1874, the Grangers won control of the legislatures in 11 Midwest states (Jones 1995), and rural discontent culminated in 1892 in the formation of the People's Party, which got 8.5 percent of the popular vote in the 1892 presidential election. In the next two elections, the Populists fell in behind the two unsuccessful Democratic campaigns of William Jennings Bryan, who made many of their issues his own.

These political movements began to have a major impact, beginning with the Interstate Commerce Act of 1887, which created the Interstate Commerce Commission and initiated federal regulation of industry. This legislation was quickly followed by the Sherman Anti-Trust Act of 1890, which began the attack on business trusts (monopolies). However, serious implementation of these only occurred later following the election of a series of presidents committed to reform, namely, Theodore Roosevelt (1901–08), William Taft (1908–12), and Woodrow Wilson (1912–20).

A key political force behind the antitrust movement and the move to impose federal regulation of industry was the farming vote. The Grangers, a organization of farmers, initiated state-level attempts to regulate railroads in the 1870s (Jones 1995). In his study of the Chicago meat packers trust, Libecap (1992) also notes the key role of farmer interests in pushing antitrust legislation. In particular,

> Of the fifty-nine petitions regarding trusts sent to the 51st Congress prior to the enactment of the Sherman Act, all but two came from Illinois, Indiana, Iowa, Kansas, Kentucky, and Tennessee and were presented by such groups as the Farmers Union, Farmers Alliance, Farmers Mutual Benefit Association, and Patrons of Animal Husbandry. The lobbying appears to have had the desired impact on members of Congress from the Midwest. At least thirteen of the sixteen antitrust bills introduced in the House, 50th Congress, 1st session, and all eighteen of the bills introduced in the House, 51st Congress, 1st session, were sponsored by Midwestern or southern representatives (Libecap 1992: 256).

From the ashes of the Populists came the Progressives. Progressivism was a heterogeneous reform movement that arose in reaction to many of the same issues that the Populists found objectionable (Cooper 1990; Wiebe 1967). Jones (1995: 369) argues that Progressives were those who were "disturbed by the rise of the trusts, the growing concentration of wealth, the spread of political corruption, the widening of social divisions, the bitterness of industrial strife." The Progressive movement initially gelled around Theodore Roosevelt, who assumed the presidency following William McKinley's assassination in 1901. In his first address to Congress, Roosevelt warned of "the 'real and grave evils' of industrial consolidation and urged Congress to establish a federal agency with power to investigate the affairs of the great combinations" (Jones 1995: 378). In 1902, Roosevelt used the Sherman Act to break up the Northern

Securities Company, affecting the interests of J. P. Morgan, and the federal government brought subsequent suits against DuPont, the American Tobacco Company, and the Standard Oil Company. Roosevelt strengthened the Interstate Commerce Act with the Hepburn Act of 1906, and his successor, William Taft, prosecuted trusts even more assiduously. The highpoint was the breakup of Standard Oil in 1910. Taft also promoted other important reforms, such as the introduction of a federal income tax, which resulted from ratification of the 16th Amendment to the Constitution in 1913.

The apogee of progressive reforms came with the election of Woodrow Wilson in 1912. As Wilson (1913: 286) notes: "If monopoly persists, monopoly will always sit at the helm of government. I do not expect to see monopoly restrain itself. If there are men in this country big enough to own the government of the United States, they are going to own it."

Wilson signed the Clayton Anti-Trust Act in 1914 and created the Federal Trade Commission. In addition, under the impetus of the Pujo Committee's investigation into the "money trust," Wilson moved to increase regulation of the financial sector, which led to the creation of the Federal Reserve Board in 1913.

Crucial to this period of reform was the role of the press. In 1906, Roosevelt had coined the term muckraker (from a character, "the man with the muckrake," in Bunyan's *Pilgrim's Progress*) for what he regarded as intrusive journalism. The term stuck and the muckrakers played an important role in exposing the ills of the existing system. Most famous were people like Ira Tarbell, whose 1904 *History of the Standard Oil Company* played a key role in moving public opinion against Rockefeller and his business interests. The newspaper magnate William Randolph Hearst also played a salient role, and his 1906 serialization in *The Cosmopolitan* of articles by David Graham Phillips called "The Treason of the Senate" galvanized the campaign to introduce direct elections for the Senate, another key Progressive reform that occurred with the enactment of the 17th Amendment in 1914. A final, much-publicized piece of muckraking that influenced the public's reception of Pujo Committee's findings was Brandeis's (1914) book *Other People's Money and How Bankers Use It*, which described a series of financial scandals.

All this antitrust activity seems to have checked, and in some cases even reduced, the extent of industrial concentration. Table 3.3 reports data on the output shares of the four largest firms in various industries in 1860, 1901, and 1963. Rapid concentration is evident in many industries between 1960 and 1901, for example,

Table 3.3 A Comparison of Industrial Concentration in
1860, 1901, and 1963
(output share of four largest firms)

| | 1860 | | | 1901 | 1963 | |
Industry	Northeast	Midwest	South	National	Regional	National
Agricultural implements	45	16	20	41	—	43
Boots and shoes	4	16	6	26	—	25
Chemicals	96		100	24	—	56
Clothing	6	15	40		—	8
Cotton goods	14	99	30	20	—	30
Flour milling	12	4	11	39	—	35
Furniture	13	18	10	—	23	11
Iron castings	32	14	66	46		28
Iron bar	29	100	37	46	71	50
Leather	7	26	11	26	—	18
Liquor	7	9	21	39	68	47
Lumber milling	10	6	9	0.5	18	11
Machinery	30	15	25	41	—	93
Meat-packing	21	32	39	39	40	16
Tobacco	17	18	9	50	—	59
Woolen goods	17	7	42	20	—	54

Source: Atack and Passell 1994: 464.
Note: — = not available.

boots and shoes, liquor, meatpacking, and tobacco, but there is
little evidence of further concentration between 1901 and 1963.
Figures 3.2 and 3.3 show that the Progressive era coincided with
the peak of inequality, after which inequality fell quite dramatically. Finally, the assault on monopolies and the power of business
trusts went hand-in-hand with sustained economic growth. Indeed,
growth was much faster during 1900–14 than it had been during
the previous decade. Figure 3.4 shows that sentiment at the time
linked the breakup of monopolies to growth, and the figure shows
President Wilson fueling the pump of prosperity by breaking up
the trusts.

Figure 3.3 The Evolution of Income Inequality, 1910–95

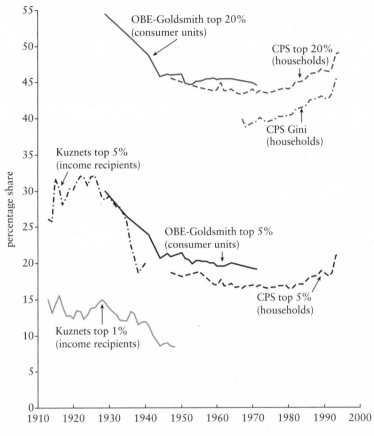

Source: Lindert 2000.

Reasons Behind the Different Outcomes in the South and the North

The contrast between the failed transition after the Civil War in the South and the successful antitrust movement can be linked to different features of the two cases.

Failure of Reconstruction in the South

If the planter elites were a major impediment to reform, why did the North not move against them? The failure of reform began as early as 1865, when it became clear that freed blacks would not get the 40 acres and a mule that they had been promised during the war. In

Figure 3.4 A Contemporary View of the Growth Effects of Antitrust Actions

addition, the planters remained in place. After the war was over, the victorious North was not prepared to pay to reorganize the South and had little economic incentive to do so. Northern industrial interests did not anticipate that the South would be a relatively important market for their goods. Not only did the North have little direct economic interest in reforming the South, but also it had conflicting political motivations. Critically, 700,000 black votes gave Ulysses S. Grant the presidency in 1868. The Northern Democrats also saw the possibilities of a coalition with white Southern Democrats.

Because the Southern states became pivotal to the outcome of national elections, this allowed them to obtain many concessions.

The most obvious was the compromise of 1877 and the disputed election of Republican Rutherford B. Hayes. The Electoral Commission gave disputed Southern Electoral College votes to Hayes, who placated Southern Democrats by withdrawing Northern troops from the South and ending Reconstruction.

Success of the Progressives

Several key factors seem to have led to the success of the Populists' and Progressives' reforms. Most important, they were preceded by decisive political reforms, particularly the introduction between 1888 and 1892 of the use of the Australian ballot in elections. The reform of the ballot massively reduced vote buying and clientelism and allowed the emergence of a much less corrupt form of politics that was more focused on programmatic issues and reform. Figure 3.5 shows a contemporary view of the connection between democracy and antitrust activities.

A realignment of politics in the 1890s followed these reforms. The South and many states of the Midwest became Democratic, while the Northeast and upper Midwest became Republican. This shift had the effect that rural interests, who were hurt by the monopolies, found common cause within the Democratic Party. The Democrats' espousal of an antitrust platform naturally influenced the policy platform of the Republicans.

Another factor, evidenced in the Wilson quote cited earlier, is that the economic elites were separate from the political elites. The

Figure 3.5 Democracy Demolishing the Trusts

New York American.]   [March 13.
Working Citizens, Do you want to Win?   Drop the old-fashioned methods—Fight with the Ballot.

political elites feared the power of the economic elites and thus had a collective interest in disciplining them and ensuring that they did not take over politics that transcended party lines.

Finally, the independence and flowering of a free press clearly played a significant role.

Lessons for Mexico

Theory and evidence suggest that monopolies and concentrated industries are less innovative than competitive ones (Aghion and Griffith 2005), and this is certainly consistent with the historical evidence from the United States. Large concentrations of wealth can also undermine democratic institutions and create political instability (Acemoglu and Robinson 2006).

The issue is whether Mexico can or will do something about the situation in relation to monopolies and wealth inequalities currently prevalent in that country. Can a political coalition along the line of the Progressives form in Mexico? Although Mexico has reformed politically and has a free press (Lawson 2002), one obvious problem is that the country's progressive coalition seems to cut across party lines. An important part of U.S. Progressivism was that it found a home in the platform of the Democratic Party. In Mexico, the rural sector has, to an extent, already been empowered by democratization, as witnessed by such social programs as Oportunidades, which have shifted policy away from its historical bias toward the urban sector. The catch is that much of the rural sector votes for the Institutional Revolutionary Party, which includes many who oppose reform, making it unlikely that the party will espouse a progressive platform.

Another interesting feature is the relationship between the economic and political elites. In Russia, President Vladimir Putin moved against the economic oligarchs because they were too strong and blocked his consolidation of power. The balance of power between these different elites in Mexico remains to be seen, but this issue is certainly a key one for those interested in reforms.

Notes

1. Scholars have hotly debated the relative poverty of the South. Even though Fogel and Engerman (1974) point out that if the South had been an independent country, it would have been among the 10 richest in the world in 1860, the consensus view is that at that time the South was relatively backward with poor institutions, a view that in its modern form goes back

to at least Genovese (1965). It was relatively prosperous compared with other parts of the world at the time because it had recently benefited from a huge boom in cotton prices (Wright 1978), and also because it was embedded in a society whose institutions were formed in the 17th century, before the development of the plantation economy.

2. Du Bois (1903: 120) describes the aftermath of emancipation as follows: "What did such a mockery of freedom mean? Not a cent of money, not an inch of land, not a mouthful of victuals, not even ownership of the rags on his back. Free! On Saturday, once or twice a month, the old master, before the war, used to dole out bacon and meal to his Negroes. And after the first flush of freedom wore off, and his true helplessness dawned on the freedman, he came and picked up his hoe, and old master still doled out his bacon and meal. The legal form of service was theoretically far different; in practice, task-work or 'cropping' was substituted for daily toil in gangs; and the slave gradually became a metayer, or tenant on shares, in name, but a laborer with indeterminate wages in fact."

3. Key (1949: 8–9), for example, notes: "Two-party competition would have been fatal to the status of black-belt whites. It would have meant in the 'nineties an appeal to the Negro vote and it would have meant ... Negro rule in some black-belt counties. From another standpoint, two-party competition would have meant the destruction of southern solidarity in national politics.... Unity on the national scene was essential in order that the largest possible bloc could be mobilized to resist any national move towards interference with southern authority to deal with the race question as was locally desired."

References

Acemoglu, Daron, and James A. Robinson. 2006. *Economic Origins of Dictatorship and Democracy*. New York: Cambridge University Press.

Aghion, Philippe, and Rachel Griffith. 2005. *Competition and Growth: Reconciling Theory and Evidence*. Cambridge, MA: Massachusetts Institute of Technology Press.

Atack, Jeremy, and Peter Passell. 1994. *A New Economic View of American History: From Colonial Times to 1940*, 2nd ed. New York: Norton.

Bateman, Fred, and Thomas Weiss. 1981. *A Deplorable Scarcity: The Failure of Industrialization in the Slave Economy*. Chapel Hill, NC: University of North Carolina Press.

Brandeis, Louis. 1914. *Other People's Money and How the Bankers Use It*. New York: Stokes.

Cobb, James C. 1984. *Industrialization and Southern Society, 1877–1984*. Lexington, KY: University Press of Kentucky.

Cooper, John M. 1990. *Pivotal Decades: The United States 1900–1920*. New York: W. W. Norton.

Du Bois, W. E. B. 1903. *The Souls of Black Folk*. New York: A. C. McClurg.

Easterlin, Richard A. 1960. "Interregional Differences in Per Capita Income, Population, and Total Income, 1840–1950." In Conference on Research in Income and Wealth: Trends in the American Economy in the Nineteenth Century, Studies in Income and Wealth, vol. 24, 73–140. Princeton, NJ: Princeton University Press.

Fogel, Robert W., and Stanley L. Engerman. 1974. *Time on the Cross: The Economics of American Negro Slavery*. Boston: Little, Brown.

Foner, Eric. 1989. *Reconstruction: America's Unfinished Revolution, 1863–1877*. New York: Perennial Library.

Genovese, Eugene D. 1965. *The Political Economy of Slavery: Studies in the Economy and Society of the Slave South*. New York: Pantheon Books.

Haber, Stephen H., Herbert S. Klein, Noel Maurer, and Kevin J. Middlebrook. 2008. *The Second Mexican Revolution: Economic, Political and Social Change since 1980*. New York: Cambridge University Press.

Jones, Maldwyn A. 1995. *The Limits of Liberty: American History 1607–1992*, 2nd ed. New York: Oxford University Press.

Josephson, Matthew. 1934. *The Robber Barons*. Orlando, FL: Harcourt.

Key, V. O., Jr. 1949. *Southern Politics: In State and Nation*. New York: Vintage Books.

Kousser, J. Morgan. 1974. *The Shaping of Southern Politics: Suffrage Restriction and the Establishment of the One-Party South, 1880–1910*. New Haven, CT: Yale University Press.

Lamoreaux, Naomi R. 1985. *The Great Merger Movement in American Business, 1895–1904*. New York: Cambridge University Press.

Lawson, Chappell H. 2002. *Building the Fourth Estate: Democratization and the Rise of a Free Press in Mexico*. Berkeley, CA: University of California Press.

Libecap, Gary B. 1992. "The Rise of the Chicago Packers and the Origins of Meat Inspection and Antitrust." *Economic Inquiry* 30: 242–62.

Lindert, Peter H. 2000. "Three Centuries of Inequality in Britain and America." In *The Handbook of Income Distribution*, ed. Anthony B. Atkinson and François Bourguignon, 167–216. Amsterdam: North-Holland.

Margo, Robert A. 1990. *Race and Schooling in the South, 1880–1950: An Economic History*. Chicago: University of Chicago Press.

Ransom, Roger L., and Richard Sutch. 2001. *One Kind of Freedom: The Economic Consequences of Emancipation*, 2nd ed. New York: Cambridge University Press.

Sanders, Elizabeth. 1999. *Roots of Reform: Farmers, Workers and the American State, 1877–1917*. Chicago: University of Chicago Press.

Schmookler, Jacob. 1972. "Time Series of Patents Classified by Industry, United States 1837–1957." In *Patents, Inventions and Economic Change: Data and Selected Essays*, ed. Zvi Griliches and Leonid Hurwicz. Cambridge, MA: Harvard University Press.

Schulman, Bruce J. 1994. *From Cotton Belt to Sunbelt: Federal Policy, Economic Development and the Transformation of the South, 1938–1980*, Durham, NC: Duke University Press.

Tarbell, Ida M. 1904. *The History of the Standard Oil Company*. New York: Macmillan.

Wiebe, Robert H. 1967. *The Search for Order, 1877–1920*. New York: Hill and Wang.

Wiener, Jonathan M. 1978. *Social Origins of the New South: Alabama, 1860–1885*. Baton Rouge, LA: Louisiana State University Press.

Wilson, Woodrow. 1913. *The New Freedom: A Call for the Emancipation of the Generous Energies of a People*. New York: Doubleday, Page and Company.

Woodward, C. Vann. 1951. *Origins of the New South, 1877–1913*. Baton Rouge, LA: Louisiana State University Press.

———. 1955. *The Strange Career of Jim Crow*. New York: Oxford University Press.

Wright, Gavin. 1978. *The Political Economy of the Cotton South: Households, Markets, and Wealth in the Nineteenth Century*. New York: W. W. Norton.

———. 1986. *Old South, New South*. New York: Basic Books.

PART II

Interactions between Equity, Institutions, and Growth in Mexico

4

The Inequality Trap and Its Links to Low Growth in Mexico

Isabel Guerrero, Luis Felipe López-Calva, and Michael Walton

Inequality and slow growth are two of the most important problems Mexico faces today. Analysts typically treat them as separate problems, with different roots and different policy solutions. This chapter argues that they are closely interconnected, and it examines a channel that can explain the link between inequality and low growth.

Social scientists generally consider inequality to be a product of historically shaped inequalities of opportunity transmitted across generations by education, ethnicity, social position, and place of

The authors would like to thank Eduardo Ortíz for outstanding research assistance and Anusha Nath and Alexandra Zenzes for excellent assistance on inputs from the Forbes database. Valuable comments were received from Raymundo Campos-Vázquez, Santiago Levy, William Maloney, Yasuhiko Matsuda, Roger Noll, Harry Patrinos, John Pencavel, and David Rosenblatt, as well as participants in seminars at the Graduate School of Public Affairs of the Tecnológico de Monterrey in Mexico City, Stanford University, the Kennedy School of Government at Harvard University, and the Mexico Public Policy Forum sponsored by the Organisation for Economic Co-Operation and Development, the World Bank, the International Development Bank, the United Nations Development Programme, and the European Communication and Language Audit Training programme.

birth. Mexico has most commonly tackled inequality as a poverty-related issue through measures that seek to assure decent education, health, and risk management instruments for all groups. Some interventions have been extremely successful, for example, the Oportunidades program.

Economists have primarily understood low growth to be a product of macroeconomic instability and structural problems, such as lack of infrastructure, high energy and telecommunications costs, high costs of doing business, lack of competition, narrow financial systems, and weak rule of law—a set of issues often grouped under the label of lack of competitiveness. With macroeconomic stability currently appearing to be more robust in Mexico, the focus today is on addressing structural constraints and prioritizing interventions to yield a stronger growth response.

However, looking at inequality and competitiveness in a piecemeal fashion misses important parts of the dynamics of low growth. Understanding the loops and reinforcing mechanisms between the structures of inequality and weak growth dynamics is an important contribution to the public debate and opens many new areas for future research.

We argue that understanding the dynamics of the entire distribution in Mexico is essential. Household surveys seldom capture the income of the elite, and the distribution of wealth and power at the top of the distributional pyramid is often more important than income alone. We then argue that inequalities of influence can result in lack of competitiveness by affecting both markets and policies. Unequal structures can cause inefficiencies in how markets and other institutions function through concentrated corporate control and union influences on product, financial, and labor markets. Influences may also occur on the choices of policy and institutional designs that favor anticompetitive and rent-seeking policies, which are bad for growth.

With a few exceptions, the six-year term of office of President Vicente Fox did not address the growth-reducing aspects of inequalities of influence. At the time of writing, what would be done during the term of President Felipe Calderón remained unclear. This is one of most important challenges behind the weak growth dynamics underlying the Mexican economy. The World Bank (2005b) argues that inequity is not only bad for poverty reduction, but also can hurt efficiency and growth. Mexico is an excellent example of how this is taking place today (see also Bourguignon and Walton 2006 for a general discussion of these issues for Latin America, and Esteban and Rag 2006 for a relevant theoretical account).

We focus on the growth-reducing influence of concentrated wealth and monopoly power in the business sector and unions in protected sectors. The influence of interconnected elites, as well as the influence of some organized corporatist groups, such as teachers, Instituto Mexicano del Seguro Social (IMSS) workers, and the farmers' lobby, are of particular relevance in underpinning inequality traps—structures of inequality that tend to perpetuate themselves over time. (For informal accounts of the concept of an inequality trap, see Rao 2006; World Bank 2005a. Also Bourguignon, Ferreira, and Walton 2007 present a formal account).

Strong institutions can countervail concentrations of power, but when a country's institutions are weak, a few predominant groups can have adverse effects on market functioning and on policy design, as schematically presented in figure 4.1. By weak institutions, we mean those that are incapable of constraining the influence of powerful groups in the interests of the broader society, including future generations. Relevant institutions include the regulatory bodies, the judicial system, the legislature, the civil service, the political parties, and the executive itself (see Glaeser, Sheinkman, and Shleifer 2003 for a discussion of how weak justice systems tend to benefit the rich and powerful). Policy can be distorted in two ways: when policy design directly serves powerful interests and when policy makers are forced to undertake suboptimal policies because of the effective veto of the powerful on first-best reforms.

Both unequal structures and overall institutional arrangements are products of the broader pattern of power and history of each country. For Mexico, we are particularly interested in whether big

Figure 4.1 How Unequal Structures Cause Suboptimal Development

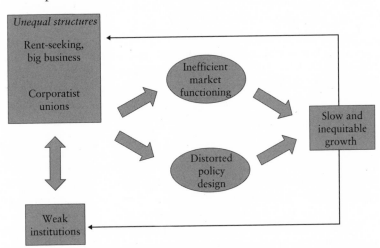

Source: Authors.

business and corporatist groups (primarily unions in protected sectors, part of the legacy of Mexico's corporatist tradition) have continued to distort policy design and market functioning in the wake of the large changes associated with economic liberalization, the North American Free Trade Agreement, and the recent democratization under President Fox.

Using the framework in figure 4.1 as a basis for analysis, this chapter examines the following questions:

- How are business elites and corporatist groups positioned relative to traditional measures of distribution in Mexico?
- What is the institutional context in which these structures operate?
- What are the potential channels of influence by each group, and is there empirical evidence that these matter?
- What is the impact of this influence on competition, competitiveness, and low growth?

Groups with substantial power currently benefit from the status quo and have no incentives to deviate from their behavior. Under the prevalent political equilibrium, they receive substantial rents at the cost of growth dynamism. We are interested in whether a different equilibrium exists in which the Mexican economy could be on a lower inequality and higher growth path. Such an equilibrium, while better for the economy as a whole, would imply that existing powerful groups were receiving smaller rents.

Wealthy and Corporatist Groups within the Overall Distribution of Wealth and Power

Both labor unions and wealthy business groups have a valuable role to play in a dynamic economy and society. However, the primary focus of this chapter is on the unequal influence of particular groups under conditions that can hurt growth and resource allocation. A useful first step is to first position both business elites and corporatist groups within the traditional measure of the distribution of income, for which our basic reference is the National Income and Expenditure Survey (Encuesta Nacional de Ingresos y Gastos de los Hogares, or ENIGH).

Influence of Wealthy Entrepreneurs

In assessing the position of the wealthy, the ENIGH indicates that Mexico is highly unequal by international standards when measured by income: in 2000, the incomes of the top 10 percent of the population were 45 times those of the bottom 10 percent. The Gini coefficient was 0.546, high by international standards, but slightly lower than in Brazil, Bolivia, Colombia, and Chile (De Ferranti and others 2004). However, as the ENIGH does not capture the truly wealthy, we complement its measures with the *Forbes Magazine* listing of the wealth of billionaires. This source has many weaknesses, but it provides an independent basis for looking at extreme wealth in Mexico over time and in an international context.[1] In 2008, the Forbes database showed that Mexico had 10 billionaires with a total net worth of US$96 billion, up from US$25 billion in 2000. Movement occurs in and out of the list, with a total of 20 individuals or families declaring a net worth of US$1 billion or more during 1996–2006, and an additional 10 who appeared for only a year or two around 1994. Most of these had inherited part of their wealth, and almost half had benefited from the privatizations of the early 1990s. Current wealth derives from businesses in a variety of sectors, including mining, banking, telecommunications, beer, cement, pharmaceuticals, retail, real estate, television, and tortillas.

The ratio of total net worth of billionaires to gross domestic product (GDP) rose from 4 percent of GDP in 2000, to around 6 percent in 2004–06, and then to an estimated 10 percent in 2008 (figure 4.2).[2]

Figure 4.2 Ratio of Net Worth of Mexican Billionaires to GDP, 1990–2008

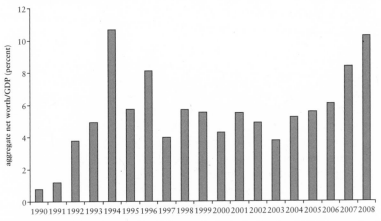

Sources: World Bank 2007; World Economic Outlook, October 2007 for actual and projected GDP data; http: //www.forbes.com for data on net worth of billionaires.

Significant changes have occurred over a longer time period. In both absolute value and as a ratio of GDP, extraordinary growth was apparent between 1989 and 1993, with a high, but short-lived, peak in 1994 at the end of President Carlos Salinas de Gortari's term. Sharp fluctuations took place during the turbulent 1995–96 period, and growth has been steady since 2003.

In an international context, the ratio of Mexico's billionaire wealth to GDP is higher than in most countries, but is not the highest (figure 4.3). In 2007, Mexico had a higher ratio of billionaires to GDP than Brazil, Colombia (both of which have higher measured income inequality according to household surveys), most other lower- and middle-income countries, Japan, and the United Kingdom. The ratio was about the same as for Chile and the United States and lower than that for India, Kuwait, Malaysia, Russia, and Saudi Arabia. Compared with the mid-1990s, India has shot up from a very low ratio, while countries affected by the East Asian crisis—notably Indonesia and Thailand—experienced significant falls in the wealth to GDP ratio.

Information about the income of billionaires that can be compared with the ENIGH is not available. To provide a purely indicative comparison, we calculated their implicit income, conservatively assuming an annual return of 5 percent on their wealth and comparing this amount with average income and the income of the top 1 percent, 0.1 percent, and 0.01 percent of the distribution in the survey (figure 4.4). For consistency, we used the same family size of three recorded for the top 1 percent of the ENIGH. Incomes are on a log scale, because otherwise putting the figures in one graph would be impossible. According to this purely suggestive calculation, billionaires have a potential income of almost 400 times the top 0.1 percent in the survey and some 14,000 times that of the population average.

Concentrations of family wealth can lead to much greater concentrations of corporate influence through pyramidal structures of corporate ownership, in which interconnected patterns of corporate ownership imply that families control assets that are a multiple of their actual ownership. For Mexico, evidence indicates that family control is important: in the mid-1990s, 100 percent of both the 20 largest firms and a sample of 10 medium-sized firms were family owned, a high ratio by international standards (table 4.1).

Complementing these indicators, securities markets are highly concentrated and play a limited role in financing the bulk of the private sector. Among listed firms, 15 represent more than 80 percent of the sample used in the stock market index (Índice de Precios y Cotizaciones) and more than 40 percent of total stock market capitalization. This is an underestimate of the extent of big

Figure 4.3 Net Worth of Local Billionaires in Relation to GDP, Mexico in International Context, 2007

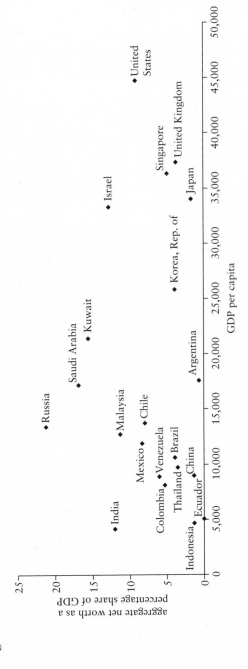

Sources: http://www.forbes.com; World Bank 2007.

Figure 4.4 Implicit Income of Billionaires Compared with the Incomes of the Richest Groups in the ENIGH, 2004

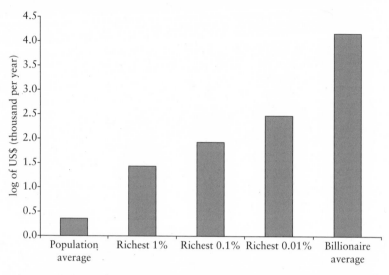

Sources: Authors' calculations from the ENIGH 2004; http://www.forbes.com.

business control, as accounting for pyramidal structures would show a higher concentration. Mexican stock market legislation makes assessing the importance of such a phenomenon difficult given the absence of information about minority shareholding with control rights. Castañeda (2000) analyzes the potential implications of pyramidal structures in Mexico's corporate sector using existing information to track the actual control rights structure in several Mexican corporations. In particular, he shows that control rights are highly concentrated, both because family members own large holdings of stock in these firms, and also because using pyramids and issuing nonvoting shares are common practices. More important for the purposes of our argument, control rights in the hands of a few large shareholders can provide incentives for extracting rents from the controlled firms at the cost of other shareholders (a phenomenon known as tunneling in the corporate governance literature) and can reduce aggregate productivity.

A similar picture emerges in the financial sector, where the banking system has traditionally been highly concentrated in a few banks (and with lending going to larger firms, often connected to bank owners, and at favorable terms) (see Haber, Maurer, and Razo 2003 on history; Haber 2005 on the 1994 tequila crisis and cleanup;

Table 4.1 Measures of Family Control, Selected Economies, 1995
(percent)

Country	20 largest firms		10 medium-sized firms		Country	20 largest firms		10 medium-sized firms	
	20% threshold	10% threshold	20% threshold	10% threshold		20% threshold	10% threshold	20% threshold	10% threshold
Argentina	65	65	80	80	Japan	5	10	10	10
Australia	5	10	50	50	Korea, Rep. of	20	35	50	80
Austria	15	15	17	17	Mexico	100	10	100	100
Belgium	50	50	40	40	Netherlands	20	20	20	20
Canada	25	30	30	50	New Zealand	25	45	29	36
Denmark	35	35	40	40	Norway	25	25	40	40
Finland	10	10	20	20	Portugal	45	50	50	50
France	20	20	50	50	Singapore	30	45	40	60
Germany	10	10	40	40	Spain	15	25	30	30
Greece	50	65	100	100	Sweden	45	55	60	60
Hong Kong	70	70	90	90	Switzerland	30	40	50	50
Ireland	10	15	13	25	United Kingdom	0	5	40	60
Israel	50	50	60	60	United States	20	20	10	30
Italy	15	20	60	80					

Source: Morck and Yeung 2004.

Note: Family control is inferred if the largest shareholder is a family and if its stake is greater than either a 20% or 10% voting-control threshold. Samples are the 20 largest publicly traded firms, ranked by December 1995 market capitalization, in each country, and the 10 firms with market capitalization just greater than US$500 million in December 1995.

119

La Porta, López-de-Silanes, and Zamarripa 2003 for evidence on related lending). The reforms following the 1994 crisis cleaned up the system, but they led to an even more concentrated system. The share of assets of the five largest banks rose from 74 percent in 1994 to 88 percent in 2001, making Mexico's banking system one of the most concentrated in the world. However, in contrast to the situation before 1994, the system is almost entirely in foreign ownership, and there is no evidence of favored, related lending.

Effects of Unions

Unions can play a valuable role in protecting the interests of their members and in promoting broader public debate in a democratic society, but union influence can have costs for society as a whole when it is exercised in protected sectors and via the political process. Of particular interest in Mexico are unions in the state-owned sectors: the oil and gas company Petróleos Mexicanos (PEMEX); the electricity producing companies, namely, the Comisión Federal de Electricidad and Luz y Fuerza Centro; the IMSS; and parts of the mining, airlines, education, and health sectors. Farmers' groups in the private and the *ejido* (system of community ownership of land in rural areas) sectors are also part of the corporatist heritage. The influential Consejo Nacional Agropecuario, which represents larger farmers, falls under the business rather than union structure of organizations.

These corporatist groups are much less rich than the truly wealthy but are generally significantly better off than average citizens. Differences lie both in monetary earnings and in a wide array of benefits that workers in the protected corporatist sectors enjoy, including housing, pensions, health benefits, and loans.

Table 4.2 compares average monthly earnings for workers in four sectors—petroleum, energy (a proxy for electricity), telecommunications, and teaching—for both unionized and nonunionized workers for selected years between 2000 and 2005. As the table shows, while unionized workers in general earn more than others, unionized workers in these sectors earn significantly more, for example, Mex$7,149 per month for unionized teachers in 2005 and Mex$12,504 per month for unionized petroleum workers, compared with the average for nonunionized Mexican workers in other sectors of Mex$3,848 per month. In all sectors except petroleum (and telecommunications in some years), unionized workers earn more than nonunionized workers (in the petroleum sector, the survey is probably catching nonunionized managers or specialized nonunionized firms). Some of the earnings differences may be due to

Table 4.2 Average Earnings of Unionized and Nonunionized Workers by Sector, Selected Years
(mean monthly earnings in August 2005, Mex$)

Types of workers	2000	2002	2004	2005
Total all workers	4,362	4,327	4,383	4,416
Unionized	5,944	6,421	5,999	6,239
Nonunionized	4,066	3,955	3,998	4,016
Petroleum workers	11,197	12,396	11,439	13,781
Unionized	10,560	9,175	10,369	12,504
Nonunionized	12,152	18,079	14,473	15,668
Energy workers	6,100	6,887	8,437	8,243
Unionized	6,657	6,901	9,018	8,673
Nonunionized	5,299	6,803	7,122	7,406
Telecommunications workers	9,901	11,061	8,605	6,255
Unionized	7,134	10,357	10,100	6,640
Nonunionized	11,591	11,351	7,946	6,080
Manufacturing workers	4,756	4,395	4,512	4,512
Unionized	4,790	4,837	4,290	4,421
Nonunionized	4,749	4,307	4,547	4,482
Teachers (elementary and secondary schools)	6,066	6,794	6,349	6,467
Unionized	6,763	7,455	7,164	7,149
Nonunionized	4,253	5,027	4,494	4,640
Other workers	4,061	4,076	4,177	4,206
Unionized	6,113	6,693	6,453	6,598
Nonunionized	3,796	3,768	3,812	3,848

Source: Authors' calculations based on the ENIGH 1994, 2000, 2004, and 2005.

differences in the workers' characteristics, notably, more education and experience, which we examine later.

These results further imply that most unionized workers in protected sectors are in the top parts of the earnings distribution. For instance, in 2005, 91 percent of unionized petroleum workers and 77 percent of unionized teachers were in the top quartile (table 4.3). A small fraction lived in moderate poverty (roughly the bottom half of the distribution), and an even smaller proportion in extreme poverty. However, quite a few nonunionized teachers and telecommunications workers earned low incomes. This concentration in the upper levels of the income distribution was steady for petroleum workers and teachers, it rose for energy workers, and it decreased for telecommunications workers.

The results underscore that union densities are much higher in these sectors than in the economy as a whole, with no apparent trend over time (table 4.4). These comparisons are only for

Table 4.3 Percentage of Unionized and Nonunionized Workers by Quartile of the Earnings Distribution, 2000 and 2005

Sector	q1	q2	q3	q4
Unionized workers, 2000				
Petroleum workers	—	—	9.01	90.09
Energy workers	—	—	16.99	83.01
Telecommunications workers	—	—	31.99	68.01
Teachers	0.6	2.38	19.84	77.20
Rest of workers	3.0	17.31	37.63	42.11
Nonunionized workers, 2000				
Petroleum workers	2.55	13.72	—	83.74
Energy workers	9.82	25.45	12.86	51.88
Telecommunications workers	20.60	9.43	12.96	57.01
Teachers	15.94	17.93	28.71	37.42
Rest of workers	29.31	27.68	22.89	20.12
Unionized workers, 2005				
Petroleum workers	0.37	0.42	8.39	90.82
Energy workers	2.81	4.01	21.25	71.93
Telecommunications workers	—	24.73	27.97	47.30
Teachers	1.00	4.10	17.74	77.15
Rest of workers	4.44	12.85	30.11	52.60
Nonunionized workers, 2005				
Petroleum workers	—	0.91	1.98	97.11
Energy workers	4.74	14.53	25.33	55.39
Telecommunications workers	15.46	24.66	12.38	47.49
Teachers	17.65	17.53	27.49	37.32
Rest of workers	30.47	27.41	23.07	19.04

Source: Authors' calculations based on the ENIGH 2005.
Note: q = quarter; — = insignificant.

Table 4.4 Share of All Workers in Unions, by Sector, Selected Years

Sector	2000	2002	2004	2005
Petroleum workers	60.0	63.8	73.3	59.6
Energy workers	58.9	76.9	69.4	65.9
Telecommunications workers	38.0	29.0	30.7	30.9
Teachers (elementary and secondary schools)	71.4	72.8	69.1	72.3
Rest of workers	11.4	10.7	11.0	11.4
Total all workers	15.7	15.4	16.3	16.1

Source: Author's calculations based on the ENIGH 1994, 2000, 2004, and 2005.

reported earnings. Differences in nonmonetary benefits are substantially larger.

Farmers represent a different and more diverse group. Farming households are disproportionately represented among the poor, and even more so among the extremely poor (World Bank 2004b). However, significant inequalities are also apparent among farmers. As figure 4.5 shows, the distribution of earnings of agricultural workers (aged 15 and older) overlaps that of nonagricultural workers. Some of the more successful elements of the organized farming lobby have come from relatively well-off farmers.

Finally, table 4.5 looks at the pattern of growth of incomes or wealth of various groups during 2000–5. As the table shows, the ENIGH finds some equalization of individual incomes between 2000 and 2005, with poorer households and workers experiencing relatively faster growth and the top parts of the income distribution experiencing relatively slower growth. However, while the earnings of all workers in the top quartile of the distribution fell in real terms by 3.5 percent between 2000 and 2005, corporatist groups saw their incomes grow by as much as 18 percent for unionized petroleum workers and 30 percent for energy workers, while teachers experienced more modest growth of 6 percent. By contrast, the incomes of unionized workers in other sectors (which faced more competition) grew by 8 percent. Among the rich, the ENIGH finds large increases of some 23 percent for the top 1

Figure 4.5 Distribution of Incomes of Agricultural and Nonagricultural Workers

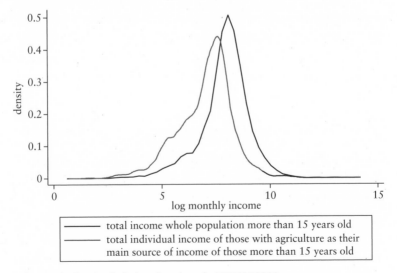

Source: Authors' calculations based on the ENIGH 2005.

Table 4.5 Real Increase in Incomes or Wealth in August
2005 Pesos, 2000–05
(percentage change)

Group	Change 2000–05
Workers, average earnings	
Total all workers	1.2
Workers in bottom quartile	17.0
Workers in second quartile	13.4
Workers in third quartile	6.3
Workers in top quartile	–3.5
Unionized workers in corporatist groups	
Petroleum	18.4
Energy	30.3
Telecommunications	–6.9
Teachers	5.7
Other sectors	7.9
Actual or implicit income of the rich	
Top 10%	0.3
Top 5%	2.7
Top 1%	22.7
Net worth of billionaires unweighted[a]	27.3
Net worth of billionaires weighted[a]	32.3

Sources: Authors' calculations based on the ENIGH 2000, 2005; http://www
.Forbes.com.

Note: All incomes are deflated by the consumer price index.

a. 2000–04.

percent,[3] while the net worth of billionaires also grew substantially
faster than the mean at around 30 percent.

Existing Institutions Imperfectly Countervail Concentrated Market Power

Every society has unequal structures of power and wealth. In developed countries, institutions that provide checks and balances partly
control this power. Such institutions range from those designed to
offset the power of the executive branch of government through
legislatures and independent judiciaries to sector-specific regulators.
However, the mere existence of a countervailing institution is not
enough. Weak regulators can be captured by the firms they are
designed to regulate; weak justice systems are more likely to serve the
interests of the wealthy and powerful (see, for example, Stigler 1971
on regulatory capture; Glaeser, Sheinkman, and Shleifer 2003 on
the judicial system). The contemporary analysis presented in this

section draws on a number of historical interpretations, in particular, Castañeda (1995); Haber, Maurer, and Razo (2003); and Tornell and Esquivel (1995). For an account of the recent period, see Haber and others (2008).

The legislature is now a genuine forum for the pursuit of interests by both parties and factions, but in many respects it remains in a transitional state. Corporatist groups have effective representation through deputies and senators linked to groups such as teachers, farmers' associations, and specific unions, notably the union for PEMEX workers. On the positive side, Mexico has the advantage of having relatively programmatic parties with distinct policy orientations. However, the party groups in the legislature have little experience with policy formulation and debate, and their incentives are to further their short-run electoral prospects rather than long-term reform processes. With the transition from dominance by the Institutional Revolutionary Party to democracy, the time horizon for policy design has been substantially reduced, with incentives shifting from long-term, repeated interactions between different groups to shorter-term opportunistic behavior. There is also a weak capacity to acquire and analyze information, which is an issue of particular importance in policy areas, such as tax reform or private participation in energy, where public opinion is poorly informed about the connections between policy choices and outcomes.

Regulatory agencies are an important set of institutions that counterbalance concentrated power in specific sectors in developed economies, but Mexican regulators lack autonomous power. The exception—and an important one—is the Central Bank of Mexico, whose independence was granted in the wake of the dramatic costs of macroeconomic instability during the 1970s and 1980s. Other regulators fall into two categories: (a) de-concentrated bodies, which have technical and operational autonomy but fall directly under the auspices of sector ministries; and (b) departments within sector ministries. None of the regulating agencies is fully autonomous, because their budgets and personnel depend on the executive branch. The least autonomous are the transport regulators, which are administrative units within the Department of Transport. All other regulators function as de-concentrated bodies, including the following:

- Comisión Nacional del Agua, Environment Department, administers and preserves water;
- Comisión Reguladora de Energía, Department of Energy, regulates natural gas and electricity;
- Comisión Federal de Telecomunicaciones (COFETEL), Transport and Communication Department, regulates telecommunications;

- Comisión Bancaria y de Valores, Treasury, supervises and regulates banks and the financial sector;
- Comisión Nacional Seguros y Finanzas, Treasury, supervises and regulates insurance;
- Comisión Nacional de Sistemas de Ahorros para el Retiro, Treasury, supervises and regulates pension funds;
- Comisión Federal de Competencia (CFC), Department of the Economy, sanctions monopoly practices and oversees competition; and
- Comisión Federal de Mejora Regulatoria, Department of the Economy, ensures transparency in the elaboration and implementation of administrative regulations.

The various agencies differ significantly from each other. The analysis in the next section focuses on the contrast between COFETEL and the CFC. COFETEL was set up with little power. It makes recommendations to the secretary of Transport and Communications rather than directly imposing sanctions. The CFC, by contrast, was set up with greater structural independence, with commissioners appointed for extended terms. It has the capacity to make decisions about monopolistic practices and to impose fines or changes in firm behavior. These decisions, however, ultimately depend on the judicial system.

An independent and well-functioning judicial system is essential for protecting the property rights that firms and financial institutions need to support investment and lending decisions. It helps to avoid biases based on the capacity to bribe or use political influence. Legal and judicial weakness can have a negative impact on economic transactions, and, even when compensatory informal mechanisms exist, the resulting distortions lead to excessive and usually unequally shared costs.

Despite several reforms, public perceptions of the efficiency of the judicial system in Mexico are among the lowest in Latin America. The courts lack legitimacy as conflict resolution bodies: a 2001 survey revealed that only 27 percent of the overall population (and only 15 percent of young people) trusted the judiciary (World Bank 2004a). A Transparency International poll of 38 government agencies placed the Mexican judiciary 28th in international rankings (where 1 is perceived as the least corrupt).

About 80 percent of all judicial cases, and the great majority of commercial cases, are initiated in state courts. The state court system receives about 800,000 cases per year, far above its capacity for processing. The state courts are also subordinated to federal courts through *amparos* (stays of action), which are designed for federal judges to review possible violations at the state level. Some 50,000 *amparos* were sent to federal court in 2000, of which 29,000 came from state judiciaries. These extend the length and cost of litigation and reduce the legitimacy of local courts. In addition, because placing an *amparo* is costly and requires specialized counsel, its use is skewed to those with greater resources.[4] The result is that the regulatory system is not a credible, independent threat to the behavior of large business interests.

Evidence on the Exercise of Unequal Power

Big business concentration is likely to be associated with a lack of competition, a resistance to tax increases, the existence of favored lending, and a narrow financial system. Corporatist union and other influences are likely to be associated with inefficient structures in the areas of social security, electricity, and petroleum production; agricultural policies favoring large farmers; and restrictive labor policies. As emphasized earlier, unequal influence can work both through the way markets and institutions function and through policy design. Furthermore, the capacity for business and corporatist groups to exercise unequal influence depends on the strength of countervailing institutions.

Evidence on the Effects of Concentrated Wealth and Big Business

In this section, we present some evidence that big business uses market power to further its private interests from new analysis of regulatory agencies' decisions, from reference to existing analysis of the workings of the financial system, and from evidence on the private gains from control over large corporations.

EVIDENCE FROM COMPETITION POLICY

For the field of domestic competition, the institutional structure (the CFC) is that of a relatively independent regulatory agency, but one that is working within a weak overall judicial context. The CFC makes assessments as to whether a company's behavior is anticompetitive and imposes fines, requires changes in behavior, or both. Market share in the relevant market is only one variable the CFC considers in its investigations. Following the spirit of most modern competition codes, having market power is not unlawful, but exercising such power and hurting consumers is considered to be a problem. A sanctioned company may appeal to the CFC, and if this appeal is unsuccessful, it can seek an *amparo* from a court. *Amparos* are more common when the

CFC's resolutions imply changing practices that involve permanent monopoly rents. Prior to a June 2006 change in the legislation, an *amparo* implied that the company could legally ignore the CFC's finding pending judicial resolution, a process that could take years.

As the CFC has a high degree of independence, the hypothesis we explore is whether the CFC is more likely to find that companies the business elites own or control are behaving in an anticompetitive fashion. As the judicial system is generally judged to be weak, we expect to find the opposite, that is, a bias in favor of these companies in issuing *amparos*.

From information published by the CFC, we constructed a database of all the resolutions issued during 1998–2004 on mergers and acquisitions and monopolistic practices. During this period, the CFC recorded a total of resolutions for 381 cases, involving 612 specific decisions, concerning monopolistic practices (figure 4.6). (Some cases involve more than one firm, and the resolution has to sanction or exonerate each specific action, thus the resolutions actually involve 612 specific decisions.)

In 39 cases, the use of *amparos* prevented resolutions that declared abuse of market power (table 4.6). In 12 of these, the *amparo* eventually resulted in judicial decisions favorable to the firms.

Some of the companies that were found guilty of monopolistic practices and have invoked *amparos* include Teléfonos de Mexico (TELMEX), RadioMóvil Dipsa (better known as TELCEL), Ferrocarriles del Sur, Fomento Económico Mexicano S.A., Grupo Modelo,

Figure 4.6 CFC Resolutions on Monopolistic Practices, 1998–2004

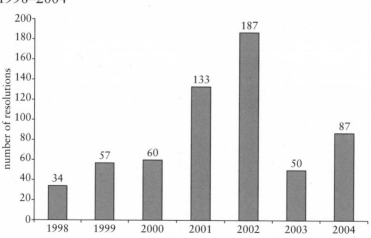

Source: CFC data.

Table 4.6 Distribution of
CFC Resolutions, 1998–2004

Resolutions	Number of cases
Guilty	206
Not guilty	367
Amparos	39
Total	612

Source: CFC data.

and Grupo Televisa. The company Avantel has sued TELMEX nine times for abusing market power. The resolutions by the CFC that have been favorable to Avantel have implied fines of about US$11 million (which does not mean that these fines have been collected). Other important cases include cable television companies (Grupo Televisa and its subsidiaries) and beer production and distribution companies (Grupo Modelo and Cervecería Cuauhtémoc Moctezuma).

To explore whether a big business bias exists, we categorized all companies for which there were resolutions with respect to whether they were controlled, directly or indirectly, by billionaires as listed by Forbes. About 24 percent of the cases of abuse of monopoly power were related to firms controlled by the Forbes billionaires. To explore statistically whether the CFC was more likely to find billionaire-controlled companies guilty of monopolistic practices, we ran a logit model using a dummy variable for billionaire control and a variety of other controls for other factors that could influence the decision. These controls included time and sector dummies and size of firm (based on the numbers of employees). We also explored the probability of a judge upholding an *amparo*. We found that billionaire-controlled companies were more likely to be found to be engaged in monopolistic practices and more likely to secure an *amparo*. Both results are statistically significant (table 4.7), and the change in probability, relative to other companies, is noticeable (figure 4.7).

The CFC also reviews mergers and acquisitions for their impact on competition and authorizes them. Between 1998 and 2006, 1,297 cases were submitted for analysis, of which the CFC prevented only 14. Of the total submitted, 106 submissions were related to billionaire-controlled firms and the CFC rejected only 1 of these. With so few rejections, a statistical analysis did not make sense.

Thus, we found that billionaire-controlled companies are more likely to be engaged in monopolistic practices than other firms and, if they are sanctioned, are more likely to obtain an *amparo*. We have no view on the rights and wrongs of individual cases, but we

Table 4.7 Statistical Results on the Probabilities of Finding Monopolistic Practice and of Securing an *Amparo* among Billionaires' Companies

Item	Coefficient	Robust t statistics	Marginal effect
Probability of finding evidence of the exercise of monopoly power			
Billionaires' companies	1.255	(4.27)***	0.299
Number of observations	569		
Probability of securing an amparo to temporarily prevent action			
Billionaires' companies	1.640	(3.78)***	0.037
Number of observations	477		

Source: Authors' calculations based on CFC data.

Note: Controlling by size of company (proxied by the number of employees) and resolutions' year and sector. Sectors are classified on the basis of the Mexican classification of activities and products.

***Significant at 1 percent.

Figure 4.7 Effect of Being a Billionaire-Linked Company on the Probability of the CFC Finding Monopolistic Practices and Obtaining an *Amparo*

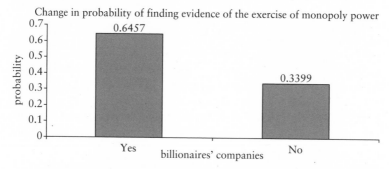

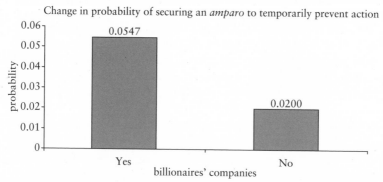

Source: Authors' calculations.

note that this statistical evidence is consistent with our hypothesis about the interaction between concentrated business influence and institutional context.[5]

EVIDENCE FROM THE REGULATION OF TELECOMMUNICATIONS

We now look at evidence from one sector, telecommunications. This is of interest for two reasons. First, the privatization carried out under President Salinas granted a temporary monopoly to one of the principal companies involved in the sector, TELMEX, that could have allowed this company to acquire a position of market dominance once competition was allowed in the sector. Second, as noted earlier, there is some presumption that the regulatory agency, COFETEL, is relatively weak, because it was set up with less structural independence than the CFC. In contrast to the case of the CFC, we would expect regulatory decisions to be biased in favor of powerful incumbent firms.

We constructed a database of COFETEL resolutions for those years for which public information is available: 1996–98 and 2003–06. Two categories of cases are important, namely,

- the award of concessions (telephony, including cellular telephony and public telephones; television and cable television; and radio)
- the decisions on sanctions in the form of recommendations to the ministry on practices that hurt consumers.

We undertook statistical analysis, using a logit model, to explore the effect of a firm being billionaire controlled (in the sense noted earlier). We found that such companies were significantly less likely to have a request for concession rejected and a sanction recommended because of practices that hurt consumers (table 4.8). The last result contrasts with the relatively large number of CFC decisions about monopolistic practices by the same companies. The effects of being a billionaire-controlled company are not trivial.

As with the analysis of CFC data, we have no views about the merits of individual cases, but again we note that the statistical pattern is consistent with our expectations about the interaction between concentrated business influence and, in this case, a less independent regulatory structure.

EVIDENCE FROM THE FINANCIAL SECTOR

The case of Mexico's financial system has been well documented in past work (see, for example, Haber 2005, 2007; Haber, Maurer, and Razo 2003). The long history is of the evolution of a highly concentrated and protected financial system, which furthered the private

Table 4.8 Statistical Results on the Probabilities of COFETEL Not Approving a Concession or Recommending a Sanction in the Telecommunications Sector

Item	Coefficient	Robust t statistics	Marginal effect
Probability that a concession request is rejected			
Billionaires' companies	–0.678	(2.06)**	–0.104
Number of observations	538		
Probability that a sanction is recommended			
Billionaires' companies	–1.399	(2.82)***	–0.1464
Number of observations	446		

Source: Authors' calculations based on COFETEL data.
Note: Controlling by resolutions' year.
**Significant at 5 percent; ***Significant at 1 percent.

interests of the intermingled banking and industrial elites. Bankers influenced laws that protected them from competition, and in turn provided finance for the government, as well as for investment in economic sectors. While independent regulation was weak, prior to the 1982 "nationalization",[6] the group of private bankers operated as a self-monitoring club with a mutual interest in sustaining financial viability.

There were two areas of post-tequila crisis resolution in the financial system. The first was a bailout, which was probably highly regressive (Halac and Schmukler 2003), sustaining the belief that market-oriented reforms supported or bailed out the rich at the cost of others. The second was a set of financial sector reforms that substantially strengthened the regulatory framework, accompanied by opening the sector to foreign ownership. The result was that more than 80 percent of the banking system was in foreign hands by the early 2000s, and the whole system has been restored to financial health. This constitutes an institutional break for this sector from the old pattern of dependence on the domestic business elite, but the sector remains highly concentrated, with unusually low lending to the private business sector by international standards. Much of the private sector, especially small and medium-sized firms, is effectively rationed out of the system. Haber (chapter 8 in this volume) discusses whether more competition is needed in the financial sector for higher growth.

EVIDENCE FROM MARKET VALUATIONS

A further source of evidence is of an indirect character and concerns market valuations of the benefits of control in the corporate sector.

Specific evidence that control rights lead to private benefits in excess of the value to noncontrolling shareholders comes from the premium of block and voting purchases (which confer control rights) to the market value (which reflects the value to noncontrolling shareholders). Data compiled from two cross-country studies by Morck, Wolfenzon, and Yeung (2005) find premiums of 34 to 36 percent for Mexico (table 4.9). This finding relates to a broader point: groups owned by the most powerful families could be the best-performing firms in a poor-performing economy if unequal influence leads to either policy design or influence over institutional functioning to create rents for these groups.

Evidence on the Effects of Corporatist Groups

We now turn to some evidence on the influence of corporatist groups, including on the rents of unions in protected sectors, on social policy design, and on agriculture policy.

Table 4.9 Estimated Private Benefits of Control Measured as Block and Voting Premiums, Selected Countries

(percentage premium over market value)

Country	Block premium[a]	Voting premium[b]	Country	Block premium[a]	Voting premium[b]
Argentina	27	—	Malaysia	7	—
Australia	2	23	Mexico	34	36
Austria	38	—	Netherlands	2	—
Brazil	65	23	New Zealand	3	—
Canada	1	3	Norway	1	6
Chile	15	23	Peru	14	—
Colombia	27	—	Philippines	13	—
Czech			Poland	11	—
Republic	58	—	Portugal	20	—
Denmark	8	1	Singapore	3	—
Egypt, Arab			South Africa	2	7
Rep. of	4	—	Spain	4	—
Finland	2	−5	Sweden	6	1
France	2	28	Switzerland	6	5
Germany	10	10	Taiwan, China	0	—
Hong Kong,			Thailand	12	—
China	1	−3	Turkey	30	—

(Continued on the following page)

Table 4.9 (Continued)

Country	Block premium[a]	Voting premium[b]	Country	Block premium[a]	Voting premium[b]
Indonesia	7	—	United Kingdom	2	10
Israel	27	—			
Italy	37	29	United States	2	2
Japan	−4	—	Venezuela, R. B. de	27	—
Korea, Rep. of	16	29			

Source: Morck, Wolfenzon, and Yeung 2005.

Note: — = not available.

a. The block premium is the average across control transactions of the difference between the price per share paid for the control block and the exchange price two days after the announcement of the control transaction, dividing it by the exchange price two days after the announcement, and multiplying the ratio by the proportion of cash flow rights represented in the controlling block and expressed as a percentage premium, (see Dyck and Zingales 2004, table 2, for details). Years are from selected transactions from 1900–2000 for the block premium and 1997 for the voting premium.

b. The voting premium is the average of estimated total vote value as a percentage of firm value, (see Nenova 2003, table 5, for details). Transactions are from 1997.

EVIDENCE ON THE EFFECTS OF UNIONIZED WORKERS IN PROTECTED SECTORS

Unions can influence outcomes in the sectors in which they work in two ways: by effective bargaining for better working conditions and by influencing overall policy for the sector. We are particularly interested in those unions, originally part of corporatist structures, in the major protected or public sectors, notably petroleum, electricity, IMSS workers, and teachers. Workers in telecommunications are also of interest given the dominant market position of billionaire-controlled firms. Unions can extract rents and can also prevent productivity-enhancing reforms from taking place or reduce aggregate productivity through their impact on the quality of health services or education. Thus, introducing more efficient and competitive union institutions has spillover effects on the overall economy.

As seen earlier, earnings in petroleum, energy, telecommunications, and teaching are, on average, above those in other sectors, especially for unionized workers in these sectors. However, to see if there is evidence of workers enjoying rents, we want to know if these premiums still hold after controlling for other influences on earnings. Using the ENIGH, we can control for the education and experience of workers, the main individual characteristics affecting earnings in the labor market. We use data for all workers with a Heckman-corrected earnings function and show the results in table 4.10. Returns to education are about 10 percent per year of education, and

Table 4.10 The Effects of Union and Sector on Workers'
Earnings, Selected Years

	2000	*2002*	*2004*	*2005*
Schooling (in years)	0.123	0.097	0.096	0.094
	(29.49)***	(35.78)***	(47.44)***	(52.50)***
Age	0.079	0.075	0.073	0.068
	(15.56)***	(18.02)***	(20.78)***	(22.02)***
Age squared	−0.001	−0.001	−0.001	−0.001
	(12.19)***	(13.32)***	(16.33)***	(17.07)***
Gender	0.177	0.122	0.188	0.167
	(5.44)***	(4.93)***	(8.06)***	(9.64)***
Union	0.389	0.384	0.333	0.382
	(11.08)***	(14.79)***	(7.09)***	(19.37)***
Petroleum	0.804	0.783	0.718	0.709
	(7.43)***	(8.29)***	(4.26)***	(7.27)***
Telecommunica-tions	0.394	0.382	0.318	0.197
	(1.93)*	(2.14)**	(3.56)***	(2.58)***
Manufacturing	0.139	0.099	0.133	0.152
	(3.37)***	(3.78)***	(5.79)***	(8.10)***
Teachers[a]	0.160	0.136	0.225	0.275
	−1.63	−1.53	(4.23)***	(4.09)***
Other (omitted)	n.a.	n.a.	n.a.	n.a.
Petroleum*union	−0.149	−0.407	−0.382	−0.357
	−0.86	(2.54)**	(1.87)*	(2.88)***
Telecommunica-tions*union	−0.353	0.002	0.101	−0.24
	−1.49	−0.01	−0.8	−0.92
Manufacturing*union	−0.134	−0.169	−0.194	−0.239
	(2.14)***	(3.52)***	(3.48)***	(6.50)***
Teachers*union[a]	−0.081	0.021	0.026	−0.122
	−0.75	−0.22	−0.35	(1.67)*
Constant	−0.527	−0.004	−0.033	0.116
	(4.55)***	−0.05	−0.45	(1.77)*
Number of observations	23,128	39,592	51,319	52,133

Source: Authors' calculations from the ENIGH 2000, 2002, 2004, and 2005.
Note: The earnings equation was estimated with a Heckman correction for labor force participation. Robust statistics are in parentheses. The coefficients represent the increase in log earnings relative to all workers in other categories and are based on hourly earnings.
a. Only elementary and secondary school teachers.
*Significant at 10 percent; **Significant at 5 percent; ***Significant at 1 percent. n.a. = not applicable.

there is a premium of around 17 to 19 for being male for most years after controlling for other characteristics. After controlling for these factors, being unionized and being in the petroleum, telecommunications, and teaching sectors confer significant premiums, and such premiums are fairly stable between 2000 and 2005. To obtain the total effects, we need to add these influences, as well as the interactions between them.[7] The results are summarized in table 4.11, which compares the apparent rents for unionized workers in protected sectors to those of nonunionized workers in other sectors (services and agriculture). The average net premium for the period is 80 percent for petroleum, 57 percent for telecommunications, and 53 percent for teachers, compared with 32 percent for manufacturing workers, who generally work in sectors facing international competition.

Manufacturing workers play an important role as a comparison group, given that manufacturing went through the liberalization process starting in the mid-1980s. Estimating the same model for 1984, prior to the liberalization process, the premium for being in manufacturing was about 28 percent, compared with an average of 13 percent for 2000–05. Thus in these two decades, the premium fell to less than half the preliberalization level. Also in 1984, the premiums were 43 percent for being in petroleum, compared with 75 percent in 2000–05, and 34 percent for being in telecommunications, compared with 32 percent in 2000–05 (authors' calculations based on the ENIGH 1984).

The ENIGH data source does not allow us to control for firm characteristics other than sector—there could be selection issues, with unobservable differences between unionized and nonunionized firms. Maloney (chapter 7 in this volume) finds that these further reduce any union premium in the manufacturing sector, supporting the view that unions in this sector bargain for employment rather than wages (see also Maloney and Ribeiro 2001).

Table 4.11 The Premium for Being Unionized and in the Following Sectors Relative to Being Nonunionized in Other Sectors, Selected Years
(percent)

Sector	2000	2002	2004	2005
Petroleum	104	76	67	73
Telecommunications	43	77	75	34
Manufacturing	39	31	27	30
Teaching	47	54	58	54

Source: Authors' calculations based on the results reported in table 4.10.

As noted earlier, earnings differences almost certainly understate the relative advantage of groups in corporatist sectors, who receive much greater nonmonetary benefits. This would imply that the foregoing results are biased downward in terms of the premiums inclusive of benefits. Indeed, in a competitive labor market we would expect monetary wages in jobs that received higher benefits to be lower than in other jobs, as workers would move between sectors to equalize their total remuneration, inclusive of benefits. Levy (2007) presents evidence of large movements of workers in and out of IMSS-related jobs (see also Maloney, chapter 7 in this volume).

Further evidence of union appropriation of rents comes from estimates of the relationship between current and contingent liabilities implied by labor contracts and asset values. Table 4.12 shows that for the two electricity companies, future labor obligations are of the same order of magnitude as assets, implying no return to capital for the public owners.[8] The net worth of the IMSS at the end of 2005 was Mex$-81,662 million after taking account of the pension liabilities of IMSS workers, but Mex$58,702 million without these liabilities. Its income was Mex$-68,047 million after taking the pension costs of its own staff into account, but Mex$200 million pesos before (*Informe al Ejecutivo Federal y al Congreso de la Unión sobre la Situación Financiera y los Riesgos del IMSS, 2005–2006*). Exactly comparable data are not available for PEMEX, but calculations from public sources indicate that PEMEX has suffered a sharp decline in net capital over the past 15 years after allowing for debt and liabilities for labor (figure 4.8).

With respect to policy and institutional design, unions in protected sectors have been active in resisting policy change, for example with respect to private investment in petroleum and energy. Le Houcq (2005) reviews the evidence on reform in relation to PEMEX. He argues that there is a "widespread consensus that PEMEX is not a well-run company.... By international standards, PEMEX has too many employees (approximately 138,000) ... 80 percent of which belong to a union aligned with the PRI [Institutional Revolutionary

Table 4.12 The Ratio of the Present Value of Liabilities in Collective Labor Agreements to Firm Value for Electricity Companies

Company	
Luz y Fuerza del Centro	1.2
Comisión Federal de Electricidad	0.8
Benchmark	$0.20 < x < 0.30$

Source: Authors' estimates based on information from the companies.

Figure 4.8 Net Accounting Capital of PEMEX, 1991–2006

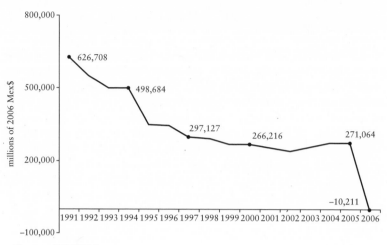

Source: PEMEX data.

Party].... A corrupt union sells posts and lets members ... will their posts to their offspring" (22). Attempts at reform to increase operational autonomy and increase efficiency have, however, been limited. President Salinas did succeed in breaking PEMEX up into four different companies. President Ernesto Zedillo sought to privatize one of these, but he never sent the bill to Congress. President Fox sent several bills to Congress, but he succeeded only in making relatively minor changes to the appropriation of oil revenues and setting up a stabilization fund for extraordinary revenues. There was a failure to reach agreement on measures to improve corporate governance, including a seemingly mild proposal to place "independent experts" on the board. While Le Houcq argues for a number of influences behind the lack of reform, including the increasing number of veto players with interests in oil revenues and public resistance to any dilution of state control, part of the story clearly lies in the behavior of the union. Lajous (chapter 11) provides an extended discussion.

EVIDENCE ON THE IMPACT OF THE TEACHERS' UNION ON EDUCATION QUALITY

The relationship between the teachers' union (Sindicato Nacional de Trabajadores de la Educación, or SNTE) and education quality is a further channel of indirect influence on institutional functioning. There is widespread concern that schooling quality is low in

Mexico: an analysis of standardized student tests places Mexico at the bottom of the ranking among Organisation for Economic Co-operation and Development (OECD) countries and among the bottom three countries in Latin America (OECD 2006). At the same time, variance in test scores across schools is relatively low. Many observers attribute this pattern to the weak links between teacher performance and learning outcomes associated with the system of centralized bargaining over many aspects of working conditions (World Bank 2006). The SNTE secured this arrangement in the 1992 agreement on decentralization, an example of how policy design is distorted relative to an optimal design.

The 1992 agreement allowed for supplementary negotiations with state governments, and this allows for further exploration of the relationship between unions and outcomes. Álvarez, Moreno, and Patrinos (2006) explore the impact of two variables on student learning: the level of conflict between the teachers' union and the state government (based on a simple categorization of low, medium, and high levels of conflict) and teachers' salaries. Relative to high levels of conflict, medium or low conflict levels increase student tests scores by 4.6 and 9.5 points, respectively (table 4.13).

The level of conflict also affects the association between salaries and student learning. Higher teacher salaries have no relationship with learning in medium- and high-conflict states, but a significant positive link in low-conflict states (figure 4.9). These results do not allow us to draw conclusions about causality, but they are indicative of a richer relationship between union behavior and learning outcomes than the nationwide results suggest. Even within a system in which the national union tends to lead to poor quality with relatively low dispersion, this suggests that change is possible or, more precisely, that incentives can make a difference in contexts in which

Table 4.13 State Characteristics, State-Level Conflict with Unions, and Student Learning

Explanatory factor	Significant	Coefficient
State accountability system		
Complete process and design intervention strategies	Yes	13.1
Conflict between state and union (relative to high levels of conflict)		
Medium	Yes	4.6
Low	Yes	9.5

Source: Álvarez, Moreno, and Patrinos 2006.

Note: Includes controls for parental participation, within-state decentralization, union influence over teacher appointments, and student and family characteristics.

Figure 4.9 Interaction between Levels of State-Level Conflict
and the Impact of Teacher Incentives

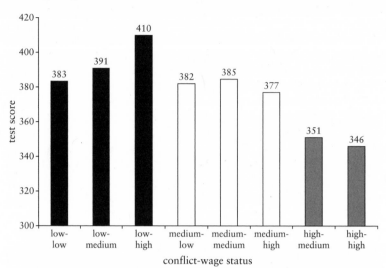

Source: Álvarez, Moreno, and Patrinos 2006.

Note: The first adjective refers to the level of conflict between the state and the
union and the second to teacher wages. For example, low-high is a low-conflict state
with relatively high teacher wages.

relationships between unions and local and state levels of government are more cooperative.

EVIDENCE ON THE DESIGN OF SOCIAL POLICY

Unequal influence also shapes social policy in a variety of ways.
We highlight two processes here: the role of the IMSS union and
the expansion of social protection spending in the past decade
(Levy 2006).

The IMSS's own workers enjoy social security benefits that are
better than those of private sector workers affiliated with the IMSS,
and IMSS workers' benefits are effectively cross-subsidized by these
other workers. After lengthy and conflictive negotiations about
reducing these privileges, Congress eventually agreed to a reform
that involved protecting the benefits of all existing IMSS workers
while treating new entrants on the same basis as private sector
workers receiving IMSS benefits. The loser was thus not incumbents
but the union, as this effectively withdrew its powers of patronage
in the allocation of IMSS jobs. The IMSS union successfully pressed
the executive branch of government to withdraw the reform. This

was a setback not only for the functioning of the IMSS, but also for the overall design of social security and social protection. (The Supreme Court eventually upheld the reform, but it is too early to assess its effects.)

The position of the IMSS's own workers is only part of the broader distortions in the structure of social provisioning. All private sector workers affiliated with the IMSS have access to a fixed package of benefits, including health care, pensions, child care, and an array of other services. As Levy (2006) argues, it is unlikely that these are fully valued by all workers because of heterogeneous needs and preferences; problems of access to and quality of services; and features of the design of benefits, for example, the years of service required to qualify for a minimum pension. This provides incentives for workers and firms to choose informal work. At the same time, social provisioning for workers outside the IMSS system has expanded considerably, driven both by social concerns and the political popularity of this category of spending. This has included increased support for conditional cash transfers to the extreme poor (under the Oportunidades program) and increased health spending for the poor (under the Seguro Popular, the health insurance program for the poor). Yet to the extent that this provides further incentives for informalization, this leads to shifts of workers into lower productivity activities.

This is less of a concern for spending oriented to the extreme poor, who would have been unlikely to be in the formal sector in any case. However, for all categories of social spending, there has not been any link with increased taxes, thus it has effectively been financed through reduced infrastructure spending, leading to losses in growth potential. This is a further example of unequal structures making first-best policies infeasible and leading to a distorted policy mix that is neither equitable nor supportive of growth.

EVIDENCE ON THE AGRICULTURE LOBBY AND POLICY DESIGN

Where groups do not have direct market power, concentrated influence can still work through the political process. Farmers' groups provide a good example. The North American Free Trade Agreement provided an extended period of protection. While this was partly to provide protection for the poor, Tornell and Esquivel (1995) argue that this was also based on political judgment. The farmers' lobby can operate through policies on input subsidies and service provision. Ample evidence points to regressive subsidies for water, electricity, and other agricultural inputs (World Bank 2004b).

Moreover, Mexico's agricultural labor productivity is one of the lowest in Latin America even though Mexico has one of the highest levels of public spending on agriculture (figure 4.10). Although some programs, such as the Programa de Apoyos Directos al Campo, reach a wide range of farmers, many subsidies to agriculture go to the richest farmers, and the aggregate impact has not solved Mexico's problem of low agricultural productivity. The World Bank's (2005a) interpretation is that the lack of dynamism is a product of inefficient biases toward subsidies and an apparently growing number of clientelistic programs, as opposed to a coherent strategy for productivity growth for small and large farmers alike.

The Impact of Unequal Influence on Growth

The impact of unequal income and wealth on growth depends on whether it is the result of dynamic, wealth-creating individuals or of rent-seeking entrepreneurs with high levels of influence. International evidence finds self-made billionaire wealth to be associated with higher growth, but evidence finds inherited billionaire wealth to be associated with lower growth (Morck, Wolfenzon, and Yeung 2005). As noted earlier, most contemporary billionaires in

Figure 4.10 Low Levels of Agricultural Productivity Despite High Levels of Public Spending: A Comparison of Mexico and Other Latin American Countries

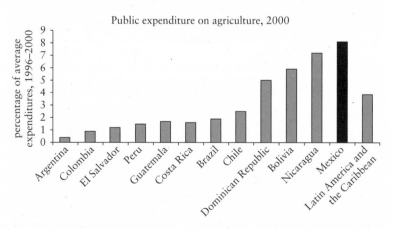

Source: World Bank 2005a.

Mexico inherited their initial wealth, while some benefited from the privatizations. Few are fully self-made.

Why should concentrated wealth hurt growth? One interpretation is that some forms of wealth concentration are associated with extensive control that distorts market functioning and policy making. As Morck, Wolfenzon, and Yeung (2005: 3) argue: "Entrusting the governance of huge slices of a country's corporate sector to a tiny collection of elites can bias capital allocation to advantage those elites, and can also reduce the pace of innovation.... In addition, to preserve their privileged positions under the *status quo,* the controlling elites arguably use political connections to stymie the institutional development of capital markets and to erect a variety of entry barriers."

In the preceding section, we documented areas where there is specific empirical evidence of the influence of either wealthy business elites or corporatist groups on economic institutions in ways that tend to preserve their economic position. The question is how these groups interact with growth processes.

By way of context, there is some cross-country evidence of a negative association between oligarchic family control and development (see table 4.14, which uses the indicators of family control shown in table 4.1). Among significant results, with greater family control, growth is lower, health status is worse, the quality of government is worse, and income inequality is higher. These results should be treated as suggestive, because they face the standard problems of potential omitted variables and endogeneity of cross-country regressions.

Of more direct relevance is work on specific constraints to growth in Mexico. The World Bank has carried out extensive analytic work on competitiveness, both in a series of programmatic reports (World Bank 2006) and through the preparation of development policy loans on competitiveness and on the financial sector and growth. This work stressed the importance of competition for growth in Mexico, as well as the lack of autonomy of regulatory agencies. What follows draws mainly from this work. We find that a number of economic institutions and policies that are shaped or affected by unequal structures are indeed constraints to Mexico's growth process.

Growth in Mexico has been much lower than in Chile, China, and India for well over a decade. Between 2001 and 2004, growth in Mexico averaged around 1.6 percent, while China was growing at an average annual rate of 8.6 percent (figure 4.11). Relative to Mexico's own history (as well as to comparators), disappointing growth since 1980—and since the tequila crisis—is associated both with lower investment in capital and, especially, lower total factor productivity (figure 4.12). We argue that one of the main reasons

Table 4.14 Economy Characteristics and Oligarchic Family Control, Controlling for Per Capita Income
(regression coefficient of oligarchic family control measure)

	20 largest firms		10 medium-sized firms		
	20% threshold	10% threshold	20% threshold	10% threshold	sample
Economic development					
Growth in real per capita GDP at purchasing power parity, 1990–2000	−2.37	−2.57	−3.31	−3.10	27
	(0.10)	(0.09)	(0.00)	(0.02)	
Physical infrastructure					
Average scores for roads, airports, telecommunications, and power for how well each meets business needs	0.398	0.431	−0.340	−0.055	25
	(0.45)	(0.44)	(0.51)	(0.91)	
Health care					
Logarithm of infant mortality rate per 1,000 live births, 1993	0.879	0.802	0.454	0.491	25
	(0.00)	(0.01)	(0.14)	(0.09)	

Human development

Percentage of respondents who agreed that the education system meets the needs of a competitive economy	−0.811 (0.26)	−0.681 (0.37)	−1.26 (0.07)	−1.05 (0.10)	25
Quality of government					
Average monthly inflation, 1990–2002	0.00483 (0.00)	0.00443 (0.01)	0.00399 (0.00)	0.00266 (0.09)	25
Social development					
Income inequality as measured by a Gini coefficient	13.6 (0.01)	14.1 (0.01)	11.5 (0.03)	10.9 (0.03)	27

Source: adapted from Morck and Yeung 2004.

Note: Numbers in parentheses are probability levels for the null hypothesis of a zero coefficient on oligarchic family control in regressions of economy characteristic of that variable and the logarithm of 1995 per capita GDP.

Figure 4.11 Mexican Growth in International Perspective and Sources of Growth

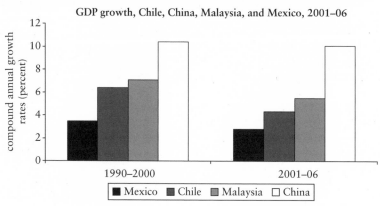

Source: World Bank 2007.

Figure 4.12 GDP Growth in Mexico and Its Components, Selected Years

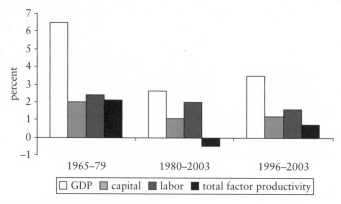

Source: Faal 2005.

behind this low productivity is lack of competition both in labor and in crucial nontradable or protected product markets.

Many studies confirm that lack of competition is a major problem holding back the possibility of strong growth in Mexico. The Instituto Mexicano para la Competitividad developed a model to assess the main factors behind the country's low and falling competitiveness. Drawing on cross-country information, the institute estimated point elasticities for the impact on investment per worker of a 10 percent change in various factors. The top four interventions that would improve competitiveness in Mexico are as follows:

- improvements in the competition environment
- changes in taxes and tax regulations
- improvements in administrative regulations and the investment climate
- improvements in education (table 4.15).[9]

Problems of logistics, corruption, finance, and energy also hurt investment. Moreover, a survey by the Centro de Estudios Económicos del Sector Privado (2005) finds that the two largest obstacles to business development identified by firms in Mexico are public and private monopolies. The *Global Competition Review* (2003) ranked Mexico near the bottom of its rankings, with a score of 2.25 (out of 5.00), which is better than only Greece and Argentina. These results are largely based on conditions for formal firms. Informal enterprises would be expected to have greater problems with lack of access to finance, electricity, and labor market regulations, though exploration of this issue would require further empirical work.

Table 4.15 Constraints to Competitiveness

Subject area	Impact on investment per worker of a 10 percent improvement in the variables underlying each subject area (percent)
Competition environment	7.5
Taxes and tax regulations	7.1
Regulatory and investment climate	6.8
Education	6.0
Trade facilitation and transport	5.8
Corruption	4.7
Innovation	3.8
Finance	3.6
Energy	2.7
Labor market	1.9
Macroeconomic environment	1.0

Source: World Bank staff figures based on Instituto Mexicano para la Competitividad data.

Note: The percentages are point elasticities, which reflect the effect on investment per worker of a 10 percent isolated improvement in each variable. Simultaneous interventions could have multiplicative effects.

These results suggest that reforms to increase competition could have a significant impact on growth in Mexico. Cross-country evidence, as well as recent research, shows that improving competition can increase productivity, promote innovation, promote investment, and increase long-run employment. One estimate finds that increasing competition can increase firm innovation by more than 50 percent (World Bank 2006). Regulatory reforms to improve competition in several U.S. industries resulted in annual gains of 7 percent in those parts of GDP. This is exactly what Mexico needs at this stage.

Table 4.15 indicates that other areas of intervention are also affected by unequal structures in Mexico. Education, as noted earlier, is an example of capture by the teachers' union; finance is difficult to access for many firms because of a history of high concentration in the banking system and capital markets; the energy sector needs much greater competition and a strategic shift to ensure its long-term sustainability; and the labor market and associated social security taxes create disincentives for formalization.

The lack of competition creates a heavy burden for Mexican producers that want to compete in international markets through increased production costs and unreliable supply. For example, both the quality and price of utilities affect competitiveness. Business opinion surveys give Mexico the lowest ranking of any OECD country in terms of energy efficiency and adequacy (IMD 2004). In addition, prices of natural gas, electricity, and fuel oil are among the highest in the world. When adjusted for fluctuations in frequency and voltage, the high electricity costs result in effective costs that are 10 to 60 percent higher than in the United States.

If we analyze the energy sector in more detail, we find that inadequate investments in infrastructure have had a significant negative impact on input costs—and thus on investment incentives—in Mexican manufacturing (Instituto Mexicano para la Competitividad 2005; World Bank 2006). The performance of the Comisión Federal de Electricidad, for example, is poor when compared with that of other Latin American companies. Mexico's electricity costs are growing and are now among the highest in Latin America, and annual interruptions in connections are much more frequent than in Argentina, Brazil, and Peru (figure 4.13). This is a difficult position for any firm that wants to compete in international markets with products that require electricity as an input. Service interruptions and voltage fluctuations affect overall productivity levels of industries and prevent the installation of modern equipment.

These are high costs despite large subsidies, which are regressive in distributional terms. A quasi-Lorenz curve of the incidence of electricity consumption subsidies shows that less than 20 percent of

Figure 4.13 High Costs and Low Quality of Service in Electricity, Selected Latin American Countries and Years

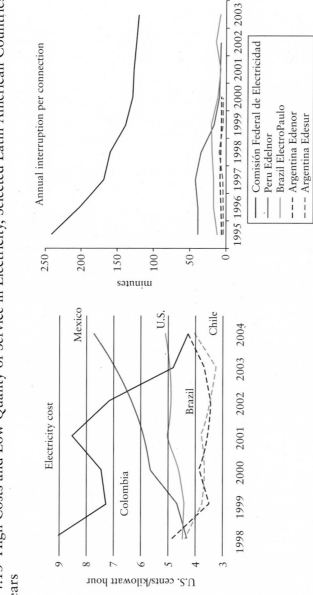

Source: World Bank 2006.

the subsidy goes to the bottom 50 percent of the income distribution (figure 4.14). Also the electric power service with the highest subsidy is for irrigated land in agriculture, which goes to wealthier farmers, while poor producers own rain-fed land.

A similar situation is present in telecommunications, where the major firms have substantial market power, as noted earlier and discussed further in del Villar and Noll (chapters 9 and 10 in this volume). Despite impressive growth in information and communication technology (ICT) in the 1990s, Mexico lags behind other Latin American and OECD countries in investment (figure 4.15). Mexico's level of ICT expenditure as a share of the overall economy (3.1 percent) is significantly below that in OECD countries such as Japan (7.4 percent), the United States (8.8 percent), and New Zealand (10 percent). It is also nearly half of Brazil's rate of 6.7 percent and Chile's rate of 6.9 percent.

As a growing number of studies have found, countries with higher levels of investment in ICT experience higher economic and social development growth (OECD 2004). Low investment in ICT has meant that fixed line growth has not kept pace with that in comparable countries and the digital divide between rural and urban areas has increased. Southern states are falling behind the rest of the country in ICT. Costs are also high when compared with other countries. Telmex dominates the long distance, local, and cellular markets; its net profit margins are more than twice those of its closest rival. In addition, telephone charges are high in Mexico compared with those in other Latin American countries, especially in relation to local prices

Figure 4.14 Bias to the Rich of the Distribution of Electricity Consumption Subsidies, 2002

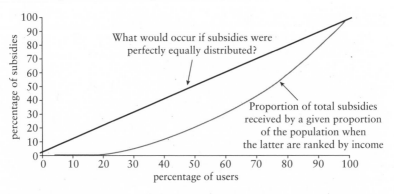

Source: ENIGH 2002.

Figure 4.15 Investment in Telecommunications, Selected Countries, early 2000s

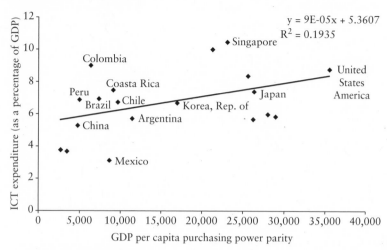

Source: World Bank 2006.

for businesses (table 4.16). Business telephone charges (factoring in installation costs, monthly fees, and per minute rates) in Mexico are more than triple those in Argentina and quadruple those in Brazil.

Lack of access to finance is an additional part of the story, especially for small and medium-sized firms and new entrants. As noted earlier, while Mexico's financial system now appears to have escaped from its long history of concentrated control by domestic economic elites, private credit remains extremely low by international standards. Foreign control undoubtedly helped solve the problem of low asset quality and connected lending, but has left Mexico with an unusually risk-averse banking system (Haber 2005 and chapter 8 in this volume).

There are also sector-specific stories related to the unequal structures discussed earlier. Low productivity and weak growth dynamics in both petroleum and agriculture hurt overall growth both directly and through links to other sectors.

Finally, we note the low levels of infrastructure spending in Mexico. The political economy of the relationship between this and unequal structures is less direct than in other areas, but is still central. In essence, infrastructure spending has been squeezed between three forces: the inability to raise taxes above a dismally low rate for a middle-income country, the growth in social spending, and the pursuit of fiscal prudence. Of these factors, only the third—fiscal prudence—is unrelated

Table 4.16 Telephone Rates, Selected Countries

Country	Monthly rate, commercial (US$)	Monthly rate, residential (US$)	Cost per connection, residential (US$)	Cost per call, three minutes (US$)
Argentina	12.94	4.56	51.72	0.02
Brazil	13.71	7.72	13.81	0.05
Chile	9.20	9.20	43.95	0.10
Korea, Rep. of	4.36	4.36	50.35	0.03
Mexico	18.35	14.51	104.73	0.14

Source: World Bank 2006.

to the political economy concerns addressed here. Failures in tax reform reflect a combination of the unwillingness of the middle classes and the elites to pay more taxes and weak administration.

Conclusion

This chapter has developed a two-part argument. First, unequal power structures continue to exert influence over policy design and the workings of economic institutions in Mexico in ways that tend to reproduce the structure of inequality. We focused on two categories of inequality: extreme wealth and corporate control in the business sector and groups that were part of Mexico's corporatist inheritance, expecially unionized workers in protected sectors.

Traditional analyses of inequality fail to capture the nature and extent of inequalities associated with these groups. In terms of income and wealth, surveys of income and expenditure never capture the truly wealthy, who have incomes way above even those of the richest households in such surveys. Corporatist groups are included in the surveys, and we find that unionized workers have incomes in the top part of the distribution. As important as the levels of income and wealth is the way in which unequal influence is exercised: this is a product of the interaction between these unequal structures and institutions. We argue that democratization did not lead to any fundamental change, and, in some respects, the resulting political equilibrium is worse with respect to the exercise of unequal influence and efficiency. We provided a series of empirically grounded examples of the exercise of unequal influence.

Second, in many areas the economic institutions that are shaped by unequal influence lie at the center of Mexico's problem of growth and competitiveness. These range from the anticompetitive conditions associated with concentrated market power to low quality in education. Unless the link between inequality and competitiveness is addressed, Mexico is unlikely to succeed in addressing its growth challenge.

Can anything be done? Although this chapter does not discuss how to effect changes in policy, we suggest exploring a general approach that seeks to define a sequence of policies as follows:

- is politically feasible in the sense that it is consistent with the initial political equilibrium,
- is designed to be resilient to capture and to increase competition, and
- helps shift the system to a political equilibrium that is both more equitable and more supportive of efficient policy design and reduced inequality of influence and that moves society away from the current inequality trap.

This approach implies not only designing policies that are socially desirable on grounds of efficiency and equity, but also doing so in ways that build the political constituency for change as part of the policy design. The variation in experience across institutions and sectors already provides examples of the potential for change. Earlier, we saw that the CFC was already a much more effective countervailing institution than COFETEL, a product in part of how it was set up. The CFC is going to be further strengthened by an amendment to the Competition Law, which will make its resolutions binding immediately and until an appeal is resolved. With respect to education, despite the centralized power of the teachers' union, in some states, a more cooperative relationship has evolved between the union and the state government, making other reforms more effective. Finally, although the financial sector needed a massive crisis to induce reforms away from a captured system, it has successfully passed through the first stage of effecting an institutional break from its prior pattern. Policy approaches will have to go further than these examples in developing political support for stronger regulation, measures that support entry of firms into protected and concentrated business sectors, and counterbalances to the power of corporatist influence. However, absent attention to the interaction between unequal structures and policy design, Mexico faces the prospect of the continuation of both slow long-term growth and entrenched inequalities.

Notes

1. The listing is based on a compilation by Forbes of all publicly available information on wealth, and so it is likely to suffer from errors of underreporting (and possibly also of overreporting.). See also de la Torre (2004) for a discussion and use of this source in an analysis of wealth in Mexico.

2. This ratio is not a "share" of GDP, because GDP measures a flow of income, and net worth is a stock of wealth. The purpose of using this ratio is to obtain a comparable scale across countries with very different income levels.

3. Much higher rates of growth were found for the top 0.1 and 0.01 percent, but the results are subject to high standard errors.

4. The *Libro Blanco de Justicia,* to be published in the future by the Federal Court, confirms this problem and adds that judges face many problems in relation to implementing their sentences and the *cumplimiento de mandatos judiciales.*

5. We treat this as a suggestive result rather than a definitive causal account, as the data do not support a clean identification strategy for the influence of billionaire-controlled companies.

6. While referred to as a nationalization, this was actually an expropriation of domestic private banking interests by the state.

7. Interactions are negative in petroleum and manufacturing, indicating that nonunionized workers are paid relatively better within these sectors. Information to assess whether this is due to the survey catching highly skilled nonunionized workers within firms or to selection effects across firms is not available. Interaction terms are generally insignificant for telecommunications and teaching, and so are assumed to be zero in the calculation in table 4.11.

8. In both cases, the denominator is an estimate of the replacement value of the firms' assets. Given that these firms and the IMSS are not publicly traded companies, it is not possible to obtain a market value.

9. The methodology does not allow identifying interactions between competitiveness dimensions.

References

Álvarez, J., V. García Moreno, and H. Patrinos. 2006. "Institutional Effects as Determinants of Learning Outcomes: Exploring State Variations in Mexico." Unpublished report, World Bank, Washington, DC.

Bourguignon, F., F. Ferreira, and M. Walton. 2007. "Equity, Efficiency and Inequality Traps: A Research Agenda." *Journal of Economic Inequality* 5 (2): 1569–1721.

Bourguignon, F., and M. Walton. 2006. "Is Greater Equity Necessary for Higher Long-Term Growth in Latin America?" In *Economic Growth with*

Equity: The Challenges for Latin America, ed. Ricardo French-Davis, 95–125. London: Palgrave Macmillan.

Castañeda, G. 1995. "A Game Theoretical View of the Mexican Economic System 1940–1980." *European Journal of Political Economy* 11 (2): 291–316.

———. 2000. "Governance of Large Corporations in Mexico and Productivity Implications." *Revista ABANTE* 3(1): 57–89.

Centro de Estudios Económicos del Sector Privado. 2005.

De Ferranti, D., G. Perry, F. Ferreira, and M. Walton. 2004. *Inequality in Latin America: Breaking with History?* Washington, DC: World Bank.

De la Torre, R. 2004. *La Riqueza en México*. Mexico City: Universidad Iberoamericana, Instituto de Investigaciones sobre Desarrollo Sustentable y Equidad Social.

Dyck, A., and L. Zingales. 2004. "Private Benefits of Control: An International Comparison," *Journal of Finance*, 59 (2) 537–600.

Esteban, J., and D. Ray. 2006. "Inequality, Lobbying, and Resource Allocation." *American Economic Review* 96: 257–79.

Faal, E. 2005. "GDP Growth, Potential Output and Output Gaps in Mexico." Working paper WP/05/93. Washington, DC: International Monetary Fund.

Glaeser, E., J. Sheinkman, and A. Shleifer. 2003. "The Injustice of Inequality." *Journal of Monetary Economics* 50 (1): 199–222.

Global Competition Review. 2003. 6 (6).

Haber, S. 2007. "Political Institutions and Economic Development: Evidence from the Banking Systems of the United States and Mexico." In *The Political Economy of Financial Development*, ed. Stephen Haber, Douglass C. North, and Barry R. Weingast. Stanford, CA: Stanford University Press.

———. 2005. "Mexico's Experiments with Bank Privatization and Liberalization, 1991–2003." *Journal of Banking and Finance* 29 (8–9): 2325–53.

Haber, S., H. Klein, N. Maurer, and K. Middlebrook. 2008. *The Second Mexican Revolution: Economic, Political and Social Change since 1980.* New York: Cambridge University Press.

Haber, S., N. Maurer, and A. Razo. 2003. *The Politics of Property Rights: Political Instability, Credible Commitments, and Economic Growth in Mexico, 1876–1929.* New York: Cambridge University Press.

Halac, M., and S. Schmukler. 2003. "Distribution Effects of Crises: The Role of Financial Transfers." Policy Research Working Paper Series 3173, World Bank, Washington, DC.

IMD. 2004. *World Competitiveness Yearbook, 2004.* Lausanne, Switzerland: IMD.

Instituto Mexicano de la Competitividad. 2005. *Situación de la competitividad de México 2004: Hacia unpacto de competitividad.* Mexico City: Instituto Mexicano de la Competitividad.

La Porta, R., F. López-de-Silanes, and G. Zamarripa. 2003. "Related Lending." *Quarterly Journal of Economics* 118: 231–68.

Le Houcq, F., 2005. "Why Is Structural Reform Stagnating in Mexico? Policy Reform Episodes from Salinas to Fox." Unpublished paper, Centro de Investigaciones y Docencia Económicas, Mexico City.

Levy, S. 2007. *Productividad, crecimiento y pobreza en México. ¿Qué sigue después de Progresa-Oportunidades?* Inter-American Development Bank, Washington, DC.

Maloney, W., and E. Pontual Ribeiro. 2001. "What Do Mexican Unions Do? A Case of Extreme Efficient Bargaining." Unpublished paper, World Bank, Washington, DC.

Morck, R., D. Wolfenzon, and B. Yeung, 2005. "Corporate Governance, Economic Entrenchment and Growth." *Journal of Economic Literature* 43: 657–722.

Morck, R., and B. Yeung. 2004. "Family Control and the Rent-Seeking Society." *Entrepreneurship Theory and Practice* 28 (4): 391–409.

Nenova, T. 2003. "The Value of Corporate Voting Rights and Control: A Cross-Country Analysis." *Journal of Financial Economics* 68 (3): 325–51.

OECD (Organisation for Economic Co-operation and Development). 2004. *ICTs and Economic Growth in Developing Countries.* Paris: OECD.

———. 2006. *PISA 2006, Volume 2: Data.* Paris: OECD.

Rao, V. 2006. "On 'Inequality Traps' and Development Policy." *Development Outreach* (February): 10–13.

Stigler, G. 1971. "The Economic Theory of Regulation." *Bell Journal of Economics* II: 3–21.

Tornell, A., and G. Esquivel. 1995. "The Political Economy of Mexico's Entry to NAFTA." Working Paper 5322, National Bureau of Economic Research, Cambridge, MA.

World Bank. 2004a. *Mexico: State Judicial Modernization Supporting Access to Justice Project.* Washington, DC: World Bank.

———. 2004b. *Poverty in Mexico: An Assessment of Conditions, Trends and Government Strategy.* Report 28612-MX. Washington, DC: World Bank.

———. 2005a. *Income Generation and Social Protection for the Poor.* Washington, DC: World Bank.

———. 2005b. *World Development Report 2006: Equity and Development.* New York: Oxford University Press.

———. 2006. *Mexico Competitiveness: Reaching Its Potential.* Washington, DC: World Bank.

———. 2007. *World Economic Outlook.* Washington, DC: World Bank.

5

Perverse Equilibria: Unsuitable but Durable Institutions

Carlos Elizondo Mayer-Serra

Economic reforms in Mexico have not resulted in a more dynamic economy offering opportunities to progressively more of the population. Growth and the creation of formal employment have been low in recent years, and it is only thanks to the informal economy and emigration that the country has been able to absorb the ever increasing number of young people entering the job market.

The economic reforms went hand-in-hand with a process of political reform that culminated in the election of Vicente Fox, the first president from outside the Institutional Revolutionary Party (Partido Revolucionario Institucional, or PRI), in July 2000 (Becerra and Woldenberg 2000). The democratization process has led to a dispersion of power. This change and an inevitable degree of erosion in the legitimacy of the economic reforms that followed the 1994 crisis, which was precisely what the reformers said would never happen again if reforms were followed, have meant that reforms designed to bring down entry barriers—primarily in the service industries and

I am grateful to Fabrice Lehoucq, Santiago Levy, Oscar Vera, Michael Walton, and two anonymous referees for their comments and to Francisco Ahued and Ixchel Cruz for their assistance. Any mistakes, of course, remain my responsibility.

labor market—have often been blocked by those who stand to be affected by such reforms. These include many business people who actually gained from the first wave of reforms. Thus, markets in which competition is minimal or nonexistent persist in both the private and the public sectors.

In terms of its direct influence on the economy and the number of processes it directly controls, the state has shrunk in size. It has not, however, become stronger in the sense of being able to protect the public's general interests over the interests of certain groups. To the contrary, powerful actors have increased their influence on the policy process, in relation to both the operation of existing regulation and the legislative process that creates new regulation.

The power the presidency used to have did not stem from a powerful state, but from a political pact derived from the president's ability to hand out rewards and punishments, including the biggest prize of all—the presidency itself. This pact shattered when the party in power lost its de facto monopoly, thereby revealing the state's true fragility. What became evident was that the state as a set of rules that permeates society to impose certain behaviors had existed in only a limited number of spheres and could not be conjured into being simply by the transition to a more democratic political system.

In recent decades, economists have gained a deeper understanding of the importance of institutions in both political and economic development (Acemoglu, Johnson, and Robinson 2005; Engerman and Sokoloff 2002; North and Thomas 1973; Parente and Prescott 2000). A country's institutions reflect its past political equilibria; therefore, any reform process comes up against actors who continue to benefit from those institutions that survive, even though the circumstances that originally made them possible may have changed. Thus, to understand the economic performance of a society, one has first to understand the relationship between de jure power and de facto power or, in other words, how institutions function given the distribution of power in that country. Institutions promote certain behaviors, impose certain limits, and give power to certain actors. Those institutions can be less than optimal in terms of growth if they allow certain sectors to extract profits or to produce goods and services of a quality inferior to what is available in other markets, if they hinder investment, or if they lead to low-quality public services.

Levels of well-being in different countries do not automatically converge just because an economy has opened up to foreign investment and the exchange of goods and services. For a country to become trapped in institutional equilibria that are suboptimal in terms of growth is much easier than achieving the complex equilibrium that underpins economies that are able to grow and to sustain their growth.

Even when certain reforms would clearly benefit society as a whole, such reforms may not come about. Similarly, those reforms that are undertaken may be applied in such a way that they do not, in essence, change the conditions that were impeding faster growth. This occurs because some actors may find that it suits them better to delay change and that they have the resources to do so.

From the point of view of growth and equity, inequality facilitates the persistence of inefficient institutions, because privileged groups have many resources they can draw on to defend their position. Indeed, the more unequal a society, the more threatening the pressure of the majority can seem, because the privileged few have much more to lose in a context where reform would imply greater sharing. By the same token, in order not to lose everything, these same privileged groups will begin to feel the incentive to reform once the threat of an even more dramatic change becomes a credible possibility. The threat of revolution, for example, is an effective spur to the sharing of power and wealth (Acemoglu 2003).

The problems of growth in the Mexican economy and the main causes of these have been well studied (see Grupo Huatusco 2004, 2006a, 2006b, 2007, 2008; for a general overview of the performance of Mexico's economy, see OECD 2007a). Mexico has found itself bogged down in an equilibrium that is less than optimal for its growth and well-being.

The central argument made in this chapter is that two sets of actors have used the power they enjoy to hinder legal reforms that would negatively affect them and their power. These two sets of actors are big business and the most powerful trade unions, particularly those representing central government workers and those in the various government agencies. Both sets of actors have managed to shield themselves from competition with the help of political parties that are also protected from competition.

Clearly, the lack of competition is not the only factor that explains Mexico's failure to grow. The country also faces serious problems in relation to human capital, infrastructure, the rule of law, and so on. However, some of these other failings are not wholly unrelated to the lack of competition to the extent that privileged groups (those who, precisely because of their power, would have the greatest capacity to redress these deficiencies) are not interested in making changes, because they themselves have no need of such changes to sustain or increase their current levels of income.

Low Growth

In the long term, growth in Mexico has been mediocre compared
with growth in other countries. Gross domestic product (GDP) per
capita in Mexico has grown at a rate above that of the United States
on only two occasions since the early 19th century: from 1885 to
1910 and from the early 1950s to 1987. As figure 5.1 shows, both
occasions ended in disaster in terms of growth, one because of the
1910 revolution and the other because of the 1982 debt crisis.

The 1982 crisis was the consequence of a system based on commercial protection that permitted accelerated industrialization, but
was politically linked to the discretionary distribution of rewards
and punishments. Indeed, the aim of the privatizing and liberalizing
reforms initiated in 1985 was to deal with the crisis this model had
provoked. The ultimate aim of these reforms was, however, political.
The group in power was facing an economy in crisis that went beyond
the financial bankruptcy of 1982 and threatened their chances of
remaining in power. What was at stake was the survival of the
government and the group that controlled it, and this group was
already facing serious doubts about its legitimacy as a result of successive devaluations and inflation and the lack of growth (Centeno
1997). Moreover, the government's relationship with investors had
been seriously damaged following the nationalization of the banks
(Elizondo 2001b).

Figure 5.1 Comparison of Per Capita GDP in China and
Selected Latin American Countries with That in the United
States, 1820–2000

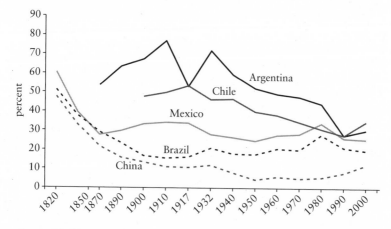

Source: Maddison 2003.

Even though the reform process was intense and painful, the government was unable to boost the economy to the rates of growth expected, and productivity and growth rates in per capita income have remained low: from 1987 to 2004, growth rates in GDP per hour worked fluctuated between 0.3 and 0.9 percent (table 5.1). This can be explained as much by the many reforms the country still needs (Lehoucq 2006) as by errors in the implementation of those reforms that actually were passed, with the most visible errors becoming apparent during the crisis of 1994.

The 1994 crisis was not, however, the most serious mistake. One of the core objectives of privatization was to increase the availability of fiscal resources. Less attention was given to solid regulation and competition.

Limited Competition

A fair amount of theoretical work and empirical evidence suggest that competition can stimulate innovation and greater productivity. When competition is limited, levels of productivity will likely remain low. In an economy open to competition, profit rates tend to be low and fairly similar. It is in the search for temporary monopolies resulting from some type of innovation where investments yielding high profit margins are to be found. Failure to innovate is what limits firms and individuals to the ordinary profitability of an economy. The search for new ways to generate value is what progressively increases productivity. If the same profits can be acquired in the political market, or if little protection is available for profits generated by innovation, then the incentive to innovate will be less.[1]

Econometric studies of the relationship between competition and productivity growth are not, however, robust. This is partly because an actor holding the biggest share of a given market today may actually be in that position because of higher productivity growth in the past (Nickell 1996). At the same time, some evidence shows that greater market power (defined as a percentage of a given market) leads to lower levels of productivity (Nickell 1996).

Given the institutions that protect them, Mexican business people in general seem to have few incentives to innovate and develop. Instead of seeking temporary monopolies through innovation, they are more likely to seek higher profits through rent seeking.

Spending on research and development is low in Mexico and is funded almost entirely by public spending. Private spending on research and development is equivalent to only 0.15 percent of GDP, the lowest level among countries of the Organisation for Economic

Table 5.1 Growth Rates in Per Capita GDP and GDP Per Hour Worked, Selected Countries and Periods
(percent)

Country	GDP per capita			GDP per hour worked (productivity)		
	1987–95	*1995–2004*	*2000–04*	*1987–95*	*1995–2004*	*2000–04*
China	5.7	6.6	7.7	4.7	6.1	6.8
Estonia	—	6.6	7.0	—	7.1	6.6
India	3.9	4.5	5.2	3.7	3.9	3.1
Ireland	5.1	6.6	4.0	4.0	4.7	3.5
Mexico	0.4	2.2	−0.5	0.6	0.3	0.9
Spain	2.5	3.2	2.6	2.1	0.0	0.2

Source: Bank of France 2005.
Note: — = not available.

Co-operation and Development (OECD). Private financing represents 34.7 percent of what Mexico spends on research and development, whereas the OECD average is 61.9 percent, and even in Turkey the figure is 41.3 percent (OECD 2006). In Mexico, a monopoly based on institutional privilege is more durable than one based on an innovation that can be made obsolete by a more skillful actor.

Figure 5.2 shows research and development as a percentage of GDP in selected economies in 2005. While Finland, Japan, the Republic of Korea, and Sweden reported the highest levels of investment, Mexico's performance was the lowest of the economies shown in the figure.

In one of the most active sectors, telecommunications (in which Mexico has a large international firm), Mexico did not register any telecommunications patents with the European Patent Office between 1991 and 2003 (figure 5.3). Other countries such as Brazil (a non-OECD member) and Turkey (an OECD member) also did not register any patents. By contrast, India (a non-OECD member), registered 5 patents in 2001 and 13 in 2003.

In Mexico, the lack of competition stemmed originally from high entry barriers and a business culture focusing more on profits than on innovation, a culture that was the result of a history of protectionism.

Figure 5.2 Research and Development as a Percentage of GDP, Selected Economies and Groups of Countries, 2005

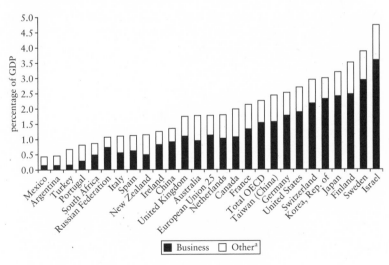

Source: OECD 2006.

a. Includes R&D performed by the government, higher education instiutions, and private nonprofit organizations.

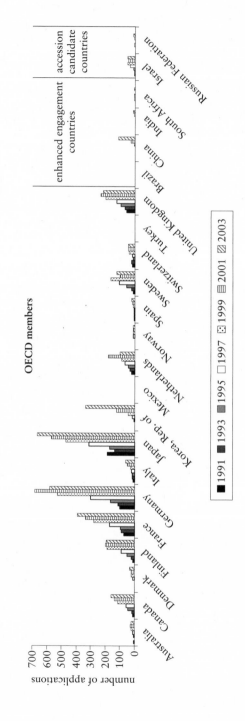

Figure 5.3 Telecommunications Patent Applications Filed with the European Patent Office, Selected Countries and Years

Source: OECD patent database.

Not much appears to have changed in this regard. A look at regulation in products markets reveals that among OECD countries, Mexico is relatively restrictive (figure 5.4).

When competition is limited, prices tend to be high. As figure 5.5 shows and as discussed in other chapters in this volume, compared with other OECD countries, Mexico has among the highest rates in the telecommunications sector. The number of users in Mexico has increased, but less than in other countries. The dominant mobile telephone firm (RadioMóvil Dipsa, known as TELCEL) is much larger than any other such firms, so users have few incentives to change to another company (OECD 2007b).

In the case of most Mexican manufactured goods, competition is wider, because imports are relatively open. Some evidence suggests that opening the market has generated more competition and greater growth in productivity (Van Wijnbergen and Venables 1993). Studies also show that those sectors of the Japanese economy that are competitive internationally today are mainly those sectors that already faced competition at home prior to market opening (see, for example, Porter and Sakakibara 2001). By contrast, the success of Korea and Taiwan (China) was underpinned by protection and

Figure 5.4 Regulation in Products Market, OECD Countries, 2003

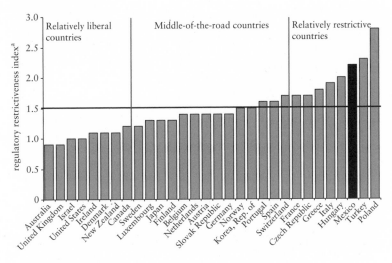

Source: OECD 2005.

Note: a = Index range goes from "0" to "6", with "0" being the least restrictive and "6" the most restrictive.

Figure 5.5 Telephone Charges, OECD Countries, August 2005

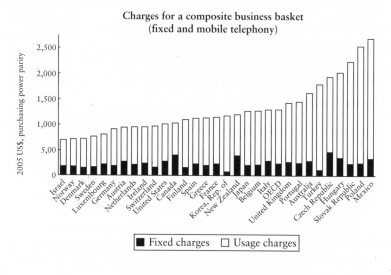

Charges for a composite business basket
(fixed and mobile telephony)

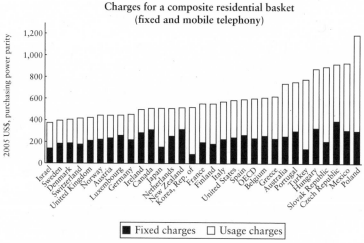

Charges for a composite residential basket
(fixed and mobile telephony)

Source: OECD 2007b.

internal subsidies; however, they were given up in exchange for being able to compete abroad (Wade 1990). In Mexico, the aviation industry is a recent example of how much the consumer can benefit from a "simple" reform that opens up the sector to new actors (table 5.2) (for the United States, see Graham, Kaplan, and Sibley 1983).

Table 5.2 Price Differences in Airline Tariffs, December
2005 to August 2006
(Mex$, real prices)

Route	December 2005	August 2006
Mexico City–Monterrey	3,200	1,500
Mexico City–Guadalajara	4,200	1,500
Mexico City–Cancún	4,000	2,000
Mexico City–Tijuana	4,000	2,500
Mexico City–Zacatecas	2,150[a]	2,000[a]

Source: Cruz 2005.
a. One-way ticket.

Many countries have had to become competitive and learn how
to live with permanent competition simply to survive as independent nations. Not to do so implied the risk of being swallowed up
by a neighbor. When one part of a country is under the control of
a government with a different development model than other parts,
and if this government were to succeed, it would displace the government ruling the rest of the country. This was the case of the Korean
peninsula and of Taiwan in relation to communist China (Cumings
1984). Mexico has never been in such a critical situation, nor has it
faced wars with its neighbors that might have threatened the country's
independence. The United States never wanted to conquer the whole
country, only the sparsely populated areas, which it annexed more
than 150 years ago.

Nevertheless, following the 1917 revolution, Mexico's strategy
was to cut itself off from the rest of the world on the premise that
the world, particularly the United States, was a threat. Even so,
Mexico never really impeded the flows of investment, tourism, and
commerce. For example, there was freedom of capital movements
throughout this period, which reassured investors that the revolutionary rhetoric was unlikely to do them any real harm. Moreover,
Mexico is blessed with a relatively abundant supply of natural
resources, and these have allowed the country to finance the wrong
type of economic policies for too long.

Mexico's border with the United States, once the source of threat,
now gives Mexico a competitive edge over other countries. This
edge is still so, even though the institutional advantages that resulted from the North American Free Trade Agreement are being eroded every time the United States signs a similar treaty with another
country and by China's entry into the World Trade Organization.

Mexico's proximity to the United States not only reduces the cost of transporting products, but also allows Mexico to import goods at which the country is not competitive, even the government services and judicial protection available north of the border when doing so is beneficial for investors. Another feature of this common border is that it allows a sizable exodus of Mexicans in search of better incomes, and this exodus has helped reduce the political pressure back home created by Mexico's poor record in relation to growth and employment.[2]

Education and Competition

The effects of the lack of competition are seen in many of the areas analyzed in this volume. One area where the effects are highly significant is the education system.

According to the OECD's Programme for International Student Assessment study of performance in secondary schools, Mexico's education system is performing dismally, but the system is surprisingly egalitarian, which indicates that both public and private education are of low quality. Figure 5.6 illustrates performance in mathematics by students in selected economies. The scale has six levels that represent different tasks of ascending difficulty, with level 1 representing tasks of low difficulty and level 6 representing tasks of high difficulty (OECD 2004). According to this scale, students who can solve tasks from levels 1 through 5 are likely to complete level 6 tasks and are A students with relatively high proficiency. B students can complete tasks from levels 1 through 3, but have a low probability of solving more difficult tasks. C students are not expected to solve tasks beyond level 1. Students below level 1 are placed in level 0, though this does not mean that they are unable to do any mathematics.

Figure 5.6 reveals that Mexico ranks way below other OECD countries, including Turkey, whose per capita GDP is lower than Mexico's, and below that of some nonmember countries such as Uruguay. It shows that 38 percent of Mexican students fall into the lowest level on the Programme for International Student Assessment scale (level 1) and 28 percent do not even reach this level (level 0). Conversely, only 0.4 percent of Mexican students fall into levels 5 and 6, while in Brazil this percentage is 1.2 percent and in Finland it is 23.4 percent.

Note that the test examined only a representative sample of students in school. It did not measure the performance of the worst students, who are generally those no longer in the education system

Figure 5.6 Percentage of Students at Each Level of Proficiency on the PISA Mathematics Scale, Selected Economies, 2003

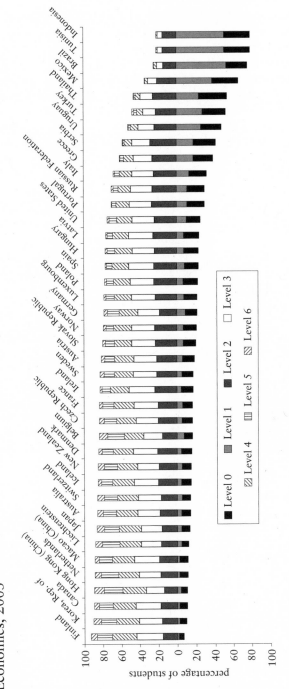

Source: OECD 2004.

because they abandoned it. In Mexico's case, this group represents a much greater percentage than the average for the other countries studied. Only 56 percent of children of secondary school age attend secondary school in Mexico, compared with 90 percent on average in OECD countries.

In Mexico, 13 percent of 15-year-old students are in private schools, which is more than the mean for OECD countries (OECD 2004). The widespread perception of public education is that it is of lower quality than private education. This is due to badly maintained infrastructure, problems of teacher attendance, and large class sizes. There is also a marked weakness in the teaching of a second language in public schools.

The performance of Mexico's private school students is, on average, slightly better than that of their peers in public schools (figure 5.7). However, taking into account that students from higher-income families already have more household resources, including greater cultural capital, and that private schools have better infrastructure

Figure 5.7 Difference in Performance between Public Schools and Private Schools, Selected Economies and the OECD, 2003

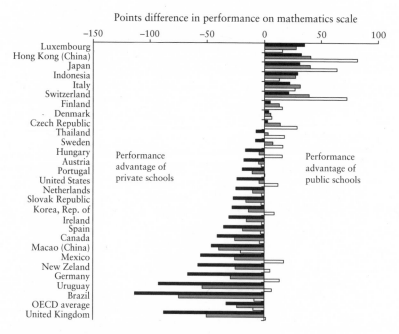

Source: OECD 2004, figure 5.18.

(which makes the teacher's job easier), public school students actually perform slightly better overall.[3]

Parents often choose to pay for private school even when an equivalent public school is available. It does not seem to matter that the quality of the service is, on average, not that good. Lack of information about each school's performance is a serious problem: it leaves parents without objective criteria on which to select a school. Until 2006, there were no national examinations that would allow schools to be compared, and all schools face the monopoly in teacher training, which limits schools' ability to provide good quality education.

The size of the private education market is not trivial: some 3.5 million students attend private elementary and secondary schools (OECD 2004). Interestingly, this market is where the country's better informed individuals are to be found. The absence of pressure to provide more objective criteria that would permit better school selection in terms of quality may indicate that quality is not the highest priority for many parents. One hypothesis is that what parents are really looking for when choosing a school is entry for their children into certain social circles that promote particular values, plus the possibility of earning a higher income because of the network of contacts made.

Many countries such as India and Korea have national public university entrance examinations, and success or failure at such examinations often determines students' professional prospects. Mexico has no such examination. Also, countries such as the United States have elite private universities with stringent entry requirements. Even though these universities may exhibit some bias toward the children of prominent citizens, particularly benefactors, the universities still remain extremely strict in terms of student selection. This type of elite private university does not exist in Mexico. At the same time, public universities in Mexico, except perhaps for some degree courses, are no longer the first choice for children from wealthier families.

Apart from having a certain minimum of skills, all students have to do to gain admission to most private universities in Mexico is to pay. Some of these universities are simply business ventures. To the extent that the job market seems to depend much more on whom one knows than on merit, parents will consider their selection validated according to whether their children find jobs or simply enter the family business. Indeed, the Instituto Nacional de Estadística y Geografía's national survey of occupation and employment reveals that more than half those employed obtained their jobs as the result of a recommendation (Rivero 2006).

In the past, education was limited to a privileged few: the gross rate of access to university education was 2.7 percent in 1960 and 20.0 percent in 2000. Overall enrollment during the same period rose from 78,753 to 1,585,408 students (Grediaga, Rodríguez, and Padilla 2004). Thus, what mattered was to have a degree, regardless of its worth. The need was even less in the context of a closed economy that had a large number of de facto monopolies in which the quality of goods and services provided had little relevance. In a global economy, however, the situation is radically different, particularly with the emergence of China and India, where highly educated workers are available at relatively low cost.

What is not clear is the incentives that would engineer a switch from an education based on people's socioeconomic position to an education based on merit. Some sectors continue to hire more on the basis of employment personal networks than on merit. This is possible for businesses in sectors with relatively little competition and is what tends to happen in the public sector and in state-owned companies, where the trade unions are actively involved in the hiring process.

Institutions of the Past

Mexico's current institutions were useful for a different development model that is based on neither economic nor political competition. The institutions made political control possible and had the capacity to stimulate investment and, therefore, growth in a context where industrialization did lead to a period of quite remarkable growth in investment and productivity rates.

Today, these same institutions have not managed to stimulate the growth that was hoped for when the reform process began. The former development model failed, and anyway, it belonged to another more closed world. Nevertheless, certain institutions continue to live on even though they are totally unsuitable, simply because powerful groups continue to benefit from them.

The distinctive feature of these institutions is their corporate nature. They organized business people, workers, and peasant laborers from the top in order to exercise political control over them (Bizberg 1990; Camp 1989; Garrido and Puga 1990). In exchange for a certain degree of political discipline, the institutions afforded their members the following privileges: commercial protection, subsidies, and low taxes. In addition, the government passed a labor law that, instead of stimulating productivity, protects the trade unions by means of money and autonomy. Finally, the government guaranteed an almost zero turnover of workers in the public sector, especially in the central government, plus the provision of attractive fringe benefits, especially pensions. These benefits have become increasingly more costly because of the tradition of improving one of the clauses of the collective contract every year.

The government actually had much less room to maneuver than is normally believed. Far from being a dictatorial system, the government was a complex balance of interests with power at the top that could demand discipline in certain extreme cases of direct defiance.[4] On the whole, the government preferred negotiation to confrontation with these interests, and it attracted allies by distributing preserves of power and influence.

The system generated remarkable political stability, in contrast to what was happening in other countries in the region. The power concentrated in the government made it possible to extend infrastructure, strengthen the financial system, and stabilize the macroeconomy—at least until the 1976 devaluation, when the first poststabilizing development crisis broke. The system, plus an initially well-designed policy of import substitution, made high growth rates possible, but it relied heavily on the capacity to distribute profits and on a closed economy that allowed business people to operate at low levels of competitiveness (Vernon 1971). Table 5.3 demonstrates the logic of this arrangement.

This pact collapsed because its wealth-generating motor, the import substitution policy, ran out of steam. Increasingly more public spending was necessary to stimulate the economy and to keep in check those actors who had an ever increasing capacity to extract profits. This client type of relationship was undermining fiscal incomes, and thus the government found itself with a growing deficit and a correspondingly increasing need to incur debt (Elizondo 2001a).

In addition, social spending was hardly progressive at all, given that corporate actors always came out on top in the budget battle. The increasing cost of this arrangement ended up bankrupting public finances and setting the scene for the 1982 economic crisis. The crisis did not happen earlier because oil and the funds generated by an increasing external debt kept the arrangement afloat even after the 1976 devaluation.

Following the 1982 crisis, the government no longer had any alternative but to acknowledge that the country's institutions had to be reformed. The issue was only partially addressed, however. Given that the government had not confronted the main trade unions of public sector workers during the years of greatest presidential power, the chances of this happening when real wages had to fall dramatically because of growing inflation were slim. Indeed, as increased fringe benefits (especially pensions) partly offset drops

Table 5.3 Main Social Agreements between the State and Society under the PRI

Credible area of commitment on the part of the state	Society's part of the deal
Government and the political elite	*Business elite*
Support for the creation of profit-making sectors (import substitution and restrictive regulation in general)	Investment in well-being and creation of profit
	Prevention of runs on capital
Selective protection for the rights of ownership and appropriation of profit	Political neutrality
	Negotiation at forums provided by the government
Exchange rate freedom	
Exchange rate stability	
Low taxes	
Forums for negotiation	
Government and the political elite	*Workers' sector*
Profit sharing	Political support, including votes
Strong labor rights	Absence of social conflicts
Union autonomy (as long as political discipline was mentioned)	Negotiation at formal forums
	Control of radical groups
Provision for social programs	
Forums for negotiation (through corporate structures)	
Government and the political elite	*Citizens*
Good macroeconomic performance: high growth, low inflation	Political acceptance of the one-party regime with little accountability
Exchange rate freedom and freedom of movement of the population	Acceptance of voting as a ritual and not as an act of empowerment
Employment	
Public security	Acceptance of the discretionary power of the authorities
Social peace	
Low tax rates with privileges for the politically most important sectors	Acceptance of a nationalist, revolutionary ideology
Gradual expansion of social services favoring political allies	

Source: Adapted from World Bank 2006: 8.

in income, the problem was made even more complex and put off to the future.

The relatively easier decisions, such as opening up the economy, were taken, but the more difficult decisions, such as reforming the Labor Law, were not taken. In other words, liberalization happened externally but not internally. There was a certain strategic logic to this approach, because it implied creating new allies to confront the adversaries who would come later. However, for the strategy to work, success was needed in relation to macroeconomic stability and growth, but hope for that was dashed by the 1994 crisis. The government did much better in situations where it simply had to make a decision (for example, whether or not to sell). It did not do so well in situations that called for the creation of sophisticated institutional infrastructure (for example, to regulate what was sold).

In terms of the value of assets in government hands, what was privatized was actually less important than is normally assumed because the energy sector, including oil, still remained in government hands. Nevertheless, the number of companies in government hands fell significantly. This reduction improved public finances in the short run and led to better functioning of those parts of the manufacturing sector that had also previously been in government hands. However, the two largest privatizations—of banks and telephone companies— ended up costing the country dearly, if for different reasons. The banking system crashed only a few years after it had been privatized; in the telecommunications sector, a colossus emerged—in the form of Teléfonos de Mexico—that was difficult to regulate.

What is left over from the corporatism of the past is now an obstacle to growth, because it extracts profits from the rest of an economy that is no longer isolated from the rest of the world. Those who have enjoyed such profits have stood in the way of effective reform. When the political system was democratized, in part as a result of the crisis of the former development model that had handed out rewards and punishments to well-organized trade unions, these same groups found themselves able to operate with more freedom from control by the executive branch, which had partially coordinated and disciplined them. If the government had not been prepared to tackle the difficult issues before democratization, when it exerted greater control, it is going to find that task even more complicated today.

Mexico's economic and political transition can be studied in comparison with the transition that the Russian Federation underwent when the Soviet Union collapsed and that China underwent when it emerged from the Cultural Revolution. In the case of Russia, the collapse of the Soviet regime resulted in an oligarchy that acquired almost complete control of the country's main resources. The state practically collapsed. As concerns labor regulation, however, those who managed to keep their jobs continued to enjoy significant protection, despite the fall in wages. Vladimir Putin has subsequently tried to re-assert government control over big business by renationalizing a sizable part of what had previously been privatized.

In China, the state has been able to choose where to promote competition among both public and private companies and among workers, who have practically no labor rights at all. It has achieved this without losing control of the process, although, of course, China is a clear case of an authoritarian state (Krussel and Rios-Rull 2002; Parente and Prescott 1999).

The situation in Mexico resembles Russia's experience more closely than China's. The government lacks the political clout to force either the biggest businesses, especially those in sectors with limited competition, or the trade unions of public sector workers to compete. The way in which legislation is applied and the government's capacity to reform legislation have been partially captured. The power of some of these groups, such as the trade unions, is so great that one part of the reform that is known to be a political hot potato (profound labor reform to produce a more efficient public sector) is no longer even on the agenda.

Big businesses in sectors with limited competition and the main trade unions are two sides of the same problem: sectors with scant competition that extract profits. In the first case, business people do this through relatively high prices and low personal taxes. Significantly, for a country with such marked inequality, the idea of an inheritance tax is not even up for consideration, something that reflects the power of those who stand to be affected. Quite apart from whether an inheritance tax is a good tax (given that it brings in little and can be evaded), it is surprising that the idea is not part of the debate, because the proportion of wealth in the hands of billionaires is greater in Mexico than in many other countries, including some of the countries in the region with the greatest inequality, and because most of Mexico's billionaires inherited their wealth.

In the case of the trade unions, they extract profits through high wages relative to those earned by workers in the manufacturing sector, which does face competition. The unions also extract profits in the form of good pensions, no accountability, and low productivity (see chapter 4 in this volume by Guerrero, López-Calva, and Walton). In general, the public sector trade unions are unaffected by low product quality or by losses their employers suffer. Even though the income that public sector workers earn is miniscule compared with the salaries of owners of large businesses, and even though these workers continue to earn less than the upper-middle class, they still enjoy working conditions that are costly to the public purse. This situation reduces the possibility of instituting more progressive and better quality social spending and saddles the economy as a whole with expensive, poor quality services. Proposing greater public spending that would narrow the inequality gap through focused transfers and better public services in education and health is difficult if one part of such spending has been captured by the trade unions and if the capacity to provide a good quality service is limited because of labor agreements that do not promote productivity.

One extreme case is Luz y Fuerza del Centro, a state-owned electricity utility company. It supplies electricity to a territorially concentrated market, central Mexico, where per capita income levels are high compared with the rest of the country. The company does not sell its electricity cheaply, but it is still losing a good deal of money. In 2008, transfers and subsidies to the company to avoid bankruptcy will amount to some Mex\$32.5 billion, which is equivalent to 157 percent of the budget of Mexico's largest public university (Secretaría de Hacienda y Crédito Público 2008).

The inefficiencies in the public sector are manifold. Some efforts have been made to quantify the problem (Lehoucq 2006), but even anecdotal evidence reveals sizable productivity problems, which are the result of a politicized corporate system that tolerates deadwood in personnel and low productivity (World Bank 2006). In Petróleos Mexicanos (PEMEX), for example, 11,450 workers on the payroll do absolutely nothing, because the collective contract makes it impossible to dismiss personnel whose jobs no longer exist. The cost to the company is Mex\$4 billion per year. These numbers do not include excess staff members in many processes who are also effectively doing nothing (Hernández 2006b). One study of PEMEX has identified potential annual savings of Mex\$17,600 million, but part of this saving would come only at the expense of confronting the trade union (Hernández 2006a).

Fragile Democracy

Despite the high expectations surrounding Mexico's democratization process, there are many concerns about the political situation and the weakness of democracy. Democracy has neither managed to discipline actors that benefit from the status quo nor opened up opportunities to other sectors; thus, majorities have not been strengthened in relation to special interest groups as was hoped. The dispersion of power has actually made controlling certain actors more difficult, because the provincial states and other groups formerly organized from above now operate with much more freedom. In contrast, society is not well organized from below, even though some organized groups have been capable of pressuring legislators and the government in their favor.

The history of President Fox's six-year term illustrates the risk of control by private interests, given that a good part of the legislation passed was driven by specific interest groups who were also able to hold back many reforms that might have affected them negatively. These groups have enough incentives to spend political and other capital to defend institutions that give them preference.

Democratization was expected to end the system of privileges or, at least, to allow the government to remove some of these privileges. However, comparing today's capacity to legislate with capacity in the past is not easy. The World Bank (2006) argues that the capacity to legislate has not been significantly inferior to what it was before democratization, but no significant progress has been made in relation to reforms that would affect the privileges discussed here. Note, however, that this analysis is based on the number of laws passed and does not distinguish between the laws according to their effectiveness. Indeed, simply calling for more legal reforms as a demonstration of efficacy would be a mistake, given that many of the new laws passed have actually been a step backward.

Congresses can easily be held hostage by well-organized special interests. In the case of Mexico, no appropriate regulation governs conflicts of interest, and even though members of Congress do not need money to run for reelection, they still pursue money to use after their term of office is over.

The only body that can, in principle at least, prevent laws devoted to special interests is the executive branch of government. Because Mexico does not permit the president to serve consecutive terms of office, presidents do not pay a cost in terms of future elections, even though they must still consider the future success of their party. By means of the presidential veto, the executive branch has managed to put a stop to some laws that might have been harmful to the general public's interests, such as the Book Law, which sought price controls in the book industry (although this law was finally approved in 2008, because President Felipe Calderón decided not to veto it). However, it has not vetoed all the laws it should have, for instance, the so-called Televisa Law.[5] The cost the executive branch pays for each veto is high, because the executive branch itself is not immune to pressures from well-organized groups, especially when the administration includes representatives of the same special interest groups that need to be reformed. During the Fox administration, the most obvious example was the appointment of the communications and transport secretary. The closer to the heart of government the special interest groups can position their allies, the more difficult the battle is, and if the battle is won, it comes at a far heavier cost.

The office of president has been losing power. Much of this power was metaconstitutional. In other words, it was the result of the PRI's hegemony and its discipline in relation to the president, who controlled the public purse and had the capacity to hire or fire not only public officials, but even governors.[6] Now that the president's party no longer controls legislative power, these metaconstitutional powers have been weakened. Thus, the true fragility of the Mexican state has become evident in relation to its basic duties, such as combating delinquency, collecting taxes, and regulating land use in towns. The personality and style of Fox's administration also served to weaken the presidency in its symbolic sense.[7]

The battle may be hard, but some laws advancing the general public's interests have been passed. The Freedom of Information Act and the Law Promoting a Career in Civil Service in the Federal Public Administration both serve to strengthen the average citizen in relation to the government and to limit the government's discretionary power in hiring and firing top bureaucrats (World Bank 2006).[8] Nevertheless, the Freedom of Information Act has not been as powerful as was hoped, for example, as del Villar explains (chapter 9 in this volume), it has not been able to declassify information about the methodology the Comisión Federal de Telecomunicaciones uses to establish its prices.

Although these laws were desirable, the net result has been to further diminish the president's power. In a context of increasing decentralization of spending in favor of local states, where transparency in the use of public money is usually much less, the relative loss of presidential power appears to be even greater.

Significant legislative changes have been made in the financial sector; however, the losers in these reforms suffer from not being part of the better organized groups. The greatest change is the increased capacity of creditors to recoup money in cases of nonpayment. Because past debtors have already been rescued, debtors' associations such as El Barzón have been losing force, and future debtors will have little political clout. One interesting reform affecting powerful interests is the reform to the Federal Law on Economic Competition. Despite resistance from big business, several parties supported the reform.

Some interesting lessons can be learned from this success. The reform process itself arose out of the stand taken against privileges in 2006 by the then candidate for the presidency, Andrés Manuel López Obrador. It was a sort of compensation for the excesses of the Televisa Law and was carried out under the leadership of the president of the Comisión Federal de Competencia. However, the reforms passed in Mexico were more limited in scope than elsewhere in the world.

The political parties have been adapting to the new environment. Even the Party of the Democratic Revolution (Partido de la Revolución Democrática or PRD) has many times opted for nonconfrontation with certain interests. The parties require the support of both big business and the principal trade unions, as much for the money they receive from business,[9] as for the organizational capacity of the unions. The parties also have their own resources to defend, which are provided by law from the public purse, are substantially higher than in other political systems, and were designed as a way of keeping dirty money out of political campaigns.

Difficulties of Reform

Transition came to Mexico in a context where the president's party no longer had an overall majority in either of the two chambers. Divided governments have made it difficult for the executive branch to assume the short-term cost of certain legal reforms and then to enjoy the medium- to long-term benefits. Nevertheless, all the reforms still needed were not passed during the years of unified government, and thus, the causality of divided government having less capacity for action is not clear (Cheibub 2007).

Even though divided government does not seem to inhibit the U.S. government's capacity to promote its own agenda, significant differences between Mexico and the United States might explain why a divided government is much more dysfunctional in Mexico, although in the United States the presence of a divided government has become more polarizing and less efficacious in recent decades (Ware 2001).

Where Mexico is concerned, four reasons that reform has been so difficult in a divided government are worth considering. The first is that the reforms still outstanding are unpopular. The 1994 crisis seriously eroded the credibility of the new economic model that the Carlos Salinas presidency had been constructing, and implied that the 1994 election had not really been about an alternative economic model. Indeed, the National Action Party candidate was not critical of the economic model, and had actively defended many of the reforms proposed by Salinas. Cuauhtémoc Cárdenas, the PRD candidate who had done so well in 1988 running on a platform that was highly critical of Miguel de la Madrid's economic model (a much more moderate model than Salinas's), not only came in a distant third, but also had even moderated his stance.

In October 1994, at the end of President Salinas's six-year term, 52.2 percent of those interviewed for a survey were in favor of privatization, 38.2 percent were against it, and the remaining 9.6 percent were indifferent. After the 1994 crisis, and only one year into Ernesto Zedillo's government, the perception of privatization had changed. In April 1995, the percentage of those in favor of privatization had fallen below 28.1 percent (that is, slightly more than half the earlier level), 35.7 percent were against it, and 36.2 were indifferent. The legislators confronting the current president, Calderón, in his attempts at fiscal, energy, and labor reform—the three most visible reform areas—have already won the media debate. The public now sees these reforms not as favorable to the interests of the majority, but as part of a sinister plan to erode its interests. According to a national poll by the polling company Parametría, 73 percent of those surveyed believe that the government should control the economy and 55 percent are opposed to any increase in private capital in the oil and electricity industries. By the same token, a 2007 Mitofsky poll shows that more than half the population is opposed to private investment in energy.

The second reason is that Mexico's electoral system and political history have led to the emergence of three major parties, plus a few small ones that often team up in coalition with the major parties. In addition, the parties are fairly well disciplined, as much because of the political culture as because the future of their members depends in good measure on keeping in with the party leadership.

The existence of three big parties complicates the mechanics of reform. Given the unpopularity of the reform agenda, if one opposition party supports the government, it risks being thought of as a traitor. Moreover, for a party to support the reforms makes little sense, because if the reforms succeed, the executive branch is more likely to reap the political benefits than the party.

The opposition is currently in the hands of two parties who are heirs to the ideological principles, revolutionary nationalism, and political practices of the PRI governments. In the case of the PRD, rejection of the most important outstanding reforms is almost automatic, because the PRD arose out of opposition to Salinas's reform agenda. In the case of the PRI, the relationship is more ambiguous; however, after the 1994 crisis, a lot of power was lost by the modernizers, who had come from the high levels of the bureaucracy controlling the party and who were not really a product of traditional PRI cadres closer to the rank and file of the party.

Moreover, as a recent World Bank (2006) study points out, the result of the 2006 election was that more than 90 percent of members of Congress came from organized groups within the PRI, in particular, trade unions and peasant laborer organizations. This is because the candidates are higher up on the lists of proportional representation candidates, from which 200 of the 500 deputies are elected. The other 300 are elected in first-past-the-post districts. The PRI itself won fewer first-past-the-post majority seats in the lower chamber than ever before. The exit of the PRI from the federal government has strengthened the provincial state governments and groups such as the trade unions who have an autonomous power base. Given the government's need for PRI support simply to be able to address most of its legislative agenda and given the PRD's reluctance to negotiate with the government, the power of the union leaders is significant.

The third reason is the fact that consecutive re-election of all members of Congress is not allowed. There is thus no incentive for collaboration based on direct pressure from the electorate. Instead of fulfilling citizens' mandate, what is important is keeping in with the party leadership and not being seen as a traitor to the cause. This argument also assumes that the electorate is in favor of the reforms that have not yet been passed. This is not, however, the case with respect to fiscal, energy, and labor reform. In the absence of the potential pressure for re-election, "going public" does not function well.

The fourth reason is the public funds the parties receive by law. The amount is staggering. In addition to tying up increasingly more federal resources, the executive branch cannot exert pressure through campaign resources as was the case in the past. The political parties are guaranteed a good part of public resources for election purposes. The three major parties enjoy pretending that they want the amount reduced, because there is some public pressure in this direction; however, as such a reduction would not really suit any of the parties, it has not happened.

An interesting debate is going on about the many institutional reforms that could be carried out to make the political system better able to promote the changes the country requires. Whether any of the proposed reforms would actually yield the hoped-for results is not clear.

The faith of many analysts and actors in Mexico regarding the possibility of controlling powerful actors simply by changing the electoral rules or by changing the power of the president relative to Congress is curious. No one would disagree that much needs to be improved, but the cost of carrying out such reforms is high and the potential gains so uncertain that it seems better to concentrate attention on reforms likely to produce more concrete results. The fact that in the case of a legal reform one knows what is being introduced into Congress but not what is going to emerge makes this type of reform much less attractive. In addition, even though a law may appear perfect in the abstract, when it is eventually implemented, it may turn out to have implications in practice that legislators had not envisaged. The country's historical context and the existing distribution of power create a certain mystery around the operation of each new law.

Even though the arrival of democracy has not led to changes in the structure of privileges, some reforms worthy of note have been passed. These include, as noted earlier, the Freedom of Information Act and the Law Promoting a Career in Civil Service in the Federal Public Administration, plus somewhat more progressive public spending. Even though we would have to better understand the mechanisms that made it possible, it does not seem to be mere chance that social spending, which is still captured to a certain degree by powerful interests, is today more progressive than it was in the past (World Bank 2004).

One part of this increase in public spending has had an inertia component that is the result of the government's legal obligations, such as universal coverage of primary education, which has occurred partly for demographic reasons. For the first time, Mexico has enacted medical insurance (known as Seguro Popular) that is, in principle, for everyone. Although socially fair, it can stimulate the informal economy, because people can now obtain some sort of social protection without paying for the expensive insurance required when they are hired in the formal sector. This can therefore backfire by reducing the capacity to grow the formal economy. It also stimulates evasion of social security, which results in fewer savings for retirement, as demonstrated by Levy (chapter 6 in this volume). Nevertheless, the medical insurance program does address a sizable deficit in terms of health coverage for the poor. The challenge now is to apply universal coverage, but with the proper incentives.

Another pro-poor program linked to the transition to democracy is Oportunidades (Scott 2003). Although the original program started before 2000, one could argue that Mexico was already a democratic country after 1997, when it became clear that the PRI had lost in the lower chamber and accepted its defeat (Przeworski and others 2000). The Oportunidades program absorbs only a small fraction of the budget compared with such extremely regressive programs as social security, higher education, and subsidies paid to the energy and agriculture sectors. Thus, much more still needs to be done to make Mexico's spending a more powerful redistributive instrument.

Mechanisms for Protecting Privileges

Big business groups and conglomerates have a range of mechanisms for protecting their privileges. The law is one of them.

Amparos (legal stays of action) can halt government regulatory action in many spheres. *Amparos* are within the reach of whoever can afford to pay for them, regardless of sector, but they really come into their own in the more heavily regulated sectors and in relation to taxation.

Contrary to what much of the discourse suggests, constructing a situation of genuine rule of law is not simply a matter of applying existing laws. Although this is part of the problem, in many cases changing laws is necessary to ensure that the rule of law extends its authority over everyone, but at the same time affords everyone some protection.

In some matters, such as those that have to do with the government's capacity to regulate and impose taxes, *amparos* seem to violate the very idea of a law within the reach of everyone and a state that can regulate everyone. A law on taxes passed by Congress that others have to abide by is not being applied to business people who can win *amparos* against that law.

This idea of legality protects the powerful and does so better than in other legal systems. It stems from a curious interpretation of Constitution Article 31, Paragraph 4, which addresses citizens' obligations. It was taken from the 1857 constitution and, until 1960, was interpreted to mean that *amparos* were not allowed in tax matters. The change in interpretation has led to an ongoing dispute about the constitutionality of fiscal laws and about the constitutionality of actions by the government that can give notable protection to big business and can grant big businesses lower tax rates than those paid by smaller businesses that cannot afford the same legal apparatus to defend themselves (Elizondo and Perez de Acha 2006). *Amparos* are a mechanism used mainly by the largest companies, which also have more success with their claims than smaller companies (González 2006).

A similar problem exists in the area of competition, where the authorities experience a great deal of trouble in applying the law. Until recently, actually collecting a fine was virtually impossible. Those affected can seek *amparos*, and even if the result goes against them, the time that passes before they can be sanctioned already gives them an advantage over their competitors (see chapter 4 in this volume). The reforms passed at the end of 2006 should change this somewhat. What interpretation the judges will make remains to be seen.

Using *amparos* allows people to protect themselves from laws that have already been passed. This has the advantage, therefore, of needing no further organization. In theory, *amparos* are available to everyone; however, if the litigation involves a lot of money, then the protection afforded by *amparos* is not available to everyone.

Even though the problem is not new, in the past the government was better able to pressure the Supreme Court in the more high-profile cases.[10]

Big businesses have always been able to affect government actions. For many decades, big businesses concentrated their actions on the executive branch with considerable success. This was the case from 1954 to 1970, the years of the so-called alliances for profit. The governing principle was support for making money in exchange for noninterference in politics (Reynolds 1970).

In a democratic world, the playing field is much bigger. Businesses seeking to influence all actors in the policy process have had to create departments to handle relationships with the government, especially Congress, and also to influence public opinion. Some business people have actively sought the presidency, as was the case with Fox. Others have played an active role in elections by contributing money and other forms of support.

Given the absence of regulation on lobbying, the room for action is wide open, and special interests have achieved notable successes. For example, the so-called Televisa Law was apparently drawn up by Televisa's own lawyers and passed unanimously and almost without discussion in the lower chamber. Despite greater resistance in the Senate because some of the press had reacted to the contents of the law, in the end it was passed exactly as the representatives in the lower chamber had left it.

The big trade unions also have enormous resources at their disposal. A trade union's power structure is largely based on a series of privileges, established by law, which give trade unions considerable organizational capacity for defending their unions and their political interests. The most important rule in the game is the monopoly over workers' representation held by registered trade unions. Every worker has to belong to a trade union and no company may have a minority trade union. The trade unions registered on a collective labor contract are unlikely to be displaced when another group in the same company tries to demonstrate that it has become the majority, in part because the burden of proof rests with the side seeking to change the status quo. Many unions have no limit to the number of times leaders may be "elected" as leaders; thus, turnover in the leadership of trade unions is extremely slow.

Another mechanism whereby unions exert their power is union dues. By law, these dues are deducted at source from all workers in the system. Thus, the economic resources the trade unions have are enormous, even though precise data as to the exact amount are not available. Saldierna and Garduño (2005) calculate that union dues collected by the Sindicato Nacional de Trabajadores de la Educación

Nacional (SNTE) are at least Mex\$2 billion a year. This sum is vast, not only in terms of its size, but also because of the associated lack of accountability. Unions also have illegal sources of income from, for example, the sale of job placements, which seems to be widespread in the case of teachers. Such practices inevitably undermine service quality.

The accounts of trade unions are almost impossible to audit. Even though, in principle, workers can demand to see them, in practice, the system is controlled from the top. In theory, the government could seek to have them audited through a legal mandate. This has never happened, and whether the judicial system would accept such request is not clear. Apart from the problems of corruption associated with a lack of accountability, having these resources available to spend at their own discretion gives union leaders a great deal of power, not only inside the unions, but also outside them.

Trade unions' power extends far beyond the money they control. Some union leaders are members of Congress, who mostly belong to the PRI and gradually account for a larger proportion of the PRI's legislators. Union leaders are increasingly found also in the ranks of the PRD. The SNTE is an extreme case. Not only has it been gathering allies in all the other political parties, but also it now has a political party of its own, New Alliance. The party was registered in 2005 and fielded candidates in the 2006 elections, winning 4.6 percent of the votes for representatives under the proportional representation scheme and 4.0 percent of the vote for the Senate.

With a political party controlled by the SNTE plus SNTE members in various other political parties, it is hardly surprising that the SNTE has been able to legislate in its own favor. The most obvious example is the 2002 reform of the Education Law, which obliged the government to spend the equivalent of 8 percent of GDP on education in 2006. The number is absurd given the level of tax revenues collected in Mexico: 8 percent of GDP amounts to almost the total of income tax and value added tax combined. This ploy is just one more in the union's search for resources, and without the SNTE being bound by any reciprocal performance commitment in return. Note that the target was not met. Public spending on education in 2006 was only 5.4 percent of GDP, itself no small sum, because it accounted for 25 percent of the federal budget (Secretaría de Hacienda y Crédito Público 2006).

The trade unions also have other power mechanisms. For example, members of the PEMEX trade union sit on PEMEX's board of directors, and the SNTE controls the Ministry of Education's structure supervising the work of teachers. This situation effectively means that the administration of a school has little control over what happens in its school. In addition, the SNTE is directly responsible for administering many of the fringe benefits given to teachers, such as loans and housing credits, and it does so with blatant discretion in most cases.

The greatest source of union power lies in being able to control who works and who is dismissed. In most cases, trade unions must approve the hiring of unionized personnel. This approval not only leads to ample opportunities for corruption, but also builds networks of relatives and cronies loyal to the leadership. Studies of the issue that have actually measured the density of these networks do not appear to be available, but such networks certainly forge strong links between the leadership and the workers. In some trade unions, leadership positions have been handed down from father to son without the son needing to have had any work experience in the sector before his designation as leader.[11]

The trade unions can also protect their members from being fired. This benefit derives not only from a labor law and collective contracts that make it difficult to dismiss workers, but also even when a dismissal is justified, if the worker has the support of the trade union, because the authorities' pursuit of the case is extremely costly politically. The problem is particularly acute in the public sector, because under Constitution Article 123, Provision B, workers contracted by the government are afforded even greater protection. Under this provision, dismissing anyone is practically impossible, even when severance pay is provided.

Another source of union power is being able to assign members to special union duties. These members can be absent from their regular employment temporarily or permanently while on full pay and benefits. The trade unions do not provide information about the numbers involved, but the newspaper *Reforma* used the Freedom of Information Act to obtain information from the federal government. The number supplied was 17,843, of which 10,187 are employees of the Ministry of Public Education (Carrillo and Rivero 2006). The employees thus assigned carry out many types of duties for the unions or are simply free to attend to other affairs, including running their own businesses on officially paid time. This means that almost 18,000 workers, equivalent to the entire workforce employed by Volkswagen in Mexico, do nothing for their employers.

The trade unions have served their members well. Their average wages are higher than in the rest of the economy (see chapter 4 in this volume). Between 1998 and 2001, that is, during the end of Zedillo's term and the beginning of Fox's administration, a teacher's basic salary rose by 52.4 percent and fringe benefits rose by 9.1 percent. Indeed, since 1993, teachers' wages have risen more in real terms than GDP (World Bank 2006). Even though their salaries continue to be low compared with those of teachers in more developed countries, they are high in comparison with Mexico's per capita GDP. In general, despite the commonly held perception, primary school teachers in the public education system earn more than those in other professions with comparable levels of qualifications (López Acevedo 2004). In addition, they have much better working conditions: more vacation days, more flexible work schedules that allow them to hold second jobs, and greater job security. No wonder that selling job placements is a profitable business.

The 2005 national survey of beliefs, attitudes, and values revealed some interesting statistics. At the national level, 65 percent of the teachers surveyed earned more than six times the minimum wage. This contrasted sharply with the earnings of parents surveyed, of whom 75 percent earned between one and five times the minimum wage. Nevertheless, in response to whether they considered that an improvement in education quality depended on an improvement in teachers' salaries, 59 percent of teachers replied in the affirmative. Even though 72 percent of the teachers claimed that they were "barely satisfied or dissatisfied" with their salaries, 81 percent answered that if they had to make a choice of career again, they would enter the same profession (Fundación Este País 2005).

Clearly, the trade unions cannot simply be thought of as puppets in the service of the government or of other interests. There is no question that the unions are sustained by the money and lack of accountability the law allows them and that this has led to abuse by union leaders on many occasions. At the same time, the unions have earned themselves a solid power base in society because of the favorable working conditions they have negotiated for their members.

The most extreme case is that of the Sindicato Mexicano de Electricistas to which Luz y Fuerza del Centro workers belong. This is probably the most democratic and independent of the public sector workers' unions. It has also achieved the best working conditions for its members, including retirement pensions at a level not found in any developed country.[12]

Because public sector firms are not subject to competition and do not live off income earned from the market, they are in a position to perpetuate inefficient union agreements that continue to be paid for out of the public purse. This is very different from what happens in the manufacturing sector, where productivity has improved dramatically, even without reform to Mexico's burdensome Labor Law. In sectors open to competition, the trade unions are limited as to what they can demand. They understand what is at stake, and most have moderated their stance accordingly. Even a combative trade union such as that of Volkswagen of Mexico knows that the company can take its investment to Brazil or back to Germany.[13]

A few cases of sector collapse have resulted from the power of the trade unions and their resistance to any changes that might affect them. The Euzkadi firm's workers are an example: they chose to defend a legal contract that was so rigid that it killed off most of the tire sector. This has not been the norm, however, and private enterprises facing competition have had to adjust their labor practices, though at no small cost.

The Labor Law imposes many restrictions, but the biggest problems occur in sectors that face little competition or that cannot go bankrupt because they are subsidized by the government. Given the political clout of the trade unions, withdrawing subsidies that allow the firms to survive is difficult. Even when this appears to have been achieved, a trade union can always renege on its decision. Luz y Fuerza del Centro was already in the hands of liquidators when Salinas halted the process, and the government ended up absorbing the company's liabilities. This was apparently in compensation for a close relationship that had proved useful to his candidacy when the oil workers union withdrew its support.

Final Thoughts

How can Mexico build a political coalition that will break with the prevailing equilibrium that is obstructing greater growth and unduly favors those who have resources and organizational power? Democracy can serve to unite the public against the special interest groups and can propagate reforms beneficial to the majority in the medium term. This condition calls for strong leadership with a clear strategy for standing up to these well-organized groups and with solid information that would enable that leadership to justify its actions. It also calls for citizens ready to involve themselves in the public policy debate and to take a stand in defense of their own interests.

The 2006 electoral campaign emphasized the need to confront privilege, even though it focused mainly on the privileges enjoyed by business people and did not link its criticism to any project for building a more efficient economy. Indeed, putting the theme of privileges squarely at the center of the debate was one of the greatest triumphs of López Obrador, the PRD presidential candidate. This asset is one that could have been used to fuel the PRD's agenda for government, especially because President Felipe Calderón's government should also be interested in reforms favoring competition and reinforcing the government's regulatory capacity.

The economy cannot grow any faster if it has to carry the dead-weight of companies and other entities, whether public or private, that face little or no competition and that provide expensive, poor quality, or both services. The public's support is key in addressing this situation. A start can be made by revealing the privileges that such entities have managed to accumulate and hold on to and that have until now been immune to a regime that gives voice to the majority.

With regard to the business sectors, the current government has the best opportunity to effect change, because it is free to move toward the center without having to neglect its right wing. There is no danger of the PRD taking over the right, although the PRI might try. If the National Action Party were to produce a coherent agenda on the issue, the PRD could do little to oppose it. Opposition is unlikely from the PRI either, because of the cost in terms of internal coherence.

The first step would be to carry out a systematic comparison of the prices of certain goods and services in Mexico with those elsewhere. The same thing needs to happen with regulations. The fines and sanctions Mexico applies to those who collude to fix prices or who fail to pay taxes should be compared with what happens in other countries.

An outcry from the business community is inevitable, but the challenge for the government is to convince business people that giving them viability in the medium term requires limiting them in the short term through better regulation for all that is more in line with what pertains in other OECD countries. In many cases, this will simply imply reinforcing the government's ability to impose existing regulation, and having a government useful to business development as a whole usually implies not favoring any one business in particular. As economist Maynard Keynes used to say, capitalism needs to be saved from the capitalists.

This first step of a systematic comparison, although important, is no guarantee of success even if it led to legal reforms that would modernize Mexico's legal framework. Take the case of the 2004 reforms to the law governing the Instituto Mexicano del Seguro Social. The 2004 reform revealed how much pensions were costing the institution and proposed a legal reform to avoid continuing to finance the pensions of future institute workers from the premiums being paid by contributors, yet the legal mechanisms for obliging the Instituto Mexicano del Seguro Social to comply with this law are not clear.

Union privileges are one of the most entrenched inheritances left behind by the old regime. The PRI government was in no position to reveal the extent of these privileges, because the privileges were the product of the regime itself: the main beneficiaries were the PRI's most loyal allies.

Fox's government pursued a somewhat erratic strategy in relation to the main PRI organizations. In the end, however, Fox chose not to upset the applecart. Despite public revelation of the illegal diversion of PEMEX union funds to finance the campaign of the PRI presidential candidate Francisco Labastida (which came to be known as PEMEXgate), no trade union leader has gone to prison, and a cordial relationship between Fox's administration and the PEMEX trade union was maintained, at least in public, until the end of his administration.

Calderón's government is in a position to pursue a more consistent strategy, and a good start would be providing better information about the nature of the privileges and their implications. Unfortunately, the appointment of the SNTE leader's son-in-law as education undersecretary does not augur well in this regard, and it smacks of a reward to the trade union for its support prior to the elections. At the same time, given that the appointment sparked significant criticism in the press regarding union power, that criticism could now be turned to good use by seeking conditions in the administration of the school system that, without affecting teachers' income, could be tied to better compliance with their obligations. This, in turn, would result in an increase in quality and a reduction in the costs of the system. A process such as this would strengthen the bodies responsible for evaluation and make proactive use of international test results such as the Programme for International Student Assessment.[14]

The government will always be limited in its ability to confront the country's most powerful actors. What is really needed is to involve society by making people understand that they are the ones who are actually paying for these privileges. In the short term at least, this would be a win-win situation for the privileged and the citizens in their role as consumers: the more efficient a company becomes, the more the economy and the market will grow, and this situation is ultimately of benefit to all business people as well. As concerns the trade unions, the losses would be less easy to compensate, but there are areas (pensions, for example) where it would at least be possible to limit the cost to future employees, although not necessarily to the current workforce.

A party such as the National Action Party, with its more citizen-based origins than the corporate origins of the PRI and the PRD, should be able to capitalize on a movement that is more critical of the government, which, by having conceded so much to the trade unions, is providing poor quality services. Citizens must be persuaded to see themselves first and foremost as consumers of public services.

The small parties, such as the Alternative Social-Democrat and Peasant Laborer Party, that do not depend on any trade union in particular, could build themselves a following by producing informed criticism of the privileges. However, as the cost of organizing society is so high, even this party needed the help of more traditional sectors simply to achieve official registration as a political party, and the fight between the two internal factions could destroy the party.

A presidential leadership that provides information could be important too, but the information would have to be accompanied by a strategy for legislative reform that would level the playing field both politically and economically.

The first reform needed is better regulation of activities inherent to the decision-making process in Congress. Rules must govern how lobbyists operate and how to deal with conflicts of interest. A start must be made by limiting the outside professional duties legislators are allowed to undertake while in office.

In terms of the electoral and political system, the reform that would have the greatest impact would be reducing campaign costs and the cost overall of engaging in politics. This second reform has already been undertaken, but in such a way that its benefits will be limited. Although the purchase of advertising space in the media for political ends was prohibited, political parties will have a vast legally mandatory space in the electronic media to promote their proposals. So-called negative campaigns were banned, which will limit the information made available to citizens. No important reduction in the prerogatives of the political parties took place, and more limits to the creation of new parties were imposed. A new council for the Instituto Federal Electoral was elected, but its autonomy is likely to be more limited, and it will also be even more expensive, because it is now responsible for regulating and allocating spots in the electronic media. A third reform must be to limit the abuse of *amparos*. These cases not only flood the legal system, making the process expensive and slow, but also generate inequities between big and small actors and erode the government's capacity to impose the law. This will be a complicated reform and must not leave average citizens defenseless against the government, a situation they are already in today unless they have the resources to afford a good lawyer. The answer lies in adapting some of Mexico's practices to those in the developed world.

The legal profession will react whatever the change in this regard, and so will the wealthiest actors who have abused the system hitherto. However, given society's demand for justice, given how this device has been misused, and given Supreme Court judges with a more modern view on the subject, putting the issue onto the agenda should now be possible and some support from society can be expected.

Labor reform is one of the most complicated areas still to be tackled and is one that costs the country a great deal in terms of competitiveness. The challenge is to craft a reform that will credibly provide more possibilities for formal employment to a majority of Mexicans, but at the same time not take away vital union protection against employer abuse.

For companies in sectors subject to competition, the current law is not as costly as for companies in sectors not currently subject to competition, because they have more leverage with their trade unions. Thus, starting with a reform to make public companies as competitive as possible and then removing their subsidies makes sense. Revealing the exact cost of the services they provide and the cost of the current labor agreements could help eventual more rational use of the country's resources.

Beyond the evident political restrictions to an effort of this nature, this strategy will be easier to apply in public sector companies than in the central government itself, where services are usually provided free of charge. To generate support from society, which is the consumer of government services, the best approach would probably be to persuade consumers to demand more and better information about the performance of all public services. A fourth reform would be to strengthen the laws protecting consumers, who are currently poorly organized. Mexico has no sizable consumers' association. There is a Federal Procurator's Office for Consumers, but it is not always headed by effective prosecutors and the law does not give it enough teeth. In addition, the law does not allow groups of supposedly defrauded people to bring class action suits. Thus, to confront big companies, where consumers have few alternatives, the answer may be to pass a law that allows collective lawsuits.

Finally, and probably an area where there is the most to gain, reform is needed in the government's regulatory agencies, in particular, the Comisión Federal de Competencia. Even though it has more legal resources today than in the past because of the reforms of June 2006, the commission still has fewer teeth than many of its counterparts in other OECD countries. For example, a U.S. entrepreneur who is shown to have tried to manipulate prices faces the risk not only of paying a heavy fine, but also of going to prison.

All these proposed reforms will run up against opposition, because they will affect some powerful interests. However, if the required actions are not taken, the loser is the public as a whole, which, being badly organized and ill-informed, sees laws being passed that only affect people adversely, even though some of those laws may be disguised as being in the general interest.

Not to carry out the reforms would be to leave Mexico with an institutional framework that, by shielding broad sectors from competition, is debilitating the economy as a whole and, thereby, undermining the well-being of the average citizen. Attracting the vote of this average person by offering pro-competition policies that put consumers and tax-paying citizens at the center of the debate is one of the greatest challenges facing the current administration.

Notes

1. This does not mean that conditions in which it is possible to stimulate productive investment in barely competitive markets cannot exist. Examples are Mexico during the period of stabilizing development (1954–70), as well as the Republic of Korea. However, it is easy to end up trapped in the inefficiencies and profits such a model generates (Parente and Prescott 2000). The main beneficiaries of protectionist policies are industrialists and unions. When these actors acquire a lot of power, change becomes difficult and the original purpose of promoting development ends up being defeated by the very actors who at the beginning helped to propel movement in this direction.

2. The net income from foreign commerce in oil products in 2006 was US$27.6 billion, equivalent to 3.59 percent of GDP. Remittances totaled US$25.0 billion, equal to 3.26 percent of GDP (http://www.pemex.com; http://www.oecd.stat; Hernández 2007). This income forced the real exchange rate up in 2006, generating additional pressure on exporters of manufactured goods.

3. This can be shown by comparing students with similar socioeconomic backgrounds attending private and public schools and by comparing schools with similar infrastructure.

4. In some high-profile cases, the president simply had to tolerate the defiance, as when President Miguel de la Madrid (1982–88) was threatened by a Petróleos Mexicanos trade union leader. De la Madrid's successor finally put the leader in prison (de la Madrid Hurtado 2004).

5. The Televisa Law is a set of reforms to the laws governing radio, television, and telecommunications. It does not confront the current concentration of telecommunications concessions. The new law grants current concessionholders the remaining space in a frequency if it is digitalized, increases entry barriers, and facilitates the possibility for radio and television concessionholders to extend their services into other areas of communications. In addition, the Comisión Federal de Telecomunicaciones was not endowed with autonomy, but has remained under the control of the Ministry of Communications and Transport. Even worse, the commissioners who have

been selected have little experience in the field, including their recently appointed president, who was one of the main promoters of the law in the Senate.

6. As Weldon (1997) argues, during the Maximato period, 1928–34 (known by this name because former president Plutarco Elías Calles maintained control of the country as "El jefe máximo de la Revolución"), widespread control had already been established by the PRI's forerunner, but the country's president was weak, because party leadership was in the hands of Plutarco Elías Calles.

7. In public events headed by President Fox, sometimes secretaries of state taking part arrived late. This virtually never happened during PRI governments. Because he was afraid of seeming authoritarian, President Fox did not exert his authority even in relation to symbolic matters.

8. Despite the advantages of greater professionalization of top bureaucrats, the law has made the appointment of certain types of public officeholders more rigid than necessary and is still working suboptimally.

9. Even though private donations are restricted, there are ways of getting around that. For example, some campaign donations are made in kind (such as the use of transport) and are difficult to monitor.

10. This is what it did to avoid the *amparo* brought by the bankers after the bank expropriation and when it opted to apply a flat rate company profit tax that seemed to be neither proportional nor equitable.

11. This happened in the Sindicato Nacional de Trabajadores Mineros, Metalúrgicos y Similares, whose lifetime leader, Napoleón Gómez Sada, handed the post down to his son, Napoleón Gómez Urrutia, in 2001. Gómez Urrutia, who was educated at Oxford, had never worked in a mine, which should have disqualified him from occupying the post.

12. The secretary general of the trade union is 35 years old and has belonged to the union for 20 years. According to the collective labor contract, Article 64: "Any worker can request and obtain retirement provided he has completed twenty-five years of service and is fifty-five years old, or provided that he has completed thirty years of service regardless of age. By the same token, women workers can request and obtain retirement with 100% (a hundred per cent) of their basic salary, when they have completed twenty-five years of service regardless of age." Thus, in 10 years' time, the secretary general will be able to retire on his full salary, which each year includes a Christmas bonus equivalent to 50 days' pay (http://www.sme.org .mx/construccion_frame/UntitledFrameset-3.htm).

13. Legal contracts are more complicated in the sugar or mining industry, for example, where they oblige all companies in the sector to have the same conditions for their workers. Some of the more troubled sectors are in this legal situation.

14. The launch of the Alianza por la Calidad de la Educación in May 2008 is an attempt to make merit the basis of all hiring and promotion of teachers within the system and seems to go in the correct direction.

References

Acemoglu, Daron. 2003. "The Form of Property Rights: Oligarchic Versus Democratic Societies." Working Paper 10037, National Bureau of Economic Research, Cambridge, MA.

Acemoglu, Daron, Simon Johnson, and James A. Robinson. 2005. "Institutions as the Fundamental Cause of Long-Run Growth." In *Handbook of Economic Growth*, ed. Philippe Aghion and Steven Durlaf, vol. 1A, 385–472. Amsterdam: North-Holland.

Bank of France. 2005. *Productivité, compétitivité et globalisation, Novembre 2005*. Bank of France. http://www.banque-de-france.fr/fr/publications/seminaires/page5.htm.

Becerra, Ricardo, and José Woldenberg. 2000. *La mecánica del cambio político en México: Elecciones, partidos y reformas*. Mexico City: Cal y Arena.

Bizberg, Ilán. 1990. *Estado y sindicalismo en México*. Mexico City: El Colegio de México.

Camp, Roderic A. 1989. *Entrepreneurs and Politics in Twentieth-Century Mexico*. Oxford, U.K.: Oxford University Press.

Carrillo, Laura, and Arturo Rivero. 2006. "Ordeñan sindicatos al erario." *Reforma*, October 11, Primera.

Centeno, Miguel Angel. 1997. *Democracy within Reason: Technocratic Revolution in Mexico*. University Park, PA: Pennsylvania State University Press.

Cheibub, José Antonio. 2007. *Presidentialism, Parliamentarism, and Democracy*. Cambridge, U.K.: Cambridge University Press.

Cruz, Lilián. 2005. "Reducen las tarifas aéreas." *Reforma*, August 28, Negocios.

Cumings, Bruce. 1984. "The Origins and Development of the Northeast Asian Political Economy: Sectors, Product Cycles, and Political Consequences." *International Organization* 38 (1): 1–40.

De la Madrid Hurtado, Miguel. 2004. *Cambio de Rumbo*. Mexico City: Fondo de Cultura Económica.

Elizondo, Carlos. 2001a. *Impuestos, democracia y transparencia*. Serie Cultura de la Rendición de Cuentas. Auditoría Superior de la Federación 2. Mexico City: Cámara de Diputados.

———. 2001b. *La importancia de las reglas: Gobierno y empresarios después de la nacionalización de la banca*. Mexico City: Fondo de Cultura Económica.

Elizondo, Carlos, and Luis Manuel Perez de Acha. 2006. "Separación de poderes y garantías individuales: La Suprema Corte y los derechos de los contribuyentes." *Cuestiones Constitucionales* 14 (January–June): 91–130.

Engerman, Stanley L., and Kenneth L. Sokoloff. 2002. "Factor Endowments, Institutions, and Differential Paths of Growth among New World

Economies." Working Paper 0066, National Bureau of Economic Research, Cambridge, MA.

Fundación Este País. 2005. "Encuesta Nacional sobre Creencias Actitudes y Valores entre Maestros y Padres de Familia (Encrave)." *Este País* (169).

Garrido, Celso, and Cristina Puga. 1990. "Transformaciones recientes del empresariado mexicano." *Revista Mexicana de Sociología* 52 (2): 43–61.

González, Hilda Gabriela Enrique. 2006. "La Suprema Corte y el acceso desigual a la justicia: ¿A quién sirve el amparo en materia fiscal?" Ph.D. thesis, Instituto Tecnológico Autónomo de México.

Graham, David. R, Daniel P. Kaplan, and David S. Sibley. 1983. "Efficiency and Competition in the Airline Industry." *Bell Journal of Economics* 14 (1): 118–38.

Grediaga, Rocío, José Raúl Rodríguez, and Laura Elena Padilla. 2004. *Políticas públicas y cambios en la profesión académica en México en la última década.* Mexico City: Asociación Nacional de Universidades e Instituciones de Educación Superior and Universidad Autónoma Metropolitana.

Grupo Huatusco. 2004. "Por qué no crecemos?" *Huatusco I.* Mexico City.

———. 2006a. "Estado, mercado y crecimiento económico." *Grupo Huatusco* II. Mexico City.

———. 2006b. "La creación y consolidación de instituciones para el crecimiento económico de México." *Huatusco* III. Mexico City.

———. 2007. "Hacia una política de estado: Crecimiento con equidad." *Huatusco IV.* Mexico City.

———. 2008. "Condiciones y limitaciones de una reforma hacendaria en México." *Huatusco IV.* Mexico City.

Hernández, Alma. 2006a. "Detecta Pemex posibles ahorros." *Reforma,* December 29, Negocios.

———. 2006b. "Mantiene Pemex a ociosos." *Reforma,* December 28, p. 1.

Hernández, Erika. 2007. "Rompen Récord Remesas." *Reforma,* February 2, Primera.

Krussel, Per, and José Victor Rios-Rull. 2002. "Politico-Economic Transition." *Review of Economic Design* 7 (3): 309–29.

Lehoucq, Fabrice. 2006. *Why Is Structural Reform Stagnating in Mexico?* Mexico City: Centro de Investigación y Docencia Económicas.

López Acevedo, Gladys. 2004. "Teachers' Salaries and Professional Profile in Mexico." Working Paper 3394. World Bank, Washington, DC.

Maddison, Angus. 2003. *The World Economy: Historical Statistics.* Paris: Organisation for Economic Co-operation and Development.

Nickell, Stephen J. 1996. "Competition and Corporate Performance." *Journal of Political Economy* 104 (4): 724–46.

North, Douglas C., and Robert Paul Thomas. 1973. *The Rise of the Western World: A New Economic History.* Cambridge, U.K.: Cambridge University Press.

OECD (Organisation for Economic Co-operation and Development). 2004. *PISA: Learning for Tomorrow's World*. Paris: OECD.

———. 2005. *Estudios Económicos de la OCDE: México*. Paris: OECD.

———. 2006. *Main Science and Technology Indicators*, vol. 2006/1. Paris: OECD.

———. 2007a. *Economic Survey of Mexico*, vol. 2007, issue 18. Paris: OECD.

———. 2007b. *Getting It Right: OECD Perspective on Policy Challenges in Mexico*. Paris: OECD.

Parente, Stephen L., and Edward C. Prescott. 1999. "Monopoly Rights: A Barrier to Riches." *American Economic Review* 89 (5): 1216–33.

———. 2000. *Barriers to Riches*. Cambridge, MA: Massachusetts Institute of Technology Press.

Porter, Michael E., and Mariko Sakakibara. 2001. "Competing at Home to Win Abroad: Evidence from Japanese Industry." *Review of Economics and Statistics* 83 (2): 310–22.

Przeworski, Adam, Michael E. Álvarez, José Antonio Cheibub, and Fernando Limongi. 2000. *Democracy and Development: Political Institutions and Well-Being in the World, 1950–1990*. Cambridge, U.K.: Cambridge University Press.

Reynolds, Clark W. 1970. *The Mexican Economy, Twentieth Century: Structure and Growth*. New Haven, CT: Yale University Press.

Rivero, Arturo. 2006. "Consiguen trabajo gracias a 'palancas'." *Reforma*, December 27, Business section, p. 1.

Saldierna, Georgina, and Roberto Garduño. 2005. "Explotan SNTE y Gordillo $2 mil millones anuales al magisterio: Diputada del PRI." *La Jornada*, November 26, Política.

Scott, John. 2003. *Progresa: Contexto y Relevancia*. Mexico City: Centro de Investigación y Docencia Económicas.

Secretaría de Hacienda y Crédito Público. 2006. *Presupuesto de Egresos de la Federación para el Ejercicio Fiscal 2006*. Mexico City: Secretaría de Haciendia y Crédito Público. http://www.shcp.gob.mx/.

———. 2008. *Presupuesto de Egresos de la Federación para el Ejercicio Fiscal 2008*. Mexico City: Secretaría de Haciendia y Crédito Público. http://www.shcp.gob.mx/.

Van Wijnbergen, S., and A. J. Venables. 1993. *Trade Liberalization, Productivity, and Competition: The Mexican Experience*. London: Centre for Economic Performance.

Vernon, Raymond. 1971. *The Dilemma of Mexico's Development*. Baltimore, MD: Johns Hopkins University Press.

Wade, Robert. 1990. *Governing the Market*. Princeton, NJ: Princeton University Press.

Ware, Alan. 2001. "Divided Government in the United States." In *Divided Government in Comparative Perspective*, ed. Robert Elgie, 21–39. Oxford, U.K.: Oxford University Press.

Weldon, Jeffrey A. 1997. "The Political Sources of Presidencialismo in Mexico." In *Presidentialism and Democracy in Latin America*, ed. Scott Mainwaring and Matthew Soberg Shugart, 225–58. Cambridge, U.K.: Cambridge University Press.

World Bank. 2004. *Mexico Public Expenditure Review*. Washington, DC: World Bank.

———. 2006. *Mexico: Institutional and Governance Review*. Report 37293, MX. Washington, DC: World Bank.

PART III

Equity and Core Institutions in Mexico: Social Security, the Labor Market, and Banking

6

Social Security Reform in Mexico: For Whom?

Santiago Levy

Social security is a centerpiece of Mexico's social policy, thereby providing workers with access to health insurance; housing loans; day care centers; and retirement, disability, and work-risk pensions. However, because social security is mostly financed by wage-based contributions that are not fully valued by affiliated workers, it acts partly as a pure tax on salaried employment, which in Mexico is the only form of employment covered by social security. Firms and workers avoid this tax legally by shifting to activities with nonsalaried contractual relationships and to self-employment, and illegally by employing large-scale evasion. Thus, the labor force is divided into a formal sector with social security coverage and an informal sector without such coverage that consists of a legal segment (self-employment and nonsalaried employment) and an illegal segment (salaried employment with firms evading social security) (Levy 2008). The resulting overemployment in the informal sector has negative effects on productivity and growth.

Legal reforms have sought to improve the functioning of social security, two of which are discussed here. The first, in 1995, changed

I want to thank Isabel Guerrero and Michael Walton for useful comments, encouragement, and support. I also thank Rafael del Villar, Ernesto Estrada, and Eduardo Pérez Mota for useful discussions on pensions. The views expressed here are my own and the usual disclaimers apply.

retirement pensions from a defined benefit pay-as-you-go system to a defined contribution pre-funded scheme, with individual accounts administered by private financial firms known as retirement fund administrators (administradoras de fondos para el retiro, or AFORES). The second, in 2004, centered on reducing the costs of the special pension regime of the Instituto Mexicano del Seguro Social's (IMSS's) own workers so that social security contributions were channeled to provide services to affiliated workers and not diverted to pay for this special pension regime.

I use these two reforms to study the link between productivity and income or power concentration. The core hypothesis is that rent-seeking by groups associated with the provision of social security services—the AFORES in the administration of individual retirement accounts and the IMSS union in labor services directly provided to the IMSS—widens the pure tax component of social security contributions, thereby lowering productivity and gross domestic product (GDP). A subsidiary hypothesis is that when the lack of social security for informal workers is remedied through parallel social programs financed out of general revenues, the implicit subsidy to informal employment magnifies the efficiency losses derived from the pure tax on formal employment, further lowering aggregate labor productivity and GDP.

Background

Three features of Mexico's social security system deserve attention. First, article 123 of the Constitution separates workers into those employed in the private sector (referred to as segment A) and in the public sector (referred to as segment B). Different social security regimes and labor laws apply to workers in segments A and B: workers in A are governed by the Federal Labor Law and the Social Security Law, while workers in B are governed by the Labor Law for State Workers and the Law of the Institute of Social Security Services for State Workers (ISSSTE Law). In what follows, I focus on the social security system of workers in segment A and the institutions associated with it.

The second feature is that the Social Security and Federal Labor laws establish that social security is a right of salaried workers only and an obligation of firms only with respect to the salaried workers they hire. Other members of the labor force, such as the self-employed and workers who have nonsalaried relationships with firms, may voluntarily join the social security system, but they are not obliged to do so.

The third feature is that social security coverage involves a wide set of benefits, namely: (a) health insurance, (b) day care services, (c) life insurance, (d) disability pensions, (e) work-risk pensions, (f) sports and cultural facilities, (g) retirement pensions, and (i) housing loans.

The first six of these benefits fall under the mandate of the IMSS. Retirement pensions take the form of a defined contribution individual accounts system administered by private AFORES regulated by the Comisión Nacional del Sistema del Ahorro para el Retiro (National Commission for the Pension System, CONSAR). Finally, the Instituto del Fondo Nacional para la Vivienda de los Trabajadores (INFONAVIT) administers housing loans. These three agencies form the core of Mexico's social security institutions for segment A workers. They have a similar governance structure with boards composed of government officials and worker and firm representatives. This tripartite composition reflects the tripartite source of the funds collected to finance social security, as well as the political conceptualization of social security as a shared responsibility between workers, firms, and the government.

Despite similarities in their legal structure, the IMSS, CONSAR, and INFONAVIT differ in critical ways. Perhaps the most important is that the IMSS, in addition to acting as a social insurance agency, is, for the most part, the main provider of the services under its mandate, particularly health services.[1] The IMSS directly operates health services for its affiliated workers and their families, making it the largest single provider of medical services in Mexico and probably one of the largest in the world. As a result, the IMSS has more than 370,000 employees, making it the largest single employer in Mexico. IMSS workers are organized in the Sindicato Nacional de Trabajadores del Seguro Social (SNTSS), the second largest union in Mexico.[2] By contrast, the other two entities serve a regulatory or financial role, but INFONAVIT does not build housing and CONSAR does not operate AFORES.

As noted earlier, coverage of social security follows the distribution of the labor force between public and private sector workers, and for the latter, between salaried and nonsalaried workers. If we associate coverage of social security with "formality" and lack of coverage with "informality," then the labor force is divided into a formal sector and an informal sector, with formal sector workers receiving social security coverage (segment A by means of the IMSS and segment "B" by means of the ISSSTE), and informal sector workers not receiving such coverage. In principle, this distinction should coincide with the distinction between salaried and nonsalaried workers, but this is not the case because of large-scale evasion of social security in segment A: many salaried workers without social security add to informal employment levels. Table 6.1 breaks down the labor force by social security coverage.

Four points made by the table are relevant. First, social security covers less than 40 percent of the labor force. Second, excluding segment B, the labor force consists of some 40.5 million workers, of whom only 13.8 million (34 percent) have social security, a telling situation more than 60 years after the creation of the IMSS. Third, more than half of formal workers earn three times the minimum wage or less a month.[3] This distinction cannot be made for all informal workers, because information is lacking on the earnings of informal (illegal) salaried workers, but if one considers only nonsalaried informal workers, 85 percent earn three times the minimum wage or less a month. All in all, at least 24 million workers, more than half the labor force, receive low wages. Finally, evasion of social security is rampant, equal to 36 percent of salaried workers in segment A.

Workers' mobility between sectors takes place on a large scale, and this mobility is greater at lower wage levels. Levy (2006) describes an exercise where the length of stay in the formal sector of 9 million workers, measured by affiliation with the IMSS, was followed from July 1997, when the current Social Security Law came into effect, to July 2005.[4] The key results are that only 11.6 percent of low-wage workers were enrolled with the IMSS for the entire nine-year period, as opposed to 42.4 percent of high-wage workers.

Table 6.1 Labor Force and Social Security Coverage, 2005

Labor force	Number (thousands of workers)	Share (percent)
Formal	17,159	39.1
ISSSTE (B)[a]	3,327	7.6
IMSS (A)	13,831	31.5
Earning more than 3 times the minimum wage	6,007	13.7
Earning 3 times the minimum wage or less	7,824	17.8
Informal	26,707	60.9
Nonsalaried earning more than 3 times the minimum wage	2,860	6.5
Nonsalaried earning 3 times the minimum wage or less	16,147	36.8
Salaried (evasion)	7,699	17.6
Total	*43,866*	*100.0*

Source: Levy (2006).

a. Includes state-level social security institutions.

At the other end, of all the low-wage workers who were enrolled in the IMSS in 1997, almost 18 percent were in the formal sector for one of the nine years, in contrast with 7.6 percent of high-wage workers. All in all, the average low-wage worker who was enrolled in the IMSS in 1997 had social security coverage for only 4.3 of the 9.0 years during which he or she could have been covered, or 48 percent of the time. The corresponding average for high-wage workers was 6.5 years, or 72 percent of the time.

More generally, workers have spells of formality with social security coverage and spells of informality without it, with these transitions being more frequent the lower the worker's wage.[5] There appear to be no substantive barriers preventing workers from entering formality and gaining access to social security.[6] Thus, the formal-informal dichotomy is a characterization of the legal status of workers at a point in time, but not a permanent separation of individual workers into two mutually exclusive subsets. Furthermore, the dichotomy is less useful the lower workers' wages are. For low-wage workers, the problem is not accessing a formal sector job with social security, but rather that for a variety of reasons their participation in social security is erratic.

Transitions between formality and informality raise fundamental questions about Mexico's social security system. Consider retirement pensions, for instance. If the patterns of mobility observed during 1997–2005 continue, the average low-wage worker will have to work 50 years to qualify for a minimum pension (because the law requires at least 25 years of contributions to qualify). Such workers will be forced to save for retirement only during the formal half of their working lives. During the informal half, they might save for retirement, and they might do so in their AFORE when they are forced to save during their formal employment, but then again they might not do so, or might do so in an instrument other than their AFORE. Similar observations apply to health benefits and work-risk coverage. If low-wage workers are ill during their formal employment, they will access IMSS health services, but not if this illness occurs during their informal employment. The same is true of an accident at work. Depending on when this health problem occurs, they may or may not have a work-risk pension or access to rehabilitation services.

I do not pursue this issue here, but it is, nonetheless, relevant for three reasons: (a) because it signals that social security is not working well, particularly for low-income workers; (b) because under these circumstances, the economy incurs important efficiency losses as the productivity of labor and capital falls; and (c) because there are important equity implications—the costs of the malfunctioning system are not absorbed by firms and workers in the formal sector only, who in principle are the beneficiaries of the system, but are spread out to informal workers also.

Equity and Efficiency Effects of Social Security

This section summarizes a framework to identify the equity and efficiency effects of social security (Levy 2008). The simplest case occurs when the total labor force, L, is divided into salaried (formal) and nonsalaried (informal) employment, with and without social security coverage, respectively. From table 6.1, L consists of approximately 40.5 million workers (excluding segment B), 13.8 million formal and 26.7 informal. In parallel, firms are divided along formal and informal lines, respectively hiring salaried and nonsalaried workers.

Let T_f be the monetary costs of social security benefits and w_f the formal sector wage so that formal firms' cost of hiring one worker with social security coverage is given by $(w_f + T_f)$. Table 6.2 shows the components of T_f for a worker earning twice the minimum wage.

Each month the worker gets Mex\$2,789, while the firm pays Mex\$3,611. The worker is then entitled to receive health and day care services from the IMSS, is covered by a disability and work-risk pension, and has Mex\$175 deposited in his or her AFORE account for retirement and Mex\$139 in his or her INFONAVIT housing loan account.[7] Social security contributions account for 30 percent of the wage.

Note that benefits are bundled together. Workers cannot choose to forego a particular benefit, such as the housing fund, saving for retirement, or day care services, because of their individual preferences. The law obliges them to participate in all of them. Similarly,

Table 6.2 Wages and Social Security Costs for a Worker Earning Twice the Minimum Wage, 2006

Item	2006 Mex\$
Monthly wage (w_f)	2,788.80
Cost of T_f	822.18
Health insurance	341.10
Work-risk pension	72.48
Disability pension, life insurance	66.24
Retirement pension	175.03
Day care, sports, and cultural services	27.89
Housing	139.44
Total labor cost ($w_f + T_f$)	3,610.98

Source: Author's calculations based on current legislation.

formal firms employing salaried workers must also pay for all the components of social security. Formal firms have a demand for labor, D_f, and hire workers up to the point where their marginal product, MPL_f, equals their cost to the firm ($w_f + T_f$). Note that participating in social security implies that workers' productivity must be 30 percent higher than their wage if they are to be hired by a formal firm.

For various reasons, formal workers might not attach a value to social security benefits equivalent to their costs; that is, they might not consider that the Mex$822 that they are getting in benefits are worth Mex$822 to them. Consider, for example, a worker living in a small urban area where the IMSS has few medical facilities. The worker expects medical care in return for the Mex$341, but if the facilities are of low quality (or nonexistent), the lines are long, the equipment is old, and the availability of some medicines is unreliable, that worker's view about paying for the medical care benefit might change. Various reasons account for low-quality services, but certainly one of them is that the IMSS uses Mex$55 of the Mex$341 contribution to pay for the special pension regime of its own workers and only Mex$286 to cover the salaries of doctors and nurses, medicines, and equipment.[8]

Or consider agricultural workers who, for reasons associated with the seasonality of production, are in salaried employment for only half of the year and would, therefore, have to be employed for 50 years to receive a minimum retirement pension. Or consider the value of the AFORES account for the approximately 350,000 workers who migrate abroad each year. Many of these workers might prefer their Mex$175 in cash today, perhaps to pay for migration costs, than a retirement pension in the distant future that they might never enjoy because they may not retire in Mexico.

Yet another case might be that of a married worker whose spouse is already covered by social security. Because the wife's or husband's health insurance already covers the other spouse, the marginal benefit of the Mex$341 for health coverage is zero.

Or, finally, consider the case of workers who have the opportunity to save in a financial instrument or a productive project with real rates of return of 5 percent.[9] This in contrast to the average annual rate of return that they received in their AFORE over the past nine years and that, net of AFORE charges, has been less than 1 percent.

Let $\beta_f \in [0, 1]$ be the valuation coefficient that workers attach to social security benefits, so that their utility from a formal job is ($w_f + \beta_f T_f$). Clearly, if workers value social security fully, so that $\beta_f = 1$, formal firms' labor costs equal formal workers' utility. Conversely, if workers do not fully value the benefits of social security, so that $\beta_f < 1$, there is a difference between what firms pay and what workers receive. This difference is equal to $(1 - \beta_f)$ T_f and is exactly equivalent to a tax on formal employment (not on labor).

The informal sector consists of the self-employed and firms with a demand for nonsalaried labor D_i hiring L_i workers, with the important difference that no social security costs are involved. Thus, if w_i is the informal wage, these firms hire workers up until the point at which the MPL_i is equal to w_i. In other words, in the informal sector, workers' productivity does not need to be 30 percent higher than their wage for them to be hired. Of course, informal workers know that they will receive only w_i as their pay and will not have access to social security: no IMSS health coverage, no AFORE, and no INFONAVIT housing loan. How much this matters to them depends on what these benefits really mean to them and the alternatives that are available to them.

Figure 6.1 provides a simple representation of the equilibrium distribution of the labor force L between formal employment L_f and informal employment L_i, with the demand for labor D_f drawn from the left-hand side of the graph and the demand for informal labor D_i drawn from the right-hand side, in the standard two-sector general equilibrium setup. Consider first the case where social security is fully valued, so that $\beta_f = 1$. In this case, the equilibrium is at point A with L_f^* workers employed in the formal sector

Figure 6.1 Social Security with a Formal and an Informal Sector

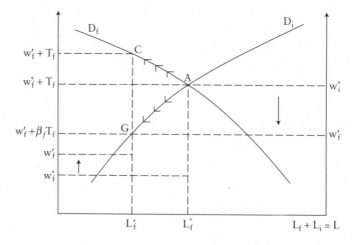

Source: Author.

with social security coverage, and L_i^*—not drawn, but equal to $(L - L_f^*)$—workers employed in the informal sector without social security coverage. Workers in the informal sector receive a wage of w_i^*, while workers in the formal sector get w_f^*. However, when the value of the social security benefits received by formal workers is considered, total utility is equalized across sectors.

This figure presents three messages. First, the MPL in the formal sector, $(w_f^* + T_f)$, is equal to the MPL in the informal sector, w_i^*, so that the allocation of labor is efficient: there is no possibility of increasing the country's GDP by reallocating workers from one sector to the other. So the first message is that a well-functioning social security system, interpreted here as $\beta_f = 1$, allows maximizing the productivity of labor in the economy and workers' wages.

The second message is that social security contributions are fully paid for by formal workers.[10] This is important. The Social Security Law states that workers, and firms must both contribute to social security, but this contribution is just a legal formality. An adjustment process in response to this law takes place in the labor market, and this process involves a reduction of wages in the formal sector, so that firms save in wages what they pay in social security contributions. In other words, social security changed only the composition of formal workers' consumption: before social security, they could freely dispose of their wage w_i^* on whatever bundle of goods they chose. With social security, they can dispose freely only of their wage w_f^*. In addition, these workers now get health insurance provided by the IMSS, are saving part of their income in an AFORE, and so on— all at a cost of T_f. However, because workers value their health insurance with the IMSS, their individual savings accounts with their AFORES, and their other benefits at exactly T_f, the sum of their freely disposed wage w_f^* and their social security benefits valued at T_f are the same to them as working in the informal sector and earning a higher wage of w_i^*, but with no social security benefits. Thus, the second message is that a well-functioning social security system is not redistributive in the sense of lowering formal firms' profits to increase formal sector workers' wages, but it does force workers to consume a bundle of goods that is important to their welfare (at least from the government's point of view).

The third message is that when social security works well, there is no change in the informal sector. Informal employment is the same with or without social security, as is the output of informal firms. Evidently, informality in the sense of lack of social security coverage is inevitable in a legal framework that excludes nonsalaried workers from the obligations of social security. In any economy, there are many valid reasons for nonsalaried employment: because firms and workers find that engaging in such relationships is profitable for risk-sharing or effort-eliciting reasons, and also because many workers might find that working on their own is profitable because they have entrepreneurial abilities or because they own some productive assets such as land. Informality in this context is as efficient as formality, except that informal workers consume a different bundle of goods than formal workers.

These three messages change in significant ways when social security is not fully valued. Note that when $\beta_f < 1$, then $(w_f^* + T_f) < w_i^*$, so that workers in the formal sector are less well-off than those in the informal sector. This induces some workers to move out of the formal sector, with formal sector employment falling from L_f^* to L_f' and, therefore, informal employment increasing (figure 6.1), but with fewer workers in the formal sector, the formal wage inevitably increases from w_f^* to w_f'. A key point here, however, is that formal firms still have to incorporate the full amount of social security contributions, T_f, into their labor costs regardless of whether workers value them fully or not, thus inevitably, their labor costs increase. This induces formal firms to move from point A to point C, where MPL_f is equal to $(w_f' + T_f)$. At the same time, if more workers are now in the informal sector, they can be employed only if their wages fall from w_i^* to w_i'. This allows informal sector firms to increase their employment from point A to point G, where $MPL_i = w_i'$. Note that at wages w_f' and w_i' workers are indifferent between formal and informal employment because $(w_f' + \beta_f T_f) = w_i'$.

Consider the first message noted earlier. The productivity of formal sector workers is $(w_f' + T_f)$, while that of informal workers is w_i'. As w_f and w_i move in opposite directions, formal workers are more productive than informal workers, but this is not because they are more educated or because of a barrier to entry into formal employment. The differences in productivity between similar workers are caused by an undervalued social security system. Note also that as formal sector firms face higher labor costs, they are less competitive than when social security was fully valued, which is why they employ fewer workers and their output is lower.

Turning to message two, because $(w_f^* + T_f) > (w_f' + \beta_f T_f)$, formal workers are not as well-off as before, and because $w_i^* > w_i'$, informal workers are also not as well-off as before. Thus, the fact that social security does not work well hurts all workers, formal and informal. In turn, because the formal sector's output is lower and its labor costs are higher, formal firms' profits are reduced. Yet this is not because profits were redistributed to wages, because workers are also worse off. It is because $\beta_f < 1$ acts like a tax on wages and profits in the formal sector. At the same time, fewer workers are covered by social security given the growth in informal employment.

Considering message three, informal employment without social security coverage results from a legal design that ex ante excludes nonsalaried workers from social security coverage and from a social security system that does not work well. The result is not surprising: if firms and workers are being forced to pay for something but they are receiving less than what they paid for, they will turn to informality. The fall in gross domestic product (GDP) as a byproduct of their behavior is something that they are probably unaware of and may not care about.

As $\beta_f \to 0$, incentives for firms and workers to evade social security increase. This phenomenon is widespread. Evasion by workers is mirrored by evasion by firms, but because the probability of being fined by the IMSS increases with the number of unregistered workers, evasion is mostly concentrated among small and micro firms.[11] Thus, in addition to reducing the coverage of social security, evasion also affects firms' size. Some firms will find that staying small and informal, as opposed to being larger and formal, is profitable, but this reduces their chances of exploiting economies of scale, accessing formal sources of credit, innovating, and investing in training their workers. Even though this behavior is clearly the result of many factors, a large implicit tax on salaried employment is one of them, particularly for firms where labor costs are a large share of total costs. Although not part of the foregoing discussion, the productivity costs of an undervalued social security system must also include the costs associated with a large number of stagnant firms that do not innovate, invest in training their workers, or exploit economies of scale.

The next two sections focus on some of the reasons why two central components of social security—retirement pensions and health services—reduce the performance of Mexico's social security system. Note that I do not argue that the only problems with social security are in these two areas or that the problems in these two areas are caused only by the factors examined. This is not the case. On the one hand, a revision of the functioning of INFONAVIT, of day care services, and of other components of social security would show similar problems. On the other hand, the problems facing retirement pensions and health services have multiple causes.[12] Nevertheless, the factors identified in the following sections are among some of these causes, and these factors are associated with large rents or other concentrations of power or control by two key groups involved in the administration and provision of retirement pensions and health services.

The 1995 Pension Reform

In December 1995, Congress approved the new Social Security Law, whose main feature was the replacement of a defined benefit pay-as-you-go retirement pension regime by a defined contribution pre-funded regime.

Many reasons induced the government to effect this change, including the three given here. First, given Mexico's demographic transition, the IMSS would be unable to cover the pensions of workers retiring by the end of the 1990s unless contribution rates were increased by more than 14 percent of wages, particularly as the IMSS had not created any financial reserves. Indeed, in 1995, estimates indicated that in the coming years the rate of growth of pensioners would be double the rate of growth of active workers. Second, the vertically integrated nature of the IMSS as a provider of health services and retirement pensions had implied that, in practice, contributions for retirement pensions were being invested in health infrastructure. Third, the 1994–95 economic crisis was associated with a low national savings rate, and the government thought that a pre-funded scheme would help increase aggregate savings, accompanied as it was by budget cuts to pay for the costs of the transition generation.

An important operational characteristic of the new retirement pension regime was that workers' retirement savings would be deposited in individual accounts administered by private financial intermediaries, AFORES. A new agency (CONSAR) was created to regulate the latter. As of July 1, 1997, when this new scheme came into effect, the IMSS would no longer be responsible for workers' retirement pensions.

It is important to separate two features of the 1995 reform that are usually lumped together: a pre-funded defined contribution pension scheme on the one hand, and administration of workers' contributions in individual accounts by private financial firms on the other. A pre-funded defined contribution scheme with individual accounts could be administered by a public agency (not necessarily the IMSS) or by a public–private entity. The choice is not so much associated with macroeconomic considerations as it is with agency and political economy issues. Who can manage the funds with the best risk–reward combination? What institutional arrangement avoids the potential deviation of funds to other uses? The 1995 reform tried to solve these problems by making workers the owners of the funds in the accounts and by having private firms manage the accounts. Clearly, however, many other combinations are possible while keeping the pre-funded nature of the regime and its positive effects on aggregate savings and the country's financial system.

The 1995 law established a transition regime for all workers affiliated with the IMSS up to June 30, 1997. Although these workers, referred to as the transition generation, would have individual accounts with an AFORE, they would retain the option of retiring under the provisions of the 1973 Social Security Law. If they did so, savings accumulated in their AFORE account would be transferred to the federal government, which, in turn, would pay for their pensions out of general revenues. If they chose instead to retire on the basis of the 1995 law, savings accumulated in their AFORE account would be used to purchase an annuity at the time of retirement, just as for workers enrolled after July 1997, referred to as the new generation. That is, the difference between the transition and the new generation was that the former could choose between the pay-as-you-go defined benefit scheme of the 1973 law or the pre-funded defined contribution scheme of the 1995 law, while the latter were obligated to retire under the provisions of the 1995 law.

Savings channeled to an AFORE account derive from two sources: from workers' and firms' wage-based contributions, equivalent to 6.5 percent of the wage, and from a new government subsidy of equal amount for all workers, known as the social subsidy and paid for out of general tax revenues. This social subsidy is set at 5.5 percent of the 1997 minimum wage indexed to the consumer price index and is approximately equivalent to Mex\$1,030 (2006 pesos) a year (about US\$94). When the uniform social subsidy is added to the wage-based contribution by firms and workers, the average contribution to the AFORE account is 8.4 percent of the wage. In addition, there is a contribution of 5 percent of the wage for INFONAVIT, which is also deposited in the AFORE account. This implies that for those workers who do not get a housing loan (particularly low-wage workers), the savings rate is around 13.4 percent of the wage, 11.5 percent out of wages (6.5 percent + 5 percent), and 1.9 percent equivalent from the social subsidy.

The social subsidy has two purposes. The first is to incorporate a redistributive component to retirement pensions, because it is proportionately larger for lower-wage workers. The second is to increase the amounts accumulated in workers' AFORE accounts so that all can aspire to a pension equivalent to at least the minimum wage. This charge, in turn, would ensure that no additional fiscal contingencies would arise from the new scheme beyond the costs of the pensions of the transition generation under the 1973 law, because a government guarantee of a minimum pension equivalent to the minimum wage was another feature of the 1995 law.

An assessment of the 1995 reform must incorporate at least two dimensions. The first is the macroeconomic dimensions associated with its effects on aggregate national savings and with the potential of the AFORES to deepen and widen Mexico's financial sector by facilitating longer-term investments through a stable supply of financial savings with a long-term horizon. The second is the microeconomic dimensions associated with the reform's effects on workers' pensions, the AFORES' profits, the incentives to save, and the contribution of forced retirement savings to workers' overall valuation of formality and social security coverage. CONSAR's role as a regulatory agency encompasses these two dimensions: on the one hand, the regulation of the investment regime of the AFORES (composition of the portfolio, risk levels, time profile of investments, and the like); on the other hand, the regulation of the industrial organization aspects of the industry (entry of new AFORES, information to workers, rules for changing workers' accounts from one AFORE to another, and commission levels). The remainder of this section focuses on the second dimension, thereby providing only a partial assessment.

AFORES' Profits and Workers' Valuation of Retirement Savings

By definition, any system of forced savings imposes costs on workers to the extent that the composition of their consumption between the present and the future is altered contrary to their preferences. Many governments mandate that workers save for retirements as part of their social security systems to preclude potentially myopic behavior by workers, free-riding by some—or for other reasons not explored here. In the absence of cross-subsidies between workers and of external subsidies, a scheme in which forced savings occur in individual accounts has potentially larger benefits for workers, because their savings efforts are fully reflected in their future pensions. Furthermore, their individual accounts follow them from their entry into to their exit from the labor force. Contributions and benefits are, in principle, brought closer together.

For these reasons, a reasonable supposition is that if workers are forced to save, and if per worker subsidies are the same for any system of forced saving, workers will prefer individual retirement accounts. This judgment, however, needs to be modified by the net risk-adjusted rate of return on workers' individual accounts resulting from the interplay between the gross rate of return on the portfolio invested on their behalf by their AFORES and the commissions AFORES charge to manage their accounts. Thus, from workers' point of view, the superiority of individual accounts managed by private firms over an alternative scheme of forced savings is not absolute.

The 1995 reform relied on competition between AFORES to bring commissions in line with AFORES' administrative costs, in principle maximizing the benefits of the new scheme for workers. Implicit in this mechanism were three critical assumptions: (a) that the regulatory regime of the AFORES would be conducive to intense competition between them, (b) that workers would have access to and be able to understand the information needed to make a rational choice among AFORES, and (c) that workers would have the incentives to make choices compatible with a competitive outcome. That is, the 1995 reform implicitly assumed that a market for forced retirement savings could be created, as well as that under proper regulation, this market could produce a competitive outcome, with AFORES' commissions basically reflecting AFORES' marginal costs. Nine years after the reform, however, these three critical assumptions have clearly not been a reasonable approximation to the nature of the industry, at least so far. To the contrary, what has been observed to date are net rates of return to workers that have been substantially below expectations and, in parallel, substantial rents accruing to the AFORES.

Table 6.3 compares AFORES' profits (approximated by their earnings before income taxes, depreciation, and amortization) and AFORES' income from commissions with government subsidies to

Table 6.3 AFORE's Profits, Commissions, and Subsidies, 1998–2005

(Mex$ millions)

Year	Profits (earning before income taxes, depreciation, and amortization)	Income from commissions	Pension subsidies (social subsidy)
1998	1,283	4,778	5,297
1999	3,083	6,958	7,201
2000	3,868	8,779	8,343
2001	5,175	10,390	9,798
2002	6,160	10,960	9,984
2003	7,240	12,173	8,778
2004	6,996	13,119	11,081
2005	6,070	13,726	11,947

Source: Pension subsidies: Ministry of Finance and Public Credit data; profits and income from commissions: http://www.consar.gob.mx/estadisticas/index.shtml.

Note: Data for 1997 are not provided, because the reform operated for only six months of that year.

Table 6.4 Real Annualized Net Rates of Return, 1997–2005 (percent)

Wage level	2	3	5	7
	Contribution density			
AFORE	47%	61%	77%	79%
Santander	0.8	0.5	0.2	0.1
Banco Bilbao Viscaya	1.1	0.8	0.5	0.3
Grupo Nacional Provincial	1.2	0.9	0.6	0.5
ING	1.3	1.0	0.7	0.5
Banamex	1.5	1.2	0.9	0.8
Inbursa	2.1	2.1	2.1	2.1

Source: Author's calculations based on http://www.consar.gob.mx.

Note: The wage level is measured in multiples of the minimum wage. Contribution density measures the share of time that a worker contributes to an AFORE.

workers' AFORE accounts (the social subsidy) during 1998–2005. For six of the eight years, AFORES' incomes from commissions have exceeded government subsidies for workers' retirement pensions. For the period as a whole, AFORES' income was 1.1 times the social subsidy. The implication is simple but powerful: since the start of the 1995 reform through 2005, AFORES' commissions have absorbed the full amount of government subsidies to workers' retirement savings. Indeed, their commissions have exceeded government subsidies by 10 percent, meaning that the AFORES have also absorbed part of workers' and firms' contributions into the system.

Table 6.4 presents the annualized real rates of return to workers' savings net of commissions during 1997–2005 for six AFORES that jointly represent 70 percent of all accounts (with the first five listed accounting for 50 percent). These rates of return differ between AFORES and wage levels for the following reasons. First, rates of return on AFORES' investment portfolios differ as a result of variations in investment strategies across AFORES. Second, the composition of commissions differs between AFORES.[13] Third, the variations in the composition of commissions have a different incidence depending on workers' wage levels: although the social subsidy is the same for all wage levels, the flow commission is not charged on this component of the resources channeled to the account, and this component is relatively more important for lower-wage workers.

The results are striking. The simple average of these rates of return over the period is less than 1 percent.[14] The rates of return are comparable to what workers would get in an ordinary savings account at a bank, except that workers cannot make withdrawals from their AFORES account until they have reached retirement age and that their

AFORES accounts cannot serve as collateral for a loan, although they could make withdrawals from ordinary savings accounts at any time and could use such savings as collateral.

These results provide a measure of the costs that workers incur not because they save, but because they are forced to do so in an AFORE. Consider, for example, a worker who saved Mex$100 each year for the past eight years. If that worker had done so in a savings account with a rate of return of 3.5 percent, at the end of the eighth year, he or she would have Mex$936. If the worker had instead been forced to save in an AFORE with a rate of return of 0.9 percent, he or she would have Mex$833, a difference of Mex$103 or 12 percent in just eight years. Depending on the length of the worker's working life, such differences in rates of return, if maintained in the future, could account for a pension that is 30 percent lower than it might have been.

The other side of the net rates of return to workers' savings are AFORES' profits, which have been extremely large. A recent official opinion by Mexico's Comisión Federal de Competencia (Federal Competition Commission) (2006) provides evidence of monopoly rents. In 2005, AFORES' revenues as a proportion of administered funds were 2.1 times higher in Mexico than in comparable Latin American countries. The commission also notes that rates of return on equity for the AFORES are high from any perspective and that they are not accompanied by any corresponding value to workers.

Focusing only on the industrial organization issues of the 1995 reform, one can conclude that the system of channeling workers' retirement savings to private administrators has so far generated large profits for the AFORES and low real rates of returns to workers' savings, government subsidies notwithstanding. Aside from the obvious effects on inequality, this contributes to workers' undervaluation of social security insofar as its savings for retirement component has unnecessarily high costs, and this hurts efficiency and lowers aggregate labor productivity.

More Competition May Not Be Enough

In the past few years, legal reforms and regulatory changes by CONSAR have increased competition and reduced AFORES' commissions. These measures have facilitated workers' shifts from one AFORE to another, have increased access to information, have reduced barriers to the entry of new AFORES, and have reduced the system's operating costs. As a result, entry has occurred; workers' shifts between AFORES have increased; and commissions have fallen, particularly in the higher-cost AFORES. The evidence shows that CONSAR has used its regulatory powers to steer the industry in the direction of more competition. As competition intensifies, lower commissions will imply lower AFORE rents and higher net rates of return on workers' savings in the future, although little can be done about the rents realized in the past eight years. Note, however, that lower monopoly rents need not imply a one-to-one reduction in commissions and higher pensions, because AFORES' operating costs will increase as they devote more resources to marketing, sales personnel, and the like in the context of a more competitive market.

Whether measures that only enhance competition will be sufficient to bring commissions in line with marginal costs, assuming more of these measures can be legislated and enforced, is an open question. Even if there are no barriers to entry and workers have full information—the hallmarks of a competitive market—one must ask whether the design features of the 1995 reform are sufficient to produce a competitive outcome in a reasonably short time period given the nine years that have already elapsed since the reform took effect, or whether these features will make such an outcome difficult to attain. This is important, because if the latter is the case, changes to the design of the system may be required for the 1995 pension reform to fully achieve its objectives in parallel with the promotion of more competition.

A discussion of these issues is beyond the scope of this chapter, but four remarks are pertinent. First, for many workers of the transition generation, the option of retiring under the 1973 law implies that AFORES' commissions are not very relevant. Under almost any scenario, but particularly given the rates of return observed over the past eight years, the 1973 pension will dominate the 1995 pension, and for these workers, competition or collusion between AFORES is not an issue. In other words, an important segment of the demand side of the market is price insensitive.[15]

Second, the same occurs with workers whose savings will be insufficient to reach the guaranteed minimum pension. In both this and the first case, the government bears the costs of AFORES' high commissions, because pensions will be paid out of general tax revenues (with the accumulated savings in the AFORES accounts devolved to the government).[16] This is consistent with fully rational workers acting with perfect information. Contrary to one of the implicit assumptions of the 1995 reform, these workers have no incentives to choose rationally among AFORES, because they are rationally choosing a better alternative.[17]

Third, the nature of the demand for the "product" needs to be looked at, because all workers are obligated to purchase it. Consumer choice in this context is restricted to the administrator of funds, the product of which workers will consume 20 or 30 years hence. Given this, and the complex structure of commissions, more research is required to establish whether workers who do have a stake in the level of commissions can process this information appropriately and make rational choices.[18]

Fourth, when the 1995 law was designed, perhaps insufficient attention was paid to what is probably the most troublesome issue of all: workers' mobility between the formal and informal sectors and the implications of this mobility for the length of periods during which workers are contributing to an AFORE—and thus for the size of retirement pensions.

The 1995 reform was a fundamental transformation of the retirement pension regime. Given the unviable nature of the previous pay-as-you defined benefit system, change was necessary and inevitable, but the large AFORE rents observed to date were certainly not an objective of the reform. On the contrary, they are a feature that detracts from the reform's objectives, centered as they were on making the system fiscally sustainable, more equitable, and more efficient—and with wider coverage. This is why determining whether more competition in the market for retirement savings, by itself, can achieve this result is so important.

The 2004 Pension Reform

Mexico's constitutional separation between private and public workers into segments A and B is not complete, because segment A includes some public workers, including IMSS employees (although there are no private sector workers in B). As a result, relationships between the IMSS and its union, the SNTSS, are ruled by the same Federal Labor Law as relationships between any private firm and private workers represented by a union. This is important for two reasons. First, although workers in A have the right to strike, workers in B do not. Second, workers in A can negotiate additional pension benefits beyond those established by the Social Security Law as part of their labor contracts, whereas for workers in B, their pension benefits are all established in the ISSSTE Law.

The importance of the differences between segments A and B is highlighted by comparing the labor regimes of IMSS workers and ISSSTE workers, such as doctors and nurses in both institutions who have similar qualifications and perform similar work. ISSSTE workers cannot strike nor can they negotiate their pensions with ISSSTE directors, while IMSS workers can do both. In relation to pensions, this asymmetry has resulted in a special regime for IMSS workers known as the IMSS pension and retirement system (régimen de jubilaciones y pensiones or RJP).

The first negotiations between the IMSS and the SNTSS establishing the RJP took place in 1955, 12 years after the creation of the IMSS, and resulted in a pay-as-you-go defined benefit pension that was additional to the one provided by the Social Security Law. Since then, benefits have been progressively increased in successive negotiations up to 1999, with the increased contributions being patently insufficient to cover them (IMSS 2005). The main characteristics of the RJP are as follows: there is no minimum retirement age, with women being able to retire after 27 years of service and men after 28 years of service; the pension is 130 percent of the last salary; pensions are indexed to the wage increases of active workers; and workers contribute 3 percent of their salary, with the rest covered by the IMSS. By contrast, other workers in segment A have a minimum retirement age of 65 and an endogenous replacement rate given the defined contribution nature of the system (but rarely exceeding 50 percent).

The RJP was negotiated by the SNTSS with the directors of the IMSS with no need for approval by Congress, or even the IMSS's tripartite board of directors. This institutional arrangement generates deep incentive problems. On the one hand, the IMSS is a public agency whose liabilities are implicitly guaranteed by the federal government, implying that bankruptcy does not follow when the organization's net worth is negative, nor is it a credible threat in the context of bargaining between the IMSS and the union. On the other hand, the bargaining process is carried out under a legal framework that assumes symmetry between the parties. However, the position of the IMSS as a provider of health services to around 40 percent of the country's population—making a strike a potentially catastrophic event for the government—and the absence of a credible bankruptcy threat turns this arrangement into a de facto asymmetric bargaining situation that affects the nature of the outcome.

Three more conditions have influenced the bargaining game between the IMSS and the SNTSS. First, for a long time the SNTSS was part of the corporatist structure of workers' organizations that played an important political role in supporting Mexico's quasi-monopoly political party throughout much of the last two-thirds of the 20th century, the Institutional Revolutionary Party. Second, bargaining between the IMSS and the SNTSS took place in a context of little transparency and accountability. By its very nature, the RJP establishes long-term benefits for IMSS workers and long-term obligations for the IMSS, yet until 2002, the IMSS was not obligated to reflect the RJP-derived liabilities in its balance sheet or in its financial

Table 6.5 A Comparison of the Pensions of an IMSS Worker and a Worker Affiliated with the IMSS

Category	IMSS worker (RJP)	IMSS affiliate worker (Social Security Law)
Monthly wage (Mex$)	5,000	5,000
Length of service (years)	27 for women 28 for men	40
Retirement age (years)	52.5 (average)	65
Monthly pension (Mex$)	6,450	2,106
Total income during retirement (Mex$)	2,557,425	506,415
Pension income not financed by workers' contribution (Mex$)	2,449,765	450,451
Indexing rule	Wages of workers	Consumer price index

Source: IMSS 2005, table III.4.

statements to Congress or to create reserves for these purposes. Third, the demographic structure of the IMSS's labor force implied that the costs of the RJP would be borne gradually, with little immediate implications for the operating costs of the IMSS at the time negotiations were being carried out. The costs of servicing the RJP have mattered only over the past 15 years, although these costs have grown exponentially and will continue to do so.

Table 6.5 compares the RJP with the pension regime of workers affiliated with the IMSS.[19] To facilitate the comparison, the table assumes the same wage and a flat wage profile throughout both workers' lives.[20] In addition to the obvious differences in replacement rates (that is, the ratio of pension payments to salaries) (1.29 versus. 0.42) and in years of retirement (12.5 more, on average, for IMSS pensioners), note the difference in the amount of the pension not contributed by the worker, which in this example is almost Mex$2 million (about US$180,000).[21] This sum is significant for workers who earned Mex$5,000 a month over their working lives, and it derives only from the fact that the IMSS worker has RJP rights while the worker affiliated with IMSS has the pension rights of the Social Security Law. Let us refer to this as the RJP rent.[22]

Without barriers to entry into the IMSS, this rent could not be sustained, but it is sustained because yet another feature of the IMSS–SNTSS labor contract is that entry is determined by the SNTSS. Thus, a market for entry rights into the IMSS could arise given the demand for entry into a job with a large rent, on the one hand, and control of the supply of entry into the IMSS by the SNTSS, on the other. If this hypothetical market operated, potential entrants would have to pay an entry fee to the SNTSS up to the (discounted) value of the RJP rent associated with entry into the IMSS. Of course, the total RJP rent would be the product of the per worker rent times the number of entrants, a potentially large sum, because even without any expansion in infrastructure, the number of entrants per year is more than 11,000 (because those retiring are replaced to keep the IMSS labor force constant). If such were the case, however, the per worker value of the RJP rent would clearly be a direct function of the difference between the pension regime of an IMSS worker versus the pension regime of an IMSS affiliate, that is, between the net benefits of the RJP and the net benefits of the Social Security Law pension. If this imaginary market existed, then any measures that lower net RJP benefits to new entrants into the IMSS, although not affecting the welfare of existing IMSS workers, would nonetheless reduce rents to the SNTSS.

In relation to who pays for the RJP, as mentioned earlier, IMSS workers contribute 3 percent of their salaries and the IMSS covers the rest. However, because IMSS revenues derive mostly from the social security contributions of firms and workers affiliated with it, most RJP rents are paid for by IMSS affiliate workers and by the firms that hire them.

From 1966, when workers began to retire under the RJP, to 2004, the cumulative cost of this regime has been Mex$165,590 million, of which Mex$24,198 million have come from IMSS workers' contributions (namely, their 3 percent fee) and Mex$141,392 million from the IMSS (that is, from the social security contributions of firms and workers affiliated with the IMSS). These figures do not take into account the time profile of expenditures, which are a function of the demographic dynamics of the IMSS's labor force. Two additional figures show that these costs have been incurred mostly in recent years and how they affect IMSS operations. First, during 1994 to 2004, total IMSS contributions to the RJP (excluding IMSS workers' 3 percent fees) were Mex$122,256 million. During the same period, cumulative investment by the IMSS (including investments in hospitals, clinics, medical equipment, and the like to provide medical and other services to its affiliated workers) has been Mex$32,110 million, a ratio of 3.8 to 1.0. Second, in 2005, the IMSS allocated Mex$20,206 million to the RJP out of its total yearly budget, compared with Mex$45,432 million for medicines, medical equipment, day care services, and operating expenditures to provide services to almost 40 million beneficiaries (affiliated workers and their families).

Table 6.6 shows the evolution of IMSS investment expenditures over the past quarter of a century. Given the figures shown there, the drop in the number of hospital beds per 1,000 beneficiaries from

Table 6.6 IMSS Investments per Beneficiary, 1981–2005

Years	Investment (a) (2004 Mex$ millions)	Beneficiaries (b) (thousands)	(a)/(b) (2004 Mex$ millions)
1981–85	18,579	28,339	655
1986–90	17,415	35,250	494
1991–95	15,744	36,806	427
1996–2000	17,238	41,951	410
2001–05	17,396	44,103	394

Source: IMSS 2005, table IX.35.

1.85 in 1980 to 0.83 in 2005 and in the number of doctors' offices at first-level health clinics from 0.60 to 0.42 should come as no surprise (IMSS 2006).

Unfortunately, most of the costs of the RJP have yet to be incurred. In the next decade, the number of IMSS workers reaching retirement age will double the existing stock of retired workers, and RJP expenditures will increase much more rapidly than IMSS revenues given the level of growth in formal employment. As a result, resources left over to provide medical and other services for IMSS beneficiaries will continue to decline. More precisely, estimates indicate that operating and capital expenditures per beneficiary will decline from Mex$847 in 2004 to zero by 2025. The implications for the future quality of IMSS health services are obvious, particularly given that the Mex$847 spent in 2004 for these purposes is already insufficient to provide IMSS affiliates with reasonable medical services and that no medical services can be provided in the absence of medicines and other intermediate inputs.

Preliminary Step

With the exception of a few IMSS officials and board members and some Finance Ministry officials, few were aware of the nature of the RJP and the problems associated with it. In 2001, Congress approved a proposal by President Vicente Fox to modify the Social Security Law and to make the IMSS more transparent and accountable. In particular, the reform obligated the IMSS's board to deliver to the president and to Congress an annual report certified by external auditors that included (a) an actuarial valuation of its pension liabilities, (b) a net income statement produced using the same accounting standards applied to private firms, and (c) a balance sheet showing the institution's net worth. Table 6.7 summarizes this information.

Table 6.7 Net Income and Net Worth, IMSS, 2001–05

(Mex$ millions)

Category	2001	2002	2003	2004	2005
Net income					
Without the RJP	37	63	48	241	200
With the RJP	−18,606	−19,962	−17,004	−32,210	−68,047
Net worth					
Without the RJP	78,776	61,143	63,538	68,349	58,702
With the RJP	−41,028	−61,511	−75,692	−92,669	−81,662

Source: IMSS 2002, 2003, 2004, 2005, 2006.

These annual reports include the net present value of RJP liabilities. At the end of December 2005, these were valued at Mex$775,975 million, equivalent to 9.3 percent of that year's GDP. This sum corresponds to the pension liabilities of a total of 504,054 workers, of whom 139,572 are already retired and 364,482 will retire over the next 28 years.

Transparency was not the only objective of the 2001 reform. A second relevant feature was a new provision to force the IMSS to create reserves for the RJP and, equally important, to ensure that as of the date when the reform came into effect, the future pension costs of new entrants were reserved as of the time of entry, so that at the time they retired there would be sufficient reserves in the RJP pension fund to cover their pensions. This was extremely important, because the IMSS was now obligated to internalize the full costs of hiring personnel, eliminating the possibility of ignoring these future costs in its decisions to expand its medical and other infrastructure and hire personnel. In consequence, the 2001 reform aligned the real social costs of hiring personnel at the IMSS with the costs faced by the institution in its day-to-day operations. In other words, the IMSS had to convert the pay-as-you-go nature of the RJP into a capitalized, pre-funded scheme, although without individual accounts.

Critically, the 2001 reform did not specify where the funds to be reserved for future pensions would come from. This was addressed by the 2004 reform. Nonetheless, the new regime of transparency achieved a fundamental objective: the RJP was no longer an internal problem of the IMSS only, but it was now the joint responsibility of the president and Congress. Having been officially notified of the problem, these two branches of government could no longer ignore (a) that the institution was in deep financial trouble and that its ability to provide quality health care and other services was already seriously undermined and (b) that in the absence of corrective measures, the

IMSS was heading toward operational collapse. Furthermore, after the first report was delivered to the president and Congress, the IMSS board disseminated its contents to the general public through an intense communication campaign.

Definite Step, Odd Step, or Reverse Step?

In October 2004, this time at the initiative of Congress, the Social Security Law was reformed again with a single purpose: the IMSS had to ensure that the RJP obligations of any new hires were fully funded, as stated in the 2001 reform, but it could no longer use IMSS resources to do so. If one is to understand the implications of this, three points are important. First, the reform did not modify the existing IMSS–SNTSS labor contract. Indeed, Congress does not have the power to do so. Second, Congress does have the power to legislate on matters concerning the use of public monies, and because IMSS monies are public monies, Congress can legislate what the IMSS may or may not do with the social security contributions that it collects and the subsidies that it receives from the government.[23] The reform imposed a constraint on the IMSS, not on the SNTSS or the labor contract. Third, the Federal Labor Law stipulates that the parties to a labor contract have the right to renegotiate various clauses, or even the full contract, every two years.

The implications of the 2004 reform are simple but powerful. The IMSS could no longer hire new workers without renegotiating the labor contract with the SNTSS. Moreover, at the time of such renegotiation, it could no longer sign the contract unless the new workers fully bore their RJP costs, because the IMSS could not sign any contract contrary to existing law.

The reform allowed the IMSS to continue using its resources to pay for the RJP obligations of existing workers, thereby leaving their rights untouched. The reform also left the rights of new entrants to a pension according to the Social Security Law untouched, as for any other segment A worker. It did not prohibit the IMSS from covering the share of workers' contributions to the standard Social Security Law pension (their AFORE accounts) as the IMSS was doing for workers already hired, it did not eliminate the RJP for new workers, and it did not impose any constraints on the RJP's characteristics. New entrants could continue to retire after 27 or 28 years and with a replacement rate of 1.3 if the SNTSS so wished—or with any other combination of retirement ages and replacement rates. In practice, the only point of the reform was that whatever form the RJP took for new workers, they would have to fund it fully. In other words, Congress legislated away the RJP rent.

The 2004 reform separated IMSS workers into two groups: those hired prior to the reform (the old generation) and those hired after (the new generation). The IMSS could service the accumulated RJP liabilities of the old generation, although the reform specifically stated that the terms under which these liabilities were to be serviced would follow from negotiations between the parties. As noted earlier, these liabilities will place an increasing burden on the IMSS for at least two more decades, making operation of the system practically unmanageable, but, of critical importance, they would no longer grow.

The reform has four further implications: legal, economic, political, and judicial. As mentioned before, the institutional framework in which the IMSS and the SNTSS bargained over the labor contract was unbalanced given the impossibility of bankruptcy or any other legal remedy to reduce a contractual obligation whose burden was increasingly unbearable. Congress modified this framework. In the face of IMSS's refusal to renew existing RJP obligations for new entrants during the renewal of the labor contract, the SNTSS could no longer threaten a strike because, indeed, there can be no legal strike against the provisions of a law. Furthermore, by making it illegal for the IMSS to renew the RJP under the existing terms, Congress made credible the commitment to reform the RJP. The refusal to continue using social security contributions to fund the RJP for new workers no longer reflected the will of IMSS officials or board members, but it was the fulfillment of a legal obligation.

The second implication was economic: the marginal cost of labor to the IMSS would fall by a factor of more than 60 percent, because the costs of creating reserves for the RJP liabilities of new entrants would no longer fall on its finances. To the extent that labor costs account for the largest share of providing medical services, the marginal social costs of the IMSS as a provider of health services would fall as well—dramatically. Of course, the IMSS still had to service the RJP liabilities of the old generation, but this service was now a closed set and could be treated as a sunk cost. Indeed, after some negotiation about the terms of additional contributions by the old generation to reduce the burden on the IMSS of their pensions, these liabilities could be treated like public debt whose profile and terms could then be arranged so as to minimize the distortionary costs associated with its service. By closing the RJP's liabilities and by legally prohibiting the IMSS from establishing new ones in the future, the moral hazard problem associated with the bailout of a debt that the IMSS could not service without considerable further deterioration of its health services could be avoided.[24]

The third implication was political. This was the first pension reform after the 1995 reform and the first to reduce the pension rights of public sector workers, whether in segment A or B (only for future workers). On the one hand, the precedent for other public sector unions with similar pension regimes was important. On the other hand, the 2004 reform could be interpreted as the beginning of the unraveling of the special position held by public sector unions in a context in which the economic costs imposed by these unions were increasing and their political role was being modified. In this context, support of the reform by most Institutional Revolutionary Party legislators in Congress is noteworthy.

The fourth implication was judicial. Soon after the reform was approved, the SNTSS contested its legal validity. From the point of view of the SNTSS, what was at stake was the power of Congress to modify what to the union had been gains obtained at the bargaining table. From the point of view of the IMSS, what was at stake was the power of Congress to determine the use of public monies. From the point of view of the public, what was at stake was whether Congress could intervene in public matters that had an impact on the welfare of millions. The issue was first discussed at administrative tribunals, next at labor tribunals, and eventually by the Supreme Court without the law being suspended at any time by any judicial authority. All *amparos* (stays of action) by the SNTSS were denied. At every step the courts confirmed the legality of the reforms, with matters coming to a final and definite end in March 2007 as a result of a nine-to-two vote in the Supreme Court. Since its enactment in 2004, the reform has been deemed legal.

In October 2005, the IMSS and the SNTSS faced the first renewal of the labor contract since the 2004 reform. The RJP provisions for new entrants were modified. They would now retire after 34 years of service for women and 35 for men, with a minimum retirement age of 60 and with a replacement rate of 1. Yet despite the reform, the new generation of workers will not fund fully these revised RJP benefits. To do so, the contribution rate should have been 23 percent of their salary, as opposed to the 10 percent specified in the labor contract. Thus, new workers are funding less than half the costs of their future pensions, and despite the intent of Congress, the RJP rent will still be in effect for new entrants—diminished, but nonetheless positive.

The provisions of the 2004 reform were bypassed by raising the contributions of the old generation of workers from 3 percent to 10 percent of their salaries. Their resources are not, however, used to contribute to the financing of their own RJP liabilities, which would lower the burden of servicing these liabilities on the IMSS, thereby releasing resources for capital and operating expenditures to improve services. Rather, they are used to finance the difference between what new workers should contribute according to the law to fully fund their own RJP and what they will contribute, that is, to finance the difference between the 23 percent contribution rate needed to fund the agreed-upon benefits and the 10 percent agreed-upon contribution. The bypassing of the 2004 reform thus resulted in a perhaps unique innovation: a reverse pay-as-you-go pension scheme whereby the old generation of workers subsidizes the pensions of workers that are about to enter the IMSS.

The new RJP provisions of the labor contract are unsustainable: as the generation of old workers retires, the number of people contributing 7 percent of their salary to subsidize the pensions of the new entrants shrinks, and the number of new entrants requiring a subsidy for their future pension increases. When the scheme is exhausted, a new RJP will have to be negotiated if the law is not to be further bypassed.[25] The IMSS will then have three different types of active workers with three different RJPs: the old generation hired before October 2005, the new generation hired under the auspices of the October 2005 contract, and a newer generation hired with a different RJP based on a still-to-be-negotiated contract.

In the meantime, as a result of the reverse pay-as-you-go system, the old generation of workers will contribute about Mex$50,000 million to the pensions of the new generation of workers and not to their own; their working conditions in terms of access to infrastructure, equipment, and intermediate inputs will fail to improve as a result of their additional effort; and their future pension will be no more secure. Plus, the IMSS will have lost Mex$50,000 million in workers' contributions to reduce the burden of the RJP of the old generation and will have to replace this amount with social security contributions from affiliated workers and firms, which is what the 2004 reform sought to avoid. In sum, despite the intent of Congress, the RJP rent, though diminished, will still be in place, at least for a few more years.

Discussion

Earlier sections argued that the rents associated with AFORES and the RJP reduce the benefits of social security to formal workers. Saving for retirement is one thing, but being forced to do so in an instrument that has to date paid an annual real rate of return of less than 1 percent is something else. Similarly, contributing to health insurance is one thing, but doing so through an institution that diverts increasing amounts of contributions to a different purpose is another.

Clearly, AFORE and SNTSS rents lower β_f compared with a scenario in which the IMSS fully used its contributions to provide health services and rates of return on AFORES were competitive with alternatives for voluntary saving. A direct connection exists between these rents and lower aggregate labor productivity, reduced competitiveness, and increased informality.

Other factors also contribute to this outcome, because β_f also reflects the valuation of other components of social security (housing, day care services, and so on). Nor are they the only reasons workers may undervalue AFORE accounts and IMSS health services. Nevertheless, the evidence suggests that the poor performance of AFORES and the IMSS results, at least in part, from the rent- or power-seeking behavior of the AFORES and the SNTSS. This is not to say that the 1995 and 2004 reforms were counterproductive because this is not the case. Mexico's pay-as-you-go retirement pension system was unsustainable, and the pre-funded defined contribution system is a better alternative. Equally, the RJP for new entrants is better than the previous one from the IMSS's perspective. Thus, both reforms have resulted in benefits; on balance, the situation is better with them that it was without them.

Nonetheless, weak competition and regulatory problems in the market for retirement savings and the bypassing of the 2004 reform to lower RJP costs have allowed the AFORES and the SNTSS to capture—and continue to capture—significant rents at the expense of all workers. Reducing these rents is essential. In the case of the AFORES, this can be achieved by means of a careful review of the nature of the market for retirement savings and of the appropriate combination of competition inducing and regulatory changes that could further reduce AFORES' commissions and increase the real rates of return to workers. In the case of the SNTSS, what is needed is recognition that the reverse pay-as-you-go RJP scheme negotiated in 2005—aside from bypassing the law—serves no other purpose than rent preservation for a few.

The transition to AFORES' commissions that reflect marginal costs and an IMSS–SNTSS labor contract that does not bypass the law needs to be accelerated. In the case of the AFORES, the rents already captured over the past nine years will inevitably translate into lower pensions. Even if commissions were lowered to equal marginal costs tomorrow, workers' losses could not be undone. In the case of the IMSS, hiring new workers under a pension regime condemned to collapse in a few years makes little sense. In both cases, the central point is that given the current strongly suboptimal equilibrium, the pursuit of equity through the elimination of rents is also the pursuit of productivity.

Note that there is nothing illegal about the behavior of AFORES or the SNTSS.[26] The problem is with the institutional structure and the design and implementation of the reforms. The AFORES' goal is to maximize profits. They face an extremely inelastic demand, a legally mandated supply of funds, and a market where "consumers" have substantive difficulties in valuing a product that they will consume many years from today but that they are obligated to purchase anyway. The AFORES also work in a context where information is difficult to understand. Thus, the high price-cost margins and excessive profits should not come as a surprise. The fact that workers' pensions will be low and that eventually the government may have to commit funds to pay for workers' minimum pensions is not the AFORES' problem.

The goal of the SNTSS is to maximize rents for its affiliates and for itself. It faces a quasi-monopoly situation in the provision of critical services; a firm that cannot go bankrupt and whose liabilities have an implicit government guarantee; a bargaining context where the firm has little accountability; and a political context where, until recently, its role in supporting a political party was valued by a government from the same party. That benefits for IMSS workers will be substantially larger than for other workers is, therefore, not surprising, and the IMSS's increasing inability to deliver services to affiliated workers is not the SNTSS's problem.

The AFORES and SNTSS will not internalize the negative equity and productivity effects of their behavior. That is not their role. The issue is not that the government has not responded to the excessive rents of the AFORES. As mentioned, the government has pursued various legal reforms and administrative measures to improve transparency, provide better information to workers, reduce barriers to entry for new AFORES, and facilitate workers' transfer from one AFORE to another (Madero and Mora 2006). Nor is the issue that the government has not tried to modify the RJP, as the 2001 and 2004 reforms attest. It is that the effectiveness of these measures has fallen substantially short of what is needed, that some have been too slow in coming, and that large equity and productivity costs are being paid in the meantime. The issue is why the pressures to reduce AFORES' commissions and to modify the IMSS–SNTSS labor contract are not greater.

Three reasons account for this problem. First, the government has not pursued a clear agenda to improve social security and promote formal employment; in particular, budgetary resources have not flowed in this direction. Second, social pressures to force the government to improve social security have so far not been overwhelming. Third, as a result, mustering the political capital to face the complex technical, budgetary, and political problems of the AFORES and the SNTSS has not been essential. These three reasons also help explain the behavior of Congress. Finally, a fourth reason underlies the first three: the existence of an external source of rents, derived from oil, that sustains the difference between the underlying efficiency and productivity of the economy and workers' standards of living and that allows social protection programs to partly compensate for the deficiencies of social security without the need to raise taxes.

Social Protection as a Policy Response

Even under the best of circumstances, not all workers would be covered by social security, because in any economy there are reasons for nonsalaried labor relationships between firms and workers or for workers to be self-employed.[27] As a result, over the years the government has promoted a number of social programs to provide health, housing, day care, and, more recently, pensions to workers lacking access to social security. These programs, referred to here as social protection programs, differ from social security in two relevant senses for the purposes of this discussion. First, they are not bundled, so workers can access one, such as a health program, without necessarily accessing another, such as a housing program. Second, they are not paid for by contributions from workers or firms but by general revenues. The key point is that informal workers have access to social protection programs that—even if not of the same quality as social security—are, nonetheless, unbundled and free.

Figure 6.2 shows the evolution of government subsidies for social security and social protection programs since the Social Security Law went into effect in 1997.[28] Resources for social security include subsidies for workers' AFORE accounts (the social subsidy) and for IMSS health insurance. They exclude government resources for pensions of the transition generation, because these resources do not benefit workers currently in the labor market. Resources for social protection programs include those for various federal health and housing programs, but they exclude state resources, and thus underestimate the total amount of public resources spent on social protection programs. Figure 6.2 depicts a powerful fact: federal subsidies for social protection programs have grown much faster than those for social security, and have been larger in absolute terms since 2003.[29] Over the same period, 1998–2006, no major increase in tax rates has occurred. The share of nonoil revenues in GDP has been basically constant: 14.2 percent in 1998 and 14.8 percent in 2005. Revenues from oil rents, by contrast, increased

Figure 6.2 Federal Subsidies for Social Security and Social Protection, 1998–2006

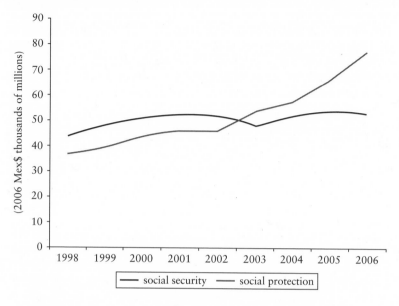

Source: Levy 2006.

from 6 percent of GDP in 1998 to 8.8 percent in 2005 (Levy 2006). The political costs to the government and to Congress of increasing social protection programs have so far not been significant.

Resources channeled to informal workers in the form of social protection programs are equivalent to a subsidy to informal employment (Levy 2008). This subsidy is in addition to the pure tax on formal employment associated with the undervaluation of social security; therefore, in terms of the composition of employment, it has the effect of further reducing formal employment and increasing informal employment.

Let us now turn to the effect of social protection programs on the three messages highlighted earlier in the context of figure 6.1. The first message was that an undervalued social security system acts like a tax on formal employment, thus reducing average labor productivity. Social protection programs accentuate this effect. In the formal sector, workers' productivity increases further as the stimulus to informal employment reduces the supply of labor to the formal sector and increases the formal wage. In the informal sector, the productivity of labor falls as the supply of labor to that sector increases. The result is that the productivity difference between formal and informal workers widens. So the first message is now that social protection programs will generate productivity losses in addition to the ones created by an undervalued social security system. The economy will be less competitive; in particular, the output and profits of formal firms will fall more.

The second message was that the costs of an undervalued social security system were paid by formal and informal workers. Now, as a result of social protection programs, both informal and formal workers are better off. Even though wages in the informal sector fall, workers now receive benefits that they were not getting before, and because there are fewer formal sector workers, their wages increase. Note that workers are better off even though they are less productive and the economy is less efficient. This improvement happens because of benefits that (apparently) nobody is paying for: the cost of social protection programs for informal workers. Of course, these programs must be paid for, but this outlay of funds is from general tax revenues or from other sources; their costs are not internalized by workers and firms in the informal sector. As a result, incentives are modified in the direction of informality, particularly because these benefits are "free" only under the condition of informality.

The third message was that informal employment resulted from a legal design that excludes nonsalaried workers from social security and from a tax on salaried employment associated with a social security system that does not work well. When social protection programs are introduced, there is a third reason for informal employment: a policy response that acts like a subsidy to nonsalaried employment (and to illegal salaried employment). Of course, many other reasons account for informality, but of the factors that explain the distribution of Mexico's labor force presented in table 6.1, the ones just mentioned are among them.

One last but critical observation: if $\beta_f < 1$ is "compensated for" with social protection benefits, the undervaluation of social security need not translate into lower workers' welfare, formal or informal. If, as suggested earlier, $\beta_f < 1$ partly as a result of the rent-seeking or power-preserving behavior of the AFORES and the SNTSS, the resulting low productivity and high income concentration equilibrium may not be reflected in lower workers' welfare if resources for social programs are increased in parallel. Because the reforms necessary for $\beta_f \rightarrow 1$ may be politically costly or complex, this low productivity and high income concentration equilibrium may persist for as long as the fiscal costs of social protection programs can somehow be paid for.

Voice and Exit

Hirschman's (1970) study of responses to the decline of firms, organizations, and states provides a valuable framework for understanding the forces supporting the high inequality and low productivity equilibrium described in the previous sections. In Hirschman's analysis, voice is the political reaction to the decline of a firm, an organization, or a state. Voice occurs through the established channels of executive and congressional action; through the active expression of opinions in the media and other forms of political action; or, eventually, through demonstrations, street protests, and the like. In parallel, exit is the economic reaction to the same phenomenon and occurs through the discipline of market forces. For example, it occurs when consumers cease to buy a firm's product or through the abandonment of a geographic space (for instance, when workers migrate to another country). Depending (a) on a country's political institutions; (b) on its cultural traditions; and (c) on specific characteristics of the firm, organization, or state, the voice and exit interplay can determine outcomes in terms of when any of the entities has the incentives and ability to correct deficiencies and poor performance generally, as well as when they fail to do so.

Consider the example of public schools and assume that educational quality is low. Voice occurs when parents express their dissatisfaction with the status quo and use their vote and other forms of political action to demand corrective measures from the executive branch and Congress. Exit occurs when parents take their children out of public schools, assuming that private schools are available and are, at least to some, affordable. If voice prevails, the performance of public schools improves. If exit prevails, bad quality persists (and the strength of voice is dampened because those most able to exercise it—that is, higher-income families—loose incentives to do so). The balance of voice and exit matters for the future of public schools. This balance depends on the responses of the executive branch and Congress, which, in turn, depend on their objectives and the costs and benefits of a particular course of action (for instance, facing the teachers' union if that is what is causing low quality or letting the public schools deteriorate while the more vociferous parents are subdued by their exit to private schools).

In this context, Mexico's social security can be thought of as a complex organization or, better still, a system made up of (a) a legal framework; (b) a set of public agencies; (c) an institutional framework characterized by the presence of two central political entities, the executive branch and Congress; (d) a set of large and dispersed private actors consisting of the firms and workers contributing to social security; and (e) a small concentrated set of private actors supplying the labor or the financial skills or assets necessary for the provision of social security services. The performance of this system is central for Mexico from two equally important perspectives. On the one hand, if the system underperforms (in the sense of $\beta_f < 1$), aggregate output and productivity losses will occur. On the other hand, if the system underperforms, workers suffer from a loss of welfare resulting from poor health services and low retirement pensions, among other benefits.

I have argued that the underperformance of social security derives partly from the rent-seeking behavior of a few of the actors associated with the provision of social security services, namely, the AFORES and the SNTSS. Their behavior is as expected of businesses and trade unions, and the resulting income or power concentration and loss of aggregate productivity is not their concern. Therefore, the central question does not concern them, but rather the institutional and incentive structure that allows their behavior to be reflected in the underperformance of Mexico's social security system. Or, to put the question in Hirschman's terms, why has the interplay of voice and exit produced such an outcome?

For voice to be effective, information must be easily accessible so that those affected by the system's underperformance are aware of the phenomenon and of its causes. That is, there must be transparency. For voice to be effective, a mechanism whereby those affected can express their concern must also be available. In other words, affected actors must be organized and represented. Finally, for voice to be effective, those that are its intended recipients must answer to those who express it. That is, there must be accountability.

Transparency, effective representation, and accountability enhance voice. One could argue that Congress would not have initiated the 2004 reform without the prior 2001 reform that made it officially aware of the problems of the RJP. One could also argue that the recent changes in AFORES' commissions have reflected the exercise of voice, as CONSAR responded to increasing concerns about these commissions. Yet another exercise of voice is the recent Comisión Federal de Competencia opinion on competition conditions in the market for retirement savings. Thus, voice has been present as a mechanism to correct the underperformance of Mexico's social security, and although not fully effective, it has mattered.

Exit has been present as well, reflected perhaps most openly in the large number of workers and firms in informality. Not all informal employment is a response to a poorly functioning social security system. Some workers will always be informal given Mexico's legal framework, and these workers did not exit into informality, but were never allowed into formality because of legal constraints. However, many more workers should legally be in formality, but they have exercised the option of exit into informality—most obviously the almost 8 million salaried workers who have been illegally hired by firms without social security coverage. The exercise of the exit option has a mirror image in an equally significant number of firms that are also in illegality.

Voice has not always been there, but when it has, the executive branch and Congress have not ignored it completely. They have also facilitated and promoted exit, even generously subsidized it, as evidenced by social protection programs that partly substitute for workers' lack of social security benefits. Given the constraints to formality and the massive exit from formality, informal employment accounts for more than half of total employment. A likely outcome is that voice will increasingly be exercised by those in informal employment, who will demand more and better social protection programs for themselves.

The interplay of voice and exit in response to $\beta_f < 1$ matters greatly for competitiveness and for workers' welfare, because social security and social protection are not the same. To reiterate just one important implication associated with pensions: in the first case, workers are forced to save for retirement; in the second, they are given the option of doing so. Plus the productivity of workers with similar characteristics is not the same, nor are firms' dynamics the same. That is why the role of voice to promote $\beta_f \to 1$ needs to be strengthened and the role of exit into informality weakened. This will occur, however, only if incentives to the executive branch and Congress, firms, and workers change. Of the many measures required for this change, two may play a critical role: forcing Congress and the executive branch to internalize the costs of exit and facilitating workers' and firms' use of voice and enhancing its effectiveness, particularly for low-wage workers and small firms.

Note that financing social protection programs from oil rents is not the same as financing them from taxes on firms and workers, particularly if such taxes are paid by formal firms and workers. To the extent that oil rents can be channeled to social protection programs, exit has no costs, while responding to voice has political costs. In other words, because the future costs of using oil rents are not fully internalized by the executive branch and Congress today, exit may dominate voice. This is an important element supporting the current high inequality and low productivity equilibrium in which almost everybody loses. Enhancing voice and removing the constraint to entry into formality (that is, moving to a universal, well-functioning social security system) is fundamental for equity and efficiency. Focusing attention on the AFORES and the RJP is a good place to start.

Postscript

In June 2008, the IMSS and the SNTSS renegotiated the RJP provisions of the labor contract, eliminating the reverse pay-as-you-go provisions negotiated in October 2005 to bypass the 2004 pension reform. Between these two time periods, events unfolded as hypothesized in this chapter: the contributions of the old generation of workers could no longer finance the RJP regime of new entrants. With no other sources of funds to bypass the law, all new workers hired by the IMSS as of June 2008 will fund their RJP with their own resources. Thus, for these new workers and for the SNTSS, there will be no RJP rent. The reverse pay-as-you-regime lasted less than three years, but because of it, the opportunity to use the increased contributions of the old generation of workers to fund their own pension liabilities, thereby releasing resources to the IMSS to provide better services, was lost. Henceforth, the IMSS can hire new workers without further compromising its future ability to offer services to affiliated workers. The problem of the accumulated RJP pension liabilities still remains, however, and needs urgent attention to avoid further deterioration in the quality of services provided by the IMSS. I argue that the federal government should absorb these liabilities in the context of a broader reform to extend the right to social security to all Mexican workers (Levy 2008).

Notes

1. The IMSS does not have a monopoly in the provision of services, but since its inception in 1943, this has been the case in practice. Some services are outsourced, but this arrangement is the exception rather than the rule. Furthermore, affiliated workers have no say in this regard, so the behavior of IMSS is very much that of a monopolist.

2. The teachers' union is the largest, with approximately 1 million workers who are, however, in segment B and whose direct contractual relationship is with state governments.

3. The minimum wage in 2005 was Mex$1,400 a month (approximately US$130). Three times the minimum wages is used here as the cutoff point between workers with high and low wages.

4. Of the 9 million workers affiliated with the IMSS in July 1, 1997, 3 million earned more than three times the minimum wage and 6 million

earned three times the minimum wage or less. Workers aged 56 or older in 1997 were excluded from the database, so that departures from formality were not due to retirement. As a result, when workers were not in the formal sector, they either were in the informal sector, were openly unemployed, had dropped out of the labor force altogether, or had migrated abroad.

5. These results are confirmed using the National Survey of Urban Employment, a panel data set that allows for following workers' formal–informal transitions (although only for a year). According to this data set, in 2005, 16 percent of low-wage workers who began the year in the formal sector ended it in the informal sector and 10 percent of low-wage workers who started the year in the informal sector ended it in the formal sector (Levy 2008). Calderon-Madrid (2006) computes transition matrixes for 1997, 2001, and 2005 and finds similar results. See also Bosch and Maloney (2006); Gong, Soest, and Villagomez (2004); and Kaplan, Martínez, and Robertson (2005). At the same time, movements from formality and informality into open unemployment are small and spells of open unemployment are short (IDB 2004). Mexico does not have unemployment insurance.

6. Evidence also suggests that the minimum wage is not binding (Bell 1997; Maloney and Nuñez Mendez 2004).

7. The mechanics associated with the Mex$139 are complex. The funds are deposited in a subaccount of the worker's AFORE account, although these resources are not managed by the AFORE, but by INFO-NAVIT. The worker may request a housing credit against the balance of the housing subaccount. If the worker does not get such a credit before retirement, the funds accumulated in the housing subaccount are added to the funds in the retirement account and are used to purchase an annuity for retirement income, so that ex post the worker is being forced to save Mex$314 a month (Mex$175 + Mex$139). In general, lower-wage workers have less access to housing loans because of their lower wages and higher mobility. Thus, they end up saving a larger proportion of their wages for retirement than workers with higher wages.

8. In 2005, the IMSS channeled 16 percent of its revenues to the special pension regime of its workers. This amount will double in the next decade (IMSS 2005).

9. Gertler, Martinez, and Rubio (2005) find that the families of workers covered by the Oportunidades program are liquidity constrained. However, when they have access to credit, some have investment opportunities with real rates of return of about 5 percent. The opportunity cost of saving for retirement in an AFORE is then too high for these workers.

10. To see this, consider what happens in the absence of social security. Formal firms' labor costs would be w_f, while informal firms' labor costs would be w_i. Given labor mobility, the equilibrium wage in the formal and the informal sectors would be the same (indeed, the distinction between the

sectors would not be meaningful). This wage could be w_i^* only where all workers are employed. When there is social security and it is fully valued, the wage in the formal sector falls to w_f^*, although when added to the value of benefits T_f it equals w_i^*.

11. The IMSS reports that in 2005 approximately 550,000 firms registered with the IMSS with up to 5 workers employed a total of 1.2 million workers, with an average firm size of 2.2 workers. The economic census for 2004 records approximately 2.8 million small and micro firms employing 6.8 million workers, with an average firm size of 2.4 workers. These numbers underestimate evasion because the census excludes firms in rural areas.

12. Mexico's epidemiological transition has increased the costs of providing health services, while the erosion of real wages associated with the country's various macroeconomic crises has reduced the IMSS's wage-based revenues (IMSS 2003, 2004, 2005, 2006).

13. Commissions are of two types: on the stock of accumulated resources in the account and on the flow of resources that are continuously deposited in the account. AFORES choose any combination of these two (although approval by CONSAR is required). In addition, AFORES can offer commission discounts after depositors have remained with them for a given length of time. In 2006, flow commissions ranged from a low of 0.5 percent to a high of 1.64 percent and stock commissions ranged from a low of 0.15 percent to a high of 1.48 percent. Discounts for time vary widely (Madero and Mora 2006). The resulting structure of commissions is, therefore, complex, because the effective cost to workers depends on their age, the length of time before they can retire, their effective time contributing to the system given their patterns of (future) transition between formality and informality, and their present (and future) wages. Workers also have to consider the rates of return on AFORES' investment portfolios.

14. This rate can be contrasted with the 3.5 percent rate usually assumed by the IMSS for its actuarial calculations (IMSS 2005).

15. On July 1, 1997, this segment of the market was the whole market, because all workers who started in the AFORES had rights under the 1973 law. This segment will decline gradually as the transition generation retires, but this decline will take a long time, because the last worker enrolled in the IMSS on June 30, 1997, may not retire until around 2027.

16. From this perspective, one could argue that for the transition generation the AFORES are an unnecessary intermediate step in acquiring a pension: resources are deposited in AFORES accounts, profits are made on these accounts, the accumulated amounts in these accounts are devolved to the government, and the government pays the pensions out of general tax revenues. This is equivalent to the government lending resources to the AFORES at an annual real rate of interest of around 0.9 percent.

17. Workers from the transition generation must be enrolled in the IMSS for at least 500 weeks to qualify for a 1973 pension, or else they obtain a pension on the basis of the amounts accumulated in their AFORES.

18. The consumers in this market are odd characters. They clearly lack perfect foresight and cannot discount the future appropriately, so they are forced to save. At this point, however, they act under perfect rationality and choose the best AFORE, discounting the expected future costs of stock and flow commissions and incentives derived from remaining with a particular AFORE. However, to protect them from the lure of some AFORE's marketing techniques, CONSAR regulations allow them to switch freely between AFORES only if they choose progressively cheaper ones.

19. All IMSS workers are subject to the Social Security Law and, therefore, are entitled to a pension under the provisions of this law. Thus, IMSS workers have their AFORE accounts. The RJP pension regime complements the Social Security Law pension regime. The IMSS must pay for any difference between RJP benefits and the Social Security Law pension.

20. This is done only for comparison purposes. The average wage of an IMSS worker is double that of a worker in an IMSS affiliate, and IMSS workers' wages are higher even for comparable occupations.

21. This formal comparison assumes that the firms' contributions to workers' retirement accounts are actually borne by the firms and not shifted to the workers through lower wages. Shifting firms' contributions to workers is probably the case for workers in private firms given free mobility of labor, but the IMSS is not characterized by free mobility of labor, and the share paid by the IMSS for workers' pensions is not shifted to them. Furthermore, the IMSS labor contract states that all social security contributions that should be paid by workers are also paid by the IMSS. As a result, the differences in the share of pensions of IMSS workers and IMSS affiliate workers not paid for by each are much larger, and so are the rents discussed later. For the purposes of argument, however, this finding is sufficient.

22. Actual RJP rents are larger, because most IMSS workers earn more than Mex$5,000 a month. Their average wage is about Mex$11,200 a month.

23. Social security contributions have the same status as taxes, and the IMSS can and must use the provisions of the Federal Fiscal Code to collect them. Furthermore, IMSS resources are subject to audit by the relevant authorities in Congress and in the executive branch.

24. The analogy with the 1995 reform is clear. Before that reform, the pension liabilities of IMSS-affiliated workers were an obligation of the IMSS, which could not service them without further reducing resources for health services. The reform transferred these liabilities from the IMSS's balance sheet to the government's. At the same time, the change to the defined contribution system ensured that there would be no new pension liabilities from new IMSS-affiliated workers (ignoring the minimum pension guarantee). Finally, the pension liabilities of the old generation of workers transferred from the IMSS to the government would be serviced by the government from

general tax revenues (social security contributions were not increased for this purpose). Therefore, these liabilities—correctly in my opinion—are not being covered by labor taxes, which is exactly what would happen if T_f were increased. Following the earlier discussion, consider what would happen to labor productivity, to the incentives to evade, to the size distribution of firms, and to informal employment if T_f were increased to service the RJP with no improvements in the quality of health services (so that $\beta_f T_f$ falls).

25. The scheme allows the financing of the future pensions of between 39,000 and 67,000 new entrants (IMSS 2006). If the IMSS replaces only retiring workers, this replacement would imply between three to five years before the reverse pay-as-you-go scheme runs out, given that the retirement rate will accelerate in the next few years from about 11,000 workers per year to 13,000 workers per year. If the IMSS expanded its medical infrastructure and hired more personnel, the scheme would be exhausted sooner. As a reverse pay-as-you-go scheme, it has the reverse properties of a traditional pay-as-you-go: the faster the growth of new entrants, the shorter the duration of the scheme.

26. The 2004 reform imposes a legal constraint on the IMSS, not on the SNTSS. The issue of whether the IMSS complied with the law by signing the 2005 labor contract or not is not relevant to the SNTSS.

27. This can be seen in figure 6.1. If $\beta_f = 1$, the equilibrium is at point A and only $L_f^* < L$ workers have social security coverage.

28. The data for figure 6.2 start in 1998 because the Social Security Law went into effect on July 1, 1997, and all data are presented on a yearly basis.

29. Even if one includes social security contributions, more resources are available as of 2003 to provide health services to informal workers than to formal workers (Levy 2006).

References

Bell, L. A. 1997. "The Impact of Minimum Wages in Mexico and Colombia." *Journal of Labor Economics* 15 (3): 103–35.

Bosch, M., and W. Maloney. 2006. "Gross Worker Flows in the Presence of Informal Labor Markets: The Mexican Experience." Research report, World Bank, Latin American and Caribbean Department, Washington, DC.

Calderon-Madrid, A. 2006. "Mobility of Workers between Formal and Informal Job Status: An Empirical Assessment of Earnings Variations and Exit Hazards in Mexico's Urban Labor Market." Research report, El Colegio de México, Department of Economics, Mexico City.

Comisión Federal de Competencia. 2006. *Opinión sobre el sistema de ahorro para el retiro*. Oficio PRES-10-096-2006-162. Mexico City: Government of Mexico.

Gertler, P., S. Martinez, and M. Rubio. 2005. *The Effects of OPORTUNIDADES on Raising Household Consumption through Productive Invest-*

ments in Micro-Enterprise and Agricultural Production. Oportunidades Technical Evaluation Paper 19. Mexico City: Secretaría de Desarrollo Social, Coordinación Nacional del Programa Oportunidades.

Gong, X., A. Soest, and E. Villagomez. 2004. "Mobility in the Urban Labor Market: A Panel Data Analysis for Mexico." *Economic Development and Cultural Change* 53 (1): 1–36.

Hirschman, A. 1970. *Exit, Voice, and Loyalty: Responses to Decline in Firms, Organizations, and States.* Cambridge, MA: Harvard University Press.

IDB (Inter-American Development Bank). 2004. *Good Jobs Wanted: Labor Markets in Latin America.* Economic and Social Progress Report. Washington, DC: IDB.

IMSS (Instituto Mexicano del Seguro Social). 2002. *Informe al Ejecutivo Federal y al Congreso de la Unión sobre la situación financiera y los riesgos del IMSS 2001–2002.* Mexico City: IMSS.

———. 2003. *Informe al Ejecutivo Federal y al Congreso de la Unión sobre la situación financiera y los riesgos del IMSS 2002–2003.* Mexico City: IMSS.

———. 2004. *Informe al Ejecutivo Federal y al Congreso de la Unión sobre la situación financiera y los riesgos del IMSS 2003–2004.* Mexico City: IMSS.

———. 2005. *Informe al Ejecutivo Federal y al Congreso de la Unión sobre la situación financiera y los riesgos del IMSS 2004–2005.* Mexico City: IMSS.

———. 2006. *Informe al Ejecutivo Federal y al Congreso de la Unión sobre la situación financiera y los riesgos del IMSS 2005–2006.* Mexico City: IMSS.

Kaplan, D., G. Martínez, and R. Robertson. 2005. "Worker and Job Flows in Mexico." Research report, Instituto Tecnológico Autónomo de México, Department of Economics, Mexico City.

Levy, S. 2006. "Productividad, crecimiento y pobreza en México: ¿Qué sigue después de Progresa-Oportunidades?" Inter-American Development Bank, Washington, DC.

———. 2008. *Good Intentions, Bad Outcomes: Social Policy, Informality and Economic Growth in Mexico.* Washington, DC: Brookings Institution Press.

Madero, D., and A. Mora. 2006. "Fomento a la competencia entre las administradoras de fondos para el retiro: Acciones y resultados en México." Coordinación General de Estudios Económicos, Documento de Trabajo 2006–1, Comisión Nacional del Sistema del Ahorro para el Retiro, Mexico City.

Maloney, W., and J. Nuñez Mendez. 2004. "Measuring the Impact of Minimum Wages: Evidence from Latin America." In *Law and Employment: Lessons from Latin America and the Caribbean,* ed. J. Heckman and C. Pages, 109–30. Chicago: University of Chicago Press.

7

Mexican Labor Markets: Protection, Productivity, and Power

William F. Maloney

Labor markets intermediate the flows of human talent and energy among enterprises. As such, their smooth functioning is critical to the growth process and to the attainment of higher levels of worker welfare. The latter can be thought of as a combination of higher incomes driven by increased productivity of workers and reduced exposure to risks that they and their families face.

That said, what set of institutions and norms will generate these outcomes? The basic neoclassical model of an infinite number of atomistic firms contracting at will an infinite number of atomistic workers offers a useful benchmark, but it applies virtually nowhere in the world. This includes Mexico, where a sizable share of the market is characterized by firms with substantial market power employing workers represented by powerful unions covered by, on paper and often in actual fact, extraordinarily protective labor legislation. At the same time, roughly half of the market, the informal sector, seems closer to the textbook model: not covered by labor protections and consisting largely of microfirms.

The striking contrast between the two halves of the labor market has led to the classic dualistic view of Mexican and, indeed, of developing country labor markets in general that focuses on the segmentation arising from distortionary labor institutions, including high minimum wages and union power. Not only do induced wage rigidities potentially lead to a misallocation of workers among jobs and sectors, but also they leave a large fraction of the workforce outside the labor protection system, thereby exacerbating inequities and leading to lower welfare as insiders benefit from access to exaggerated protections and benefits, preserving their privileged position from the outsiders who are excluded and uncovered.

I argue elsewhere (Maloney 1999, 2004) that in Mexico's case, this classic insider–outsider image largely misses the mark, and that the evidence suggests that, in practice, the formal and informal labor markets seem to be remarkably integrated. Workers frequently exit, to use Hirschman's (1970) term, formal employment and enter the informal sector voluntarily, implying that, at the margin, welfare in the two sectors is equated. Whatever risk they take on leaving the formal protection system, workers receive some compensation in terms of higher incomes, greater flexibility, or other nonpecuniary benefits. I also argue, concurring with Levy (chapter 6 in this volume), that saying the market is not segmented does not imply that all is well, because potentially important efficiency losses arise from such exit, either due to the push from the poor design of formal sector protections or the pull from implicit subsidies to informality. Furthermore, the concept of exit was conceived as a reaction to the lack of responsiveness of public institutions and, as such, suggests a poor social equilibrium where citizens lack confidence in the state and, hence, evade its mandates. It suggests that a very different lens needs to be taken to the labor code and union influence, one that, in particular, deemphasizes their distortionary impact on wages.

This alternative lens focuses on how the interaction of firm behavior on the one side and labor legislation and union interests on the other generate impediments to the accumulation and allocation of the factors of production that raise worker productivity—namely, education, capital, and knowledge. Roughly half the difference in worker productivity around the world is driven by the accumulation of physical and human capital or education. However, the other half is less well understood and is lumped under total factor productivity, which includes how resources are allocated across firms and industries and innovation, defined as the accumulation of knowledge capital captured in the adoption of new processes and technologies. The combination of these two phenomena is at the core of the process of Schumpeterian (1975) creative destruction that has been the driver of growth for the past few hundred years. Both "creation" and "destruction" are essential elements of the process: the entry of new firms will cause old capital to be scrapped, and the introduction of new ideas will render both old knowledge and previous ways of producing goods obsolete.

Both the rules of the game that firms play by and the legislation and institutions affecting labor would ideally recognize the need for the destructive aspect of modern growth and the need to cushion its impact on those who are adversely affected in the process of overall advance. Both sets of actors would see the need for localized short-term losses to support a more general long-term advance. Firms would recognize the need to produce in a competitive market, to aggressively pursue innovation, and to potentially be driven out of business. Labor would recognize firms' needs to cause short-run pain in order to advance productivity. Both firms and labor would recognize the need for institutions that provide a cushion for laid-off workers and support for the transition to new jobs. This would require changing the current protections embodied in the formal social security system and labor code that arguably protect formal workers at the same time both excessively and inadequately.

However, Mexico is arguably locked in a long-standing and self-defeating equilibrium. On the one hand, numerous chapters in this volume demonstrate the power that firms have to protect their privileged *rentier* positions and, in the process, dampen the impetus to innovation. On the other hand, the rigidities built into the labor code, and the particular modality of operation of some critical unions, although not especially segmenting, reflect a focus by labor on the redistribution of existing rents rather than on long-run productivity growth. Both work against the generation of high-paying jobs in the modern sector that, over the long run, is the most powerful tool for reducing the size of the informal sector and, arguably, reducing the risks that workers face.

Informality and Worker Protections: Beyond Segmentation to Exit

The large share of the labor force that is informal or unprotected by labor institutions has long been seen as evidence of the inequities in developing country labor markets and, often, the severe distortions. A literature with its roots in Harris and Todaro (1970) equates the informal sector with underemployment or disguised unemployment, that is, the disadvantaged sector of a market segmented by rigidities in the formal or covered sector of the economy. The classic view argues that wages that are set above market-clearing force workers to queue for preferred jobs while subsisting in the informal microfirm sector, which is characterized by an absence of benefits and by irregular work conditions, high turnover, and lower rates of remuneration. The implications for Mexico of this view are indeed dire: roughly half the country's workers are effectively second-class citizens and are excluded from labor protections, while a minority enjoys a relatively privileged position. Furthermore, labor legislation, other regulations, or union demands must be onerous and distorting to have caused this degree of segmentation.

However, another emerging view argues that the informal sector should be seen, as a first approximation, as an unregulated, largely voluntary, self-employed sector (see Perry and others 2007 for a recent survey of the Latin American literature). I argue (Maloney 1999, 2004) that, at the very least, most informal independent workers, either the self-employed or the owners of small businesses employing others, enter voluntarily from formal salaried labor on the basis of a cost-benefit analysis of being self-employed versus being salaried, and then of being formal versus being informal (see also Davila-Capalleja 1994). The corollary of this view is that regulation- or union-induced distortions that segment the labor market by providing insiders—those with formal labor contracts, and especially those covered by unions—with wages higher than market-clearing is not the primary driver of the structure of the labor market in Mexico. As already noted, in this view, labor market and social security regulations may still have significant efficiency costs, but not through the mechanisms envisaged in the traditional rationing perspective.

Segmentation in the Mexican Labor Market

Labor legislation and union power are the prime candidates for the source of segmentation and of a dual system of labor insiders and outsiders. For example, minimum wages are justified as a way of guaranteeing an income floor that permits families to at least meet their subsistence requirements. At the same time, many agree that raising the wage excessively above market-clearing levels can lead to job losses. In this case, income transfer occurs from those who lose their jobs to those who keep them at a higher level of remuneration. In some countries, this effect is pronounced and can lead to a net increase in poverty (Arango and Pachon 2003). However, although the minimum wage was binding in Mexico in the 1980s, a variety of authors conclude that it was certainly not binding in the 1990s (Castellanos, García-Verdú, and Kaplan 2004; Cunningham 2007; Maloney and Nuñez 2004). This is probably most clearly illustrated by noting that the presence of the minimum wage does not appear to have a major impact on the distribution of wages (figure 7.1). Indeed, Maloney and Nuñez argue that minimum wages may have a role in providing a floor to wages in the informal sector, suggesting that social norms exist around wage setting that transcend the formal–informal divide.

The second panel of figure 7.1 presents the cumulative distribution of wages and shows a discrete "cliff" at the minimum wage for informal workers. Castellanos, García-Verdú, and Kaplan (2004) also find some evidence that changes in the minimum wage affect changes in wages, but, overall, the conclusion holds that any impact on segmentation between formal and informal sectors is minor at best.

Unions and Wage Segmentation

The impact of unions on wages is more difficult to assess empirically. Mexico has a long tradition of unionization dating back to the revolution. Estimates of coverage range from roughly 10 to 25 percent of the total workforce of roughly 32 million (Brooks and Cason 1998). During the 1990s, Mexico had the highest union density in Latin America (O'Connell 1999). The 1992 National Survey of Employment, Salaries, Technology, and Training (Encuesta Nacional de Empleo, Salarios, Tecnologia y Capacitacion or ENESTYC) suggests that only 18 percent of manufacturing firms have no union representation and that the rest have a mean unionization rate of roughly 70 percent.

The most common view of union behavior sees unions as identifying the wage level that maximizes their utility, while firms then set the level of employment (these kinds of views are termed right-to-manage models). By pushing wages above market-clearing levels, this creates segmentation (see Guerrero, López-Calva, and Walton, chapter 4 in this volume, for how Mexican workers, especially in the petroleum sector, have acted in this classic fashion). However, an alternative view,

Figure 7.1 (a) Distribution of Wages in the Formal and Informal Sectors, Monthly, 1999 (b) Cumulative Distribution of Wages in the Formal and Informal Sectors

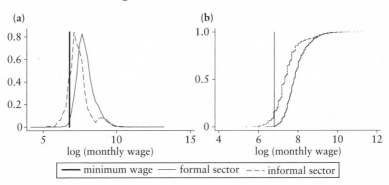

Sources: Cunningham 2007; Maloney and Nuñez 2004.

referred to as efficient bargaining, argues that if a firm is a monopolist or oligopolist and earns excess profits, then both unions and firms may be better-off by moving off the labor demand curve and bargaining over a combination of wages and employment. Bargaining to increase employment, termed featherbedding, does not necessarily lead to segmentation, but it is no less a way of transferring firms' profits to workers by creating unnecessary positions, and self-evidently leads to production inefficiencies.

The outcome of the bargaining process depends not only on the union's relative bargaining strength, but also on its relative preference for wage versus employment gains. As Pencavel (1995) notes, developing country unions may value employment over wages for several reasons, and these are clearly relevant to the Mexican context. First, like much of Latin America during the 1980s and early 1990s, job growth has been slow relative to population growth. Second, Mexico has no system of unemployment insurance; hence, workers may value employment stability more than wages. Third, since the formation of the Institutional Revolutionary Party in 1929 following the revolution, the major unions have had a long-standing and close relationship with the government and have cooperated in implementing policies to reduce inflationary pressures.[1] Particularly with the inception in 1987 of the Pact, a joint agreement of labor, business, and the government to promote price stability, unions have closely coordinated wage demands with Pact guidelines. O'Connell (1999: 41), for example, argues that in the 1992 Pact, the Confederación de Trabajadores de México "signed away salary increases of its members." Furthermore, wages showed extreme downward flexibility during the 1995 tequila crisis and showed little tendency to offset losses resulting from inflation or depreciation.[2] These factors taken together suggest an emphasis on employment creation relative to pushing up wages in the union utility function.

Empirical Evidence on the Impact of Union Power

The ENESTYC offers evidence for this kind of union behavior in the manufacturing sector as well as for efficiency wage effects.[3] Some strands of efficiency wage theory argue that firms decide on a wage relative to an outside wage that provides incentives for workers to stay with the firm and/or to work harder. The following wage equation, broadly following Dickens and Katz (1987) and Nickell and Wadhwani (1990), captures these effects:

$$w_{s,u} = \alpha_{wa} W_a + \alpha_u U + \alpha_h H + \alpha_x X + \varepsilon_w , \qquad (7.1)$$

where $w_{s,u}$ is the wage of skilled and unskilled workers respectively; W_a is a set of variables measuring the expected alternative wage a worker could get outside the firm to capture efficiency wage effects; U is a measure of union power; H is a set of variables capturing human capital; and X is set of firm-related characteristics, including a set of sectoral dummies (not reported).

Preliminary regressions suggest that, relative to nonunionized firms, firms with unions pay 15.2 percent more to skilled workers and 9.25 percent more to unskilled workers. However, ascertaining whether unions cause wage differentials or whether unions are more likely to be found in certain types of firms that also pay higher wages is difficult. Statistical tests strongly reject the hypothesis that union and nonunion firms can be taken as similar and combined in one sample. In what follows, only firms with union presence were kept in the sample to reduce the possibility of selection bias in measuring the union wage. That is, the impact of union power within the sample of firms with unions is estimated.

The annex to this chapter details the exact variables used. They include a variety of measures capturing the technological sophistication of the firm, its ownership structure, and the human capital of its workers, all of which may be correlated with union presence and hence, ideally, should be controlled for. Table 7.1 suggests that the higher the productivity of the firm, the higher the wage. The outside wage that workers can get will push up wages, although, counterintuitively, the probability of being hired elsewhere does not. The traditional measures of human capital—levels of schooling and potential experience and their squares—also have the expected influence. As discussed later, the quality of education probably also would have an important effect if good measures were available.

Among firm characteristics, more productive firms, those that have more capital per worker, those that use automated machinery (for skilled workers), those that have recently acquired technologies, those owned by foreign groups, those that are exporters (for skilled workers), and those that are larger all pay higher wages—consistent with the idea that larger, more open and externally competitive, and innovative firms—will pay higher wages. This situation could be because they demand workers with qualities unobserved in the data or pay higher wages to induce higher performance on the job and lower turnover. Either way, Mexican workers would like more of these jobs.

In a surprising result, the free-standing union density term—the measure of union bargaining power—virtually never enters significantly into the wage equations for unskilled workers (as would be predicted by the standard models of union behavior), and has a

Table 7.1 Wage Equations: Impact of Union Membership on Wages

Variable	Skilled		Unskilled	
Productivity	0.036	(0.01)*	0.039	(0.01)**
Log (outside wage)	0.300	(0.06)**	0.433	(0.09)**
Hiring rate	−0.865	(0.21)**	0.236	(0.20)
Union density	−0.065	(0.03)**	−0.002	(0.00)
Schooling	0.571	(0.06)**	0.238	(0.06)**
Schooling 2	−0.022	(0.00)**	−0.014	(0.00)**
Experience	0.027	(0.01)**	0.018	(0.01)**
Experience 2	−0.001	(0.00)**	−0.001	(0.00)**
Productivity after training	0.024	(0.03)	0.001	(0.03)
Log (capital/labor)	0.016	(0.01)*	−0.014	(0.01)*
Automated machinery	0.001	(0.00)*	0.000	(0.00)
Quality control	0.094	(0.19)	0.238	(0.20)
Research and development	0.010	(0.03)	−0.035	(0.03)
Technology acquisition	0.097	(0.02)**	0.135	(0.03)**
Dummy competitiveness	−0.008	(0.02)	−0.003	(0.02)
Dummy corporate	0.028	(0.03)	0.067	(0.03)**
Dummy foreign ownership	0.179	(0.03)**	0.025	(0.03)
Dummy export	−0.108	(0.03)**	0.024	(0.03)
Dummy medium	−0.229	(0.03)**	−0.091	(0.03)**
Dummy small	−0.676	(0.03)**	−0.335	(0.03)**
Constant	3.523	(0.68)**	3.082	(0.73)**
R^2	0.2895		0.1191	
F test	49.43**		16.39**	

Source: Author's calculations based on the ENESTYC.

Note: * = significant at the 10 percent level, ** = significant at the 5 percent level. Numbers in parentheses are standard errors. Samples sizes: nonunion n = 731, union n = 3,422. Chow tests for equality of union and nonunion coefficient (27d.f.) 86.66. a (skilled), 42.37 a (unskilled).

Also includes industry dummies (not shown).

negative relationship with skilled wages. More detailed work suggests a positive union effect for workers who earn little given measured human capital. If, for example, workers' unobserved characteristics (such as reliability and diligence) dictate a low wage relative to those who, on paper, appear similar, then unions will push them toward the average for their class. Overall, however, union density does not appear to have a major impact on unskilled wages for this sample of industries, but it does increase employment levels. The counterintuitive result of a negative impact of union density on skilled wages and employment is less easily explained. It might reflect unobserved characteristics across skilled workers, with firms with lower union densities attracting or training more productive workers.

These findings may differ from other similar exercises (Guerrero, López-Calva, and Walton, chapter 4 in this volume; Panagides and Patrinos 1994) partly because of the approach taken to avoid endogeneity and the inclusion of a more complete set of regressors to soak up firm effects that might be associated with union power. In addition, the results presented here give an average effect for a set of manufacturing industries, whereas in selected industries, such as the petrochemicals industry, there is clear evidence of classic wage-augmenting behavior. The *Wall Street Journal* (2006), for instance, details the pay demands of Petróleos Mexicanos (better known as PEMEX) and educational unions in recent years.[4] As noted in chapter 4 in this volume, wage-setting behavior may be different in competitive manufacturing sectors than in other sectors, especially the public sector, that do not face product market competition.

Evidence of Exit into Informality as an Option for Formal Workers

Two of the primary potential sources of segmentation of the labor market thus appear to have little influence on the overall wage level and, hence, on segmentation. Other evidence also suggests that workers behave as if the formal and informal sectors are well integrated and that the kind of crude insider–outsider paradigm fits poorly. Several types of evidence suggest that mobility of workers among firms is extensive and that much of this mobility is of voluntary moves from the formal sector to the informal sector. First, turnover in the Mexican labor market is high, and much of it seems to be voluntary. The ENESTYC indicates that every six months, 26 percent of unskilled workers and 9 percent of skilled workers separate from their jobs and that 85 percent of these separations are quits, even from large corporations.

Second, the National Microenterprises Survey suggests that roughly 70 percent of those leaving formal jobs enter informal self-employment voluntarily, either for higher earnings or for more flexibility (Maloney 1999).

Third, gross workers flows using the National Urban Employment Survey support these reported motivations. If we think of the labor market as highly segmented, then informality is a holding pattern in inferior jobs and one would expect an overall pattern of graduation whereby workers enter the workforce in informality, queue up until they get better formal jobs, and then retire. The reverse transition would occur only during downturns when displaced workers seek some form of income to stay afloat. Alternatively, if informal jobs offer different qualities—independence, tax evasion, exercise of entrepreneurial skills—but are not necessarily inferior, then we might expect patterns of transition among sectors corresponding more closely to what we find in the United States: workers search across sectors and move more or less symmetrically among them, and they are more likely to search during booms when the labor market is tighter and success as a micro-entrepreneur is more likely. Figure 7.2 supports the latter view: a reallocation of workers across sectors that is both more or less symmetrical and procyclical. That is, more people search for jobs in and enter informality during upturns than downturns. Indeed, the rise of net flows into informality at the same time that informal earnings relative to formal earnings rose during the boom of 1987–92 again suggests substantial voluntary opening of microfirms when the economy is doing well. These patterns are broadly echoed for the informal salaried sector.

The traditional segmentation view holds more clearly during downturns, although recent work suggests that the adjustment mechanisms are somewhat different from those conventionally imagined. During the 1995 crisis, Bosch and Maloney (2007) show that formal sector hiring ceased while informal sector hiring did not, much as Shimer (2005, 2007) documents for downturns in the United States. This occurs among other changes that are somewhat counter to what is usually thought: the informal sector actually sheds more labor into unemployment than the formal sector, and fewer

Figure 7.2 Gross Labor Flows between Formal Salaried and Self-Employed Sectors, 1987–2003

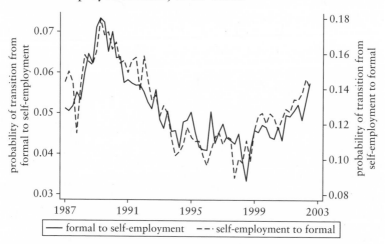

Source: Bosch and Maloney 2007.

workers transit into informality from formality (as displaced labor, for example) than is the case during good times. However, the continued hiring of the informal sector from unemployment dominates the other effects. The informal sector expands and its relative earnings decline relative to those in the formal sector. The share of workers preferring formal sector jobs rises.

What drives the shut-down in formal sector hiring is not clear, even in the United States, where the formal sector accounts for most of the labor force. Bewley (1999), for instance, argues that firms prefer not to lower wages during downturns to avoid an across-the-board deterioration in morale. Workers soon forget their fired colleagues and never meet the ones not hired. However, the U.S. literature is not even sure whether wage rigidities can explain the shut-down in formal hiring. Simulations suggest that they account for little, and Haefke, Sonntag, and van Rens (2007) argue that the relevant wage—that of the last worker hired—is actually extremely flexible.

Taking both the evidence on segmentation and the discussion of worker transitions into account, the bottom line appears to be that for much of the time, a large fraction of the workforce moves easily and voluntarily between formal and informal sector jobs.

Implications of the Exit View

I argue (Maloney 2004) that this view moved the policy focus away from segmentation-driven inefficiencies to the incentives workers face to be formal or informal. One can think of workers as undertaking an analysis of the benefits and costs of different job types and, rather than being rationed out of formality, they may decide that they are better-off being in the informal sector. Emphatically, this does not imply that they are happy or well-off or that things are optimal. It implies only that informality may represent the best among poor choices given the options available. This is obviously especially the case among poorly educated workers who choose between bad jobs in the formal sector and bad jobs in the informal sector. However, the logic of exit raises an important agenda for labor market reform away from cutting minimum wages, bashing unions, or undertaking more intense brute enforcement of existing labor regulations that emerge from the traditional segmentation view: governments need to work on eliminating the inefficiencies in the design of worker protections, either formal or informal, or the elements in the labor code that provide a disincentive to formality.

This vision of informality as an exit option was developed more thoroughly by Perry and others (2007), and Levy formalizes and further explores it for the social security dimension of the formal–informal divide (chapter 6 in this volume). Levy offers a revealing exploration of disincentives to formality caused by the poor design of pensions arising precisely from the high rates of transition of poor workers into and out of the Mexican Social Security Institute (Instituto Mexicano del Seguro Social, or IMSS), effectively the informality–formality transition patterns that we see in figure 7.2: workers may never accumulate enough seniority to earn the pensions to which they contribute.

This is consistent with interviews of informal workers in Guadalajara by sociologist Roberts (1991), who notes that "the absence of welfare coverage is a drawback, but, on the other hand, many informants cited the deductions made for welfare as a disadvantage of formal employment, particularly since the services they received were poor" (50). Put differently, perceived costs and benefits of formality are misaligned. Realigning these, James (1999) notes, was an important part of the rationale for defined contribution pension plans. By guaranteeing that workers would get back what they contributed, they "reduce labor market distortions, such as evasion by escape to the informal sector, since people are less likely to regard their contribution as a tax" (James 1999: 7). Kugler and Kugler (2003) discuss a similar logic for Colombia. It is also plausible to imagine a micro-entrepreneur, perhaps faced with borrowing constraints to expand a business, being reluctant to hand over current resources to a government of dubious trustworthiness for a promise of an old-age pension in the distant future. Barr and Packard's (2002) work on Chile supports this view. They find that participation in the government's voluntary pension scheme, a private individual account scheme with no redistributive dimension, is extraordinarily low, around 4 percent. This low participation suggests that these entrepreneurs are choosing to be unprotected even by the scheme that arguably best aligns costs and benefits in the region. In general, any program where workers value benefits below the costs to them, because of either poor performance or inappropriate bundling of programs, will lead to the same effect.

This logic extends to other dimensions of labor legislation. The rigid promotion ladder that values seniority over worker performance may leave exit as the preferred option for talented workers frustrated by a lack of promotion. Severance payments may also not be what they seem. As Davila-Capalleja (1994) and Kaplan and Sadka (2008) calculate, the litigation process surrounding unjust dismissals may leave workers with far less than promised on paper.

That exit is voluntary does not imply social optimality in a larger sense. A worker's conclusion that the cost of state-provided benefits substantially exceeds the likely benefits still leaves the family at least partially unprotected in important ways. Family- or community-level substitutes for pensions or unemployment insurance may be available, but these are likely to be imperfect. Health services raise major issues in relation to insurance market failures and tend to require facilities for service delivery not easily substituted for in the informal sector. Pension systems are designed in part with the idea that agents are myopic and do not plan well for their retirement. The exit option frustrates the attempt to ensure that they do plan well. Policies to directly protect informal workers, what Levy calls social protection, have unexpected implications. Any policy that makes informality relatively more attractive also leads to a reallocation of workers. Social protection policies that provide services without explicit taxes effectively provide a subsidy to informality. This provision is problematic. A government may reasonably argue that formal and informal workers have a right to certain transfers or benefits, but to the degree that this right leads to exit, this view encourages workers to leave formality, shifting the labor supply curve to the left and raising wages in the formal sector. This implicitly adds a tax on the formal sector and makes it less competitive. Hence, addressing the genuine needs of the families of informal workers implies a tradeoff with competitiveness more generally.

Levy (chapter 6) examines several ways that this exit can affect the productivity of the economy. A few more follow. First, although evidence to date is weak, microfirms probably have fewer prospects for productivity gains than bigger firms. Hence, shifting workers into informality may imply less aggregate growth. Second, de Soto's (1989) classic story of firms not growing to avoid excessive taxes or regulatory burdens is also subject to the same cost-benefit considerations: firms may stay suboptimally small if the benefits of becoming formal, such as access to credit, lower bribes, and better utility services, are low relative to the costs (Davila-Capalleja 1994; Levenson and Maloney 1996). Another potential productivity loss may arise from exactly the turnover induced by the exit option. If firms risk losing their investment in training, they will hire fewer workers, train less, or pay efficiency wages to keep those workers. Evidence from Mexico suggests that roughly 50 percent of firms offer higher remuneration of various types in response to resignations by recently trained workers, while roughly 10 percent reduce the training offered (Ribeiro and Maloney 1999). Finally, Krebs (2003) and Krebs, Krishna, and Maloney (2005) argue that, as with any other asset, the higher the risk on the return to human capital given an average return (in this case, the wage), the lower the investment. If Mexico were to have the level of wage uncertainty characterized by the United States, worker welfare would be higher by the equivalent of roughly 0.5 percentage point in growth in year, and the resulting higher accumulation of human capital would add another 0.5 percentage points. Because microfirms, which across the world offer riskier earnings than salaried jobs, dominate the informal sector, some productivity drag from this source is likely.

Size of the Exit Effect

In assessing the effects of the processes described here, useful knowledge would be how much an increase in the pure tax on formal wages—that is, income surrendered without corresponding benefits, or a pure subsidy to informality—affects the decision to be informal. Empirics are in their infancy in this regard, and I can offer only a couple of approaches that, regrettably, give a wide range of estimates. The first is to exploit the now well-established finding that self-employment, which can be used as a proxy for informality, decreases almost log linearly with the level of development (figure 7.3). One argument is that, all things being equal, workers would prefer not to have a boss, but as the opportunity cost of operating one's own micro-enterprise increases—that is, as higher-paying jobs emerge in the modern salaried sector—fewer people enter the microfirm sector. If this is the case, then the imposition of the tax or the granting of a subsidy can be thought of as reducing this opportunity cost. The second approach uses data from Mexican worker employment transitions and a two-sector model of the formal and informal sectors to simulate the impact of the same policies on formal firm hiring and the rate at which formal sector workers quit to enter self-employment (Krebs and Maloney 1999).

The two methods offer substantially different estimates of how much the share of informal self-employment in total employment would increase in response to a 1 percent increase in the relative attractiveness of informality. The first approach gives a value of between 0.03 percent (using data from Maloney 2001) and 0.05 percent (using data from Loayza and Rigolini 2006), depending on the precise assumptions. The simulation method gives a value of 0.3 percent. That is, if we assume that 10 percent of formal sector earnings are absorbed in unvalued benefits (pure tax), and say another 10 percent of the value of earnings is given to informal workers in untied social protection programs (subsidy), leading to a decrease in the relative attractiveness of formal work of 20 percent, then in the first case, the size of the informal self-employed sector increases by 0.6 to 1.2 percentage points of the workforce and, in the second, by 6 percentage points.

Figure 7.3 Self-Employment Versus Level of Development, Selected Countries, 1990s

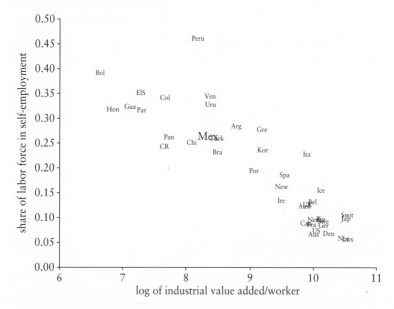

Source: Maloney 2001.

Using an alternative approach, Fernandes, Gremaud, and Narita (2006) simulate the impact of eliminating the labor tax on workers earning up to the minimum wage, thereby effectively providing formal sector benefits for free, while maintaining revenue neutrality. They find a decrease in formality of 1.5 percent.

The first and third approaches suggest modest, although non-trivial impacts. The second suggests that the disincentive effects of a low benefit-cost ratio could be a major determinant of the relative size of the informal self-employed sector with the potential to account for much of the variance observed among countries at similar levels of development (figure 7.3).

Broader Implications of the Exit Option

The exit option has implications far beyond the social security and social protection issues discussed earlier, with larger issues relevant to improving the social contract. Exit occurs at many levels: is it referred to as informality when poor workers choose to be unregistered and as tax evasion when large firms or wealthy individuals opt out? At whatever level, it can be viewed as both a cause and a manifestation of a troubled social contract. Under such circumstances, two functions of government, addressing inequities and providing public goods, become problematic. First, any attempt to redistribute income across workers necessarily implies that those who are better-off will be taxed more than they receive back from the government. As Perry and others (2006) state, a substantial increase in progressive transfers would be required; informality, in this case tax evasion of better-off workers, is both an obstacle to and a result of attempts to redress inequities. Second, the nature of public goods (such as defense, general infrastructure, and public education) is such that not contributing will not lead to any loss in benefits to the person evading the taxes required to finance them. Thus, the marginal benefit of paying taxes for these services is, by definition, zero.

The universality of these considerations leads all societies to implement mechanisms or foster norms supporting compliance. On one side, governments monitor evasion and assess fines. However, the size of penalties is generally too small to provide straightforward private incentives for compliance, and the literature on tax morale stresses that in most Organisation for Economic Co-operation and Development countries, people pay partly because they trust that others will pay too and feel some obligation to the overall national agenda. In this sense, the "warm glow" effect that some economists (and recently neurobiologists) argue can accompany paying taxes decreases the incentives to evade. By contrast, in countries where feelings of trust and reciprocity are weaker, we would expect more exit. As Perry and others (2007) argue, Latin America, including Mexico, may be in a bad equilibrium where the glow is weak: there is little sense of community or shared well-being, few pay, and many seek to evade. As a result, the state underprovides public goods and has mustered inadequate distributional efforts.

Labor Markets and Productivity Growth

Ideally, Mexico would be in a better equilibrium where all thought well of the government and felt drawn, not merely compelled, to interact with it as the incarnation of the social contract. The previous section explored the implications of a view of the labor market where segmentation is not a dominant feature, and where informality is, at the margin, a choice that workers are making voluntarily. Hence, the focus on the distribution of the largesse of the state or on worker protections through the optic of insiders and outsiders is probably misplaced. This section will explore another equilibrium that has potentially larger negative implications for Mexican growth, but which is arguably independent of whether or not the labor market is segmented in the traditional sense. In a nutshell, the Mexican labor code and union–employer relations appear more oriented toward allocating a fixed or slow-growing stock of rents than toward facilitating the accumulation and reallocation of physical and knowledge capital while effectively protecting workers from the dislocations these processes necessarily imply.

Importance of Reallocation and Creative Destruction

The international literature has recently focused on the importance of the ease of reallocating factors of production across sectors and from firms with low productivity to firms with high productivity. Thus, the discussion concerns net accumulation, with the understanding that the process of creative destruction implies that the entry of new firms will cause old capital to be scrapped and that the introduction of new ideas will render old knowledge obsolete. Barriers to this type of reallocation of factors can have dramatic impacts on total factor productivity and, hence, on income levels. Caselli and Tenreyo (2004) argue that convergence in both Italy and Spain occurred largely by moving the workforce from low productivity to higher productivity sectors and by increasing the productivity of those sectors through general advances in organization and management. Productivity growth within sectors similarly depends greatly on the most productive firms absorbing a larger share of markets and resources. Hsieh and Klenow (2007) argue that if barriers to the allocation of factors are removed as their marginal products are equated across sectors, manufacturing total factor productivity would rise 25 to 40 percent in China and 50 to 60 percent in India (see also Banerjee and Duflo 2005). In a competitive market, labor benefits greatly from such increases in higher wages and employment growth.

Consistent with this view, Bergoeing and Repetto (2006) calculate that much of the gain in Chilean total factor productivity in the 1970s and 1980s was due to precisely these types of reallocations, including the displacement of less productive firms by new, higher productivity firms. Only in the 1990s, with the consolidation of the reforms, did "unbounded, *within-plant* [emphasis added] efficiency gains driven by technology adoption and innovation occur" (Bergoeing and Repetto 2006: 3). Bergoeing, Hernando, and Repetto (2006) argue that the adoption of better technologies and production processes by both incumbents and new firms was facilitated, in particular, by the reform of financial markets and the traded goods markets.

The greater appreciation of the role of such reallocations, and of creative destruction more generally, has intensified the focus on the microeconomic flexibility necessary to ensure that this process occurs. Lack of flexibility may arise because although institutions or actors may favor the accumulation of capital, they may actively resist the adoption of new technologies and processes. Although the idea that the creative destruction process is critical to growth has been accepted since Schumpeter (1975), the destruction part of the phenomenon can nonetheless lead to intense dislocation for either owners of firms likely to be displaced or workers whose jobs are imperiled.

That firms may resist the forces of competition that might drive productivity growth and may prefer a more rentist existence is well documented in Latin America and elsewhere. Rajan and Zingales (2004) examine *rentier* mentalities among advanced country corporate elite and the need for active financial markets to ensure the pressure of new entry. Even though Schumpeter argues that more innovative firms are those that enjoy some market power and rents, Aghion and others (2005) provide evidence of the importance of competition for innovation. Firms that are close to the technology frontier, but that suddenly face lower barriers to entering firms or trade liberalization, will innovate, in a sense to escape from the competition and sustain their market position. Without such competition, they will not.

The leaden protectionism of the period of import substitution industrialization in Latin America sheltered industries from exactly these competitive forces, and many firms clearly resisted the reallocations of assets occurring in the wake of trade reforms. However, if we are to believe the estimates of Hsieh and Klenow (2007) and Banerjee and Duflo (2005) and the evidence from Chile, such reallocations are essential for productivity growth and, with it, wages. This volume suggests that Mexico is no exception to the Latin American rule. For example, Haber (chapter 8) documents how, historically, a highly concentrated financial system has permitted sheltering financial and industrial elites from competition, and Guerrero, López-Calva, and Walton (chapter 4) discuss the apparent use of influence, including the use of *amparos* (stays of action) to deflect challenges to monopoly power in key sectors.

For organized labor, a similar tension is apparent between the need to adopt new technologies to raise worker productivity, and hence the standard of living of workers in the future, and to protect the livelihoods of current workers. Prescott and Parente (2000) argue that, historically, a bias toward the latter—in particular, resistance by guilds and organized labor to the adoption of new technologies— is the critical contributor to current income disparities among countries. In this light, excessively strong regulation on the reallocation of workers or high firing costs may be impediments to the necessary adoption of technologies as well as to the more general flexibility discussed earlier.

For Chile, Caballero and others (2004) measure the relative ease with which firms adjust their levels of employment, either up or down, to productivity shocks across countries and argue that differences in such flexibility can account for roughly a percentage point in growth.[5] Furthermore, they argue that reduction in their measure of microeconomic flexibility (the speed at which firms close the gap between current and desired levels of employment) in Chile since the 1997 Asian financial crisis may account for a substantial fraction of the decline in total factor productivity growth since 1997 and, potentially, could account for a permanent reduction of 0.5 percent in the growth rate.

In both the historical and Chilean examples, the focus on labor flexibility is probably excessively narrow and the concerns of the investigators cited earlier (Aghion and others 2005; Guerrero, López-Calva, and Walton, chapter 4 in this volume; Haber, chapter 8 in this volume) need to be maintained in the center of the debate as well. However, labor legislation and union approaches differ greatly across countries and are thought to have important impacts on productivity growth. U.S. labor legislation is among the most conducive to reallocation, and ongoing debate surrounds the role of more rigid European legislation in European countries' lower levels of growth.

Menezes-Filho and Van Reenen (2003) survey the theoretical and empirical evidence available for advanced countries and note the varying roles of unions in different countries. Unionized companies tend to have a lower rate of turnover by reducing grievances, and unions can induce firms to increase incremental training expenditures to motivate workers, thereby favoring the entrance of new technology. The Scandinavian unions go further, providing an example of how unions may promote productivity-enhancing industrial policy and investment and emphasizing the rationalization of firms (Blomström and Meller 1991). Hjalmarsson (1991), for example, suggests that Swedish unions take as axiomatic the link between technological upgrading and wage increases and aggressively encourage firms to adopt new techniques and to shed less productive operations. Hence, unions can be vital partners with management in ensuring productivity growth. Clearly, the necessary complement to this flexibility is a strong safety net for workers. Unemployment insurance programs are features of all Organisation for Economic Co-operation and Development legislation, and retraining programs for displaced workers are central elements of the Scandinavian package for high-growth labor relations.

Arguably, Mexico's overall approach to labor relations is the opposite, that is, rooted less in the pursuit of increasing efficiency and growth than in a defensive stance in a context where job growth is slow and society is geared toward dividing current rents. For instance, the absence of a system of unemployment insurance and the lack of portability of some pension funds, particularly in the public sector, has led to excessive emphasis on job stability, costly severance payments, and involved litigation. The job security provisions first set forth in Article 123 of the 1917 constitution and then expanded in the 1931 Federal Labor Law (amended in 1970) establish that, with the exception of temporary workers and those hired to undertake specific assignments, the relationship between employer and employee is a permanent one. For workers to be legally dismissed, employers must prove that the employees committed certain unacceptable behavior such as stealing, unauthorized absence from work, or drunkenness. Even in these cases, workers can appeal to the labor courts and can be awarded the constitutional right to be reinstated along with the payment of all back wages. Critically, the legal treatment of dismissal for economic grounds (redundancy) is the same as for arbitrary dismissals,[6] and if the dismissal occurs because of technological change, the compensation is even higher.

As figure 7.4 shows, together, restrictions on hiring and firing make Mexico one of the more rigid labor markets in the world (Heckman and Pages 2004; López-De-Silanes and others 2004). From a theoretical point of view, such restrictions do not necessarily translate into segmentation; they just reduce the number of jobs for a given level of output. Once again they highlight a fundamental choice facing workers in an era of rapid technological change: how much to value short-run employment stability over the potential for longer-run productivity and standard-of-living gains. Losing a job and finding a new one clearly entails large costs. If workers see these factors as necessary elements of a system that generates continuing productivity gains that will make them and their progeny better-off with time, then the factors are accepted, as is the case in the United States and much of Europe. However, if productivity growth is slow and, hence, rising living standards depend on increasing a share of relatively fixed rents, then the existing model may seem more compelling.

In practice, the current fight-for-rents model protects workers badly, and a better designed employment security system would somewhat mitigate the tradeoff discussed earlier. Although high severance payments are a disincentive to firing, and therefore should, in principle, insulate workers from shocks arising from employment loss, workers often demand such payments at exactly the moment when a firm is least able to honor its obligations, leading to increased

Figure 7.4 Firing Rigidities Index, Selected Economies, 1990s

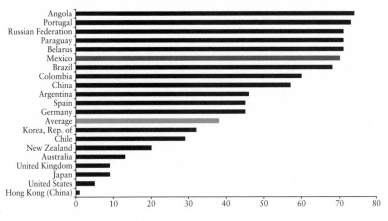

Source: López-De-Silanes and others 2004.

stress on weak firms and exacerbated uncertainty for workers about the firm's ability to pay. In practice, most severance packages are renegotiated and workers receive substantially less than the amount mandated by law.

Unions

Unions, too, behave in a way that privileges job stability over productivity. As noted earlier, the outcome of the bargaining process between unions and firms depends on the union's relative bargaining strength, but it also depends on the relative preference for wage versus employment gains and the lack of rapid job growth, and a strong safety net may lead toward a greater privileging of employment.

Labor demand is estimated analogously to the previous section as

$$N_{s,u} = \beta_w W + \beta_q q + \beta_{wa} W + \beta_u U + \beta_x X + \varepsilon_n, \qquad (7.2)$$

where $N_{s,u}$ is the log of labor demand for skilled or unskilled labor; W captures both the skilled and the unskilled log wages; and q, log firm output, and the other groups of variables remain the same as in the wage equation, albeit with some variation in the exact set.

Table 7.2 shows that, as expected, higher levels of output, larger firm size, and higher capacity utilization lead to higher employment levels and that higher levels of wages (or lower levels of wages for the substitute type of worker—blue collar for white collar and vice versa) lead to lower employment. The age of the firm appears to be correlated

Table 7.2 Labor Demand Equations: Two-Stage
Least Squares

Variable	Skilled		Unskilled	
Log (output)*	0.480	(0.02)**	0.405	(0.02)**
Log (wage) skilled	−0.379	(0.02)**	−0.024	(0.02)
Log (wage) unskilled	0.037	(0.02)**	−0.591	(0.02)
Log (outside wage) skilled	−0.091	(0.07)	0.195	(0.08)**
Log (outside wage) unskilled	−0.002	(0.12)	−0.244	(0.13)*
Hiring rate skilled	0.081	(0.03)**	0.067	(0.04)*
Hiring rate unskilled	0.008	(0.00)**	0.001	(0.00)
Union density	−0.417	(0.24)*	2.689	(0.26)**
Age	0.004	(0.00)**	−0.003	(0.00)
Age 2	−0.002	(0.00)	0.008	(0.00)**
Capacity utilization	−0.001	(0.00)*	0.003	(0.00)**
Automated machinery	0.000	(0.00)	0.000	(0.00)
Quality control	−0.060	(0.18)	0.048	(0.19)
Research and development	0.042	(0.02)*	−0.039	(0.03)
Technology acquisition	−0.016	(0.02)	−0.027	(0.03)
Dummy corporate	0.080	(0.03)**	0.059	(0.03)**
Dummy foreign ownership	0.155	(0.03)**	0.010	(0.03)
Dummy export	0.068	(0.03)**	0.234	(0.03)**
Dummy medium	−0.339	(0.03)**	−0.612	(0.03)**
Dummy small	−0.524	(0.05)**	−1.129	(0.05)**
Constant	1.986	(0.69)**	3.212	(0.75)**
R^2	0.6339		0.6918	
F test	210.25**		269.56**	
DHW	72.44**		151.53**	

Source: Author's calculations based on the ENESTYC.

Note: * = significant at the 10 percent level, ** = significant at the 5 percent level.
Numbers in parentheses are standard errors. Samples sizes: nonunion n = 731, union
n = 3,422. Chow tests for equality of union and nonunion coefficient (26d.f.) 36.23*
a (skilled), 130.89** (unskilled).

Estimation: Two-stage least squares. Instruments for output: capital stock, its
square, sector dummies, and its interactions and technology variables.

(through the quadratic term) with more unskilled employees. With the
exception of research and development spending for skilled workers,
traditional innovation variables—automation, quality control, and
technology acquisition—do not appear to be labor displacing.

Union density does have a strong positive effect on the level of
unskilled employment, suggesting an extreme case of efficient bargaining where unions accept the market wage, but cause firms to
move off the demand curve to hire more labor.[7] For each 1 percent
of the workforce that is unionized, unskilled employment appears to

increase by roughly 2.5 percent. Furthermore, as might be expected, estimates of the impact of unions on productivity (not shown) confirm the intuition that the additional labor hired gives rise to a significant adverse effect. Somewhat counterintuitively, the regressions for skilled workers find a negative union effect. This might suggest that among firms with high levels of employment, given their characteristics, unions represent primarily unskilled workers and crowd out those more skilled or force the use of less skill-intensive technologies. Alternatively, perhaps when unions seek to organize, they pick firms with large labor forces but, within this group, choose those with relatively more unskilled workers.

These findings, taken together with the wage regressions of the previous section, suggest that, at least for relatively unskilled workers, union power is directed more toward increasing employment and is not particularly focused on wages. This is consistent with limited anecdotal evidence. For instance, early surveys of 206 Mexican workers found that "the members themselves state that unions make an almost insignificant contribution to obtaining higher wages," although "an overwhelming majority of the workers interviewed stated that the union had helped them find a job" (Germidis 1974: 30).

In relation to this discussion and the discussion of wages in the previous section, three points are important. First, strong union power can be consistent with an unsegmented labor market and, indeed, an increase in formal employment. As Layard and Nickell (1990) note, the general equilibrium effects on the overall level of labor employed in the economy are clear: if unions bargain over employment as well as wages, and if the elasticity of substitution is less than unity (Ribeiro and Maloney 1999), employment in the union sector should be higher than in the absence of unions. So far, as they reduce the level of employment by rationing workers into the informal sector, Mexican unions may be preserving low-skilled jobs at the cost of lower wages.

Second, variables associated with innovation, firm growth, and technological progress tend to raise wages and do not have obvious negative impacts on employment within firms. To the extent that technological progress may cause individual firms to fail, there is obviously a loss of employment in those firms, although, in the aggregate, the effects are less clear.

Finally, whatever the logic of the observed union behavior in a context where job growth is slow and society is geared toward dividing current rents, it is potentially costly in terms of long-run worker welfare exactly because it impedes such growth and modernization of firms. If the union perceives that new technology will modify the labor intensity structure of the firm with a consequent job cut, it can attempt to undermine the adoption of new technologies.

The lower worker productivity in union firms observed in the regressions may arise from such dynamics—forcing firms to stay with more labor-intensive technologies—or it may simply imply make-work jobs. The evidence that might offer insight is largely anecdotal and not specifically from the manufacturing sector, but it suggests both types of behavior that, in the perspective of Prescott and Parente (2000), are damaging to long-run worker welfare and development. García-Verdú (2004) argues that unions drastically increased the cost of adopting new technologies in the Mexican aviation industry, if not impeded them altogether. In one instance, the union representing flight attendants argued that limits on the maximum workday prohibited Aeroméxico's plans to fly nonstop flights to São Paolo and Santiago in Chile that new planes permitted. Similarly, the pilots' union effectively blocked the airline's plans to replace ageing DC-9s with the Boeing 737s needed to comply with U.S. environmental restrictions. The flight attendants' union also blocked the reductions from four to three attendants made possible by the better-designed Boeing 737-700 on technical and safety grounds.

The international press has covered similar resistance to techno-logical upgrading in the electric power industry. The Sindicato Méx-icano de Electricidad, one of the earliest unions, dating back to the revolution, is portrayed as opposing modernization and enjoying exceptional perquisites: one generating plant was overstaffed, by union calculations, by a factor of almost 100; stable hands are still employed even though dray horses have not been used in decades; and rigid work rules lead to productivity-inhibiting absurdities. According to the *Wall Street Journal* (1999, A1) "The union won't permit the use of premixed concrete lest the worker who hand-mixes concrete lose his job. The union wants productivity pay for secretar-ies when a new photocopier is installed that allows for, say, 400 copies an hour instead of 80. It takes three workers to change a light bulb: one to carry the ladder, a second to change the bulb and a third to supervise. The union contract, says an aide in the energy secre-tariat, 'is something out of Alice in Wonderland.'"

The concern is not just that the Sindicato Méxicano de Electrici-dad can shut down Mexico City's power with the flip of a switch, but that, over the longer term, the inability of power generation to keep up with demand poses a serious threat to economic growth. The union strongly opposed private investment in the sector and President Ernesto Zedillo's attempt to privatize the industry. As the *Wall Street Journal* (1999) notes, the fear is precisely that privatiza-tion would lead to massive job losses such as were reported to be the case when Mexico privatized its railways. Another possibility is that, as the unions claim, lack of upgrading and low performance is due to insufficient funds being dedicated to infrastructure. However, the picture that potential businesses abroad get is one of a country paralyzed by conflictive unions and archaic work rules.

Less directly, union power has also become associated with a severe deterioration of critical services to workers and their families that, in all probability, has hampered Mexico's growth and poverty reduction. Levy (chapter 6) argues that the IMSS union has created an inequitable pension system whereby affiliates receive 42 percent of their last salary while IMSS employees receive roughly 120 percent of their final salary. More critically, the scheme is not sustainable given projected contributions. Levy argues that IMSS affiliates will see a progressive reduction in the coverage and quality of their health benefits, and calculates that by 2025, all affiliate contributions will be dedicated to paying union pensions, thereby leaving no resources for health programs.

Similar concerns surround union resistance to improving the quality of Mexico's education system. Figure 7.5 reveals two critical facts. First, students in Mexico, indeed, Latin American students in general, score abysmally on international standardized mathematics tests. The literature suggests that this may have important impacts

Figure 7.5 Education Expenditure and Mathematics Scores, Selected Economies

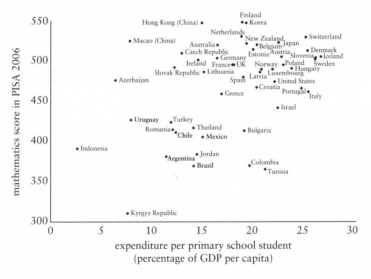

Source: OECD 2001, 2003; Vegas and Petrow 2007.
Note: GDP = gross domestic product, PISA = Programme for International Student Assessment.

both on how much Mexican workers earn and on how fast Mexico grows. Hanushek (2005) demonstrates that for the United States, a 1 standard deviation change in education quality is worth about a 10 percent increase in earnings, more in developing countries. Jamison, Jamison, and Hanushek (2006) show that Mexican workers arriving in the United States will earn 65 percent less per year of education that those educated in the United States, partly because of the lower quality of education in Mexico.

Second, the issue is not the available resources for education. Internationally, there does not appear to be a relationship between performance and money spent (Hanushek 2005; Hoxby 1996). Mexico spends more as a share of gross domestic product than the Czech Republic, Hong Kong (China), and Ireland and only slightly less than Australia, Finland, the Netherlands, and New Zealand—all of which are at the top of the quality rankings. The issue is also not one of lack of development. The Czech Republic, Hungary, Latvia, Poland, the Russian Federation, and the Slovak Republic all have similar levels of income, but they have radically higher scores.

Many factors impinge on this situation, but teacher union power emerges in the international literature as a major explanation for why more resources dedicated to education do not translate into quality, including in Latin America. Hoxby (1996) finds that globally, teachers' unions increase school inputs, but reduce their productivity, resulting in a negative overall effect on school performance, especially where students have few alternatives: in sum, more money, poorer results. More recently, Woessmann (2003) finds that schools in which unions had substantial control over the curriculum performed worse. In Chile, Foxley (2004), the finance minister in the first elected government following the Pinochet regime, sees the education unions as the largest barrier to further reductions of poverty in the country. Despite a substantial budget increase that accompanied the return to democracy, education performance did not improve because of union resistance to education quality evaluation measures and other reforms.

A similar picture emerges from various sources in Mexico, with that painted by the international press as perhaps the most extreme: education unions are seen as corrupt vehicles for patronage that block even basic quality standards, such as requiring that teachers show up for class. They also participate in the buying and selling of teaching positions, which occurs irrespective of the quality of the applicants (*Wall Street Journal* 2006; *Washington Post* 2004).

The Sindicato Nacional de Trabajadores de la Educación Nacional, the largest education workers' union in Latin America with 1.3 million members and with strong historical links to the Institutional Revolutionary Party, blames the reduced budget for leading to outdated technology, low teacher salaries, and poor infrastructure. However, as noted earlier, Mexico does not spend particularly less than comparable countries, and according to Guerrero, López-Calva, and Walton (chapter 4), teachers are paid more than other workers with similar characteristics.

A recent study by the Inter-American Development Bank (2006) concludes that the long association with the Institutional Revolutionary Party, mandatory membership fees, and a guaranteed monopoly resulting from a law barring competing unions maintains the union's extraordinary power, despite some recent, but relatively toothless, reforms aimed at improving education quality: "The union's approach was not to oppose the performance evaluation reform head on, but rather to make sure that it would stay under its control and acquire features that would prevent any substantive impact on core policies" (230). This continuity is also noted by Órnelas (2004), who argues that despite expectations of change arising from the installation of Vicente Fox's administration, reforms, in the end, were highly constrained by the militant union (see also Vegas and Petrow 2007).

From Rent Seeking to Competitiveness and Equity

These examples of the exercise of union power and the previous discussion of the labor law illustrate the extraordinary challenges facing Mexico as it tries to develop a labor market that both protects all workers and facilitates a rise in their long-run standard of living. In a sense, Mexico is in a bad equilibrium where both institutions and agents on the firm side, and those on the side of labor, are dedicated to preserving a share of current rents.

Presumably, most parties might agree that moving to the Swedish equilibrium would promise a brighter future for all. So why does this not happen? I offer three possible categories of motivation for staying with the status quo. First, the high degree of exit across all income classes to both informality and tax evasion in most countries of Latin America suggests low commitment to a state that, in many eyes, is unreliable and often ineffective. Even though existing safety nets serve workers imperfectly, trading away a lifetime right to a job enshrined in a labor code dating from the revolution for the promise of a well-funded unemployment insurance program, for instance, at the same time that public health institutions are heading toward bankruptcy, might seem an unwise tradeoff.

Second, implicitly, workers are being asked to take on potentially more risk, even if good unemployment programs are instituted, for the promise of a higher rate of growth in the wage they earn. However, as Fernandes and Rodrik (1991) argue, the true outcome of reforms is always uncertain. Some Mexicans will come out ahead, and some will come out behind. Not knowing in which group they will fall ex ante can lead agents to vote against reforms, even when they would actually come out ahead.

Finally, as Rajan (2006; chapter 2 in this volume) points out, even in the absence of uncertainty and under democratic rule, in countries inheriting great inequality, competitive rent preservation could lead to a preference to hold onto existing rents rather than to support reforms that would promote economy-wide productivity. Competition to preserve rents among labor groupings may lead to reform paralysis.

In the first two categories of motivation, the IMSS, airline, electricians, and education unions are doing what unions do—looking out for their members—and they should not be faulted for pursuing their interests as they see them in the context in which they live. Although the current approach of many unions helps perpetuate the bad equilibrium, their defensive rent seeking will be difficult to change so long as business overall is perceived as being so much about enjoying high rents. Mexican union leaders know that they do not live in Sweden. For them to acquiesce to the hard budget constraints imposed by privatization would probably be easier if the divestment of public sector banks and corporations had been handled in a transparent, competitive way. This would require demonstrable evidence that Mexico's future will be less about exploiting monopoly rents and really about embracing an agenda dedicated to raising its citizens' quality of life through innovation and other productivity-enhancing measures. Again, this will require that workers are guaranteed a better safety net for when they are adversely affected by this process.

At the same time, Rajan is right in pointing out that the game is not simply between labor and capital or between rich and poor. Not only are the education unions extracting rents from capital by restricting the supply of educated workers, but also they are extracting them from poor people who cannot afford private schools. The pensions of the IMSS union may be paid for partly by oil revenues, but they are also being paid for by workers in declining coverage and quality of health care. Getting to a point where all groups would benefit in the long run potentially implies losing rents in the short run and, hence, implies some complex political economy dynamics (as Bourguignon and Dessus, chapter 1 in this volume, also discuss in a more abstract way).

Shifting to such a better equilibrium is Mexico's imminent and inescapable challenge. One of Argentina's foremost economic historians, Di Tella (1985: 51), describes how fundamental this agenda is in his study of his country's difficulty in weaning itself from passive exploitation of another type of rents, those arising from natural resources:

> It must be acknowledged that the ability of the United States, Australia and Canada to continue a process of vigorous growth, even at the end of the expansion of the frontier, has been an extraordinary feat and one that cannot be taken for granted. Further development for the United States and Canada was more based on innovation. For Argentina it arose exclusively from collusive quasi-rents. *To the extent that development was based on innovation, these countries were switching to an alternative and unlimited source of growth. To the degree that it was based on collusion, it opened up a limited, alternative path* [emphasis added].

The lessons are fully applicable here. Mexico's competitors are switching to this alternative and unlimited source of growth. Mexico must as well.

Annex: Variables Used for the Regression Analysis

Core Variables

Wages and employment: Following Roberts and Skoufias (1997) and others, the wage and labor stock of skilled labor (W_s and N_s, respectively) and unskilled labor (W_u and N_u, respectively) are derived as weighted averages of subcategories within each. The weights for constructing the labor variables are the full wage (wage, social security, and other nonwage benefits) per worker that capture the relative marginal product of each subclass. This generates a compound measure of efficient units of skilled or unskilled labor with the least productive subclass of labor as the numeraire in each.[8] The wage is then the total payments to the subclasses of labor divided by the labor measure, which, in practice, is simply the wage of the numeraire subclass. The average schooling of the unskilled is about half that of the skilled workers.

Value added (Value Add.): The value of total 1991 output minus the expenses in materials and energy in millions of pesos.

Human Capital Variables

Schooling (School and School 2): Average years of schooling of the employed workers at each skill level in the firm, where the years of schooling were obtained from seven levels.

Experience (Experience and Experience 2): Average tenure in the firm of workers within each subclass of labor. As Dickens and Katz (1987) note, the most thorough tests for efficiency wages are those that can cross individual-level human capital variables with plant-level characteristics and control for both. Controlling only for the mean level of schooling in the plant and the mean tenure of each category of workers within the plant is possible. Though not a good measure of individual experience, the latter is a good proxy for the accumulation of firm-specific human capital and arguably better than the potential experience variable (age-education) found in many articles (see, for example, Lam and Schoeni 1991).

Union and Efficiency Wage Variables

Union density (Union): The 1995 National Survey of Employment, Salaries, Technology and Training (Encuesta Nacional de Empleo, Salarios, Tecnologia y Capacitacion, or ENESTYC) tabulates union density (ratio of firm employees affiliated with a union) by individual firm, while the 1992 ENESTYC tabulates only a dummy for the presence of unionization in the firm. Under the assumption that union structure changes little over the period, we assign a value of zero to the union density variable if the 1992 dummy is zero, and we assign the median sectoral value from the 1995 survey if the 1992 dummy is unity.

Outside (alternative) wage (Wa): Log of the median sectoral wage is at the four-digit industry level.

Hiring rate (Hiring): In the cross-sectional context, the aggregate unemployment rate that Nickell and Wadhwani (1990) use is not useful.[9] Instead, the sectoral hiring rate (number of hires over level of employment in the sector) is used as a measure of the probability of finding a job if a worker separates. This is more consistent with a labor turnover view of efficiency wages.

Quality control (Qual. Con.): Dummy is for firms that have quality control of outputs.

Productivity after training (Training): Dummy is for firms that indicated increases in productivity after implementing training programs.

Two-firm size and eight sectoral dummies.

Shift Parameters

Capacity utilization (Cap. U.): Average capacity utilization is as reported by the firm in 1991.

Productivity: Labor productivity is measured as output per unit of labor.[10]

Capital labor ratio (K/L): Log is of the ratio of the reported value of capital stock over labor force.

Corporate: Dummy is for firms that belong to a corporation with multiple branches.

Foreign: Dummy is for firms with more than 50 percent foreign ownership.

Age (Age and Age 2): Age of the plant is in years.

Export: Dummy is for firms with 10 percent or more of their sales going to other countries.

Automated: Value of automated machinery is as a percentage of the value of capital stock.

Competiveness: Dummy is for firms that identify their product as competitive against imports.

Research and Development (R & D): Dummy is for firms with positive research and development expenses in 1991.

Technology acquisition (Tech.): Dummy is for firms with positive expenses on technology acquisition.

Observations with missing, incomplete, or zero entries for employment, output, or capital stock were dropped. Only privately owned firms and those with more than 16 employees are included. Micro-firms (up to 15 employees) are extremely underrepresented in the sample, and their heterogeneity cannot be captured with the sample weights provided.

Notes

1. These unions include the massive Congreso del Trabajo (CT) or Labor Congress, which embraces the Confederación de Trabajadores de México (CTM), or Confederation of Mexican Workers (2 million to 6 million workers); the Confederación Revolucionaria de Obreros y Campesinos (CROC), or Revolutionary Federation of Workers and Peasants (1 million to 4 million workers); the Federación de Sindicatos y Trabajadores al Servicio del Estado (FSTSE), or Federation of Government Workers (2 million workers); and roughly 38 other labor organizations.

2. Note, however, that in November 1997, the Unión Nacional de Trabajadores (UNT) or National Union of Workers (0.7 million to 1.5 million workers) split from the CTM largely over what it perceived to be excessive responsiveness to government initiatives. Across the period analyzed here, some analysts have seen a decline in union influence both within the Institutional Revolutionary Party and overall (Brooks and Cason 1998; Collier and Collier 1991).

3. This section draws heavily on Ribeiro and Maloney (1999).

4. PEMEX workers "got an average 10 percent pay increase each of the past six years, almost double the rate of inflation. Rising pension costs at the state-run firm, which is struggling to prevent a fall in oil output, are also expected to climb steadily in the coming years, leaving much less money available for critical investment in exploration.... Every spring since 1981, the (Oaxaca) teachers have gone on strike to get a pay raise above the one negotiated by the national union" (A6).

5. Using a dynamic labor demand specification, they estimate the effects of job security using a sample of 60 countries for 1980–98. They find that increasing job security significantly lowers the speed of adjustment to shocks in one-third of the countries and reduces productivity growth by almost 1 percent for countries with strong rule of law, including Chile.

6. Workers who are legally dismissed are entitled to severance compensation equal to 3 months' salary, plus 20 days per year of service (with a cap of double the monthly minimum wage per year of service), plus 12 days per year of work in the case of workers with 15 or more years of seniority. In the case of technological change, the compensation is the same except that firms must pay four months' salary, not three.

7. Ideally, the labor demand equation would be estimated using instruments for wages because of possible measurement error and random productivity shocks and because unions may bargain over both wages and employment simultaneously. However, good instruments are difficult to find (Ribeiro and Maloney 1999).

8. This approach is arguably preferable to simply assuming that each subclass of workers has identical productivity in the aggregation. In the skilled category are found directors, professionals, technical workers, administrative employees, and supervisors. Among the unskilled are professional workers, specialists, and general workers.

9. The cross-sectional nature of the data and the impossibility of identifying firms' regional location precludes the use of a regional average wage or typical informal sector earnings.

10. To avoid a division bias in the productivity coefficient, I use the previous year's productivity as in Borjas (1980). Dropping this variable from the regressions does not noticeably change the results in general.

References

Aghion, Philippe, Nick Bloom, Richard Blundell, Rachel Griffith, and Peter Howitt. 2005. "Competition and Innovation: An Inverted-U Relationship." *Quarterly Journal of Economics* 120 (2): 701–28.

Arango, C., and A. Pachon. 2003. *Distributive Effects of Minimum Wages on Household Incomes: Colombia 1997–2002*. Bogotá: Banco de la República.

Banerjee, A., and E. Duflo. 2005. "Growth Theory through the Lens of Development Economics." In *Handbook of Economic Growth*, vol. 1, part A, 473–552. Amsterdam: Elsevier.

Barr, A., and T. Packard. 2002. "Revealed Preference and Self-Insurance: Can We Learn from the Self-Employed in Chile?" Policy Research Working Paper 2754, World Bank, Washington, DC.

Bergoeing, R., A. Hernando, and A. Repetto. 2006. "Market Reforms and Efficiency Gains in Chile." Working Paper 372, Central Bank of Chile, Santiago.

Bergoeing, R., and A. Repetto. 2006. "Micro Efficiency and Aggregate Growth in Chile." *Cuadernos de Economía* 43 (May): 169–91.

Bewley, T. 1999. *Why Don't Wages Fall in Recessions*. Cambridge, MA: Harvard University Press.

Blomström, M., and P. Meller. 1991. "Issues for Development: Lessons from Scandinavia-Latin Comparisons." In *Diverging Paths: Comparing a Century of Scandinavian and Latin American Economic Development*, ed. Magnus Blomström and Patricio Meller, 1–14. Washington, DC: Inter-American Development Bank.

Borjas, G. 1980. "The Relationship between Wages and Weekly Hours of Work: The Role of Division Bias." *Journal of Human Resources* 15 (3): 409–23.

———. 1996. *Labor Economics*. New York: McGraw-Hill.

Bosch, M., and W. Maloney. 2007. "Gross Worker Flows in the Presence of Informal Labor Markets: The Mexican Experience, 1987–2002." Policy Research Working Paper 3883, World Bank, Washington, DC.

Brooks, D., and J. Cason. 1998. "Mexican Unions: Will Turmoil Lead to Independence?" *WorkingUSA* (March–April): 23–35, 88–91.

Caballero, R. J., K. N. Cowan, E. M. R. A. Engel, and A. Micco. 2004. "Effective Labor Regulation and Microeconomic Flexibility." Cowles Foundation Discussion Paper 1480, Yale University, New Haven.

Caselli, F., and S. Tenreyo. 2004. "Is Poland the Next Spain?" Public Policy Discussion Papers 04-8, Federal Reserve Bank of Boston, Boston.

Castellanos, S. G., R. García-Verdú, and D. S. Kaplan. 2004. "Nominal Wage Rigidities in Mexico: Evidence from Social Security Records." *Journal of Development Economics* 75 (2): 507–33.

Collier, R., and D. Collier. 1991. *Shaping the Political Arena: Critical Junctures, the Labor Movement, and Regime Dynamics in Latin America*. Princeton, NJ: Princeton University Press.

Cunningham, W. 2007. *Minimum Wages Social Policy: Lessons from Developing Countries*. Washington, DC: World Bank.

Davila-Capalleja, E. 1994. "Regulaciones laborales y mercado de trabajo en México." In *Regulacion del Mercado de Trabajo en America Latina,* ed. Gustavo Marquez, chapter 6. Santiago: Ediciones Instituto de Estudios Superiores de Administracion and Centro Internacional para el Desarrollo Economico.

de Soto, H. 1989. *The Other Path.* New York: Harper and Row.

Dickens, W. T, and L. F. Katz. 1987. "Inter-Industry Wage Differences and Industry Characteristics." In *Unemployment and the Structure of Labor Markets,* ed. K. Lang and J. S. Leonard, 48–89. New York: Blackwell.

Di Tella, G. 1985. "Rents, Quasi Rents, Normal Profits and Growth: Argentina and the Areas of Recent Settlement." In *Argentina, Australia and Canada: Studies in Comparative Development, 1870–1965,* ed. D. C. M. Platt and G. di Tella, 19–37. London: MacMillan Press.

Fernandes, R., A. Gremaud, and R. Narita. 2006. "Tax Reform and the Formalization of the Economy: Simulating Different Alternatives for Brazil." Working paper, Universidade de São Paulo, São Paulo, Brazil.

Fernandes, R., and D. Rodrick. 1991. "Resistance to Reform: Status Quo Bias in the Presence of Individual-Specific Uncertainty. *American Economic Review* 81 (5): 1146–55.

Foxley, A. 2004. "Successes and Failures in Poverty Eradication: Chile." Paper presented at Scaling up Poverty Reduction: A Global Learning Process and Conference, Shanghai, May 25–27. http://info.worldbank. org/etools/docs/reducingpoverty/case/24/fullcase/Chile%20Full%20 Case.pdf.

García-Verdú, R. 2004. *Barreras a la adopción de nuevas tecnologias y mejores prácticas organizacionales en la industria de la aviación: Un estudio de caso.* Dirección de Estudios Economicos. Mexico City: Banco de México.

Germidis, D. 1974. *Labor Conditions and Industrial Relations in the Building Industry in Mexico.* Employment Series 11. Paris: Organisation for Economic Co-operation and Development, Development Centre Studies.

Haefke, C., M. Sonntag, and T. van Rens. 2007. "Wage Rigidity and Job Creation." Working paper, Institute for Advanced Studies, Vienna.

Hanushek, E. 2005. "The Economic Value of Improving Local Schools." In *Proceedings,* 59–72. Cleveland, OH: Federal Reserve Bank of Cleveland.

Harris, J., and M. Todaro. 1970. "Migration, Unemployment, and Development: A Two Sector Analysis." *American Economic Review* 60 (1): 126–42.

Heckman, J., and C. Pages. 2004. *Law and Employment: Lessons from Latin America and the Caribbean.* Chicago: University of Chicago Press.

Hirschman, A. 1970. *Exit, Voice, and Loyalty: Responses to Decline in Firms, Organizations and States.* Cambridge, MA: Harvard University Press.

Hjalmarsson, L. 1991. "The Scandinavian Model of Industrial Policy." In *Diverging Paths: Comparing a Century of Scandinavian and Latin*

American Economic Development, ed. M. Blomström and P. Meller, 245–65. Washington, DC: Inter-American Development Bank.

Hoxby, C. 1996. "How Teachers' Unions Affect Education Production." *Quarterly Journal of Economics* 111 (3): 671–718.

Hsieh, C.-T. and P. J. Klenow. 2007. "Misallocation and Manufacturing TFP in China and India." Working Paper Series 13290, National Bureau of Economic Research, Cambridge, MA.

Inter-American Development Bank. 2006. *The Politics of Policies: Economic and Social Progress in Latin America*. Washington, DC: Inter-American Development Bank.

James, E. 1999. "Coverage Under Old Age Security Systems and Protection for the Uninsured: What Are the Issues?" Policy Research Working Paper Series 2163, World Bank, Washington, DC.

Jamison, E., D. Jamison, and E. Hanushek. 2006. "The Effects of Education Quality on Mortality Decline and Income Growth." Working Paper 12652, National Bureau of Economic Research, Cambridge, MA.

Kaplan, D., and J. Sadka. 2008. "Enforceability of Labor Law: Evidence from a Labor Court in Mexico." Policy Research Working Paper Series 4483, World Bank, Washington, DC.

Krebs, T. 2003. "Human Capital Risk and Economic Growth." *Quarterly Journal of Economics* 118 (2): 709–43.

Krebs, T., P. Krishna, and W. Maloney. 2005. "Labor Market Risk and Human Capital Investment in Developing Countries." Unpublished paper, World Bank, Washington, DC.

Krebs, T., and W. Maloney. 1999. "Quitting and Labor Turnover: Micro-economic Evidence and Macro-economic Consequences." Policy Research Working Paper Series 2068, World Bank, Washington, DC.

Kugler, A. 2000. "The Incidence of Job Security Regulations on Labor Market Flexibility and Compliance in Colombia: Evidence from the 1990 Reform." Working Paper R-393, Inter-American Development Bank, Washington, DC.

Kugler, A., and M. Kugler. 2003. "The Labor Market Effects of Payroll Taxes in a Middle-Income Country: Evidence from Colombia." Discussion Paper 852, Institute for the Study of Labor, Bonn.

Lam, D., and R. Schoeni. 1991. "Effects of Family Background on Earnings and Returns to Schooling: Evidence from Brazil. Paper presented at the Annual Meeting of the American Economic Association, New Orleans.

Layard, R., and S. Nickell. 1990. "Is Unemployment Lower if Unions Bargain over Employment? *Quarterly Journal of Economics* 105 (2): 773–87.

Lazear, E. 1990. "Job Security Provisions and Employment." *Quarterly Journal of Economics* 105 (3): 699–726.

Levenson, A., and W. Maloney. 1996. *Modeling the Informal Sector: Theory and Empirical Evidence from Mexico*. Urbana, IL: University of Illinois at

Urbana-Champaign, College of Commerce and Business Administration, Center for International Business Education and Research.

Loayza, N., and J. Rigolini. 2006. "Informality Trends and Cycles." Policy Research Working Paper 4078, World Bank, Washington, DC.

López-De-Silanes, F., J. Botero, S. Djankov, and R. La Porta. 2004. "The Regulation of Labor." *Quarterly Journal of Economics* 119 (4): 1339–82.

Maloney, W. 1999. "Does Informality Imply Segmentation in Urban Labor Markets? Evidence from Sectoral Transitions in Mexico." *World Bank Economic Review* 12 (2): 275–302.

———. 2001. "Self Employment and Labor Turnover in Developing Countries: Cross-Country Evidence." In *World Bank Economists' Forum*, ed. S. Devarajan, F. H. Rogers, and L. Squire, Part III, 137–67. Washington, DC: World Bank.

———. 2004. "Informality Revisited." *World Development* 32 (7): 1159–78.

Maloney, W., and J. Nuñez 2004. "Measuring the Impact of Minimum Wages." In *Law and Employment: Lessons from Latin America and the Caribbean*, ed. J. Heckman and C. Pages, 109–30. Chicago: University of Chicago Press.

Menezes-Filho, N., and J. Van Reenen. 2003. "Unions and Innovation: A Survey of the Theory and Empirical Evidence." Discussion Paper 3792, Centre for Economic Policy Research, London.

Nickell, S., and W. Wadhwani. 1990. "Employment Determination in British Industry: Investigations Using Micro-Data." *Review of Economic Studies* 58 (5): 955–69.

O'Connell, L. D. 1999. "Collective Bargaining Systems in Six Latin American Countries: Degrees of Autonomy and Decentralization, Argentina, Brazil, Chile, Mexico, Peru, and Uruguay." Working Paper 399, Inter-American Development Bank, Office of the Chief Economist, Washington, DC.

OECD (Organisation for Economic Co-operation and Development). 2001. *Knowledge and Skills for Life—First Results from PISA 2000: Publications 2000.* Paris: OECD.

———. 2003. *The PISA 2003 Assessment Framework.* Paris: OECD.

Ornelas, C. 2004. "The Politics of Privatisation, Decentralisation, and Education Reform in Mexico." *International Review of Education* 50 (3–4): 397–418.

Panagides, A., and H. Patrinos. 1994. "Union–Nonunion Wage Differentials in the Developing World: A Case Study of Mexico." Policy Research Working Paper Series 1269, World Bank, Washington, DC.

Pencavel, J. 1995. "The Role of Labor Unions in Fostering Economic Development." Policy Research Working Paper 1469, World Bank, Washington, DC.

Perry, G., O. S. Arias, J. H. López, W. F. Maloney, and L. Servén. 2006. *Poverty Reduction and Growth: Virtuous and Vicious Circles.* Washington, DC: World Bank.

Perry, G., W. Maloney, O. Arias, P. Fajnzylber, A Mason, and J. Saavedra-Chanduvi. 2007. *Informality: Exit and Exclusion*. Washington, DC: World Bank.

Prescott, E., and S. Parente. 2000. *Barriers to Riches*. Cambridge, MA: Massachusetts Institute of Technology Press.

Rajan, R. 2006. "Competitive Rent Preservation, Reform Paralysis, and the Persistence of Underdevelopment." Working Paper 12093, National Bureau of Economic Research, Cambridge, MA.

Rajan, R., and L. Zingales. 2004. *Saving Capitalism from the Capitalists*. Princeton, NJ: Princeton University Press.

Ribeiro, E., and W. Maloney. 1999. "Efficiency Wage and Union Effects in Labor Demand and Wage Structure in Mexico." Working Paper 2131, World Bank, Washington, DC.

Roberts, B. 1991. "Employment Structure, Life Cycle, and Life Chances: Formal and Informal Sectors in Guadalajara." In *The Informal Economy*, ed. A. Portes, M. Castells, and L. A. Benton, Part 2, 41–59. Baltimore, MD: Johns Hopkins University Press.

Roberts, M., and E. Skoufias. 1997. "The Long Run Demand for Skilled and Unskilled Labor in Colombian Manufacturing Plants." *Review of Economics and Statistics* 79 (1): 330–34.

Schumpeter, Joseph. 1975. *Capitalism, Socialism, and Democracy*. New York: Harper.

Shimer, Robert. 2005. "The Cyclicality of Hires, Separations, and Job to Job Transitions." *Federal Reserve of St. Louis Review* 87 (4): 493–507.

———. 2007. *Reassessing the Ins and Outs of Unemployment*. Chicago: University of Chicago.

Vegas, E., and J. Petrow. 2007. *Raising Student Learning in Latin America: The Challenge for the 21st Century*. Washington, DC: World Bank.

Wall Street Journal. 1999. "Power Play in Electrical Union." December 3, A1.

———. 2006. "Union Muscle Goes Unchallenged in Mexico." October 4, p. A6.

Washington Post. 2004. "A Union's Grip Stifles Learning." July 14, p. A1.

Woessmann, L. 2003. "Schooling Resources, Educational Institutions and Student Performance: The International Evidence." *Oxford Bulletin of Economics and Statistics* 65 (2): 117–70.

8

Why Banks Do Not Lend:
The Mexican Financial System

Stephen Haber

In recent years, the Mexican government has been engaged in an ambitious program to increase the amount of credit available to business enterprises and households. During Ernesto Zedillo's administration, Mexico's banks were rescued from collapse, the deposit insurance system was reformed, accounting standards were modernized, private credit reporting was instituted, and foreign multinationals were allowed to purchase controlling shares of the country's largest banks. Vicente Fox's administration built upon and went beyond those initiatives. It improved contract enforcement by reforming the federal judiciary and by beginning pilot programs to organize property registers. It made loan contracts easier to enforce by reforming the bankruptcy laws, thus allowing banks and debtors to write contracts that placed assets being collateralized outside of the debtor's bankruptcy estate. Finally, it injected funds directly into the market for housing credit through the Sociedad Hipotecaria Federal, a development bank that acts as a second-tier lender.

These programs have, to some degree, borne fruit. The banking system is now stable and prudently managed. Moreover, the dramatic decline in the availability of bank credit since 1995 was finally reversed in 2004. Indeed, total bank credit to firms and households, expressed as a percentage of gross domestic product (GDP), grew

An earlier draft of this chapter benefited from helpful comments by Augusto de la Torre, José Antonio González, and Roger Noll.

from 7.7 percent in 2003 to 9.9 percent in 2005 (the last year for which complete data are available). This improvement in credit access was most notable in consumer lending, a fact that the Fox government was quick to trumpet as evidence that its policies were working. Note, however, that the difference between rates of growth and levels of development is huge. For example, bank credit to consumers grew by 36 percent per year from 2000 to 2005, but that was an easy feat, because the level of bank credit to consumers in 2000 was close to zero (0.6 percent of GDP). Thus, even after five years of rapid growth, the level of bank lending to consumers is only 2.8 percent of GDP, a stunningly low level by any reasonable international comparison.

Figures 8.1 and 8.2 clarify the situation. Whether Mexico is compared with other members of the Organisation for Economic Co-operation and Development (OECD) or other countries in Latin America, its banking system extends extremely low levels of credit to business enterprises and households. As figure 8.1 demonstrates, private credit as a percentage of GDP (the standard metric in the literature) in Mexico is the smallest of any OECD country. Moreover, it is small by a wide margin, even when compared with the economies of southern and eastern Europe. Mexico also does not fare well when compared with other Latin American countries. As figure 8.2 shows, in Mexico, private credit from deposit money

Figure 8.1 Private Bank Credit as a Percentage of GDP, OECD Countries, 2005

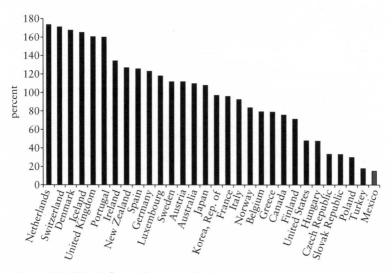

Source: World Bank financial structure database.

Figure 8.2 Private Credit from Deposit Money Banks as a Percentage of GDP, Latin American Countries, 2005

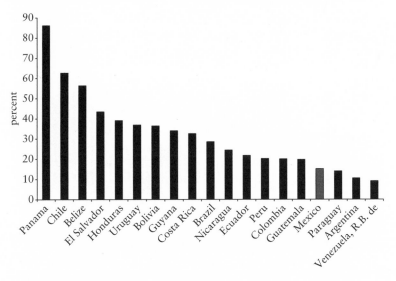

Source: World Bank financial structure database.

banks as a percentage of GDP is dwarfed by that in Panama, Chile, Belize, and even Nicaragua. It is even small by the standards of Ecuador, Peru, Colombia, and Guatemala. Indeed, only three countries in the region extend less private credit than Mexico: Paraguay, Argentina, and the República Bolivariana de Venezuela.

Mexican banks also extend lower levels of credit today, as a percentage of GDP, than they did in earlier periods. As figure 8.3 shows, bank credit as a percentage of GDP is currently less than half its level in the early 1970s. Indeed, it was lower on only one occasion in the past half century, the 1980s, when the government expropriated the banks and used them to finance its budget deficits.

Equally striking is that the decline in credit since 1995 has not been uniform: business enterprises have been hit harder than households. As table 8.1 shows, from 1997 to 2003, commercial credit (loans to manufacturing firms, farms, and service enterprises) as a percentage of GDP declined steadily. Even with a minor increase from 2003 to 2005, at the end of 2005, commercial credit as a percentage of GDP was still one-third below its 1997 level and, at only 4.6 percent of GDP, was low by any reasonable comparative international metric. As a result, the percentage of business enterprises that relied on the banking system for credit fell steadily from 1998 to 2005, so much so that as figure 8.4 shows, by the end of 2005,

Figure 8.3 Private Credit from Deposit Money Banks as a
Percentage of GDP, Mexico, 1950–2004

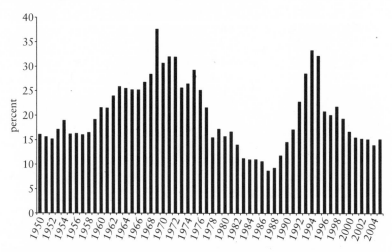

Sources: 1950–61: International Monetary Fund/international finance statistics
database, 1961–2005; World Bank financial structure database.

fewer than 20 percent of small firms, 28 percent of medium firms,
27 percent of large firms, and 38 percent of very large firms obtained
credit from domestic banks.

The focus of this chapter is to understand the causes of credit scarcity in Mexico and to offer recommendations for policy makers based
on an assessment of four hypotheses, namely, that the limited amount
of bank credit in Mexico is caused by alternative (noncommercial
bank) sources of finance, by an unintended outcome of the specific
features of the government bailout of the banking system in 1990s, by
an outcome of an oligopolized market, and by an outcome of a legal
environment in which enforcing contract rights is difficult.

Hypothesis 1: Alternative Sources of Finance

One hypothesis is that low levels of bank credit do not indicate
capital scarcity. Other sources of capital, such as government development banks, organized markets for debt and equity, foreign direct
investment (FDI), and direct lending by international banks can substitute for a domestic banking system.

This hypothesis is, however, problematic, because it is not consistent with the evidence. Take, for example, the argument that
government development banks are a substitute for the commercial

Table 8.1 Commercial Bank Credit as a Percentage of GDP, 1997–2005

Year	Commercial credit	Consumer credit	Housing credit	Credit to non-bank financial institutions	IPAB bonds	Credit to government[a]	Total credit	Total credit to firms and households	Credit to firms and households minus IPAB bonds
1997	6.5	0.7	3.0	0.2	7.1	1.6	19.2	17.6	10.4
1998	7.0	0.6	3.1	0.2	8.1	1.8	20.8	19.0	11.0
1999	5.2	0.6	2.3	0.2	7.5	1.7	17.5	15.9	8.4
2000	4.9	0.6	2.0	0.2	5.0	2.6	15.4	12.8	7.8
2001	4.8	0.9	1.9	0.2	4.5	2.5	14.9	12.3	7.8
2002	4.7	1.1	1.9	0.3	4.2	3.1	15.2	12.2	8.0
2003	4.2	1.5	1.6	0.3	2.8	2.9	13.4	10.5	7.7
2004	4.5	2.0	1.5	0.5	2.3	2.0	12.7	10.7	8.5
2005	4.6	2.8	1.9	0.6	0.6	2.1	12.6	10.5	9.9

Source: Haber and Musacchio 2006.
Note: IPAB = Instituto para la Protección al ahorro Bancario (Bank Savings Protection Institute).
a. Does not include treasury bonds issued by the federal government. These bonds are included in banks' investment portfolios. Government credit is primarily loans to states.

Figure 8.4 Percentage of Firms Using Bank Credit, Year
End, 1998–2005

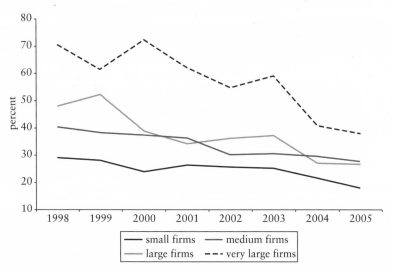

Source: Bank of Mexico data.
    Note: Small firms: sales of less than US$12.5 million in 1997; medium firms: sales
of US$12.5 million to less than US$65 million in 1997; large firms: sales of US$65
million to US$650 million in 1997; very large firms: sales of more than US$650 million in 1997.

banking system. Figure 8.5 presents data on commercial lending by
development banks as a percentage of total commercial lending
(including development banks and commercial banks) and as a
percentage of GDP. If development banks were substituting for
commercial banks, both percentages would increase over time, but
as the figure shows, the opposite has occurred. From 2003 to 2006,
development banks accounted for a declining proportion of total
commercial lending to the extent that by 2006, they accounted for
only 7.4 percent of the bank credit obtained by business enterprises. Note that this measure of development bank lending over-
states its importance in private finance, because it excludes loans
for housing and consumption. If housing and consumption loans
are included in the numerator and denominator, then development
banks accounted for only 4.4 percent of total bank lending for
private purposes. Development bank lending for commercial purposes as a percentage of GDP shows equally astonishing results: at
its peak in 2002, development bank lending for commercial purposes accounted for only 1.2 percent of GDP, and by 2005, the
figure was only 0.5 percent.

Figure 8.5 Development Bank Credit to Private Enterprises, 2000–06

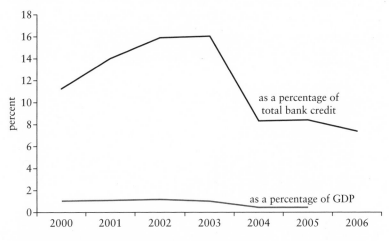

as a percentage of total bank credit

as a percentage of GDP

Source: Bank of Mexico data.

Mexico's securities markets also do not serve as substitutes for the banking system. Figure 8.6 presents data on the size of Mexico's stock and private bond market compared with other OECD and Latin American countries in 2005. As the data show, Mexico is on the right tail of the distribution, with a ratio of only 27 percent. Worse, as figure 8.7 demonstrates, in 2005 Mexico's securities markets were smaller than they had been a decade earlier. In the mid-1990s, capitalization of the stock market as a percentage of GDP hovered around 40 percent, but by the end of 2005, it was 23 percent. The corporate bond market underwent some modest growth during this period, but even as late as 2005, its total market capitalization was only 3.6 percent of GDP.

Another alternative source of finance for business enterprises is direct investment by foreign firms. The evidence indicates, however, that FDI is not a substitute for a domestic banking system in Mexico. Indeed, as figure 8.8 shows, the absolute level of FDI flows to Mexico has declined dramatically since 2001, so much so that in 2005 the nominal level of FDI was the same as it had been when the North American Free Trade Agreement first went into effect in 1994. As a result, FDI in 2005 was a much lower percentage of GDP than it was in 1994.

A fourth alternative source of finance for business enterprises is direct loans by international banks. Estimates of the extent to which Mexican business enterprises borrow outside the country are not available, but indirect evidence from surveys of business

Figure 8.6 Sum of Stock and Private Bond Market
Capitalization as a Percentage of GDP, Latin America
and the OECD Selected Countries, 2005

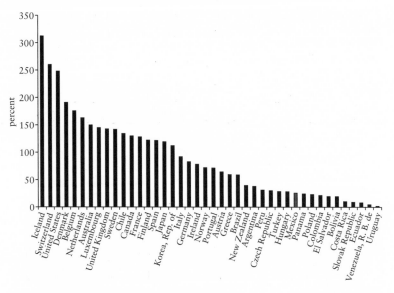

Source: World Bank financial structure database.

Figure 8.7 Private Bond Market and Stock Market
Capitalizations as a Percentage of GDP, 1990–2005

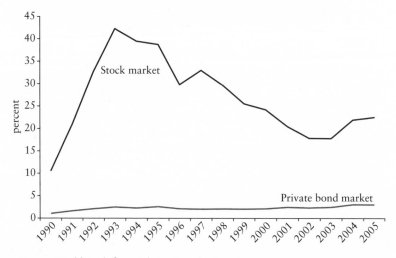

Source: World Bank financial structure database.

Figure 8.8 FDI Flows to Mexico, 1980–2005

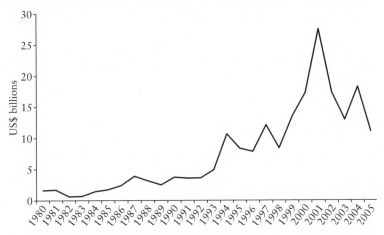

Source: http://www.inegi.gob.mx.

enterprises regarding their use of the domestic banking system suggests that direct lending from foreign sources has not replaced lending by domestic banks. The logic is that large firms are much more likely to be able to borrow in New York or other money centers than small and medium firms. If Mexico's largest firms are borrowing abroad, one would expect to see a decline in the extent to which those firms rely on the domestic banking system, but would not expect a decline in the use of the banking system by small and medium firms. Figure 8.4 indicates, however, a monotonic contraction in the use of bank credit by firms of all size categories.

One might be tempted to argue that all these measures of alternative sources of business finance are imperfect. Indeed, the Bank of Mexico's surveys of business enterprises indicate that many firms can obtain credit from their suppliers, suggesting that some firms are able to replace bank credit with other sources. Nevertheless, direct evidence on gross fixed capital formation as a percentage of GDP (figure 8.9) indicates a contraction in investment in Mexico over the past five years. In 2005, gross fixed capital formation as a percentage of GDP was 19 percent, down from 21 percent in 2000. This means that Mexico's current investment rate is no higher than when the North American Free Trade Agreement went into effect in 1994, no higher than it was when Mexico joined the General Agreement on Tariffs and Trade in 1986, and well below its pre-debt crisis levels of the early 1980s.

Figure 8.9 Gross Fixed Capital Formation as a Percentage of GDP, 1980–2005

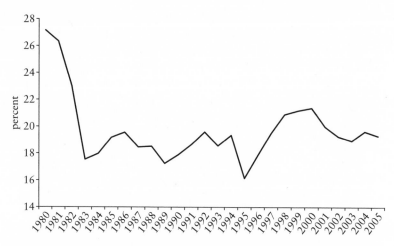

Source: International Monetary Fund international financial statistics database.

In short, the evidence suggests that the scarcity of bank credit in Mexico is not a product of alternative sources of finance. The evidence suggests instead that the supply of credit faces constraints.

Hypothesis 2: Disincentives to Lend from the 1990s Bailout

One possible explanation for the low levels of bank lending in Mexico is that the government's bailout of the banks in the 1990s through its deposit insurance agency, the Banking Fund for the Protection of Savings (Fondo Bancario de Protección al Ahorro, or FOBAPROA), created disincentives for banks to lend. This view was first put forward in a seminal paper by González-Anaya (2003), which points out that banks' inability to trade the promissory notes that they had received from FOBAPROA in exchange for their bad loans undermined their incentive to lend. Their incentive was instead to earn a secure return from their FOBAPROA notes.

This hypothesis might have been consistent with the facts during 1995 to 2000, the period studied in detail by González-Anaya, but it does not explain lending patterns after 2000. In the first place, why FOBAPROA bonds should provide any more of a disincentive to lend than any other kind of government security is not conceptually clear. In 1998, Congress disbanded FOBAPROA and replaced it with a new and more autonomous deposit guarantee agency, the Bank Savings Protection Institute (Instituto para la Protección al Ahorro Bancario, or IPAB). Most FOBAPROA bonds were swapped for similar IPAB bonds, and IPAB assumed responsibility for recouping and liquidating the assets backed by those bonds, a de facto admission that the loans that had originally been swapped for FOBAPROA promissory notes could not be recovered. Congress also agreed that the government would pay for the annual costs of the IPAB program out of each year's budget (McQuerry 1999). Thus, from the point of view of a bank, holding an IPAB bond is little different from holding a treasury bill: both are tradable, and both are backed by the government. If banks can earn higher rates of return by selling their IPAB bonds and making loans with the proceeds, nothing prevents them from doing so.

In the second place, the evidence indicates that banks have been liquidating their IPAB bonds and replacing them with other investments, to the extent that IPAB bonds are now a trivial component of bank loan portfolios. As figure 8.10 shows, in early 2000, IPAB bonds accounted for 29 percent of all outstanding bank credit. By the end of 2005, however, IPAB bonds accounted for only 3 percent of total outstanding bank credit. Thus, reconciling the view that IPAB provides a disincentive to lend when IPAB bonds now account for only a tiny fraction of bank assets is difficult.

Figure 8.10 FOBAPROA–IPAB Bonds as a Percentage of Bank Credit Portfolios, September 1997–December 2005

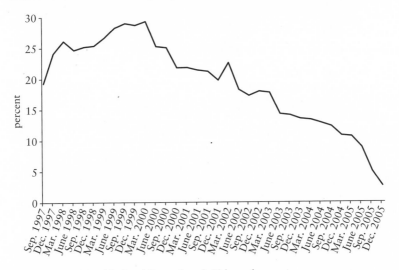

Source: Comision Nacional Bancaria y de Valores data.

Hypothesis 3: Oligopolistic Behavior of Mexico's Banks

Perhaps Mexico's banks act as oligopolists, that is, they constrain credit to drive up rates of return. The banking system is certainly highly concentrated. As figure 8.11 shows, the entire retail banking business comprises only 19 banks. Two of these banks (BBVA Bancomer and Banamex, denoted by gray columns, control just over 50 percent of total bank assets. The three next largest banks (Banorte, HSBC Mexico, and Santander Serfin, denoted by white columns, control an additional 30 percent of assets. The remaining 14 banks (denoted by solid blocks) tend to be quite small, with the largest having a market share of 7.5 percent and the smallest having a market share of 0.1 percent

Data and Methods

Detecting oligopolistic competition is less straightforward than documenting a market structure that is consistent with oligopoly. To estimate the impact of market structure on output and prices, one may use bank-level data compiled by the Comisión Nacional Bancaria y de Valores (the National Banking and Securities Commission). These

Figure 8.11 Market Share by Assets, Mexican Retail Banks, 2002–05 Averages

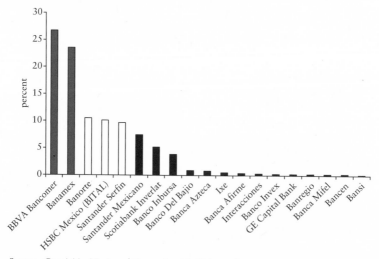

Source: Comisión Nacional Bancaria y de Valores data.

data include standard measures of bank performance (income, expenses, administrative costs, and nonperforming loans), bank size (assets and earning assets), and outputs (loans by broad type, that is, consumer, commercial, housing, nonbank financial intermediary, and government). The data are reported on a quarterly basis. Haber and Musacchio (2006) link the commission's quarterly data over time by tracking mergers and acquisitions to construct a panel data set.

In an ideal world, fixed effects regressions would be used to measure the impact of changes in a bank's market share on its pricing and output decisions. However, that empirical strategy requires a high degree of variance in banks' market shares over time, large numbers of observations over time, and no changes in the institutional environment that affects banks' output and pricing decisions independently of their market share.

These factors mean that fixed effects regressions cannot be employed in the case of Mexico. In the first place, the banking market has always been highly concentrated: a small number of banks has dominated the banking system for the past 120 years, with four or five banks stubbornly accounting for some 60 to 70 percent of market share (Haber 2006). In the second place, a major reform of accounting standards in 1997 makes linking Comisión Nacional Bancaria y de Valores data before and after 1997 impossible (Del Angel Mobarak, Haber, and Musacchio 2006). In the third place, in 2001, the government undertook a series of reforms to the bankruptcy laws designed to allow banks and borrowers to write loan contracts such that collateral could be placed outside an individual's or firm's bankruptcy estate. These reforms did not affect the probability of collateral recovery uniformly across different types of loans. At the same time, the federal government carried out a major reform of its own housing loan programs, which resulted in a dramatic expansion of government lending for housing and the growth of nonbank financial intermediaries that took advantage of these new federal programs. The combined impact of these legal and administrative reforms was that banks had incentives to reallocate their credit portfolios independently of changes in their market shares.

These constraints require that the empirical analysis undertaken here starts in 2002, after all the accounting, administrative, and legal reforms had taken place. In turn, the short span of data available requires exploitation of variance in market shares not within banks, but across banks. I, therefore, estimate ordinary least squares regressions on a panel data set of quarterly observations running from the first quarter of 2002 through the fourth quarter of 2005.

Analyzing the data in cross-section implies, however, that the ability of the largest banks to act as market makers, by constraining lending in order to drive up the price of credit, is likely to be under-estimated. The presence of a few market makers may allow their smaller competitors to follow similar pricing strategies, producing high net interest margins, low rates of nonperformance, and stable returns on capital for all banks. For this reason, the estimates of the impact of market structure on lending volumes, prices, and profit-ability presented should be understood as lower-bound approxima-tions of the impact of concentration on the availability and pricing of credit.

Returns on Equity

The most direct test of oligopoly pricing is to estimate the effect of market power on rates of return on equity. One must, however, be careful to control for the possibility that larger banks may have higher rates of return on equity because they can take advantage of scale economies. One must also be careful to control for the possibil-ity that larger banks may be willing to bear more risk than smaller banks, because their larger size allows them to absorb losses from risky loans that would be ruinous for smaller banks.

The second column of table 8.2 estimates a regression on the impact of market shares on rates of return on equity that controls for scale economies by including the ratio of administrative costs to assets and that controls for the level of risk that banks are willing to bear by including the ratio of nonperforming to total loans.[1] Quarterly dummies to control for outlying quarters are also included and (robust) standard errors are clustered at the quarterly level to control for serial correlation. Alternative functional forms, such as panel corrected standard errors, Prais-Winstin (AR1), and Prais-Winstin (PSAR1), are also employed. These produce similar qualitative results and are, therefore, not reproduced here.

The regression results reported in the second column of table 8.2 indicate a strong, positive association between market share and risk-adjusted returns on equity, even when controlling for scale economies. As market shares double, quarterly rates of return increase by 0.07 percentage point. Given the wide variance in mar-ket shares and a sample mean of 0.026, an increase of 0.07 per-centage point is extremely large. In short, the results indicate that large banks practice oligopoly pricing. The question remains, however, as to exactly what products they price above the com-petitive level.

Table 8.2 Performance of Mexican Banks, Ordinary Least Squares Regression Results

Item	Return on equity	Private credit as % of assets[1]	Consumer credit as % of assets[1]	Housing credit as % of assets[1]	Commercial credit as % of assets[1]
Market share (by assets)	0.069	−0.9782	0.0199	0.3675	−1.2028
	(2.76)**	(25.69)***	(0.73)	(18.34)***	(32.66)***
Administrative costs/assets	−0.1143				
	(0.15)				
Nonperforming loan ratio	0.0224				
	(0.45)				
Equity ratio		−0.1043	−0.1071	0.0285	0.0262
		(2.22)**	(3.34)***	(3.12)***	(0.69)
Quarter dummies	Yes	Yes	Yes	Yes	Yes
Robust standard errors clustered by quarter	Yes	Yes	Yes	Yes	Yes
Constant	0.0145	0.5669	0.0423	0.0206	0.4524
	(1.07)	(65.57)***	(6.92)***	(10.34)***	(74.54)***
Number of observations	297	297	297	297	297
R-squared	0.1	0.14	0.06	0.37	0.2

Source: Author's calculations.

Note: ** = significant at 5%; *** = significant at 1%. Robust t statistics in parentheses.

a. Private lending does not include IPAB bonds. For that reason, IPAB bonds are also netted out from assets in the lending regressions. Alternative specifications that include IPAB bonds in assets and that add a control variable for the ratio of IPAB bonds to assets produce qualitatively similar results and are, therefore, not reported here.

Lending Volume

One interpretation of the rates of return on equity regressions is that large banks constrain the volume of lending to push up the price of credit. As a first step in testing this hypothesis, figure 8.12 graphs the average volume of credit that banks granted to households and business enterprises as a percentage of total assets during 2002 to 2005.[2] Following the organization of figure 8.11, the banks are ordered from largest to smallest and bank size categories are denoted in the same way: the two largest banks (market shares of more than 24 percent each) are in gray columns, the next three largest (market shares of 10 percent each) are indicated by white columns, and small banks are indicated by solid black.

The graphed averages suggest that the largest banks in the system extend less private credit than their smaller competitors. For example, neither of Mexico's two largest banks have private loan-to-asset ratios of more than 40 percent, but 11 of the 14 smaller banks have ratios that exceed 40 percent, most of them by a wide margin. The pattern holds if the next three largest banks are included in the group of oligopolists: none of the five large banks have private loan to asset ratios of more than 50 percent, but 8 of the 14 smaller banks have loan to asset ratios of more than 50 percent.

One might argue that the graphed averages do not control for banks' equity ratios (lower equity ratios tend to be associated with

Figure 8.12 Credit to Consumers and Private Firms as a Percentage of Assets, Mexican Retail Banks, Quarterly Averages, 2002–05

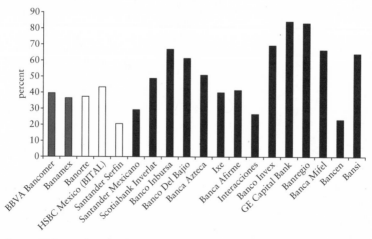

Source: Haber and Musacchio 2006.
Note: Assets are net of IPAB bonds.

more risk taking, and hence more lending). Similarly, the graphed results might be driven by one or two quarters of data. I, therefore, estimate an ordinary least squares regression in the ratio of equity to assets and control for outlying quarters by including quarterly dummies. To control for serial correlation, the robust standard errors are clustered by quarter.

The regressions, reported in the second column of table 8.2, suggest a strong relationship between market power and the volume of credit granted: as market shares double, the ratio of private credit to assets falls by nearly a full percentage point. Given the wide variance in market shares (from 0.1 to 26.7 percent), and given that the sample mean for private lending is only 49 percent of assets, this result is of large magnitude.[3]

Given the strong relationship between market shares and loan volume, the question arises whether large banks constrain credit across the board or constrain only particular types of credit. The same loan volume regression as in column 2 of table 8.2 is, therefore, estimated, but substituting commercial lending, consumer lending, and housing lending for total private lending, and the results are reported in columns 3, 4, and 5, respectively. The results are striking: large banks do not constrain credit across the board; they constrain lending for commercial purposes. Indeed, no relationship at all is apparent between market power and the volume of consumer lending, and a strongly positive relationship exists between market power and housing lending. When it comes to commercial lending, however, the relationship is strongly negative: as market shares double, the ratio of commercial loans to total assets declines by 1.2 percentage points.[4] In other words, all of the reduction in lending associated with large market shares is attributable to reduced levels of commercial lending. This relationship is graphically displayed in figure 8.13.

Net Interest Margins

If banks with market power make fewer loans but earn higher rates of return on equity, then perhaps they charge higher risk-adjusted net interest margins (the spread between what banks pay for deposits and what they charge for loans). That is, the source of their greater profitability may be that they either pay less for deposits or, charge more for loans, or both. I, therefore, estimate a regression in which I measure the elasticity of net interest margins as a function of market share, controlling for risk (as proxied by a bank's ratio of nonperforming to total loans) and for the allocation of credit across loan types (as measured by the ratio of loans to commercial,

Figure 8.13 Commercial Loans as a Percentage of Assets, Mexican Retail Banks, Quarterly Averages, 2002–05

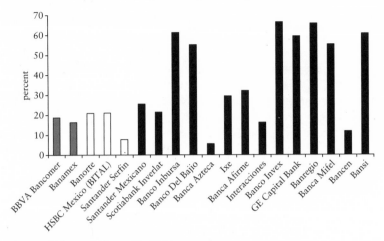

Source: Haber and Musacchio 2006.
Note: Assets are net of IPAB bonds.

consumer, housing, and nonbank financial intermediaries to assets). As before, quarterly dummies and cluster robust standard errors by quarter are included.

The first column of table 8.3 reports the results of these net interest margin regressions. The results indicate that, controlling for risk and for portfolio allocation, larger banks charge lower net interest margins. One could argue that this unexpected result is an outcome of larger banks being able to afford to charge lower interest rates because they enjoy scale economies. The second column of table 8.3 therefore adds a control for scale economies (the ratio of administrative costs to assets). Administrative costs enter the regression with the expected sign and significance: higher administrative costs are strongly correlated with higher net interest margins. The coefficient on market share is now no longer statistically significant, indicating that the lower margins detected in the previous specification are a product of the scale economies that larger banks enjoy. Nevertheless, the regression is consistent with the null hypothesis: it provides no evidence that large banks charge higher risk-adjusted net interest margins than do smaller banks. Indeed, the change in statistical significance of market share from the first specification to the second suggests that larger banks pass along the savings from their scale economies to consumers.

Table 8.3 Income of Mexican Banks, Ordinary Least Squares Regression Results

Item	Net interest margins	Net interest margins	commissions and fees as % of equity	Return on equity (net of fees and commissions)
Market share (by assets)	−0.0376 (2.55)**	0.0132 (1.57)	0.161 (22.57)***	−0.0662 (1.73)
Administrative costs/assets		1.907 (11.13)***	1.0799 (5.10)***	−0.7118 (0.82)
Commercial credit/assets[a]	−0.027 (3.77)***	−0.0192 (7.67)***		
SOFOL credit/assets[a]	−0.0306 (1.71)	−0.0275 (3.23)***		
Consumer credit/assets[a]	0.1783 (7.52)***	−0.0049 (0.35)		
Housing credit/assets[a]	−0.1313 (6.58)***	−0.1338 (5.15)***		
Nonperforming loan ratio	−0.0457 (3.04)***	−0.0211 (2.12)*		−0.0558 (1.38)
Quarter dummies	Yes	Yes	Yes	
Robust standard deviation errors clustered by quarter	Yes	Yes	Yes	

(Continued on the following page)

Table 8.3 (Continued)

Item	Net interest margins	Net interest margins	Commissions and fees as of equity	Return on equity (net of fees and commissions)
Constant	0.0292	0.0013	0.0065	0.0036
	(6.17)***	(0.48)	(2.46)**	(0.25)
Number of observations	297	297	297	297
R-squared	0.67	0.88	0.28	0.17

Source: Author's calculations.
Note: * = significant at 10%; ** = significant at 5%; *** = significant at 1%. Figures in parentheses are robust t statistics.
a. Private lending does not include IPAB Bonds. For that reason, IPAB bonds are also netted out from assets in the lending regressions.

Commission and Fee Income

How can large banks make more money by providing less credit if they do not charge higher risk-adjusted net interest margins? One possible answer is that their market power allows them to charge commissions and fees above the competitive level.

This hypothesis is tested in two steps. The first step is to estimate the percentage of total income from commissions and fees and graph the averages by bank (figure 8.14.) The graphed data suggest that market power is associated with higher income from commissions and fees. On average, the two largest banks earn 21 percent of their total income from commissions and fees, the next three largest banks earn 18 percent, and the remaining (small) banks earn 9 percent.

The second step is to estimate a regression of the return on equity from commissions and fees on market share. Scale economies are controlled for by including the ratio of administrative costs to assets and quarterly dummies and by clustering the (robust) standard errors by quarter. The results, presented in the third column of table 8.3, indicate a strong association between market power and the rate of return on commissions and fees. As market shares double, commission and fee income (as a percentage of equity) increases by 0.16 percentage point per quarter.

Figure 8.14 Commissions and Fees as a Percentage of Income, Mexican Retail Banks, Quarterly Averages, 2002–05

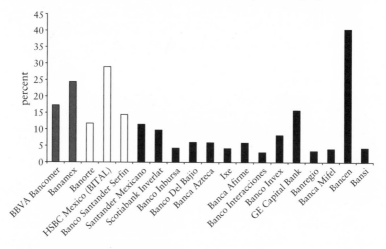

Source: Haber and Musacchio 2006.
Note: Assets are net of IPAB bonds.

As a double check on the results, the regression on returns on equity presented in the first column of table 8.2 are re-estimated, but commissions and fees are now stripped out of income. If the assumption that the higher rates of return for larger banks are driven by their ability to charge higher commissions and fees is correct, the coefficient on market share should no longer be statistically significant. The results, presented in the fourth column of table 8.3, bear out this intuition.

Conclusion

Taken together, the regressions indicate that Mexico's largest banks earn rents from market power. The evidence suggests that they do so through a somewhat subtle oligopoly pricing strategy that can be outlined as follows. Consumers and businesses can open accounts anywhere they like, but they cannot obtain loans anywhere they like. Obtaining a loan requires a number of steps, but one of them is to have an account at the bank that is making the loan. This provides the largest banks—which make the vast majority of loans—with an opportunity to earn rents through the fees and commissions they charge to maintain accounts and process payments. They, therefore, do not charge interest margins any higher than their smaller competitors. Indeed, the evidence suggests that large banks may charge lower net interest margins by passing on the savings from scale economies, but they more than recoup the lower net interest margins by hitting borrowers and account holders with fees and commissions on every transaction they make.

Hypothesis 4: Weak Contract Rights

The summary statistics on lending by type (table 8.1) suggest that the contraction of credit since 1997 has not been uniform. As of December 2005, the ratio of commercial credit to GDP was one-third below its 1997 level. Lending to consumers, by contrast, quadrupled over the same period. Note that the 2005 level of consumer lending (2.8 percent of GDP) is extremely low by any reasonable comparative metric. Nevertheless, the sharp divergence in the trends for commercial and consumer credit requires explanation. Why have banks favored consumer lending over commercial lending?

One answer is that banks find that assessing risk and enforcing contracts is more difficult in the commercial credit market than in the market for consumer loans. This is not to argue that the contract rights environment is good for consumer lending, but that the assessing of risk and enforcing of contracts is generally difficult in Mexico, and that the environment facing commercial lenders is particularly difficult.

History of Contract Enforcement

Banks' ability to enforce contracts requires that they be able to repossess collateral. One form that collateral takes is physical: a house, a farm, or an inventory of raw materials. To repossess physical collateral, banks need access to a system of property and commercial registries to verify the ownership of the collateral and a system of laws, courts, and police that allows them to take legal and physical possession of the collateral. Another form that collateral takes is reputational: the knowledge that failure to repay will prevent borrowing in the future. Typically, banks assess reputational collateral through two means. First, banks themselves develop internal systems of credit analysis. Second, they share this information with other banks, or other creditors generally, through a credit reporting agency.

Virtually none of the institutions required to assess and attach collateral efficiently existed in Mexico until relatively recently. Physical collateral was extraordinarily difficult to repossess. Mexico did not (and still does not) have an efficient or accurate real property register (Joint Center for Housing Studies 2004). The Ministry of Commerce did maintain a commercial property register, but it was not (and is not) available to the public. Thus, for banks to attach property was difficult, because whether the person or business that pledged the property actually owned it was not always clear. In addition, in those cases when bankers did move to foreclose, debtors could take advantage of Mexico's extraordinarily inefficient bankruptcy laws. Not only did Mexico have few bankruptcy judges, but also the bankruptcy laws required judges to pass resolutions on each and every objection debtors presented. Debtors could, therefore, delay the recovery of property by raising a long string of objections. In addition, even when favorable judgments were rendered, the police did not always enforce them.

Banks also could not assess the quality of reputational collateral. The banks themselves had weak internal systems of credit analysis. As Del Angel Mobarak (2002, 2005) shows, prior to the bank expropriation of 1982, Mexico's industrial conglomerates typically owned both a commercial bank and an investment bank, and the portfolios of these banks tended to consist of shares held in the enterprises that were part of the conglomerates. The commercial and investment banks were, in essence, the treasury divisions of the industrial conglomerates. They bore little resemblance to the impersonal credit intermediaries of economic theory. That is to say, much of the private lending from the 1950s through the 1970s captured in figure 8.3 was insider lending: banks lent primarily to firms owned or controlled by their own directors. The banks, therefore, had weak incentives to develop internal systems of credit analysis. During the period when the government ran the banks (1982–91), whatever systems of credit analysis that banks had developed were allowed to languish, because the banks were used primarily as a vehicle for financing government deficits. The net result was that when the banks were privatized in 1991, their internal systems of credit analysis were virtually nonexistent (Mackey 1999).

Banks could not rely on information that private credit bureaus gathered in place of their own systems of analysis, because, until recently, private credit reporting did not exist in Mexico. The Asociación de Bancqueros de México started to pool credit information in the early 1930s, but in 1933 the central bank arrogated this authority from them. In 1964, the responsible department of the central bank was constituted as a government-run credit agency. The problem with government-run credit reporting is that bankers have weak incentives to provide the government with information about their client bases. The government, for its part, has weak incentives to provide accurate information to banks, because it is not motivated by the need to make a profit. As a result, the information available from this government-run credit bureau was out-of-date and limited in scope (Negrin 2000). The first private credit bureaus were finally founded starting in July 1993, but rules governing their operation were not in place until February 1995 (Mackey 1999).

Under normal circumstances, when bankers lack the ability to repossess collateral through the legal system and cannot assess the quality of reputational collateral, they do not make arm's length loans. Instead, they do what Mexico's bankers did before 1982: they lend primarily to their own enterprises (Del Angel Mobarak 2002, 2005; Maurer and Haber 2007).

When Mexico's banks were privatized in 1991, however, the circumstances were far from normal. The banks had weak incentives to engage in prudent lending because neither their directors nor their major stockholders had much of their own capital at risk. The government had allowed them to buy the banks with funds that they borrowed from the banks (Mackey 1999).

The absence of effective monitoring meant that credit expanded at a prodigious rate. From 1991 to 1994, the compound rate of growth of bank lending was 24 percent per year. Even more rapid than the expansion of lending was the growth of nonperforming loans. As early as December 1991, the ratio of nonperforming to total loans was already 14 percent. By December 1994, it had hit 17 percent. It then skyrocketed to 36 percent by the end of 1995 and to 53 percent by the end of 1996 (Haber 2005). At the same time that nonperformance rates surged, bankers found that they could not easily repossess collateral. Even given the lax standards by which Mexican banks determined a loan to be nonperforming, which allowed banks to count loans as in good standing that would be considered nonperforming in the United States or other developed countries, collateral recovery rates were amazingly low: 5 percent in 1991 and 1992, 7 percent in 1993, and 9 percent in 1994. If more standard definitions of nonperformance are used, then collateral recovery rates were probably some 2 or 3 percent (Haber 2005). This situation resulted in the collapse of the banking system and a government-financed bailout.

As the banks emerged from government intervention and restructuring in 1997, the Zedillo government carried out a series of reforms designed to put the banks on a more sound institutional footing. For example, it limited loans to related parties, required banks to follow accounting practices that more closely approximate those in the rest of the OECD, placed limits on deposit insurance, and allowed multinationals to purchase Mexico's major banks. It also introduced a regulatory system that establishes reserve minimums that vary in accordance with the risk level of a bank's portfolio. In particular, banks are required to access borrowers' credit records through a private credit bureau. Loans made without regard to this requirement, or loans made to borrowers whose credit records are poor, must be provisioned at 100 percent (Mackey 1999).

These reforms did not, however, solve the weakness of contract rights. To this end the government implemented a series of reforms designed to make repossessing collateral easier. In 2001, the Fox government pushed through a bankruptcy reform, one of whose innovations was to sidestep the inefficient bankruptcy courts by allowing banks and borrowers to write contracts that put the assets being collateralized outside of a borrower's bankruptcy estate by assigning those assets to the lender. A simple example of such a contract is the recently developed lease-to-own automobile finance agreements. Under this kind of arrangement, a borrower does not technically purchase a car with financing from a bank, but instead the bank purchases the car and then leases it to the borrower. The depreciation and interest rates used to calculate the lease payments are then structured so that the bank recoups its principal and interest during the lease period. When the lease expires, the title passes to the borrower, but until that time, the bank holds title to the car and can seize it as soon as a lease payment is missed.

A second example of this type of innovation was the 2001 reform of mortgage contracts that replaced liens on property with bilateral trusts in which the bank is both the trustee and the beneficiary of the trust. When payments are missed, the bank can evict the debtor and sell the house at auction. Debtors can legally contest the repossession, but they are unable to remain in the house during that process, which gives them strong incentives to negotiate an amicable repossession with the bank (Caloca González n.d.).

Difficulties in Assigning Assets to Creditors

Despite these steps, Mexico still has a difficult contract rights environment. For example, not all assets can be assigned to creditors so as to avoid the legal process of foreclosure and bankruptcy. As a practical matter, the types of assets that consumers use as loan collateral are far easier to assign to creditors than the types of assets that business enterprises pledge as collateral.

To be assignable, an asset has to be tangible, identifiable, and have value in a liquid market. As a result, some types of assets are easier to assign to creditors than others. At one end of the spectrum is a typical consumer asset, an automobile. The bank can easily write the contract in the form of a lease; thus, the automobile is the bank's property, not the borrower's. Repossessing the car is a simple matter: it is tangible, is identifiable (by vehicle identification number), has ongoing value, and can be sold in a liquid market for used cars. Moreover, the cost of repossessing the car (the cost of renting a tow truck, some muscle, and a baseball bat) is low relative to the value of the car.

Some assets that businesses own can be pledged in much the same way. For example, trucks, cranes, and earthmoving equipment can be leased from the bank and are tangible, are individually identifiable, depreciate slowly, have secondary markets, and can be repossessed by driving them off the property. Other commercial assets have characteristics that make them difficult to assign to the bank. Receivables, for example, are not tangible and can be difficult to identify. Indeed, firms can write sales contracts in such a way that their income is not credited to the category of receivables that has been assigned, but to some other category. The assignee can, of course, use the legal system to undo this subterfuge, but that presupposes the existence of an efficient legal system. Inventories of raw materials, to cite another example, are almost impossible to identify individually (is the pile of coal that has been assigned the one in warehouse A or the one in warehouse B?). Moreover, inventories of raw materials are used up in production. Even most production machinery departs from the criteria for easy assignability. Although production machines can be identified individually and tend to depreciate slowly, the problem is that most are designed for specific tasks in a specific setting and, as a result, do not always have liquid secondary markets. In addition, much of the cost of such machines is embodied in their installation, not in the cost of the machine per se. In short, much production machinery tends to be expensive to remove relative to its value in a secondary market.

The Mortgage Market

Mortgage contracts can be written in such a way as to assign the assets being collateralized to lenders. The problem is that it is not always clear that the borrower actually holds clear title to the property being mortgaged. The shortcomings of Mexico's property registers are numerous:

- They cannot be accessed online, but must be accessed manually by consulting the sheaves of paper that compose the file for each parcel.
- The individuals who consult the register often have access to the original documents in a parcel's file, not photocopies of the documents, which gives them opportunities to tamper with the file.
- Many property sales go unrecorded in the property register, because purchasers seek to avoid paying property registration fees.
- Mechanics liens on property are not recorded.
- Multiple owners are often recorded for the same parcel.
- The boundaries of parcels are not clearly specified.
- The public property registry is not integrated with the property tax registry. This reduces the incentives of the municipal governments that collect property taxes to make sure that the public registry is up to date.
- The public property registry does not cover village lands held in common, which are included in a separate agrarian property registry. This means that such lands that have been converted to private use—typically by their sale to housing developers, who then create parcels that are resold to homeowners—do not have clear title histories (Rajoy n.d.).

As a result, it is highly uncertain whether the person who owns a parcel of land actually has clear title to it (Joint Center for Housing Studies 2004). Because titling is so uncertain, in 2004, banks made only 18,601 loans for the purchase of existing housing. Even more shocking, this was a dramatic improvement compared with previous years, when almost no loans were made (Centro de Investigación y Documentación de la Casa and Sociedad Hipotecaria Federal 2005).

As concerns new construction, banks do not finance most lending for new construction either. New construction tends to be financed either by loans from a government housing agency or by specialized nonbank financial intermediaries that are linked to construction and development companies. The latter, in turn, are partially financed by loans from a government development bank (the Sociedad Federal Hipotecaria) that also guarantees the mortgage. In short, lending for new housing has recovered because much of the risk of such lending has been shifted to the government.

The Problem of Assessing Reputation

Credit reporting also favors consumer lending over commercial lending. Since 1995, Mexico's new private credit bureau has been gathering data on consumers and business enterprises, but this credit bureau is a pale reflection of credit bureaus in developed countries. Its fundamental problem is that it is owned by the largest banks, which have weak incentives to provide credit information about their best borrowers to their smaller competitors. Thus, the range of information that the credit bureau collects is restricted to borrowers' payment history for bank loans. Payment histories to other creditors, such as utility companies, department stores, or automobile financing companies, are not included. Similarly, mechanics liens against borrowers are not recorded and neither are other kinds of legal judgments. In addition, there is a fundamental problem that confronts creditors everywhere: tracking consumers is much easier than tracking businesses, especially small ones. Consumers cannot readily change their identities. Business enterprises, especially small ones, can change their corporate identities virtually at will.

The Judicial System

Finally, the ability of consumers and of business enterprises to use the legal system to delay repossession differs significantly. The vast majority of cases involving contract enforcement are not adjudicated in federal courts, which have undergone a prolonged process of reform since the mid-1990s, but in state courts, which are woefully inefficient. Because Mexico has a federal system, state courts and other judicial agencies (prosecution, defense, judicial councils, and court clerks) are organized independently of the federal judiciary and operate according to their own procedural and substantive laws. State governors continue to name judges, who are subject to a high degree of partisan influence. They and their staffs have a great deal of discretion, carry enormous caseloads, and are grossly underfunded compared with the federal judiciary. What is true of the courts is even more true of the police, who continue to be poorly paid and highly corrupt (Domingo 2000; Giugale, Lafourcade, and Nguyen 2001; Magaloni and Zepeda 2004; Ríos-Figueroa 2007).

Thus, business enterprises, especially those with considerable financial resources, can take advantage of the disorganization, inefficiency, and corruption of state judicial systems to delay judgments against them and the repossession of collateral. For consumers to marshal the necessary resources to do so is much more difficult.

The Joint Determination of Oligopoly and Weak Property Rights

From 1929 to 2000, Mexico was ruled by a single party, the Institutional Revolutionary Party (Partido Revolucionario Institucional, or PRI), which not only won all presidential elections, but also dominated both houses of the legislature, controlled all the state houses, named the judiciary, controlled the press, and ran the education system. So complete was the PRI's hegemony that knowing exactly where the party ended and the government began was difficult.

The lack of checks on the government's authority and discretion created a thorny problem for the business class: nothing prevented the government from expropriating private assets once they had been deployed, which meant that the incentives to invest were weak. Weak incentives for investment, in turn, created a problem for the PRI: it needed to generate jobs for the core constituencies that assured it electoral dominance. The PRI solved this problem the way many authoritarian governments do, namely, it awarded a select portion of the country's business class with special privileges designed to raise rates of return high enough to compensate them for the risk of expropriation. These privileges included low levels of taxation, trade protection, and barriers to entry. This is to say, high levels of market concentration were endogenous to Mexico's authoritarian political institutions (Haber and others 2008).

The special privileges that the government crafted had an unforeseen consequence: low levels of tax collection. Mexico essentially had two economic sectors: a rapidly growing sector that received special privileges and was lightly taxed and a slowly growing sector that was subject, at least on paper, to heavy tax rates. The irony of this system is obvious: the part of the economy that produced most of the output paid little in taxes, while the rest of the economy produced so little that there was almost nothing to tax. The result was that until the oil boom of the late 1970s, government revenues were less than 10 percent of GDP. Even after the oil boom, total government revenues typically amounted to only 15 percent of GDP. As a consequence, the government provided little in the way of public goods. Education, health care, old-age pensions, and other public programs were targeted to subsets of the population, that is, those who the PRI needed to keep winning elections.

The special privileges granted to a subset of the business class had a second unforeseen consequence: weak property rights institutions. As an emerging body of economic theory has demonstrated, wealth holders who are politically influential have strong incentives to invest little in the institutions that protect property rights, because they can obtain all the property rights protection they need through private arrangements with public officials. In addition, their political power, when coupled with weak property rights institutions, allows them to prey on the assets of other members of society (Sonin 2003). Indeed, weak property rights institutions serve as a barrier to entry to would-be competitors. Consider, for example, two entrepreneurs: entrepreneur A, whose political connections allow him to win all contract disputes brought against his firm, and entrepreneur B, who knows that he will lose all disputes brought against him by entrepreneur A. Entrepreneur B is beaten even before he begins. He therefore does not invest in the first place.

Not only did privileged elites have weak incentives to invest in property rights institutions, but also the government did as well. Establishing and maintaining property and commercial registers, as well as providing sufficient levels of funding to create courts and police that are not corrupt, comes at a fiscal cost. Funds spent on property rights institutions are funds not spent on satisfying the demands of core constituents (in Mexico's case, social insurance for unionized workers) and not available for extraction by public officials (which is to say, not available to be stolen).

Policy Implications

The transition to democracy swept away some of Mexico's authoritarian institutions. Elections are now closely contested, the president no longer rules as a virtual dictator, and the PRI is now one of three major parties and is struggling for its existence. This means that the political institutions that gave rise to concentrated markets and weak contract rights no longer operate. It does not mean, however, that barriers to entry and weak contract rights automatically disappeared once the PRI was voted out of office.

The policy implication is straightforward: Mexico could increase the amount of credit available either by reforming the institutions necessary to enforce contract rights or by making it easier to obtain a bank charter. These are not, of course, mutually exclusive policies. Indeed, they are likely to complement each another. As more banks enter the market, they will develop relationships with borrowers who currently do not access the banking system, and in so doing, they will help those firms and households develop credit histories. Those banks are also likely to lobby for reforms to the institutions that underpin contract rights. Similarly, as contract rights become more easily enforced, incumbent banks will have incentives to extend credit to groups that they currently do not serve.

The first policy goal—more liberal bank chartering—is likely to be obtained more easily. Increasing the number of chartered banks can be accomplished at the discretion of the secretary of the treasury. Moreover, the political pressures to do so are strong, because constituents are demanding increased access to credit. At the same time, the political pressures to restrict entry have weakened. Mexico's largest banks are now foreign owned; thus, their major stockholders are not constituents of the government.

The second policy goal, better contract rights, is likely not to be easily obtained except in the long run. The secretary of the treasury can, at the stroke of a pen, increase the number of bank charters. He or she cannot, however, decree a better contract rights environment. This is because establishing a system of property in which claims and contracts can be enforced universally and at low cost is impossible without first establishing the rule of law. Obviously, if the courts and police are corrupt, then enforcing even the most carefully crafted contract or protecting even the most clearly demarcated asset from encroachment is impossible. Rule of law requires the creation of a broad range of institutions, and no road map for generating such institutions is available. Indeed, not all of the institutions necessary for rule of law are legally codified; many are embedded in sets of attitudes and beliefs among citizens about how the legally codified institutions of government should work. Thus, societies tend to find their way to the creation of the institutions that produce rule of law through processes of experimentation. The empirical evidence strongly suggests that this is a slow process that is accomplished over generations, not something that comes about in a few years.

What is true about establishing the rule of law is also true about establishing and maintaining property and commercial registers. The Fox government began a program to modernize property registries. This program is still, however, in its pilot phase. The government provided funding of US$4 million to convert paper files to an electronic database in three states, Sonora, Colima, and Baja California (Centro de Investigación y Documentación de la Casa and Sociedad Hipotecaria Federal 2005), but many of the other problems with the property registry remain, even in these states. In short, resolving the problem of uncertain titling remains a major challenge.

The implication is clear. In the short run, the most efficient way to increase credit is to facilitate market entry. A number of small banks, such as Azteca in the consumer market and Mifel, Bansi, and Banco del Bajío, have shown that specializing in particular market niches and earning positive rates of return is possible by developing long-term relationships with borrowers that allow the banks to assess credit risk. During the last days of the Fox administration, the secretary of the treasury granted bank charters to six retailers, including Wal-Mart. This will almost certainly increase the amount of consumer credit available and may also have an impact on the ability of the largest banks to charge fees and commissions above those that would prevail in a more competitive market. It is, however, just a step in the right direction.

The cost to Mexico of not increasing the availability of credit is not trivial. The economy has grown anemically since the signing of the North American Free Trade Agreement more than a decade ago. From 1994 to 2005, real per capita GDP grew at only 1.3 percent per year, a slow rate by any comparative metric. Mexico's rate of growth was 38 percent slower than the growth rate for comparable middle-income developing countries (2.1 percent per year), 43 percent slower than the U.S. growth rate (2.3 percent per year), and 54 percent slower than Mexico's own growth rate from 1950 to 1980 (2.8 percent per year) (Haber and others 2008). It was also slow compared with the growth rate that would have been needed to provide employment for the roughly 1 million new entrants to the labor market each year. More than half of those new workers did not find employment in Mexico and, instead, migrated to the United States. As the chapters in this volume make clear, many reasons account for Mexico's sluggish economic performance, but as Tornell, Westermann, and Martínez (2004) show, one crucial reason is the scarcity of credit.

Notes

1. The administrative cost ratio enters the regression as nonsignificant, but a regression of administrative costs on market shares not reported here detects significant scale economies. As market share doubles, the administrative cost ratio falls by 0.02 percentage point per quarter. The nonperforming loan ratio enters the regression as not significant, and dropping it from the regression has no qualitative impact on the other estimated coefficients. A separate regression of nonperforming loans on market shares finds a strong inverse relationship: as market shares double, nonperforming loans fall by 0.2 percentage point.

2. Private credit is the sum of commercial, consumer, and housing loans, plus credit granted by banks to nonbank financial intermediaries. IPAB bonds are not included as a form of private credit and are thus also netted out from assets. The results are not, however, sensitive to the inclusion of IPAB bonds in the numerator and the denominator.

3. I report assets and estimate loan-to-asset ratios, net of IPAB bonds, to control for differences in the degree to which banks hold these federal bailout bonds in their portfolios. Alternative specifications that include IPAB bonds in assets and that then add controls for the ratio of IPAB bonds to total assets produce qualitatively similar results.

4. I report assets and estimate loan-to-asset ratios, net of IPAB bonds, to control for differences in the degree to which banks hold these federal bailout bonds in their portfolios. Alternative specifications that include IPAB bonds in assets, and that then add controls for the ratio of IPAB bonds to total assets, produce qualitatively similar results.

References

Caloca González, Manuel. N.d. "Mortgage-Backed Securitization: New Legal Development in Mexico." Unpublished paper, Mexico City.

Centro de Investigación y Documentación de la Casa and Sociedad Hipotecaria Federal. 2005. "Current Housing Situation in Mexico." Unpublished report.

Del Angel Mobarak, Gustavo. 2002. "Paradoxes of Financial Development: The Construction of the Mexican Banking System, 1941–1982." Ph.D. dissertation, Stanford University, Stanford, CA.

———. 2005. "La banca mexicana antes de 1982." In *Cuando el estado se hizo banquero: Consecuencias de la nacionalización bancaria en México*, ed. Gustavo del Angel Mobarak, Carlos Bazdresch Parada, and Francisco Suárez Dávila, 43–56. Mexico City: Fondo de Cultura Económica.

Del Angel Mobarak, Gustavo, Stephen Haber, and Aldo Musacchio. 2006. "Normas contables bancarias en México: Una guía de los cambios para legos diez años después de la crisis bancaria de 1995." *El Trimestre Económico* 73 (4): 903–26.

Domingo, Pilar. 2000. "Judicial Independence: The Politics of the Supreme Court in Mexico." *Journal of Latin American Studies* 32 (3): 707–35.

Giugale, Marcelo, Olivier Lafourcade, and Vinh Nguyen. 2001. *Mexico: A Comprehensive Development Agenda for the New Era.* Washington, DC: World Bank.

González-Anaya, José Antonio. 2003. "Why Have Banks Stopped Lending in Mexico Since the Peso Crisis of 1995?" Working Paper 118, Stanford Center for International Development, Stanford, CA.

Haber, Stephen. 2005. "Mexico's Experiments with Bank Privatization and Liberalization, 1991–2003." *Journal of Banking and Finance* 29 (8–9): 2325–53.

———. 2006. "Por qué importan las instituciones: La banca y el crecimiento económico en México." *El Trimestre Económico* 73 (3): 429–78.

Haber, Stephen, Herbert S. Klein, Noel Maurer, and Kevin J. Middlebrook. 2008. *Mexico Since 1980.* Cambridge, U.K.: Cambridge University Press.

Haber, Stephen, and Aldo Musacchio. 2006. "Foreign Entry and the Mexican Banking System." Unpublished paper, Stanford University, Stanford, CA.

Joint Center for Housing Studies. 2004. *The State of Mexico's Housing 2004.* Cambridge, MA: Harvard University, Joint Center for Housing Studies.

Mackey, Michael W. 1999. *Report of Michael W. Mackey on the Comprehensive Evaluation of the Operations and Function of the Fund for the Protection of Bank Savings (FOBAPROA) and the Quality of Supervision of the FOBAPROA Program, 1995–1998.*

Magaloni, Beatriz, and Guillermo Zepeda. 2004. "Democratization, Crime, and Judicial Reform in Mexico." In *Dilemmas of Political Change in Mexico*, ed. Kevin J. Middlebrook, 168–97. London: University of London, Institute of Latin American Studies, and University of California, San Diego, Center for U.S.-Mexican Studies.

Maurer, Noel, and Stephen Haber. 2007. "Related Lending: Manifest Looting or Good Governance? Lessons from the Economic History of Mexico." In *Growth, Institutions, and Crises: Latin America from a Historic Perspective*, ed. Sebastian Edwards, 213–42. Chicago: University of Chicago Press.

McQuerry, Elizabeth. 1999. "The Banking Sector Rescue in Mexico." *Federal Reserve Bank of Atlanta Economic Review* Third Quarter: 14–29.

Negrin, José Luis. 2000. "Mecanismos para compartir información crediticia: Evidencia internacional y la experiencia mexicana." Working Paper 2000–05, Banco de Mexico, Dirección General de Investigación Económica, Mexico City.

Rajoy, Enrique. N.d. "El registro de la propiedad en México: Principios y reformas." Unpublished paper, Mexico City.

Ríos-Figueroa, Julio. 2007. "Fragmentation of Power and the Emergence of an Effective Judiciary in Mexico, 1994–2002." *Latin American Politics and Society* 49 (1): 31–57.

Sonin, Konstantin. 2003. "Why the Rich May Favor Poor Protection of Property Rights." *Journal of Comparative Economics* 31 (4): 715–31.

Tornell, Aaron, Frank Westermann, and Lorenza Martínez. 2004. "NAFTA and Mexico's Less Than Stellar Performance." Working Paper 10289, National Bureau for Economic Research, Cambridge, MA.

PART IV

How Unequal Structures Hurt Competition in Major Sectors

9

Competition and Equity in Telecommunications

Rafael del Villar

The lesson drawn from both theory and experience is that an economy's incentive structure is critical to its performance. An economy with a healthily competitive incentive structure is likely to lead to

- a more efficient use of resources, and consequently greater aggregate output
- a wider variety of higher quality goods and services available to consumers at lower prices
- the availability of more job opportunities with remuneration in line with productivity
- the availability of more possibilities for entrepreneurs to turn their creativity into material returns and successful projects.

For markets that do not operate under conditions of competition, welfare losses can often significantly exceed the rents being received by the sheltered sectors. This leads to less efficient allocation of resources and, to the extent that rents accrue to wealthier groups, worse income distribution.

The author would like to thank Eduardo Martínez, Everardo Quezada, and Arcelia Rodríguez for the excellent assistance provided in preparing this chapter. He would also like to thank Roger Noll, Jessica Serrano, and Michael Walton for valuable comments. The opinions expressed in this chapter are those of the author and do not necessarily represent those of the Bank of Mexico or the Ministry of Communications and Transport.

The concept of equity goes beyond income distribution. As Bourguignon and Dessus discuss (chapter 1 in this volume), the concept refers to the ability of members of society to access opportunities that allow them to lead productive lives. As society grants more equity (ex ante), this will be reflected, over time, in improved distribution (ex post) of income and wealth and an improvement in the overall standard of living.

Equity and competition are closely linked. These concepts are particularly relevant for broadly used inputs such as labor, telecommunications, and energy. Any change in these sectors affects not only consumers, but also the activities for which they are inputs. Where lack of competition leads to restrictions in access, this amounts to an inequitable outcome: those firms or individuals with influence or connections have preferential, exclusive, or cheaper access to inputs than others. The other side of this is that for certain activities, the social rate of return is greater than the private rate of return (for example, ensuring an educated and healthy society and providing basic infrastructure). In the context of this chapter, ensuring extensive broadband penetration in Mexico is essential for both efficiency and equity reasons, and should be a priority objective of public policy. Thus, the purpose of this chapter is to analyze several issues that have a bearing on competition and equal opportunities as they relate to the telecommunications sector.

Economic Overview of the Privatization of Teléfonos de Mexico

The telecommunications sector has been among the economy's most dynamic over the past 40 years. The key event during this period was the privatization of Teléfonos de Mexico (TELMEX) in 1990, which continues to influence and mold the sector.

Between 1965 and 1980, the number of telephone lines increased more than 12 percent per year. During the 1980s, Mexico underwent a serious external debt and macroeconomic crisis that led to economic stagnation: annual gross domestic product (GDP) growth fell from 6.7 percent between 1965 and 1980 to just 1.8 percent in the 1980s. During that same decade, the average annual increase in the number of telephone lines fell to 7 percent. The precariousness of the economy and public finances not only had an effect on the sector's growth, but also on the quality and reliability of telephone services. The government viewed TELMEX's revenues as a source of funds to be used for other areas of the economy and for servicing its debt (Casasús 1994). Thus, the necessary investments to support

TELMEX operations were not made, and it had to rely on increasingly obsolete technology. The 1985 Mexico City earthquake paralyzed the telecommunications system and revealed the frailness of its infrastructure and the growing need for investment.

All led to the development of a modernization policy for the sector that included the privatization of TELMEX. In September 1989, the government announced its intent to privatize the company. The government's strategy was based not only on improving the company's efficiency, but also on possibly improving its public finances basically by decreasing government subsidies.

In August 1990, the government changed TELMEX's license (known as a title of concession under Mexican law), giving the company an ambitious set of obligations. These were aimed at preventing the privatized company from engaging in monopolistic or excessive practices and ensuring that third parties would have nondiscriminatory access to the company's key facilities and infrastructure, such as interconnection.

The government's overriding goals were, however, to maximize revenues from the privatization and to do so as quickly as possible so it could proceed with other privatizations. This approach ultimately meant that the privatization took place without a sound institutional framework. Indicative of this was the fact that the Ministry of Finance was responsible for the privatization and not the Ministry of Communications and Transport.

To maximize revenues from the privatization, the government sold a package of firms to a single group of investors. It included TELMEX and Teléfonos de Noroeste (the telephone carrier in northwest Mexico), both state-owned fixed telephony companies that operated in exclusive geographic zones; the only existing nationwide cellular telephony concession; the federal microwave network; and several frequency bands.

To eliminate subsidies and make the company more attractive to potential buyers, the government allowed TELMEX to credit up to 65 percent of the special tax on telephony (equal to 29 percent of the company's revenues) against its investments. This implied lowering the effective tax from 29 percent to 10 percent. Before the privatization, it also increased rates considerably. As a result, annual revenues per line rose from US$440 in 1989 to US$710 in 1990, a 61 percent increase (Casanueva and del Villar 2003).

In addition, the government negotiated with the Telephone Workers' Union of the Republic of Mexico (Sindicato de Telefonistas de la Republica Mexicana, or STRM) to modify the collective bargaining agreement to make labor conditions more flexible. In exchange, the workers received stockholding interest in the privatized company.

In 1989, months before the federal government announced the privatization, the STRM and TELMEX agreed to change the collective bargaining agreement and decrease STRM interference in the company's modernization (for example, the STRM had had the right to intervene in the implementation of technological changes and the startup of new services).

Improved labor flexibility was achieved by eliminating the previous structure that regulated all details of labor relations through so-called department agreements. These were now replaced by position profiles, which were much less regulated and gave much more general definitions of workers' duties and categories. It also allowed TELMEX to have more say about moving its personnel internally among departments without having to be subject to STRM approval.

The government guaranteed that TELMEX would not face competition in domestic and international long distance for the first six years following its privatization. At the time of privatization, revenues from international and domestic long distance telephony represented slightly more than twice the revenues the company earned from local telephony (this market was left open to competition after privatization). The share of local telephony in the company's overall revenues increased drastically, rising from a little more than 20 percent of total revenues in 1989 to slightly more than 41 percent in 1992.

The owner of the television monopoly in Mexico was barred from acquiring TELMEX because of the government's concerns about this type of concentration. In exchange, the government blocked the possibility of TELMEX offering television and video services indefinitely in its title of concession.

Finally, although the government had stipulated obligations for the privatized company regarding coverage and network expansion in the modification to the title of concession, the main responsibilities concluded in 1994—for example, the requirement that telephone lines had to increase a minimum of 12 percent annually. (Other requirements, such as reducing the period of time consumers must wait before being serviced or increasing the number of public telephone booths, which extended beyond 1994, are not as economically important.) This was the last year in office of the administration of President Carlos Salinas, which was responsible for carrying out the privatization of the company. In an example of political opportunism, the authorities did not set conditions regarding the growth of the company, considering them not to be particularly relevant, even though monopolies are motivated to restrict supply in order to increase prices.

Thus, even though the concession forbids monopolistic practices and discrimination against third parties and obligates TELMEX to

provide interconnection and nondiscriminatory access, the administration did not take the necessary steps to ensure that competition
would materialize. It did not grant concessions or set interconnection conditions so that third parties could enter the local telephony
market that, on paper at least, had been left open to competition,
and even though third parties were indeed interested in competing
in this market.

The government's actions and omissions turned TELMEX into an
extremely profitable quasi-monopoly and its owners into economically powerful people virtually overnight. By 1993, TELMEX's gross
profits were roughly equivalent to 1 percent of GDP, while the added
value was only 2 percent of GDP. The administration that carried
out the privatization essentially ignored the problems this enormous
private economic power would, in all likelihood, pose in the future
for the authorities responsible for regulating the company.

Importance of Telecommunications

The impact of telecommunications services and information technologies in the economy has been thoroughly documented and discussed. According to Jorgenson and Vu (2005), the adoption of
information and communication technology explains more than
15 percent of the growth the world economy experienced from 1995
to 2003. The contribution of information and communication technology to growth varies among countries: although it accounted for
almost 30 percent of economic growth, on average, in the Group of
Seven countries (and 47 percent in Germany), it accounted for only
8 percent in Eastern Europe and 10 percent in Sub-Saharan Africa.

In Mexico, national account statistics also confirm the increasing
contribution of information and communication technology to the
economy. The share of telecommunications has increased drastically
in recent years, rising from 1.1 percent in 1990 to 5.0 percent in 2005,
while the weight of telecommunications service rates in the national
consumer price index has risen to 2.16 percent for local telephony,
similar to that of electricity (2.27 percent) (figures 9.1 and 9.2).

All population deciles in Mexico account for significant consumption of telecommunications services. In 2006, household expenditure on telecommunications in the poorest income decile accounted
for 2.9 percent of total household expenditure, whereas for the
second-richest decile telecommunications expenditure represented
5.7 percent of household expenditure, the highest of any decile (table
9.1). This high percentage is explained primarily by the high rates
consumers pay for telecommunications services.

Figure 9.1 Weight of Telecommunications Services Rates in the Consumer Price Index, Selected Years

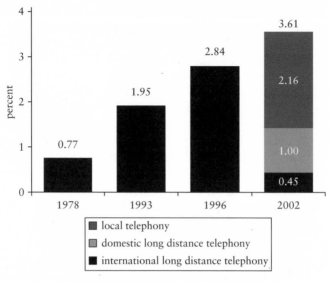

Source: Bank of Mexico data.

Figure 9.2 Share of Communications Services in Gross National Product, Selected Years

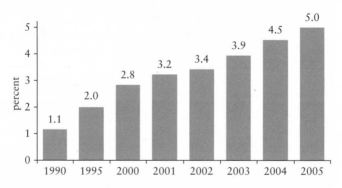

Source: President, Fifth State of the *Union* address, September 2005.

In addition, according to household income and expenditure surveys, since 2004, households from all population deciles have stated that they spend money on Internet services, but the disparity in expenditure between the highest-income decile and the two lowest

Table 9.1 Household Expenditure on Telecommunications Services by Population Decile, 2006 (percentage of household expenditure)

		Poorest				Household deciles[a]					Richest
Category	Total	1	2	3	4	5	6	7	8	9	10
Total communications[b]	4.8	2.9	3.2	3.5	3.9	4.3	4.7	4.7	5.6	5.7	5.0
Local service[c]	1.7	1.3	1.4	1.5	1.6	1.8	2.1	2.0	2.1	2.0	1.4
Long distance service	0.6	0.3	0.4	0.5	0.5	0.5	0.5	0.6	0.7	0.8	0.7
Mobile telephony[d]	1.9	0.8	1.0	1.0	1.3	1.5	1.5	1.7	2.3	2.4	2.3
Internet service	0.3	0.1	0.1	0.2	0.1	0.2	0.2	0.2	0.3	0.4	0.5

Source: Author's estimates are based on the 2006 national survey of household income and expenditures.

a. According to monetary income.

b. Includes public telephony and other services such as mail, telegraph, public fax, beeper, and others.

c. Includes telephone installation and local calls.

d. Includes initial payment, equipment acquisition, prepaid cards, and mobile telephony service.

Table 9.2 Penetration of Telecommunications Services by
Population Decile, 2006
(percentage of households)

Population decile	Fixed telephony	Mobile telephony	Internet
1 (poorest)	11.34	7.56	1.13
2	17.62	14.68	2.55
3	25.09	20.28	4.65
4	31.14	29.54	6.25
5	39.70	38.53	7.66
6	46.56	40.54	7.73
7	52.02	48.00	10.06
8	62.15	58.83	14.96
9	71.18	69.57	20.22
10 (richest)	84.68	82.11	39.03
Total	44.15	40.96	11.42

Source: 2006 national survey of household income and expenditures.

income deciles is 87 to 1, whereas the difference between the income of the highest decile and the lowest is 33 to 1. Moreover, Internet penetration in the seven lowest income deciles is still low (table 9.2). Ninety percent of households have little or no Internet access, with the main reason cited for lack of access being a lack of resources.

The TELMEX Price Cap

This section discusses TELMEX's pricing regime and its impact on competition and consumers.

Evolution of Telephone Rates

Telephone rates—in real terms—have behaved irregularly. Thus, figure 9.3 shows that real telephone rates increased 50 percent between 1988 and 1994, remained stable until late 1997, and exhibited a downward trend as of December 1997. The decreases in rates have occurred primarily in the markets that have faced stiffer competition, such as long distance telephony and local business telephony.

In addition, tables 9.3 and 9.4 show the significant discrepancy between the evolution of the real rates for residential and business telephony services and the drop in costs from 1990 to 2005. For example, whereas residential and business service rates fell 24.8 percent

Figure 9.3 Evolution of Telephone Rates Relative to the Consumer Price Index, Selected Months and Years

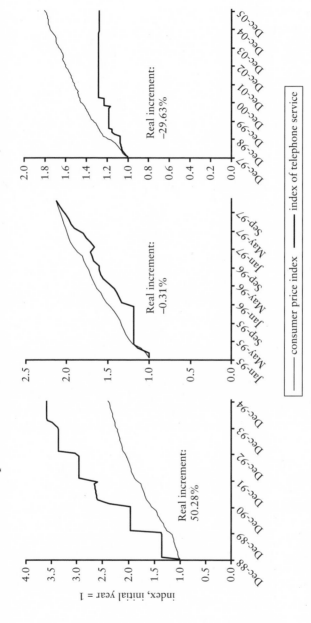

Source: Bank of Mexico data.

Table 9.3 Evolution of TELMEX Rates, 1990–2005
(percentage change)

Category	Residential	Commercial
Local service	13.9	–27.7
Connection charge	–79.9	–88.4
Monthly rent of fixed line	83.7	–8.4
Average service charge	–28.5	–28.5
National long distance	–79.0	–79.0
International	–80.8	–80.8
Weighted average	–24.8[a]	–48.3[b]

Source: Author's estimates based on TELMEX data.

a. Telephone services for residential customers are based on the weights that local, national long distance, and international long distance each have in the consumer price index (basis: last two weeks of June 2002).

b. Telephone services for business customers are based on the weights that local, national long distance, and international long distance each have in the producer price index (basis: December 2003).

Table 9.4 Indicators Explaining the Drop in TELMEX Costs, December 1990–December 2005
(percentage change)

Indicator	Change
Employees per telephone line	–74.0
Employees per local call	–80.1
Employees per minute of domestic long distance	–78.2
Employees per minute of outgoing international long distance	–78.0

Source: Author's estimates based on TELMEX annual reports.

and 48.3 percent, respectively, cost indicators decreased between 74.0 percent and 80.1 percent.

Establishment of the Price Cap

TELMEX's title of concession establishes a price cap mechanism for controlling basic services (local telephony, domestic long distance, and outgoing international long distance for residential and business users). As specified in the concession contract, as of January 1999 and in four-year cycles thereafter, the price cap mechanism contemplates two types of adjustments to the controlled services basket. First, the Federal Telecommunications Commission (Comisión Federal de Telecomunicaciones, or COFETEL) must set the price level that will be in force at the start of the new cycle for the controlled services basket. Second, every quarter COFETEL must apply a productivity gains adjustment factor to the index of the rates of the controlled services so that the latter does not increase more than inflation, as measured by the consumer price index, minus this adjustment factor (called X).

Condition 6–7 of the title of concession states that a technical-economic study will be carried out every four years, following the established methodology, to determine long-term incremental costs and to specify the initial level of the basket and adjustment factor X that will produce sufficient revenue levels to obtain an internal rate of return on the controlled services basket equal to the weighted average cost of capital.

Estimation of the Initial Price Increase and Adjustment Factor X

Incremental cost studies for controlled basic services are considered confidential, and only the Ministry of Communications and Transport, COFETEL, and TELMEX have access to them. For the purposes of this section (which draws on del Villar and Serrano 2003), the calculation methodology used publicly available information related to the mandated accounting separation of local telephony, domestic long distance, and international long distance.

The study made two assumptions to estimate the initial increase that the price cap must have undergone in early 2003. First, that COFETEL fixed the initial level of the basket at the correct level in early 1999 during the review of the price cap for the 1999–2002 cycle. Second, that between 1999 and 2002, TELMEX operated with a reasonable degree of efficiency, and therefore the costs it reported for the period did not evolve very differently from the incremental costs. These assumptions entail that the implied initial 2003 change in the price cap can be estimated by the cumulated difference between the annual 4.5 percent adjustment factor X established for 1999–2002 and the annual adjustment factor X estimated on the basis of the information reported by the company during this period. According to these data, the price cap should have undergone a 17.67 percent downward adjustment in 2003. Contrary to this result, COFETEL decided that the price cap would not have to be adjusted.

After the initial change in the level of the price cap for controlled services for 2003 was determined, a cash flow model was developed to endogenously establish the productivity adjustment factor X for the 2003–06 basic services basket such that the internal rate of return equals the weighted average cost of capital. The annual adjustment factor X that resulted from the relevant cash flow model was 5.28 percent. Contrary to this result, COFETEL decided on an annual adjustment factor of 3.00 percent.

The same steps were taken to estimate the required initial change in the price cap for the next cycle in early 2007 by cumulating the difference between the estimated adjustment factor and the established adjustment factor from 1999 to 2006. The result (table 9.5) was that the price cap should have been adjusted down 33 percent in 2007. Contrary to this result, COFETEL decided again that the price cap would not be adjusted.

Impact of the Initial Changes in the Price Cap on Consumer Expenditure

From 1999 to 2006, TELMEX lowered its real rates faster than required by the price cap that COFETEL defined. This change means TELMEX could increase the rates of the controlled services basket by roughly 9.5 percent without violating the price cap. A 33 percent drop in the price cap would have forced TELMEX to reduce the price-controlled services basket by approximately 24 percent.

The direct impact of a 24 percent decrease in TELMEX's basic service prices on the consumer price index would have been between 0.4 and 0.5 percent, because the controlled services basket has a 2.7 percent weight in the consumer price index. Although TELMEX does not account for the entire market, other basic telephone service providers would have likely found themselves obliged to lower their rates if the rates of the main carrier had.

Table 9.5 Estimate of Required and Established Initial Price Increases, 1999–2006
(percent)

Year	Estimated X factor	Established X factor	Difference
1999	14.0	4.5	9.47
2000	4.6	4.5	0.05
2001	15.7	4.5	11.17
2002	1.1	4.5	−3.36
2003	6.0	3.0	2.99
2004	9.4	3.0	6.40
2005	6.7	3.0	3.68
2006[a]	2.5	3.0	−0.48
Cumulated difference			33.04

Source: Author's estimates based on TELMEX and COFETEL annual reports.
a. Figures for the fourth quarter are estimates.

Dominance

This section discusses how TELMEX's economic and political power affects its relationship with its regulatory authorities and the impact of TELMEX's behavior on competition in the industry.

Difficulties of Establishing Healthy Competition in the Telecommunications Sector

The lack of competition in the telecommunications sector has occurred in part because the resolutions issued by the Federal Competition Commission (Comisión Federal de Competencia, or CFC) have in large measure been turned down in the courts (see also chapter 4 in this volume). The CFC determined that TELMEX had engaged in monopolistic practices in nine instances; however, TELMEX has not complied with any of the CFC's resolutions either because the courts have taken too long to hand down their rulings or because TELMEX has been granted *amparos* (injunctions or stays of action) that have prolonged procedures and even prevented the substance of the litigation from being resolved.[1]

The most important case the CFC and COFETEL have lost so far is probably the one regarding Article 63 of the Federal Telecommunications Act. According to this article, the Ministry of Communications and Transport is empowered to establish specific obligations on concessionaires holding substantial power over the market in accordance with the Federal Antitrust Act. The ministry could exercise this power through COFETEL, a decentralized agency of the Ministry of Communications and Transport. In December 1997, the CFC determined that TELMEX held substantial market power in five fixed telephony markets (local telephony services, access or interconnection services, domestic long distance service, interurban transportation services, and international long distance service). TELMEX immediately started an *amparo* to prevent any action in this regard.

In sum, almost nine years after the CFC issued its declaration of substantial market power and six years after COFETEL established specific obligations,[2] the courts overruled the substance of the CFC resolution. Even though the CFC has appealed the decision, it might have to start from scratch in defining TELMEX as a dominant player.

TELMEX filed a motion before the CFC for reconsideration of the 1997 ruling, but the CFC confirmed it in 1998. TELMEX delayed implementation of the decision by means of several *amparos*. COFETEL ultimately issued a resolution that established certain obligations on TELMEX in 2000, but TELMEX appealed it through an *amparo* that held up implementation of the said obligations. In 2001, the courts annulled the original CFC decision, and as a consequence, TELMEX was able to reverse all the resolutions that had derived from the original decision, including the one issued by COFETEL. The CFC later issued a new ruling declaring TELMEX to be a dominant player, but the company once again appealed and won an *amparo* in May 2004. In August 2004, the CFC promulgated another decision that TELMEX also appealed. In October 2006, the courts overturned the substance of the CFC decision.

Article 63 of the Federal Telecommunications Act implies that for COFETEL to impose obligations on a company, the CFC first must declare that the company has substantial power in the relevant market. This system is inefficient in practical terms and poses problems as follows:

- The delays it causes are considerable, because decisions by CFC and COFETEL are sequential and TELMEX can appeal the decisions of both before the courts. This hinders COFETEL from imposing pro-competition regulations in a timely manner, because it has to wait for the CFC to issue a resolution on the matter.
- The authorities have to make public their intent to regulate and affect private interests, thereby allowing TELMEX to take measures to preempt the acts of the authorities.
- The resolutions issued by the CFC are not guaranteed the expected reaction by COFETEL.

Note that the CFC's annual budget is equal to two days worth of profits by TELMEX and RadioMóvil Dipsa (TELCEL) combined. The disparity in the economic power of the authority and that of the regulated entity has probably contributed to the CFC's low effectiveness. Antitrust agencies need resources to hire the best law firms because of the economic power wielded by the companies they face.

Foreign Investment

Foreign direct investment (FDI) is recognized as a key mechanism for the diffusion of new technologies among countries. The relationship between FDI and competition is complex. Companies on the receiving end of FDI can put significant competitive pressure on sectors that had previously been dominated by large domestic companies, or they can come to hold a dominant position in a segmented market. That, is why competition policies are fundamental in realizing the benefits of FDI. Restrictions on FDI are particularly counterproductive when they are asymmetric in closely linked markets. This is the case of fixed telephony and mobile telephony. FDI is limited to 49 percent for the former, where competition is limited, whereas there is no limit for the latter, where levels of competition are high.

This situation has led to low levels of investment in the sector. Between 1990 and 2003, average investment as a share of total industry revenue was 30 percent, which does not compare favorably with other countries with similar per capita income levels. Figure 9.4 shows that the level of investments in telecommunications in Mexico was below the average of selected emerging countries of the Organisation for Economic Co-operation and Development (OECD) between 1991 and 2003. As the constant drop in investment levels between 1990 and 1995 indicates, investment performance in Mexico worsened after the privatization of TELMEX.

By its nature, the telecommunications sector requires huge investments, profound market knowledge, and access to specialized equipment. Opening the fixed telecommunications market to FDI would promote the entry of foreign carriers that have the financial leverage, knowledge, and technology needed either to start up new companies or to acquire or enter into partnerships with existing companies.

Figure 9.4 Investments by Telecommunication Companies, Mexico and Selected Emerging OECD Countries, 1991–2003

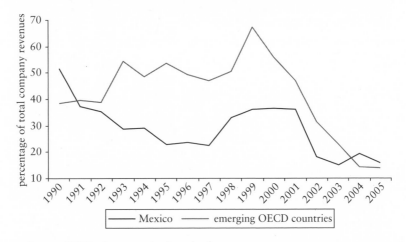

Source: OECD telecommunications database.

Note: The emerging countries include the Czech Republic, Greece, Hungary, Poland, the Republic of Korea, the Slovak Republic, and Turkey.

Importance of TELMEX's and TELCEL's Main Shareholders on the Stock Exchange

TELMEX has earned net profits of US$2.0 billion to US$2.5 billion per year since 1990, earning roughly US$30 billion in profits between 1991 and 2003. (Note that TELCEL was split from TELMEX in 2000.) These earnings are being shared by fewer shareholders over time. In December 1990, the Grupo Carso, TELMEX's main shareholder, held 5.7 percent of TELMEX's shares and currently holds 48 percent of the voting shares of TELMEX and 71 percent of the voting shares of TELCEL. Furthermore, companies associated with

Figure 9.5 Market Value of TELMEX and TELCEL Controlling Group Companies, November 2006

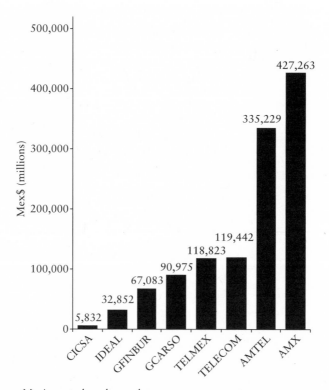

Source: Mexican stock exchange data.

Note: AMTEL = Axtel; AMX = America Movil, CICSA = Carso Infraestructura y Construccion; GCARSO = Grupo Carso; GFINBUR = Grupo Financiero Inbursa; IDEAL = Impulsora del Desarrollo y el Empleo en America Latina; TELECOM = Carso Global Telecom.

Figure 9.6 Weight of TELMEX and TELCEL Controlling
Group Companies in the Mexican Stock Index,
November 2006
(percent)

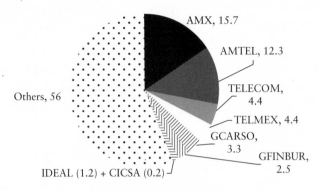

Total weight of the
group in the stock index = 44%

Source: Mexican stock exchange data.
Note: AMTEL = Axtel; AMX = America Movil, CICSA = Carso Infraestructura y
Construccion; GCARSO = Grupo Carso; GFINBUR = Grupo Financiero Inbursa;
IDEAL = Impulsora del Desarrollo y el Empleo en America Latina; TELECOM =
Carso Global Telecom.

the Grupo Carso have substantial weight in the Mexican stock
exchange (figures 9.5 and 9.6).

Even though TELCEL's market value was 3.6 times greater than
TELMEX's in November 2006 (US$38.9 billion compared with
US$10.8 billion), TELMEX's earnings before interest, taxes, depre-
ciation, and amortization were 50 percent greater than TELCEL's in
2005. Both companies generate large profits, but even though it
operates in a less competitive market, TELMEX apparently has a
much higher profit rate.

Commercial and Financial Ties with Competitors

In 1995, TELMEX's main shareholder bought 49 percent of
Cablevisión—the cable television company that serves the Mexico
City area and is owned by Televisa, Mexico's largest television
broadcasting company. In 2000, the CFC forced TELMEX to divest
itself of these shares. Nevertheless, the Grupo Carso later bought
25 percent of the shares of Televisa through Inbursa Bank (another
company of the Grupo Carso) that, according to a CFC ruling, it
should also have sold off a few years ago.

At the same time, close financial connections also exist between TELMEX owners and other carriers, which weaken competition. In 2001–02, TELMEX bought 20 percent of Alestra's debt, worth US$80 million, before Alestra carried out its restructuring plan in November 2003. Later, TELMEX's partner, the Southern Bell Company, acquired American Telephone and Telegraph (better known as AT&T) in the United States.

In 2002 and 2003, TELMEX bought MCI debt worth approximately US$340 million, which it recently sold to Verizon for US$1.1 billion after it was converted into stock. (MCI holds 49 percent of Avantel's stock.) TELMEX became MCI's main stockholder, with 13.8 percent of the company's stock, when MCI emerged from bankruptcy in 2004.

Another example is the purchase of Unefon debt and the sale of radio-electric spectrum to TELCEL in late 2003 for US$288 million. In addition, Inbursa (the Grupo Carso's bank) granted Televisión Azteca a US$300 million credit in 2004. Televisión Azteca is Mexico's second-largest television broadcasting company.

Status of Interconnection between Carriers

The interconnection framework has played an important role in shaping the current market structure of the industry. When TELMEX was privatized, mandatory interconnection was incorporated into its title of concession to allow the development of competition. This condition was later extended to all carriers when the Federal Telecommunications Act was enacted in 1995, but this obligation has not been enforced in a cost-effective and timely manner for three main reasons. First, COFETEL, perhaps because of regulatory capture, has been reluctant to enforce the time frame and conditions specified in the law. Carriers have used this lack of enforcement to delay interconnection, sometimes for years. The same holds true for dispute resolution. According to the Federal Telecommunications Act, disputes should be resolved within 60 working days, but this does not happen. The CFC and COFETEL can also intervene by imposing special conditions on dominant carriers, but this avenue has not yet been applied because TELMEX has been successful in using the courts to reverse all CFC decisions (for more details, see Solano, del Villar, and García-Verdú 2006).

The second reason why mandatory interconnection has not been effectively enforced is that the law does not recognize key issues such as collocation and billing and collection services as interconnection services. This has allowed TELMEX to soften competition by denying interconnection services such as collocation.

The third reason is that COFETEL and market participants have poor access to commercial and technical information about carriers. Interconnection agreements and information about the location and technical specifications of a carrier's network are not publicly available. This allows discriminatory treatment among carriers and inhibits the development of business plans, because firms have no certainty about the required investments for entry. For example, the lack of transparency has allowed TELMEX and TELCEL to engage in agreements with preferential conditions.

To address some of these loopholes, COFETEL recently issued a set of interconnection rules for public consultation, but they still have to undergo a lengthy review process before becoming effective.

Long Distance Interconnection

On July 1, 1994, when Mexico decided to open up long distance telephony, the authorities established that, as of January 1, 1997, new carriers could interconnect with TELMEX in 60 cities and that interconnection would gradually be increased until all facilities with switching capabilities were covered by January 1, 2001. This has not happened.[3] Of the 397 local service areas the country has been divided into, non-TELMEX long distance carriers can interconnect in only 198. The 199 areas not open to competition hold 18.7 percent of all lines and are home to 25 percent of the population, most of whom have relatively low incomes. To terminate calls in non-open areas, the competition has to pay TELMEX a so-called resale tariff. Even though the interconnection rate (which is equivalent to the termination rate in local areas open to competition) has dropped from US$0.03 or US$0.05 per minute (depending on how it is measured) to slightly less than US$0.01 per minute, the resale tariff has remained well above the interconnection rate and is currently US$0.07 per minute.

Although COFETEL recognized resale services as an interconnection service and, hence, subject to regulation, in a resolution issued in 2001, TELMEX obtained an *amparo* against this decision. An alternative avenue taken recently by COFETEL to lower the resale tariff was to merge non-open areas with open areas; however, a decision that merged 70 non-open areas with other open areas made in early 2007 has not yet been implemented because TELMEX obtained an *amparo* from the courts.

In relation to international traffic and despite a regulatory scheme aimed at maintaining high international settlement rates, growing bypass practices have led to significant drops in these rates. In 2000, the United States brought Mexico before a World Trade Organization panel. As a result, on August 11, 2004, Mexico eliminated the exclusive privilege of the long distance carrier with the highest share

of the outgoing long distance market (TELMEX) to negotiate settlement rates, proportional return systems, and the uniform settlement
rate scheme. The reduction in international settlement rates has been
huge, falling from approximately US$0.40 per minute in 1997 to
approximately US$0.02 in 2007, provided that the calls terminate
in areas open to long distance competition. In the 199 areas not open
to competition, rates are US$0.08 to US$0.09 because of the high
resale charges.

Interconnection among Local Carriers

With the dawn of competition in local telephony in 1999, COFETEL
made a distinction between local telephony carriers that would be
subject to symmetric interconnection rates because they had certain
coverage obligations, on the one hand, and local telephony carriers
that would not be subject to coverage obligations and that would
therefore be subject to asymmetric interconnection rates, on the
other hand. The former initially consisted of Axtel, Maxcom, and
TELMEX, among others. They were later joined by other companies
that were granted long distance telephony concessions such as
Alestra and Avantel. The latter group included a consortium from
the cable television sector, Megacable.

COFETEL promoted a bill-and-keep regime to interconnect new
carriers in the first group with TELMEX. According to this strategy, carriers would not charge each other for interconnection. The
carriers originally negotiated with TELMEX to continue with the
bill-and-keep scheme as long as the imbalance in incoming and
outgoing traffic was not more than 40 percent. If it were more, then
long distance interconnection rates for calls exceeding the allowed
imbalance would apply. If, however, the imbalance was greater
than 70 percent, interconnection rates would apply for the total
imbalanced traffic. Over time, TELMEX lowered the allowed traffic imbalance, which currently stands at only 5 percent, on the
ground that part of the domestic and international long distance
traffic is introduced into the TELMEX network as if it were local
traffic and, therefore, avoids paying long distance interconnection
fees. This may be hampering competition, because it increases the
interconnection costs of new entrants, which usually generate more
outgoing traffic than incoming when starting operations. It also
facilitates price collusion among carriers, because it penalizes price
reduction strategies that create traffic imbalances and because it
limits the expansion of services such as public telephony that would
generate traffic imbalances (public-telephone-booth traffic is exclusively outgoing in Mexico).[4]

As for the Megacable interconnection with TELMEX, COFETEL decided that Megacable would pay TELMEX the domestic long distance interconnection rate and TELMEX would pay Megacable a little less than 40 percent of that rate (Gil 2000). Because of this policy, cable television companies were, in practice, excluded from the market. In late 2003, the Ministry of Communications and Transport issued agreements that allowed cable television companies to lease their infrastructure to concessionaires that had been authorized to provide local telephony services. The ministry did not permit cable television companies to provide telephony services directly. This ban was not consistent with the Federal Telecommunications Act and was eliminated in late 2006. At the same time, cable television companies were allowed to negotiate bill-and-keep agreements, enabling them to compete in the market.

Interconnection on Mobile Networks

Initially, a decision was reached whereby TELMEX would not pay the interconnection rate for termination of calls on mobile networks, although mobile telephony carriers had to pay an interconnection rate for calls terminated on the TELMEX fixed telephony network. In 1999, when the calling party pays (CPP) scheme for local calls came into force, a decision was reached whereby fixed networks would pay mobile networks a US$0.19 per minute interconnection fee. In exchange, fixed networks were allowed to charge users a US$0.06 per minute fee for billing and collection on calls made to mobile networks. COFETEL decided that it would review the billing and collection charge each year, but has not done so for the past eight years. Most important, the billing and collection charge represents a double charge for fixed telephony users, because the monthly fixed telephony rent already includes billing and collection (see Noll, chapter 10 in this volume). This charge represented close to US$0.4 billion annually in revenues for TELMEX during 2002–05 (figure 9.7).

At the same time, in 1999 a decision was reached that the US$0.19 fixed-mobile interconnection rate would also apply to the interconnection rate that mobile telephony carriers would pay each other. This rate remained constant in nominal terms during 1999–2004 and then fell 10 percent over 2005 and 2006.

TELMEX does not allow competitors to interconnect directly with TELCEL within its facilities where TELCEL is collocated. TELMEX charges US$0.3 per minute, which is the same as the mobile termination rate, to interconnect other carriers with TELCEL.

As figure 9.8 illustrates, in recent years interconnection fees from fixed networks to mobile networks have been less important for

Figure 9.7 TELMEX Revenues from Billing and Collection
Charges, 1999–2005

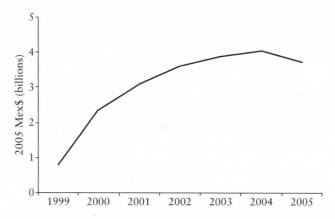

Source: Author's estimates based on TELMEX annual reports and Merrill Lynch
2006.

Figure 9.8 Mobile Carrier Revenue from Fixed-Mobile
Interconnections, 2000–2005

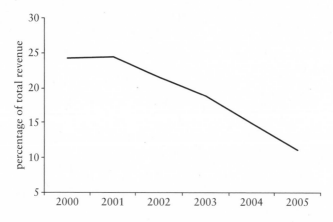

Source: Author's estimates based on TELMEX annual reports and Merrill Lynch
2006.

mobile carriers. This is because the relative size of fixed networks in
relation to mobile networks has decreased and because users often
make their calls from mobile networks instead of fixed networks
because doing so is less expensive.

Table 9.6 Tariffs, Lines, and Network Traffic, 1999–2006

Category	1999	2000	2001	2002	2003	2004	2005	2006
General tariff (U.S. cents)								
Fixed-mobile	2.50	2.50	2.50	2.50	2.50	2.50	2.25	2.03
Interconnection tariff (U.S. cents)								
Fixed-mobile	1.900	1.900	1.900	1.900	1.900	1.900	1.710	1.540
Mobile-mobile	1.900	1.900	1.900	1.900	1.900	1.900	1.710	1.540
Mobile-fixed	0.300	0.316	0.117	0.094	0.105	0.110	0.106	0.106
Lines (millions in service)								
Mobile network	7.7	14.1	21.8	25.9	30.1	38.5	45.1	56.4[a]
Fixed network	10.9	12.3	13.8	15.0	16.3	18.1	19.2	20.9[a]
Network traffic								
Mobile network (millions of minutes)	5,152	10,975	15,919	19,990	26,386	38,188	50,236	73,000[a]
Fixed network (millions of TELMEX calls)	23,426	24,738	25,567	25,679	26,494	26,782	26,680	26,666[a]

Source: COFETEL and TELMEX data.
a. January–November.

Distortions Caused by High Mobile Interconnection Rates

Table 9.6 suggests that high fixed-mobile rates for users have had a significant impact on the development of fixed and mobile networks. Fixed network traffic only increased slightly more than 10 percent between 1999 and 2006, whereas the number of fixed lines almost doubled. The opposite is the case for the mobile network. Between 1999 and 2006, mobile network traffic increased 14-fold, even though the number of mobile lines increased only 7-fold. This is because with the introduction of the CPP scheme, making calls from fixed telephones to mobile telephones became more expensive than making them from mobile telephones, which tended to reduce fixed network traffic and increase mobile network traffic. The spike in the number of fixed lines during this period seems to be associated with the low penetration of telephone service in the country. That is, it reflects the fact that fixed telephony is still reaching many households for the first time given the large coverage lags in Mexico. In addition, fixed telephone lines are the main vehicle for access to the Internet.

Fixed-to-mobile and mobile-to-mobile interconnection rates are much higher than mobile-to-fixed rates. To compare the mobile termination rate with the fixed termination rate, one must add an additional 25 percent to the former, because mobile termination services are billed on a full per-minute basis. As a result, the mobile termination rate is 15 times higher than the fixed termination rate.

The high mobile termination rate has generated important price differences between calls that originate and terminate on the same mobile carrier network (on-net) and those that originate on one network and terminate on another (off-net). This is because high termination rates put a floor on off-net prices while channeling competition through on-net prices.

High termination rates dissuade healthy competition. They let TELCEL (the incumbent carrier) offer rates that, although high, discourage consumers from belonging to the competitors' networks. That is, elevated interconnection rates disproportionately increase costs for smaller mobile competitors, which is why the incumbent is able to fix relatively costly on-net rates.

Consider the example of a mobile telephony user who makes calls to mobile telephones only. Assume that call traffic is uniformly spread out between all the companies, that is, it is in the same proportion as the companies' market share.[5] TELCEL's market share is 80 percent and Telefónica's is 13.6 percent. Assume that the final fee TELCEL and Telefónica charge their users for their on-net calls is US$1.00 and US$0.00 per minute, respectively. As far as the off-net calls are concerned, assume that TELCEL charges US$2.00 per minute whereas Telefónica charges its users the interconnection rate of only US$1.54 per minute. Even if TELCEL charges more than Telefónica for on-net and off-net calls, the average cost per minute for users would be less if they opted for TELCEL over Telefónica because of the high interconnection rate (note that under this scheme, Telefónica would not be earning revenue from its users).

If one assumes that calls are distributed in accordance with the overall market shares in the population, the average cost per minute for TELCEL users is $0.8 \times US\$1.00 + 0.2 \times US\$2.00 = US\$1.20$. The average cost per minute for Telefónica users is $0.136 \times US\$0.00 + 0.864 \times US\$1.54 = US\$1.30$. If the mobile interconnection rate were lowered to cost, competition among mobile carriers would be on a level playing field. In addition, resources would no longer be transferred from fixed telephony users to mobile networks and users. Fixed telephony rates would drop, and increased competition in mobile telephony would also tend to lower mobile telephony rates.

Even though this would decrease the interconnection revenue these carriers received, the subsequent fall in rates for consumers would significantly increase the use of mobile services, which could more than compensate for the decline in revenues from interconnection rates. This effect can be seen in table 9.7, which shows that economies with lower mobile termination rates have higher minutes of use per mobile subscriber.

Table 9.7 Revenues, Usage, and Termination Rates, Selected Economies, 2005

Economy	Average revenue per minute (US$)	Average number of minutes of use per subscriber per month	Average revenue per user (US$)	EBITDA margin (%)	Mobile termination rate (US$)
Argentina	0.10	116	11	23.6	0.134
Chile	0.14	106	14	34.6	0.124
China	0.02	323	10	49.2	0.010
Hong Kong (China)	0.05	399	21	19.6	0.006
India	0.02	445	9	36.2	0.007
Korea, Rep. of	0.11	315	44	33.9	0.044
Mexico	0.14	115	18	41.0	0.140
Peru	0.16	68	14	28.7	0.168
Singapore	0.08	320	32	44.3	0.006
United States	0.06	822	53	33.2	0.010

Sources: Merrill Lynch 2006; Sárl Switzernet data.
Note: EBITDA = earnings before interest, taxes, depreciation, and amortization.

CPP Scheme in Long Distance

In November 2006, the CPP scheme was extended to domestic and international long distance calls, which, until that time, had been under the receiving party pays (RPP) scheme. With the exception of TELMEX, fixed telephony carriers have filed to nullify implementation of this scheme and some have been granted permanent injunctions.

The benefits of operating under a CPP scheme in long distance are being hotly debated. The literature and international evidence has shown that in many countries, particularly in Europe, use of the CPP scheme makes the price per minute of calls to mobile telephones high, because interconnection rates are much higher than costs. This is evidenced by interconnection rates under the CPP scheme more than compensating for the air time charged to users in the RPP scheme.

In Mexico, the CPP scheme in long distance has led to an increase in the price of domestic and international long distance calls to mobile telephones. In domestic long distance calls made from fixed telephones to mobile telephones under the previous RPP scheme, the user originating the call and the user receiving it together paid an average of US$0.24 per minute (not including the cost of the local call that is charged to the fixed telephone consumer). Under the new CPP scheme, these calls cost US$0.30 per minute, not including the cost of the local call.

When one compares charges included in long distance calls from fixed telephones to mobile telephones under the CPP and RPP schemes, the cost of domestic long distance service is the same under both. The average price differs because a billing and collection fee was introduced under the CPP scheme, which constitutes a double charge and was presumably added because of TELMEX's demands to ensure it would accept the new scheme.

Moreover, the interconnection rate is higher than the average air time rate that mobile carriers charge to their users under the RPP scheme. The difference between the air time rate and the interconnection rate is probably due to the air time rate being determined by each mobile telephony company in competition with other mobile telephony companies, whereas carriers reach agreement as to the interconnection rate.

As far as the long distance CPP interconnection rate is concerned, it was essentially agreed upon by TELMEX and TELCEL, which belong to the same group of shareholders. Even though the negotiation of interconnection rates between two connected companies with different concessions does not constitute a violation of the Federal Telecommunications Act, it is contrary to its spirit and objectives.[6] The objectives of the Federal Telecommunications Act are

(a) to promote the efficient development of telecommunications, (b) to set the basis for the government's regulatory functions, and (c) to foster healthy competition. Hence, fixing high interconnection rates, and thereby establishing elevated rates, is contrary to the law's goals of efficiency and competition.

Even though, as noted earlier, some fixed telephony carriers have been granted *amparos* by the courts that allow them to continue operating under the RPP scheme, mobile carriers have introduced systems that make completing calls difficult (for example, voice mail). In highly competitive markets, such as the incoming international market, this type of restriction tends to displace those carriers that were granted *amparos* by the courts. International traffic is being passed through TELMEX or other carriers that follow the CPP strategy for long distance.

Coexistence of the RPP and CPP Schemes for Incoming Domestic and International Long Distance Service

Letting long distance calls to mobile telephony users operate under both schemes without any type of restriction to completing calls would be advantageous. Each time users want to make long distance calls to a mobile phone, they would choose the preferred billing scheme, either the CPP with the 045 prefix or the RPP scheme with the 01 prefix. Users receiving calls would know, thanks to caller identification, when a call was made under the RPP scheme and would have the option of not taking the call. Current technology could allow the coexistence of the two regimes.

This proposal would be efficient, because it would let the maximum number of calls be completed. Calls not made under the CPP scheme would be made under the RPP scheme. In addition, because the RPP is cheaper, most traffic would be made under this scheme, which would eventually force CPP rates down.

The coexistence of both strategies would benefit both low-income mobile telephony users by means of the CPP scheme and mobile service users who value being connected to mobile telephony and fixed telephony users and who would thus be willing to pay the air time rate, as is mainly the case for companies.

Factors that Influence the Performance of Mobile Telephony

This section includes an econometric analysis using panel data of the main variables that affect mobile telephony (Eduardo Martínez

Chombo prepared the econometric model estimation). The mobile telephony performance variables employed in this analysis were average revenue per minute, average minutes of use per user, and mobile telephony penetration. The explanatory variables were GDP per capita in thousands of U.S. dollars (as the economic performance proxy for each economy), the percentage of prepaid lines, a dummy variable for the payment modality (CPP scheme = 1, other schemes = 0), a dummy variable for number portability, the market share of the two major carriers, and the number of carriers in the market. (Note that for the market share of the two largest telephone companies and the telephone number portability dummy, the coefficients were insignificant.) The analysis used annual information (calculated as the average of quarterly values) from 50 economies for 2001–05 as reported by Merrill Lynch (2006). In the case of information on dichotomous variables that do not vary over time, such as payment mode and number portability, the estimation used the random effects method. Table 9.8 summarized the results of the estimations. The estimate was performed on unbalanced panel data. In the final report, variables with less than 10 percent significance were sequentially eliminated.

The main results are as follows:

- When compared with the RPP scheme, the CPP scheme tends to reduce the use of mobile telephony while increasing revenues per minute.[7] This confirms that the CPP scheme is linked to

Table 9.8 Panel Data Regression Results

Variable	Revenue per minute (U.S. cents per minute)	Minutes of use (minutes per month)	Penetration of mobile telephones (percentage of all calls)
Number of companies	−1.4643*	—	4.7284*
CPP	6.2210*	−95.792*	17.416*
Prepaid	—	−0.7933*	—
Per capita GDP	0.2719*	1.7808*	1.9039*
Constant	13.165*	260.06*	−5.3488
R^2	0.33	0.39	0.52
Number of observations	224	176	247
Number of countries	48	46	50

Source: Author's calculations based on data from the International Monetary Fund's world economic outlook database and Merrill Lynch 2006.

Notes: * = 1 percent significance. — = Not included in the regression.

high interconnection rates. High rates lead to a decreased use of mobile telephony, which is particularly inefficient because of the high price of terminal devices and the tendency of mobile carriers to replace them periodically, regardless of how much they have been used. When the cost of the terminal device has to be amortized in fewer air time minutes, the cost of providing air time increases.

- Penetration levels are higher with the CPP strategy. Interconnection rates place limits on off-net rates, so the competition focuses on offering subsidized terminal devices, replacing the devices frequently, and/or maximizing on-net call rates. In addition, this payment scheme fosters the connection of terminal devices whose main objective is to receive calls.

- GDP per capita has a positive relationship with minutes of use and mobile telephony penetration variables. GDP per capita also has a positive effect on revenue per minute, which is explained by the presence of 16 European countries in the sample (32 percent of the total). In those high-income countries, interconnection rates were elevated, which was evidenced by high usage per minute prices.

- Of the two variables used to measure competition in the market (number of companies in the industry and market share of the two largest companies), the results suggest that the number of participating companies is the most relevant. This is probably explained by the high entry barriers to the telephony market that make competition dependent on the number of current competitors. The results also highlight that the fewer the number of companies, the more revenue they earn (negative sign of the coefficient). They also indicate that countries with few mobile telephony companies have less penetration (positive sign of the coefficient). All this suggests that in countries with few participants in the industry, the companies hold market power.

- As concerns the existence, or not, of the portability of mobile numbers, this variable did not significantly affect any of the three mobile telephony indicators analyzed.

- The prepayment variable was important only in the regression of the minutes of use. Extensive use of a prepayment system reduces the time of use of mobile telephony. This might be because prepayment system prices are higher than those of postpayment systems and prepayment users face temporary liquidity limitations, and thus, when they are recurrently left without credit, prepayment users are briefly compelled to reduce their consumption.

Development of Broadband

The telecommunications industry has undergone rapid technological change in recent decades. Network capacity has been doubling every 6 to 12 months since 1997. This change has allowed the introduction of new and better quality services, including those related to the Internet, that require huge amounts of bandwidth. These services have improved business productivity and welfare, as Crandall and Charles (2001) find for the United States, estimating an annual consumer surplus gain of between US$270 million and US$420 million because of more rapid adoption of broadband services.

As defined by the OECD, broadband is an Internet connection at one-way speeds greater than 256 kilobits per second where the user is permanently connected. Broadband development has been strongly linked to that of the Internet, because the delivery of new content demanded greater bandwidth.

The positive impact of broadband use on economic performance has been well documented (Crandall and Charles 2001; Ford and Thomas 2005; Jorgenson 2004; Lehr and others 2005; Litan and Rivlin 2001; Minges 2006). For the United States, Lehr and others (2005) show that broadband use is connected to favorable economic development, employment, wages, and investment. In the case of developing countries such as Mexico, the benefits of this technology are significantly higher, because it can be a valuable instrument for educating and training large and scattered segments of the population. By promoting broadband penetration, governments could foster equity as well as growth within society. In addition, broadband could help make public administration more efficient by enabling the provision of public services, facilitating the payment of taxes, fostering greater transparency, and improving accountability.

Broadband in Mexico

Until 2001, TELMEX introduced broadband Internet services over its copper lines, known as digital subscriber lines. Broadband adoption in Mexico has been slow compared with countries that started to introduce broadband at the same time, such as the Czech Republic, Hungary, and Poland, and with countries where it started later, such as Ireland and the Slovak Republic (figure 9.9).

Mexico's delay in adopting broadband is a consequence of several factors, among which the following stand out: (a) the lack of a policy to increase competition by unbundling or leasing local subscriber loops, (b) the delayed authorization to cable television companies to

Figure 9.9 Broadband Penetration Per 100 Inhabitants, Selected Countries, 2006

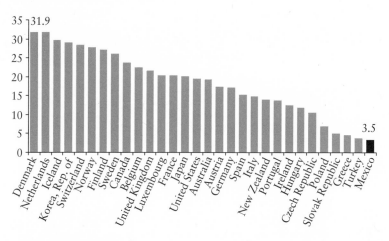

Source: OECD 2006.

provide broadband services, and (c) the restrictions that TELMEX has imposed on broadband use.

Local loop unbundling is particularly useful in fostering competition in countries with few broadband access alternatives where conventional telephony networks dominate. Unbundling allows users with telephone service to access broadband through providers that lease the local loop from the dominant carrier's network. Mexico is the only OECD country that has not introduced broadband competition by unbundling or leasing local loops. In light of TELMEX's opposition, the possibility of unbundling local loops has not even been discussed. By contrast, TELMEX has backed unbundling outside Mexico, notably in 2004, when the Chilean government asked for responses to its proposed framework for network unbundling.

One example of the impact that unbundling could have on telephone rates and quality of service is Orange in Spain, a subsidiary of France TELECOM. This carrier leases local loops from Telefónica and is currently offering a €39 (US$54) package per month that includes ultra-broadband service (20 megabits per second) that is five times faster than the fastest service TELMEX offers (4 megabits per second) at one-tenth the price, unlimited local and long distance calls, and 1,000 minutes of international long distance calls to 25 countries.

Another clear example can be seen in figure 9.10. Even though both Japan and Mexico introduced digital subscriber line offerings at roughly at the same time, Mexico has far fewer broadband users.

Figure 9.10 Evolution of Number of Broadband Internet
Subscribers, Japan and Mexico, 2000–05

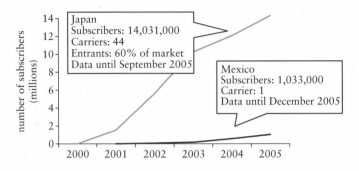

Sources: OECD, COFETEL, and Japan Ministry of Public Management data.

One of the reasons for this difference is that Japan allowed the
unbundling of loops whereas Mexico did not.

Even though the 1995 Federal Telecommunications Act did not
restrict public telecommunications networks from providing new
services, the authorities did not let cable television companies begin
to supply Internet access until 2003. In contrast, by 2002, cable
television companies in 26 other OECD countries were already
offering their users broadband Internet access.

The entry of cable television companies into the broadband market in Mexico could have significant effects on welfare, because their
networks cover up to 55 percent of the population. These effects
include the following:

- Cable television companies would offer the same services
  TELMEX does but at lower prices. Cable television companies
  have entered the market with lower rates: a 2 megabits per
  second connection costs residential cable television users
  between 8 to 35 percent of what TELMEX charges and business users 28 to 47 percent of what TELMEX charges.
- By competing, the cable television industry would stimulate
  lower rates, faster speeds, more innovation, and/or better quality
  of services. TELMEX recently decided to increase its users' broadband Internet speed without raising its rates, probably because
  of increased competition from cable television companies.
- Users would have more options to choose from. Note that
  TELMEX's slowest residential speed is 512 kilobits per second,
  whereas several cable television companies offer slower speeds
  at much lower prices, which would help an important segment
  of the population be incorporated into the market, especially

lower-income users, and would let users select the price and speed combination that is best for them.

Finally, TELMEX has limited the applications and services offered over the Internet. TELMEX's service contracts ban customers from using broadband for voice over Internet protocol (VoIP) services, which are much less expensive than traditional switchboard network technology. TELMEX has also forbidden broadband resellers from providing VoIP through its network.

Broadband and Content

Demand for broadband depends on the applications and content available to users. The more applications broadband can offer, such as VoIP, the greater the demand and, therefore, the faster it is adopted.

A connection exists between broadband supply and broadband providers' access to content such as television channels, and it is in the interests of broadband providers to obtain exclusive content to have a competitive edge on the market. If a broadband provider has limited or no access to content or must operate under unfavorable conditions in relation to another provider, it might be unfairly pushed out of the broadband market. For example, one of the main reasons Direct TV left the pay television market in Mexico was because it could not have access to Televisa's free-to-the-air programming, while its rival SKY could.

So far, the Internet has fostered free distribution of content and applications, which has led to a boom that has benefited users and that has, in turn, spurred broadband demand. However, the possibility that Internet access providers might follow discriminatory practices is high, particularly given the enormous concentration of broadband provision and content in Mexico whereby two television broadcasting companies dominate the content market. This could lead to agreements among the major broadband and content providers that would limit both content offerings and competition in the broadband market. The economic costs could be high in terms of lower broadband penetration, little content variety, and higher prices.

Concern is not limited to agreements between two or more broadband and content providers, but also applies to vertically integrated companies such as TELMEX, because it is not always in their interests to allow users to have unlimited access to applications and content. As noted earlier, this is particularly true for services that compete with those broadband providers offer such as VoIP services. Thus, the service contract of TELMEX's broadband offering bans customers from simultaneously using other available applications.

In relation to this issue, the U.S. Federal Communications Commission defined its stance in its Internet freedom principles published in 2005. These principles stated that to foster broadband penetration and to preserve and advance the open and interconnected nature of the public Internet, consumers have the right to use the applications of their choice. Allowing telecommunications service providers to make unrestricted offerings to broadband users may have a similar effect to that of local loop unbundling. Indeed, the U.S. Federal Communications Commission forbade AT&T the privilege of degrading any applications transmitted through its broadband.

More recently, as a result of a lawsuit by an Internet service provider and the Office of the National Economic Attorney, the Chilean Court for the Defense of Free Competition fined the dominant fixed telephony carrier approximately US$1 million for blocking VoIP providers. The court ordered the carrier to eliminate any clauses from its contract that banned or limited the use of services provided by independent vendors. It also ordered the company to abstain from restricting or hampering broadband use, in any manner, contractually or in practice, in the future.

Broadband access providers can restrict or discriminate against content or applications on their networks in several ways. For example, they can prioritize certain types of services or applications on the network, thereby affecting the quality of the content or services provided by third parties. Network providers can also use a variety of tools to block content. For instance, bit caps limit the number of bits a user can send out per month, notwithstanding bandwidth, while so-called walled gardens block third party's content or services (as is currently the case for the VoIP provider Skype), which the authorities in Mexico justify by noting that these providers require concessions that the authorities have not been willing to grant.

The following is a list of alternative measures the government could use to foster access to telecommunications content and services and, thereby, stimulate Internet demand:

- Ban Mexican companies from making exclusive or discriminatory arrangements with content or broadband providers. Free content, such as local television and radio, should also be available for free on the Internet (maintaining the restriction that local television advertising must be broadcast). The aim would be to increase Internet content, attract users to the Internet platform, and avoid the traditional television platform from being favored over the Internet.

- Encourage alternative broadband access platforms.
- Introduce competition by unbundling loops on TELMEX's network.
- Counteract the market power of Televisa and Televisión Azteca in the field of content by promoting competition in the television industry and allowing entry by foreign companies that broadcast in Spanish and are committed to creating domestic content.
- Require structural separation between providing broadband services and providing access to content, at least for the major content and broadband providers.

Municipal Use of the Radio-Electric Spectrum to Provide Broadband Services

One way to encourage broadband is to allow cities, municipalities, or states to offer this service jointly with telecommunications carriers. Several municipal projects to deploy wireless broadband networks are currently under way in cities such as San Francisco, Philadelphia, and Singapore. The governments of these cities plan to offer broadband Internet access for free at speeds of 256 to 512 kilobits per second and at reasonable prices at speeds above 1,000 kilobits per second.[8]

Development of these types of projects is partially due to the emergence of new wireless access technologies, namely, Wi-Fi and Wi-MAX, that allow entrants to deploy citywide networks in a short period of time and with only a small investment. Compared with wire-line networks, wireless deployments are faster and cheaper, because a single antenna may cover large areas. Chaska County, Minnesota, for example, installed a wireless network that covers the whole county with an investment of only US$600,000. As a result, the monthly rate consumers pay for broadband service is US$15.99 (Tropos Networks 2004).

Another driver of such municipal projects is the availability of unlicensed frequency bands. Experts have indicated that designating a greater portion of the radio-electric spectrum as unlicensed, particularly in the low frequency bands, would trigger broadband service offerings and innovation in mobile technologies and applications (Lehr 2004). The availability of unlicensed spectrum and relatively inexpensive equipment has led to an increase in the number of hotspots: public sites with wireless Internet access such as coffee shops, airports, and universities. The United States, for example, has more than 150,000 hotspots serving close to 30 million users (Federal Telecommunications Commission 2006).

POTENTIAL BENEFITS OF MUNICIPAL WIRELESS BROADBAND NETWORKS

According to a report by the U.S. Federal Telecommunications Commission (2006), municipalities should provide broadband services for three basic reasons. First, dominant telecommunications carriers have restricted broadband service offerings; thus, municipalities could represent an alternative for consumers. Second, municipalities could use the networks to improve the services they provide. Third, wireless broadband services could produce positive externalities, such as attracting or keeping companies or accelerating the adoption and use of new, beneficial technologies in a community.

Wireless networks could also let states and municipalities offer long distance health and educational services, thereby lowering coverage costs. Other services for which wireless networks might prove useful are consulting criminal, driving license, and fingerprint databases; providing wireless communication services for fire fighting and ambulance operations; and undertaking distance metering and billing of public utilities such as water and power.

Another argument for municipal wireless broadband networks is that installing wireless networks could be less expensive than installing wire-line networks, especially in areas with low population densities. In addition, public provision of wireless broadband could be more efficient than private provision, because it avoids costs related to the negotiation of rights of way to install antennas. Note that municipalities should consider equity issues when deciding to provide services; subsidies may be justified to provide service in unprofitable areas.

Finally, municipal wireless networks could represent an alternative to the dominant carrier network; thus, telecommunications carriers could offer telephony services to the community.

STATUS OF WIRELESS BROADBAND IN MEXICO

Mexico currently has few wireless broadband providers. Multivision is a wholesale and retail wireless broadband service provider that provides service to the three main cities using pre-Wi-MAX technology in the 2.5 gigahertz band. Another carrier that recently started offering wireless broadband services is Iusacell in the personal communication system band. Some frequency bands have already been assigned, but concessionaires are not using them. In 1998, TELMEX and UNEFON each obtained access to 50 megahertz in the 3.5 gigahertz band, which has been declared suitable for providing broadband services based on Wi-MAX technology, but have not yet provided any service on it.

Unlicensed spectrum could represent a means for encouraging wireless broadband deployments. In Mexico, certain spectrum ranges were declared unlicensed for broadband services according to a 2006 agreement (*Federal Official Gazette* 2006). TELMEX is currently using the 2.4 gigahertz unlicensed band to offer wireless broadband services to its clients through its Prodigy Móvil (Wi-Fi) brand.[9]

Under current regulations, states and municipalities could operate broadband networks on unlicensed frequency bands, as occurs in other countries. These networks should offer nondiscriminatory access to all carriers interested in providing services through them. In the United States, bills to this end have already been introduced. Because Mexico's Federal Telecommunications Act allows only concessionaires to negotiate interconnection agreements, municipalities will have to strike alliances with concessionaires so that they can offer not only wireless broadband Internet services, but also telephony services.

Aside from the unlicensed bands, the federal government could assign dedicated-use frequency bands, through the social coverage mechanism of the Federal Telecommunications Act, to public–private partnerships in municipalities or cities. For example, some frequencies in certain bands have not yet been assigned. Those bands could operate with Wi-MAX equipment, which transmits data at faster speeds and over longer distances than Wi-Fi (OECD 2006).

With the advent of digitalized television signals, the United States has begun to auction off spectrum in the 700 megahertz band to companies offering wireless broadband services, among others. Although Mexico is also transitioning toward digital television, the government has still not established a policy to release spectrum as soon as possible for other uses. The policy for the transition to digital television in Mexico sets deadlines for television station concessionaires to make digital replicas of the analog channel, but does not specify a date for turning off the analog channels (*Federal Official Gazette* 2004).

Consumer-Related Issues

This section discusses the impact of Mexico's telecommunications regulatory framework on consumer welfare.

Empowering Consumers

Class action suits are important to lower the costs of legal representation to dispersed clients, each of whom may have only a small claim. Mexico has made progress in this regard, because the 2004 Federal Consumer Protection Act states that the Federal Consumer Advocate's Office can file class action suits before the courts without needing to present any guarantees. However, the office is constrained by the need for interested parties to prove that they have suffered damages, which, in some cases, makes the class action nonviable (for example, in the case of gas stations or distributors that cheat consumers by charging for full liters but do not dispense full liters). Why the Federal Consumer Advocate's Office is the sole legal entity that can file these types of suits is still unclear.

Double Billing Calls

On November 30, 1994, the Ministry of Communications and Transport authorized TELMEX to charge the cost of a local call to all long distance calls, to calls to 1–800 numbers, and to mobile telephones, which means customers are being billed twice for using the local network. In the case of long distance calls, consumers pay for the long distance call to the long distance carrier that, in turn, pays two interconnection rates: one to the local carrier originating the call and another to the local carrier terminating it. Interconnection rates cover the costs local carriers incur for originating and terminating long distance calls. In addition, local carriers of originating calls charge their customers for a local call, which once again covers the cost of originating and terminating the call. Therefore, local infrastructure is paid for twice; that is, both the long distance carrier and the subscriber pay.

For international long distance calls originating in Mexico, essentially three payments are made for using the local infrastructure of origin, one by the long distance carrier and two by the subscriber. In 2005, TELMEX revenues from double billing long distance calls amounted to US$0.48 billion (figure 9.11), or 3.9 percent of its total revenues in Mexico.

On calls to 1–800 numbers, the subscriber pays the carrier providing the service for the calls it receives, whether local or long distance. The local carrier also charges the subscriber for a local call when these numbers are dialed. In addition to this charge to the consumer, carriers also have to pay TELMEX for billing and collection services.

Rounding Up Minutes or Charging Per Minute

In Mexico, calls to mobile telephones and long distance calls are charged per minute, and these charges are rounded up to the next minute. For example, if a customer makes a 1.5-minute call, the

Figure 9.11 TELMEX Revenues from Charges to Fixed
Telephone Consumers on Long Distance Calls, 1999–2005

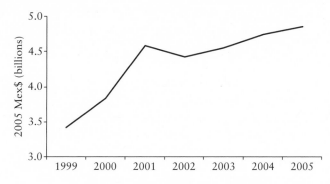

Source: Author's estimate based on TELMEX annual reports.

customer is billed for a 2-minute call, representing a surcharge of
33 percent. In other words, consumers pay an additional percentage
on top of the cost of their call for time they never used. This kind
of rounding up is not transparent for consumers and violates the
Federal Consumer Protection Law, which prohibits charging users
for a service that is not used. Technology permits tracking calls by
the second.

Enabling Portability of Numbers

In Mexico, number portability is technologically feasible and has
been legally binding for a number of years. At present, however,
subscribers are made to change telephone numbers when they switch
carriers, which is extremely inconvenient and poses a barrier to making the change.

The benefits of number portability include the following:

- cost savings for subscribers who switch service providers,
  because portability eliminates the expense of having to inform
  third parties of the new number and subscribers do not miss
  possible business opportunities or other calls;
- cost savings for subscribers making calls to users who have
  switched providers, because portability eliminates the costs
  and time connected with users who have to obtain the new
  number; and
- enhancements to service efficiency and quality, as well as price
  reductions because of increased competition.

COFETEL began a process to allow for the portability of geographic and nongeographic numbers. Portability is expected to be implemented by late 2007. Users would incur a charge for administrative expenses only.

Conclusions

When TELMEX was privatized in late 1990, a significant part of the country's infrastructure was concentrated in the hands of this one company, which was also granted a substantial rate increase and tax reduction. Moreover, when TELMEX was privatized it was shielded from competition for six years in the profitable domestic and international long distance markets. For all practical purposes, the company was also sheltered from competition in local telephony, because the government failed to establish interconnection rules until 1999. Furthermore, the more relevant coverage obligations were imposed on TELMEX until only 1994.

TELMEX has exercised its substantial market power unchecked. With the privatization, the Ministry of Communications and Transport took on key supervision, sanction, and control functions for which it was poorly prepared. Improving its skills in these areas was discouraged, because each time ministry technical departments tried to impose sanctions on TELMEX for noncompliance, they were rejected by their superiors. This rejection obviously frustrated the ministry staff, which, in turn, led to no follow-up of TELMEX's compliance with its concession-related obligations.

When the 1995 Federal Telecommunications Act was enacted, the government had an opportunity to create an agency with technical autonomy to supervise and regulate TELMEX and the industry. Initial drafts envisaged a telecommunications commission with that authority, but the articles dealing with the detailed enforcement powers of the regulatory entity were deleted. COFETEL was set up by a general article as an agency of the Ministry of Communications and Transport in such a way that it lacked the power required for effective regulation.

Mexico was also short of other institutions that could countervail TELMEX's market power. For example, in November 1994, when the Ministry of Communications and Transport authorized TELMEX to charge both the long distance rate and the cost of a local call for long distance calls, no consumer advocacy groups were in place that could have challenged the authorization. The opaque manner in which this charge was introduced meant that for years most consumers were unaware of what they were being charged for. The Federal Consumer

Advocate's Office was not involved in the problem and, in any case, would probably have been unable to disallow the charge.

The defense of consumers' rights before the federal courts faces two significant limitations. First, *amparos* do not have effects on all parties, but rather are binding only upon the parties involved in the proceedings. Second, contrary to the custom in other countries, when juridical proceedings are filed before the federal courts regarding regulatory measures issued by the telecommunications regulating agency, users (individually or collectively) cannot participate in the corresponding *amparo*. This is the case for the suits currently filed against the CPP scheme in long distance. The rationale is that— according to judicial criteria—users have only an economic, not juridical, interest in COFETEL's rulings and, therefore, cannot be party to the suit.

As for competition policies, even though Mexico's constitution bans monopolies, it did not have both the legislation and the agency to deal with economic competition issues until mid-1993, plus the CFC's capacity to enforce its resolutions before the courts has been limited. It has been unable to implement many of the sanctions it has imposed, as was the case with the declaration of TELMEX's dominance in the market in late 1997, which the courts recently rendered null and void.

Because of the country's institutional weaknesses, it has been unable to prevent practices that harm competition and consumers. In light of the huge technological changes in the sector and to foster competition, preventing existing dominant carriers from forming monopolies with new technologies or standards is extremely important. This would be the case for Wi-Fi, power line communications, digital subscriber lines, VoIP, and so on, because these technologies have the potential of opening increasingly important telecommunications markets to competition. To date, the authorities' performance has been lackluster. TELMEX has monopolized digital subscriber line technology, which uses telephone-line copper pairs to provide broadband access, because no policy regarding local loop unbundling is in place. Power line communications technology runs a similar risk of monopolization if, instead of being operated by the Federal Electricity Commission, a decision is reached for its commercial applications to be undertaken by a dominant company.

Mexico can, however, overcome its tardiness in embracing broadband and place itself on the cutting edge. Proper management of the radio-electric spectrum by the state is crucial. So far, allocation of the spectrum has been concentrated among just a few players. Those players sometimes seem to acquire the spectrum either to warehouse it and prevent it from falling into the hands of third parties who would then offer services or to secure it so they can resell it to major carriers. In the case of Wi-Fi standards, because equipment operates on bands that have recently been declared unlicensed, cities or municipalities, in association with concessionaires, might be able to develop low-cost broadband networks for offering competitive telecommunication services to citizens.

The underlying question is therefore how Mexico can change the status quo. It now has the Telecommunications Law, which, although obsolete in certain regards, has fundamentals that are still valid. In addition, Mexico has signed international agreements such as the World Trade Organization's Fourth Protocol to the General Agreement on Trade in Services. The protocol includes a reference paper on basic telecommunications that clearly stipulates key issues regarding proper interconnection of networks, anticompetitive practices, and even appropriate operation of a regulatory agency. The paper notes that regulatory agencies are to be independent of all basic services vendors and that agency decisions must be impartial with regard to market participants.

Mexico could achieve a good deal simply by complying with the provisions of the Federal Telecommunications Act and the reference paper, as well as by ensuring clear separation between the major carriers and the regulatory agency.

Notes

1. Condition 8–4 of the concession certificate requires that if TELMEX engages in monopolistic practices in any or several of the services it provides and cannot prove otherwise, the Ministry of Communications and Transport can (a) revoke authorization according to the terms and conditions established in the law or in regulations in effect, or (b) ban TELMEX from providing services for a five-year period or for an undefined period of time.

2. In 2000, COFETEL established 39 specific obligations for TELMEX: 18 pertaining to rates, 12 to quality of service, and 8 to information, and 1 stating the goal of the regulation and the relevant markets it covered.

3. According to the July 1, 1994, resolution and the long distance rules of June 20, 1996, all local areas are open to competition through the presubscription service (whereby competitors interconnect with TELMEX in areas where it has digital connections). TELMEX's network has been entirely digital since 2000. Thus, it could provide this presubscription service throughout the country, but has yet to do so.

4. Apparently, some local carriers are unwilling to enter the market to avoid payment of the long distance interconnection rate, and so to provide public telephony services, they lease lines from TELMEX.

5. The assumption that call traffic is uniform overestimates the average cost if we consider that users prefer to make more on-net calls than off-net calls. The Telefónica average cost per minute would decrease by a smaller proportion than the TELCEL average cost, because Telefónica users cannot minimize their off-net calls as much as TELCEL users. In this scenario, the negative effects of high interconnection rates on the competition could be greater than estimated.

6. The act assumed that negotiations would be carried out to determine interconnection rates because one of the parties would want to lower the rates while the other party would want to keep them high. The law did not consider the case in which both parties would be willing to keep interconnection rates high for the benefit of one or both of the companies involved, albeit to the detriment of competition and consumers.

7. There is a double accounting of minutes per user in countries using the RPP system. This is because on-net calls are billed twice, once for the calling party and again for the receiving party. Under the CPP system, only the party making the call is billed. Data for countries using the RPP system have been adjusted downward by 20 percent as a way to compensate for the double billing.

8. For more information, visit http://www.sfgov.org/site/tech_connect_index.asp?id=36612; http://www.wirelessphiladelphia.org/; http://www.ida.gov.sg/idaweb/marketing/infopage.jsp?infopagecategory=factsheet:wireless&versionid=2&infopageid=I3928.

9. For more information, visit http://www.telmex.com/mx/hogar/ai_pdgyMovilInicio.html.

References

Casanueva, C., and R. del Villar. 2003. "Analysis of the Reform in the Basic Telecommunications Industry in Mexico (1990–2000)." In *Critical Infrastructures: State of the Art in Research and Application*, ed. W. A. H. Thissen and P. M. Herder, 179–207. Kluwer Book Series, International Series on Operations Research and Management Science, vol. 65. Boston: Academic Publishers.

Casasús, C. 1994. "Privatization of Telecommunications: The Case of Mexico." In *Implementing Reforms in the Telecommunications Sector: Lessons from Experience*, ed. B. Wellenius and P. Stern, 177–84. Washington, DC: World Bank.

Crandall, R., and J. Charles. 2001. *The $500 Billion Opportunity: The Potential Economic Benefit of Widespread Diffusion of Broadband Internet Access.* Washington, DC: Criterion Economics.

del Villar, R., and J. Serrano. 2003. *Estimate of Teléfonos de México 2003 Controlled Services Rate Level and the Adjustment Factor for 2003–2006.*

Mexico City: Banco de México, Departamento de Investigación Economica.

Federal Official Gazette. 2004. "Agreement to Adopt the Technological Standard of Terrestrial Digital Television and Establish the Policy to Transition to Terrestrial Digital Television in Mexico." First section, July 2.

———. 2006. "Agreement to Establish Policies for Broadband Services and Other Applications." First section, March 13.

Federal Telecommunications Commission. 2006. *Municipal Provision of Wireless Internet.* Staff Report. Washington, DC: Government Printing Office.

Ford, G., and K. Thomas. 2005. "Broadband and Economic Development: A Municipal Case Study from Florida." *Review of Urban and Regional Development Studies* 17 (3): 219–22.

Gil, J. 2000. "La interconeccion en el sector Mexicano de telecomunicaciones desde la privatizacion de TELMEX: Un analisis teorico y empirico," B.A. thesis, Instituto Tecnológico Autónomo de México, Mexico City.

Jorgenson, D. W. 2004. "Accounting for Growth in the Information Age." In *Productivity and Cyclicality in Semiconductors: Trends, Implications and Questions.* Washington, DC: National Academies Press.

Jorgenson, D. W., and Khuong Vu. 2005. "Information Technology and the World Economy." *Scandinavian Journal of Economics* 107 (4): 631–50.

Lehr, W. 2004. *Economic Case for Dedicated Unlicensed Spectrum Below 3GHz.* Cambridge, MA: Massachusetts Institute of Technology, Research Program on Internet and Telecoms Convergence.

Lehr, W., C. Osorio, S. Gillett, and M. Sirbu. 2005. "Measuring Broadband's Economic Impact." Paper presented at the 33rd Research Conference on Communication, Information, and Internet Policy, October, Arlington, VA.

Litan, R. E., and A. M. Rivlin. 2001. "Projecting the Economic Impact of the Internet." *American Economic Review* 91 (2): 313–17.

Merrill Lynch. 2006. *Global Wireless Matrix 2Q06.* New York: Global Securities Research and Economics Group, Research Department.

Minges, M. 2006. *Revisiting Jipp.* Research report. Washington, DC: Telecommunications Management Group.

OECD (Organisation for Economic Co-operation and Development). 2006. *The Implications of WiMax for Competition and Regulation.* Paris: OECD. http://www.oecd.org/sti/ict/broadband.

Solano, O., R. del Villar, and R. García-Verdú. 2006. "Challenges to the Effective Implementation of Competition Policy in Regulated Sectors: The Case of Telecommunications in Mexico." *Northwestern Journal of International Law and Business* 26 (3): 527–46.

Tropos Networks. 2004. *Metro-Scale Wi-Fi as City Service.* Chaska Case Study. Minnesota: Tropos Networks.

10

Priorities for Telecommunications Reform in Mexico

Roger G. Noll

In the preceding chapter, del Villar provides extensive details about telecommunications policy and performance in Mexico. As documented there, although prices have fallen and utilization has increased, the telecommunications sector remains more expensive and less developed than it could be, mainly because of the continued dominance of a largely unregulated provider, Teléfonos de Mexico (TELMEX), and its mobile sibling, RadioMóvil Dipsa, known as TELCEL.

This chapter is intended as a companion to chapter 9 in two ways. First, it provides additional information about and analysis of the performance of Mexico's telecommunications system in comparison with systems in peer nations. Second, this chapter examines the relationship between the performance of the telecommunications industry and its structure and governance institutions and identifies changes in the structure, rules, and procedures of telecommunications regulation that would likely improve the sector's performance.

Overview of Telecommunications Reform

Research on privatization and regulatory reform reaches two profoundly important conclusions: privatization almost always improves performance, but postprivatization governance institutions and market conditions are extremely important in determining the magnitude of the improvement (see, for example, Armstrong, Cowan, and Vickers 1994; Levy and Spiller 1996; Noll 2000; Ramamurti 1996; Wellenius and Stern 1994; World Bank 1995). The history of telecommunications in Mexico is consistent with both conclusions.

From the Great Depression until the late 1980s, in nearly all nations, developing and industrialized, a ministerial state-owned enterprise operated the telephone system.[1] Mexico was among the last to nationalize telecommunications, converting the firms in the industry to ministerial state-owned enterprises only in 1972. During the period of nationalization, the telecommunications sector suffered from underinvestment, high operating costs, and prices that were too low to recover costs. The central government financed the resulting operating losses. As a result, Mexico, like many other nations, began to consider major reform in the 1980s, and by 1989 it had concluded that the best option was privatization.

The political origins and intent of telecommunications restructuring in Mexico were unexceptional. Poor performance, stricter fiscal controls, and commitment to a more open economy led Mexico to consider privatizing a long list of industries. Telecommunications was an attractive target because of its strategic significance in a trade-oriented growth policy, the potential for significant improvements in service, the opportunity to derive substantial revenues from the sale, and the prospect of using the political cover that privatization offered to raise prices and eliminate a fiscal drain on the budget.

Since the decision to restructure the industry was made, Mexico's telecommunications sector has undergone a dramatic transformation. In December 1990, the government sold TELMEX to a consortium that included a large Mexican company, Grupo Carso, and Southwest Bell, an American local exchange carrier. The reformed entity started operating in 1991. In the amendments to its concession that accompanied privatization, TELMEX was given a seven-year monopoly in domestic and international telecommunications services, accompanied by investment and pricing commitments. Initially, TELMEX was not regulated except in terms of the enforcement of the concession by the Ministry of Communications and Transport (Secretaría de Comunicaciones y Transportes, or SCT). Thus, for the first few years, TELMEX was an almost completely unregulated monopoly.

In 1995, the Federal Telecommunications Law was passed. This law adopted a policy to create a fully private and, eventually, competitive industry, and established a regulatory framework to apply during the period in which TELMEX would dominate the industry. A 1996 presidential decree created the Federal Telecommunications

Commission (Comisión Federal de Telecomunicaciones, or COFETEL) to implement the regulatory framework. Although headed by an independent commission, COFETEL was designed to be under the control of the SCT. In the next few years, some competition emerged as entrants were given concessions to operate in long distance, mobile, and fixed local access telephony, but competition suffered because COFETEL was a weak regulatory agency that could not cope with Telmex's entrenched power as the incumbent former monopolist.

Converting a ministerial, state-owned enterprise into a reasonably independent corporation,[2] whether mostly publicly owned or completely privatized, usually results in a substantial improvement in performance. Because of the legal status of corporations in most nations, corporatization increases a firm's financial security and independence, which in an industry like telecommunications—with little risk and substantial demand—virtually guarantees that a firm will be financially viable. Consequently, after corporatization, investment increases, service quality improves, capacity grows more rapidly, waiting lists for new service and repair become shorter, financial performance is stronger, costs are lower, and prices become better aligned with costs.

Research on telecommunications restructuring in developing nations concludes that the types of reforms introduced in Mexico should improve performance. Fully privatized firms usually perform better than corporations that are mostly publicly owned, but this difference is small compared with the advantages that both organizational forms have over ministerial state-owned enterprises. The key point is that efficiency is substantially improved if the telecommunications operator faces a hard budget constraint and is relatively free from political interference in its day-to-day business decisions. If competition is strong, even if limited to a few firms, performance is improved even more.

Mexico's experience is consistent with these generalizations. After the telecommunications sector was restructured, its performance improved significantly. From 1990 to 2005, the number of wire-line telephones in service almost tripled, increasing from 6.4 million to 18.9 million. Wireless telephony grew from nothing to nearly 50 million telephones by 2006. Yet the limited scope of competition apparently caused the improvements to be less than could have been achieved.

Mexico's performance in telecommunications is not impressive when compared with other nations at a comparable state of development. Table 10.1 contains data about telecommunications penetration for Mexico and 12 nations that form a reasonable peer group

Table 10.1 Telephone Penetration, Mexico and Selected Peer Nations, 2005

Country	Per capita GDP (US$ thousands purchasing power parity)	Population (millions)	Penetration of selected services per 100 households			
			Fixed	Wireless	Total fixed and wireless	Internet utilization rate
Argentina	13.9	39.3	22.4	56.2	78.6	25.4
Brazil	8.2	186.1	22.8	46.3	69.1	13.9
Bulgaria	8.6	7.5	33.3	82.7	116.0	29.3
Chile	11.5	16.0	21.3	66.3	87.6	41.9
Colombia	7.4	43.6	17.7	50.2	67.9	10.8
Malaysia	10.3	24.0	18.3	81.3	99.6	45.8
Mexico	10.0	106.4	18.3	44.6	62.9	17.5
Romania	8.9	22.3	19.7	60.1	79.8	22.0
Russian Federation	10.6	143.4	28.0	83.7	111.6	16.5
South Africa	12.1	44.3	10.6	76.7	87.4	11.5
Tunisia	7.9	10.1	12.9	56.4	69.3	9.4
Turkey	8.4	69.7	27.3	62.6	89.8	23.0
Venezuela, R. B. de	6.4	25.4	14.2	49.2	63.4	12.0

Sources: CIA 2006; World Bank World Development Indicators database.

for Mexico. Telephone penetration per 100 households is the most commonly used indicator of the sector's development. The list includes all nations except the Islamic Republic of Iran for which per capita gross domestic product (GDP) is within US$2,000 of Mexico's and that have populations of more than 5 million, plus three Latin American nations that fall outside this income range, namely, Argentina, Colombia, and the República Bolivariana de Venezuela. All other Latin American nations are either poorer than the lowest-income nation in the group (the República Bolivariana de Venezuela) or have fewer than 5 million inhabitants.

In this peer group, Mexico is in the middle with respect to use of the Internet; however, Mexico's Internet utilization rate is less than half that of the best-practice nations within the peer group, Chile and Malaysia, and is substantially behind that of Argentina, Bulgaria, Romania, and Turkey. With respect to access, Mexico has the lowest wireless penetration and the lowest total penetration of fixed line plus wireless in the peer group. Colombia, Tunisia, and the República Bolivariana de Venezuela, the poorest nations in the peer group with per capita incomes more than US$2,000 below that of Mexico, all have more wireless telephones and higher total telephone penetration than Mexico. Even Ecuador, which has a per capita GDP of US$4,100, had wireless penetration of 46.3 percent in 2005, exceeding that of Mexico, and it had a total telephone penetration of 59.0 percent compared with Mexico's 62.9 percent. Thus, Mexico's telephone penetration represents the norm for nations with per capita GDP of around US$6,500 and best practice for countries with per capita GDP of roughly US$4,000.

The most plausible explanation for Mexico's poor performance is that the industry was initially privatized as an unregulated monopoly and remains dominated by one firm that is only weakly regulated. The decision to create a temporary monopoly in telecommunications was controversial when it was made and remains so today (for a detailed history of the reform, see Mariscal 2002). At the time of privatization, the Mexican government intensely debated the form that privatization would take. Eventually, following the advice of management consultants, prospective investors, and some officials from international organizations, it decided to allow TELMEX to be a temporary monopoly and to postpone setting up regulatory institutions (the author was on the losing side of this debate; see Noll and Salas 1990).

The decision to create a monopoly was based on three arguments. First, foreign investors would pay substantially more to purchase TELMEX if it were a monopoly. Second, a monopoly facilitated the pursuit of a universal service objective: to serve households that could not afford service that was priced to recover its full cost and to bring service to areas that were underserved because of difficult terrain, low population, or generally low incomes. Third, a monopoly was regarded as necessary to get a private firm to commit to a major investment program to improve service even to businesses and high-income households. Major investment would be required simply to eliminate the long waiting list for service and the high rate of failure in completing or holding calls.

The argument that monopoly leads to more investment and greater utilization is inconsistent with elementary economics. When privatized, a monopoly sells for more than a competitive firm if the monopoly is either unregulated or loosely regulated, because the purchaser of a monopoly buys a stream of monopoly profits, which is more valuable than a stream of competitive returns. By granting TELMEX a period of exclusivity and by deferring the establishment of a regulator, Mexico created a temporary monopoly that had the opportunity to earn substantial excess profits for many years. As a result, Mexico probably received a higher price for TELMEX than it would have received under privatization to either an effectively regulated monopoly or competition.

A high privatization price and subsequent monopoly prices for services do not lead to greater investment and more service. In the absence of a substantial state subsidy for customers with a low ability to pay, high prices reduce the quantity of service that is demanded, so that a monopoly will undertake less, not more, private investment than a firm that—because of regulation or competition—charges lower prices (but prices that are still above the average cost of service). Meanwhile, under an unregulated monopoly, customers and, more generally, the Mexican economy suffer from an underdeveloped telecommunications infrastructure. Research on the privatization of telecommunications in developing countries bears out these simple economic arguments. Granting a temporary monopoly reduces network expansion by between 10 and 40 percent and the annual growth of telephone penetration by more than two percentage points (Wallsten 2004).

The results for Mexico show that creating a monopoly in telecommunications did not deliver the benefits that were said to have motivated the reform. Table 10.2 shows the penetration of telephone service in Mexican states in 1998, the year after TELMEX's exclusive rights came to an end. The table shows that telephone penetration in states with less than US$3,000 per capita GDP in 1999 was about 5 lines per 100 households. Thus, the monopoly period did not result in anything remotely close to universal service in underserved areas.

The reason for the slow growth in telephone penetration during the exclusivity period is apparent in table 10.3, which shows the financial performance of TELMEX in 1998 compared with that of

Table 10.2 Teledensity by District/State, 1998

District or state	Population (thousands)	Main lines per 100 households	Per capita GDP (1999) US$	Per capita GDP (1999) Growth (%)
Aguas Calientes	921	10.0	5,607	5.5
Baja California	2,333	16.3	6,235	5.9
Baja California Sur	397	13.7	6,828	5.0
Campeche	696	5.6	9,027	6.7
Coahuila	2,277	11.4	6,462	4.0
Colima	531	11.3	5,006	4.2
Chiapas	3,689	3.1	2,045	3.1
Chihuahua	3,003	11.5	6,502	4.4
Distrito Federal	8,582	27.5	7,334	3.3
Durango	1,463	7.7	4,276	3.7
Estado de México	12,635	9.4	7,334	3.3
Guanajuato	4,559	7.2	3,508	4.9
Guerrero	3,064	5.6	2,523	2.2
Hidalgo	2,225	5.1	3,071	3.4
Jalisco	6,284	13.3	4,777	4.7
Michoacán	3,978	6.9	2,635	1.8
Morelos	1,562	10.9	3,797	1.1
Nayarit	912	7.4	3,008	2.0
Nuevo León	3,778	17.8	8,420	5.6
Oaxaca	3,306	3.4	2,029	1.8
Puebla	4,894	6.7	3,346	6.2
Querétaro	1,344	9.0	5,803	6.1
Quintana Roo	831	9.2	8,944	9.0
San Luis Potosí	2,289	6.4	3,311	1.6
Sinaloa	2,553	8.4	3,733	0.6
Sonora	2,270	10.5	5,658	3.3
Tabasco	1,878	4.7	3,178	2.7
Tamaulipas	2,703	11.4	5,138	3.5
Tlaxcala	938	5.5	2,894	6.1
Veracruz	6,974	5.8	2,740	1.0
Yucatán	1,679	8.2	3,807	4.4
Zacatecas	1,339	4.9	2,711	2.0

Source: http://www.banamex.com/banamex/esem/c_indexesem_eng.htm, accessed May 2000.

private telephone companies in the United Kingdom and the United States. Among these companies, TELMEX had by far the largest operating margin, with more than a third of its revenues going to operating profit.[3] Typically well-managed telephone companies have operating costs in the range of 75 to 80 percent of revenues, whereas TELMEX's operating costs are in the range of 60 to 65 percent of revenues. TELMEX also had the lowest fraction of revenue and

Table 10.3 Financial Performance of Selected
Telecommunications Firms, 1998

Item	TELMEX	Ameritech	Bell Atlantic	GTE	British Telecom
Total revenues (US$ millions)	8,187	17,154	31,566	25,473	25,138
Operating income (US$ millions)	3,111	4,193	6,627	5,336	5,151
Percentage of revenues	38	24	21	21	20
Capital expenditures (US$ millions)	1,235	2,954	8,675	4,940	4,775
Percentage of revenues	15	17	27	19	19

Source: http://yahoo.marketguide.com/mgi/MG.asp?rt=aincomstd&m=A0484,
0444N, 1082N, 3642N, and 1306N, accessed May 2000.

profit going to investment, despite the much more underdeveloped
state of telecommunications in Mexico. These data show that privatization to monopoly succeeded in creating monopoly profits, but
the change did not succeed in inducing TELMEX to reinvest these
profits to increase service.

Regulatory Institutions and Policies

Given that the industry was going to be a monopoly for nearly a
decade and was highly concentrated for an indefinite period thereafter, a well-designed regulatory system was essential to protect consumers and—when competition was finally introduced—to prevent
monopolistic abuses by the incumbent against entrants. Unfortunately, Mexico never developed an effective regulatory system. The
regulatory system governing the transition from state-owned monopoly to privatized competition was put in place long after privatization, is still not fully developed, and has not worked well because it
has too little authority.

Economics research (for example, Estache and Rossi 2008; Kessides 2004; Levy and Spiller 1996; Noll 2000) concludes that the design
of regulatory institutions has a substantial effect on the performance
of a regulated industry. Specifically, performance is better if

- regulators are independent of both the legislature and the
  executive branch of government
- regulatory processes are open and transparent

- judicial review is speedy and the standards for judicial review focus on substance, that is, whether the agency acted within its mandate and had a reasonable basis for its decisions
- regulatory policy is designed to favor largely unregulated competition, as opposed to monopoly or managed competition, wherever competition is feasible
- regulators are given substantial authority to compel the release of information from regulated firms to control the prices of monopoly services and to compel pro-competitive behavior
- regulation of the residual monopoly is oriented toward maximizing economic efficiency, including suppressing monopoly pricing and anticompetitive behavior.

Moreover, privatization is likely to be more successful when most, if not all, of these governance institutions, including the commitment to competition, are in place before privatization occurs.

Despite problems with its governance structure, Mexico's telecommunications policy produced several positive results. In 1996, 1997, and 1998, the government held successful auctions for electromagnetic frequency assignments for paging, cellular telephones, local microwave distribution, and wireless personal communications services. Several companies entered wireless telephony, especially mobile service. The introduction of prepaid calling for radio telephones increased both penetration and usage, because these policies allowed customers to gain firmer control of the money they spent on telephone service.

Nevertheless, all the major regulatory issues about interconnection rules and prices remain incompletely resolved, primarily because (a) the front-line regulatory agency, COFETEL, lacks a statutory policy mandate; (b) the procedural and decision-making authority to issue decisive, timely regulations on issues that create significant conflicts among the players in the industry; and (c) the power to enforce its regulations effectively after they have been adopted. As a result, the prospects for achieving high penetration and competitive pricing are not good.

Successful privatization of an infrastructure provider that was previously a state-owned monopoly requires an effective regulatory institution to cope with the incumbent's power before competition can be firmly established. This institution must have several key features if it is to be effective in optimizing the industry's performance.

One requirement for effective regulation is that regulation must not become a de facto instrument for re-expropriating the capital investments of private companies. This goal requires that firms be able to charge reasonable prices that recover their costs.

Regulation must also encourage efficient investment. To do so, regulation must not impose requirements on regulated firms that raise their costs, but that do not improve the value of their service to their customers, and it must give regulated firms a significant degree of latitude in making decisions about investment and employment.

At the same time, effective regulation must also avoid becoming an instrument simply for advancing the interests of firms in the industry. Efficiency requires that prices be capped somewhere near the level that would emerge under competition and that carriers make sufficient investments to provide all services that consumers demand at these prices. The 1990 revised TELMEX concession attempted to achieve this objective by including growth targets in relation to the number of lines in service, but after these targets expired, growth slowed. Post-1996 regulation has not proven to be effective in increasing fixed access penetration. Even though growth in wireless telephony has partially made up for Mexico's deficit in wire-line penetration, an unfortunate consequence of the under-developed wire-line network is that it inhibits the growth of high-speed Internet access by households.

A competitive market structure is an effective means of increasing penetration and use of the system. Consequently, regulation must be proactive in supporting the development of competition where this is feasible. Where technology does not create a natural monopoly, a regulated monopoly is not as efficient as unregulated competition in preventing monopoly prices and increasing service. Moreover, incumbent monopolists in one component of the industry can frequently extend their monopoly into other parts that clearly could be competitive, which further reduces efficiency. This issue has been the center of controversy in long distance telephony and is a serious policy controversy in Internet services.

In a network industry such as telecommunications, an incumbent monopolist in local access has the potential to exploit two anticompetitive advantages over competitors. First, customers may prefer to buy all services from the same source. If the incumbent's monopoly is not the result of superior efficiency, but arises because entry is difficult caused by some combination of business practices by the monopolist and regulatory policies, then customer preferences for one-stop shopping will cause an unwarranted monopoly to extend into related markets. Second, competitors in one market must buy services from the incumbent monopolist to offer their own services. Examples are terminating access service and interconnection service. If these services have prices substantially in excess of costs or are of low quality, competitors are crippled.

At some point, all nations that have tried to introduce competition into some aspect of the network, such as in long distance service, mobile telephony, and Internet access, have been forced to face these issues. In some cases, regulators have prevented local access companies from entering competitive markets. An example was the U.S. ban on entry into long distance by Bell Operating Companies, the local access carriers of the formerly integrated American Telephone and Telegraph Company, which was in effect for 15 years. In some cases, regulators have imposed an equal access requirement, which means that all competitors must be provided monopoly telecommunications services on the same price and technical terms as affiliates of the monopolist. An example is the U.S. requirement that Bell Operating Companies provide equal access to all Internet service providers and all long distance carriers.

Mexico has formal policies in place that provide protection against anticompetitive activity by TELMEX. The basic Federal Telecommunications Law states that competition is the preferred market structure and establishes policies against pricing services below cost and in favor of providing technically acceptable interconnection. These policies imply that TELMEX has a responsibility not to subsidize its affiliates in the industry and not to disadvantage competitors by providing technically inferior interconnection. Nevertheless, the regulatory system continues to subsidize access service from usage charges and has not adopted clear rules regarding acceptable and unacceptable policies in relation to TELMEX's operation and obligations in competitive markets. Hence, long-standing controversies about interconnection among competing firms in long distance, local access, and Internet services remain unsettled.

Finally, to induce adequate investment, regulatory policy should be stable, predictable, and timely. Stability and predictability mean that policies change only when significant changes have occurred in the environment in which the industry operates, and timely decision making means that the agency responds reasonably quickly when such changes arise. These features of regulation enable regulators to avoid becoming an important source of business uncertainty, which, if not avoided, inhibits economically and financially warranted capital investments by regulated firms. In practice, regulatory policy in Mexico is not stable, predictable, or timely.

Importance of Structure and Process

Whether regulatory institutions can be relatively effective at improving the efficiency of telecommunications, or of any other infrastructure industry, depends on the details of their structure and process. The structure and processes of regulation determine who is empowered to make which decisions and what they must do to implement those decisions successfully (McCubbins, Noll, and Weingast 1989). Scholars who have studied regulatory reform generally agree that an effective regulatory system has the ingredients described in the following paragraphs (Kessides 2004; Levy and Spiller 1996; Noll 2000).

INDEPENDENCE

Regulatory decisions about prices, entry, and technical interconnection arrangements should be removed from the day-to-day pressures of ordinary politics if they are to avoid being viewed as a means for rewarding political allies. This requirement does not mean that democratic politics should not constrain and direct regulatory policy, as discussed next, but it does mean that regulators should have considerable autonomy in the short run. The main economic functions of prices are to recover costs and to send appropriate signals to other businesses about which markets to enter; however, in the political sphere, prices of state-operated entities tend to be treated as just another tax. Likewise, in the regulated domain, investment and employment decisions are expected to be driven by the desire to provide efficient service to a large base of customers, not as means to reward political allies through patronage and procurement.

To ensure that short-term political interference does not lead to inefficiencies in prices, investments, and service attributes, regulators need to be independent, that is, insulated from day-to-day politics. Independence is provided in two ways. First, regulators have the authority to make decisions without review or approval by elected officials except in the area of passing new laws that repeal a regulation. A useful way to measure this element of independence is the number of separate political actors who must agree to overturn a policy decision by a regulator, with a greater number of "veto gates" implying greater independence.[4] Second, regulators can have fixed terms that prevent their removal from office until their term has expired (except in the case of malfeasance). Regulators should not be removed simply because the president, minister, or legislature would have made a different regulatory decision.

CLEAR MANDATE

Democratic responsiveness in independent regulatory agencies is created by clearly crafted laws that tell the agency with some precision what it is supposed to do and how it is supposed to do it. In the case of telecommunications, the underlying mandate of the agency should specify that its task is to provide services to as many citizens as possible at prices that fairly reflect the cost of service, and that where possible, it should accomplish this task by creating a sufficiently competitive market in which little or no regulation is necessary. Moreover, this mandate must tell the agency how to make decisions and what it must do to ensure that its decisions have the force of law. A clear legislative mandate not only gives the agency objectives, but it tells the agency how it should develop rules that achieve these objectives. The next few features of an effective regulatory system are the most important elements of this process.

COMPETENCE

Regulation is a technically demanding activity that requires considerable expertise in engineering, accounting, finance, and economics. To succeed, a regulatory authority must have access to talented people in these disciplines, either by employing them or by contracting with them. Fundamentally, competence primarily requires a sufficient budget to afford skilled professionals and the flexibility to acquire their services solely on the basis of merit, as opposed to patronage or other political factors. Competence within the regulatory agency is necessary for decisions to promote efficient operation of the industry.

TRANSPARENCY

Transparency applies not only to the policies and implementing rules, but also to the process for making rules. Transparency means that the regulatory rules and policies are clear, so that regulated firms and their customers know, or can easily find out, what regulations apply to them and how to comply with those regulations. In addition, transparency means that regulated firms, their competitors, and their customers understand how to initiate a regulatory proceeding to resolve a dispute and what kinds of information regulators will expect from them to render a decision. In short, those who are affected by regulatory rules need to know how these rules can be changed to make regulation predictable and responsive.

OPENNESS

An open regulatory process is one that allows all who are significantly affected by a regulatory decision to participate in it effectively. The heart of this requirement is that regulation must not be a secret, bilateral bargain between the regulator and a regulated company that is unobservable to anyone else except for the ultimate announcement of a decision. For example, if the issue is pricing by a firm, and if the policy is that prices should bear a reasonable relationship to cost, the customers and competitors of a firm must have access to the methods used to estimate costs and, hence, to set prices, and the right to challenge these methods in front of the regulator and the regulated firm.

COMPETITION ADVOCACY

Advocacy of competition should be institutionalized in the regulatory process. Regulation and competition are inherently conflicting policies: regulation uses a centralized process to make decisions about prices, entry, investment, and service quality, while competition is a decentralized process in which each competing firm makes independent decisions that are driven by the goal of profitably winning customers by offering them a superior combination of products and prices. To prevent regulation from destroying competition requires vigilant attention, which can be accomplished by creating a competition advocate. A common way to institutionalize competition advocacy is to grant standing in regulatory proceedings to the agency that is responsible for enforcing competition law.

FORMAL OVERSIGHT: JUDICIAL REVIEW

To protect against error, incompetence, corruption, or simply laziness, the regulatory system should include opportunities for external review of individual decisions and of overall policies. Judicial review can play an important role by giving the parties affected by a decision the opportunity to challenge it on either of two grounds: the agency exceeded its authority or otherwise did not carry out its objectives as stated in its legal mandate, or the agency did not base its decision on the information that was presented to it. In both cases, agencies need to be given some discretion about how to make difficult decisions when neither the law nor the evidence is clear, so that the standard of review should be reasonableness (that is, a rational person, after considering the law and the facts, could have made this decision). Judicial review must also be timely. Because technology and market conditions evolve rapidly, judicial decisions about the validity of a regulation can impose substantial uncertainty and costs if they are made years after the regulation has been promulgated.

FORMAL OVERSIGHT: STATUTORY REVIEW

Independence of the regulator does not mean that the statutes granting regulators a mandate should never be reconsidered. Indeed, requirements for periodic reporting to political leaders about how laws are being implemented, including identification of vague or inconsistent laws and suggestions for amendments, are the most effective means for democratic oversight of the direction of regulatory policy. Such requirements enable elected authorities and their ministerial appointees to review the overall policy without becoming involved in specific cases or minor details.

Mexico's Regulatory System

The history of Mexican telecommunications reform began with preparations to privatize TELMEX. This privatization was initiated in 1990 and completed in 1991. Until 1995, the only formal regulatory system was the SCT's enforcement of the revision of the TELMEX concession that permitted privatization. The concession granted the newly privatized TELMEX a temporary monopoly in domestic and international long distance telephone service, but in return required TELMEX to expand its wire-line network. In theory, competitors could have entered local service, but in practice, no concessions were granted. Two companies, Iusecell and Pulsar, sought, but were denied, concessions for fixed wireless local service. Others did not seek to provide local service until they were also permitted to enter long distance or mobile telephone services.

The revised concession agreement also specified that a general tariff regulation would apply to a basic basket of core services: installation fees, monthly service charges, usage charges for local calling, and prices for domestic and international long distance calls, with the first two tariffs differentiated between residential and commercial customers. The concession agreement stipulated that the method of tariff regulation would be a price cap for the bundle of these services, with the proviso that no service would be cross-subsidized.

As a practical matter, TELMEX has set prices so that the price cap ceiling has not been reached. The price cap is stated as a maximum value for a price index of basic residential and business services. Initially, the cap was a weighted average of historical prices adjusted for inflation. The cap increases each year by the rate of inflation minus 4.5 percent. Because of rapid technological progress, increased usage that captures scale economies in parts of the network, and improved operating efficiency, TELMEX has experienced productivity gains in excess of the 4.5 percent target, allowing it to earn increasing profits while not raising prices as fast as is permitted under the price cap formula.

The 1995 Federal Telecommunications Law and the 1996 presidential decree that implemented it elaborate upon the rules and policies regarding the industry and establish an institutional framework for carrying them out. Although creating an independent regulatory agency by statute was considered at the time the act was being drafted, the final version of the act lodged authority for regulating telecommunications in the SCT. The act also retained the concept of concessions as a means of licensing entry, which entails a far more elaborate specification of the facilities and services that the carrier will offer than would be the case if carriers received licenses or permits.

The presidential decree that implemented the act created COFETEL and delegated most day-to-day regulatory functions to this agency. The law included the provision that facilities-based telecommunications firms had to file tariffs and that Telmex could be subjected to regulation of specific prices upon a finding by the antitrust authority, the Federal Competition Commission (Comisión Federal de Competencia, or CFC), that TELMEX was a dominant carrier in that market. The decree gave COFETEL the responsibility for implementing this part of the law as well as overseeing compliance with the price cap rule.

COFETEL can regulate interconnection arrangements, including pricing, if operators request intervention after failing to negotiate an agreement. The premise of interconnection policy is that the carriers should resolve interconnection issues. This approach to interconnection creates two problems. First, because some interconnection issues inherently bring carriers into conflict, bilateral negotiation cannot be expected to work well, and the presumption in favor of negotiation inevitably causes delay. Second, in other cases, carriers may be in a position to use interconnection agreements to engage in price collusion. For example, interconnection prices between competing local access carriers, including mobile telephone operators, place a floor on local calling prices, thereby limiting the extent to which competition can drive prices to cost.

COFETEL is, in some ways, a well-designed agency. At the top are five commissioners, four of whom are required to have relevant technical expertise. Because Mexico has many well-educated civil servants, the agency's technical competency does not appear to be a problem. Likewise, in many ways the 1995 Federal Telecommunications Law provides reasonable policy guidance for the regulator. Price regulation properly focuses on monopoly markets and adopts the policy that regulated prices are to be cost based and free of cross-subsidy. Moreover, granting the CFC the role of deciding whether a carrier is dominant gives an important function to the competition advocacy agency.

Nevertheless, the new regime has several features that prevent effective regulation. To begin with, COFETEL is not independent. In most cases, the SCT must approve COFETEL's decisions before they are adopted, which makes these decisions more political than is necessary or desirable. In addition, even though COFETEL's commissioners are appointed to fixed terms, the secretary of SCT can remove them at will. Moreover, the principal means for controlling the structure of the telecommunications industry and the operating responsibilities of the carriers is concession agreements, which are periodically renegotiated by the SCT. The continued involvement of the SCT in day-to-day decisions makes COFETEL a weak regulator and vitiates the more natural function of the SCT, which is policy oversight—assessing industry developments, reviewing the adequacy of policy in light of these developments, and proposing changes in the laws and decrees that underpin the current system.

COFETEL's procedures are neither transparent nor open. In nearly all cases, and especially with respect to pricing, the agency develops regulations by engaging in secret bilateral negotiations on a case-by-case basis, as opposed to undertaking open rule-making proceedings in which all firms in the industry, users, and disinterested experts such as scholars of communications policy are allowed to participate. No other parties have the right to participate in these bilateral negotiations, including the CFC, which is naturally concerned with the competitive effect of regulations that affect relationships among competitors, such as interconnection rules. COFETEL believes that existing law dictates this procedure.[5]

The information that is developed during these negotiations and that is the basis for COFETEL's decisions is typically not made public, because COFETEL believes that the information that it receives from carriers must be treated as confidential. COFETEL lacks the authority to compel regulated firms to release information, and thus has no leverage to resist a carrier's demand to provide information only on a confidential basis. Because published regulations are neither explained nor supported by evidence, the agency's underlying policies and procedures are unclear.

The Federal Telecommunications Law also retains a system of concessions for all facilities-based carriers that does not differentiate between competitive and monopolized services. All carriers must have a concession, and to grant one COFETEL is required to review an entrant's detailed business plan and its technical and financial competency to provide the service described in the plan. If a firm decides to alter the configuration or capacity of any component of the network while building it, the firm must seek an amendment to its concession. Because the SCT is solely responsible for amending concessions, the requirement to revise the concession with every minor change in service inevitably forces the SCT to be heavily involved in regulating the industry.

The premise behind concession review is that public oversight is needed to ensure that a carrier offers adequate service at reasonable prices. Such reviews can have substantial value in a monopolized market or when a licensee uses a public resource that offers limited opportunities for competition, but careful reviews of entrants serve no valid public purpose when a market is competitive. In a competitive market, customers decide whether to patronize a new entrant, and the government has no real competency to do a better job than the entrant and its potential customers in assessing the adequacy of the entrant's services. Thus, a concession process is unnecessary for these cases and forces the agency to use its resources in unproductive ways. Moreover, frequent concession renegotiation undermines the regulator's authority and effectiveness.

COFETEL has also been unable to react in a timely and predictable way to the tasks that have been assigned to it. COFETEL's proceedings do not have a time limit, and even though COFETEL usually sets a reasonable goal in terms of the length of a negotiation, it frequently does not meet these goals and negotiations are protracted.

Part of COFETEL's problem in implementing effective regulation arises from its inability to convince the courts that its regulations are reasonable and necessary. An important aspect of judicial review in Mexico is the *amparo*. An *amparo* is a form of temporary injunction that the courts can grant if a private party believes that a decision by the government will cause it financial harm. The *amparo* stays the implementation of a decision—in this case, a regulation promulgated by COFETEL—pending an evidentiary hearing by the court. Because the courts operate slowly, an *amparo* can remain in place for years, by which time the regulation is obsolete because of subsequent developments in the industry. The same problem affects the CFC. The CFC initially declared TELMEX to be a dominant carrier—a necessary step for COFETEL to adopt pro-competitive regulations—in 1998, but its action was stayed by a series of *amparos*, amendments to its declaration, further *amparos*, and eventually a court decision in 2006 that vacated the CFC's finding because the evidentiary basis for it was now outdated.

Participants in the Mexican telecommunications industry hold very different views about the *amparo* process. Some believe that an *amparo* is too easy to obtain, while others believe that obtaining an *amparo* should be easy if the government fails to offer a reasonable justification for its decisions. Regardless of the general validity of *amparos*, the system as currently practiced makes effective regulation unworkable.

Because the results of COFETEL's regulatory negotiations are secret, proposed regulations are not supported by evidence and arguments, which makes the agency vulnerable to *amparos* as long as the court requires some justification for a decision. Just about every regulation that COFETEL has promulgated has been stayed successfully by either TELMEX or its competitors. Hundreds of *amparos* concerning telecommunications are pending resolution. The result of all these successful *amparos* is confusion and disruption with respect to exactly what is required of each carrier in terms of its legal obligations regarding prices and service.

To solve this problem requires creating a statutory regulator, one with well-defined and transparent procedures and the authority to carry out its mandate. Regulated firms should be permitted to challenge the agency, but an agency decision should not be enjoined if the agency has followed its procedures and written a transparent, comprehensive justification for its decision. Of course, subsequent litigation may reveal an error in the agency's decision, but the most efficient solution to this problem is to enable the firm that experienced an unjustified cost to recover the cost, either through subsequent price increases or from the government.

The 1995 Federal Telecommunications Act lacks clarity regarding several important issues. Because the act is silent about COFETEL, it fails to define the agency's powers in relation to gathering information and places the agency in a weak position to enforce its regulations. In addition, the act is not clear about policy objectives with regard to telephone penetration, price rules, interconnection arrangements, or universal service. For example, the prohibition against cross-subsidies, which implicitly requires that no price should be below long-run incremental cost, is interpreted as applying to the entire bundle of basic services rather than to each separately. As a result, interconnection prices contain a contribution to cover local access costs, thereby subsidizing access through usage charges despite the prohibition against cross-subsidies.

Recommendations for Reform

The preceding review of the regulatory system suggests several changes that would probably improve the performance of the telecommunications sector, namely:

- *Grant COFETEL true independence.* The Federal Telecommunications Act should be amended to make COFETEL a statutory agency with the authority to regulate. Whereas the SCT can be granted the right to participate in COFETEL's decisions, its role should be no different than that of other participants. The

SCT should have the right to submit evidence and arguments in an open regulatory process, to propose regulations, and to comment on submissions by others, but should not have the right to communicate secretly with COFETEL or to overturn COFETEL's decisions. The responsibility for making a decision should belong to COFETEL, and COFETEL's decisions should be reversible only by the courts through judicial review or through new legislation, not by a presidential decree or an intervention by the SCT. In addition, true independence also requires that COFETEL be able to compel the release of information from the carriers it regulates and that its commissioners be appointed to a secure fixed term of several years, removable only for malfeasance (corruption or failure to perform their duties).

- *Require open decision-making processes for regulatory proceedings.* The act should authorize COFETEL to conduct open rule-making proceedings and to make case-by-case decisions. These proceedings should be open to participation by anyone who is affected by them, and all participants should have access to the evidence that is submitted for the purpose of evaluating it.

- *Require that COFETEL explain the legal and information basis for its decisions.* If proceedings are open and COFETEL can compel the production of information, the agency will be able to explain the basis for its decisions, including why it rejected alternative proposals.

- *Focus judicial review on whether decisions have a reasonable basis.* Clear standards for judicial review are useful in shaping how the agency explains and justifies its decisions. The appropriate standard is that COFETEL has a reasonable basis in law and fact for its decisions. That is, a decision should be upheld if a reasonable person can believe that the agency's underlying statutes give it the authority to act and that the evidence and analysis justify the regulation.

- *Grant standing to the CFC on matters related to the competitive effects of COFETEL's decisions.* The CFC is the expert on competition policy and ought to have the responsibility to assist COFETEL in understanding the competitive implications of its regulations. Because the act envisions a competitive industry, among the issues to be resolved in judicial review is whether COFETEL reasonably took into account the effects of its regulations on competition and dealt adequately with the CFC's views.

- *Make concession requirements simpler for competitive entrants.* In a competitive environment, a government agency need not be responsible for dictating carriers' specific investments and business plans. The legal requirements for a concession derive from a belief that both competition and regulation are either not present or are weak. A license need only require that a carrier subject itself to reporting requirements and agree to operate under COFETEL's regulations. In most parts of the industry, licensing should be virtually automatic and could be implemented by creating a standard application form that includes an agreement by the firm to be bound by regulations and to submit information when COFETEL asks it to do so. Only the dominant carriers—TELMEX and TELCEL—should be required to have their investments approved, and this approval should be by COFETEL and only for the purpose of allowing these carriers to recover the costs of these investments in regulated services.

- *Assign the responsibility for periodic assessments of the performance of the telecommunications sector to the SCT.* The SCT ought to be the entity responsible for overseeing the sector's performance and offering a separate opinion about the adequacy of existing policies and laws. The SCT should not have direct responsibility for making decisions about prices, interconnection arrangements, and entry.
- *Clarify national policy on universal service and provide explicit directions to COFETEL about how to implement this policy.* Legislation should define universal service in terms of both the services it entails and the benchmarks that should be used to measure whether progress toward these objectives is adequate. For example, does universal service mean that every residence has a separate, dedicated telephone connection to the public network, or does it mean that shared lines and pay telephones are available in reasonable proximity to every residence?
- *Ensure that once a universal service objective has been adopted it does not interfere with policies to set prices for each service roughly equal to long-run average incremental cost, and eliminate regulatory impediments to investment and competition.* If the government seeks to increase penetration by more than would occur in an environment in which prices reflect cost, the best approach is direct subsidies that are targeted at low-income households and financed either by general taxes or by a competitively neutral tax that falls equally on all telecommunications services and providers. If specific benchmarks are to be adopted, the act should specify them and address exactly how these goals are to be adjusted in the future and how

COFETEL is to achieve them. COFETEL once proposed a universal service fund, created by a tax on services, to be used to subsidize residential service in low-income areas. Whereas this approach is better than cross-subsidization of all residential access service by other services (especially long distance, international, and mobile calling), an attractive alternative is simply to ensure that regulation encourages provision of service at prices equal to the cost of an efficient carrier, which means encouraging competition and avoiding unnecessary costs from regulation itself.

Conclusions

Mexico's telecommunications policy and performance has improved since reform began. The state-owned monopoly carrier was successfully privatized, and before privatization, its performance was substantially improved by increasing its rate of investment and by bringing prices more in line with cost. After an initial period of monopoly, competition was introduced in the late 1990s in long distance, then in mobile telephony, and then in local service, especially fixed wireless service. Meanwhile, the penetration and usage of phone service more than doubled.

Nevertheless, the telecommunications industry has not yet reached its full potential. The incumbent former monopoly is extremely powerful and does not have a particularly impressive investment record, while competitive entrants have enjoyed limited success. Competition is hampered by slow and ineffective regulation, created by limitations to the authority of the primary regulator, COFETEL; by an opaque, secretive, and cumbersome regulatory process; and by an inadequate oversight system in the courts and the political branches of the government.

No doubt, economic growth and TELMEX's profit incentive will continue to increase the penetration of telecommunications, and rapid technical progress will probably cause some reduction in prices. However, this progress is unlikely to propel Mexico to leadership within Latin America in terms of the performance of its telecommunications sector, despite Mexico's natural advantages arising from its proximity to the United States. For Mexico to achieve its full potential in this industry, further reforms of telecommunications regulation are necessary to make it simpler and more focused on promoting competition while controlling the remaining pockets of market power.

Notes

1. A ministerial state-owned enterprise is an entity in which managers are political appointees who serve at the pleasure of elected officials. Many, if not all, positions are regarded as patronage; prices and revenues are treated like taxes; and expenditures are part of the government's budget. In comparison, a corporate state-owned enterprise is one in which the government owns the company, but its revenues and expenditures are not part of the government's budget and its managers are professionals who cannot be removed except for cause and who have both the authority and the responsibility to assure that revenues cover costs.

2. The meaning of "independent corporation" and "independent regulator" are discussed in detail elsewhere in this chapter. The basic idea is that both are sufficiently isolated from elected political leaders that the firm and its regulator can make decisions without the approval of or intervention by the latter. Independence does not mean beyond political control. Rather, it means that political control is exercised through the more open and deliberative processes of legislation and judicial review of decisions for conformance with legislative mandates.

3. Since 1998, TELMEX's operating income as a fraction of revenues has fallen below 30 percent, but it remains among the highest in the world.

4. For a useful application of this concept, see Keefer and Stasavage (2003). In this article, the authors show that as the number of veto players increases, the ability of an independent central bank to control inflation and avert financial crises also increases.

5. A COFETEL (2000) press release announcing a procedure to develop regulations in response to the CFC's finding that TELMEX is a dominant carrier states that federal law requires that the proceedings be closed.

References

Armstrong, Mark, Simon Cowan, and John Vickers. 1994. *Regulatory Reform: Economic Analysis and the British Experience.* Cambridge, MA: Massachusetts Institute of Technology Press.

CIA (Central Intelligence Agency). 2006. *The World Factbook.* Washington, DC: U.S. Government Printing Office. https://www.cia.gov/cia/publications/factbook/index.html.

COFETEL (Comisión Federal de Telecomunicaciones). 2000. "The Procedure to Establish Specific Obligations to TELMEX Due to Its Substantial

Market Power Begins." Press release, COFETEL, Mexico City, March 27 (English translation).

Estache, Antonio, and Martin A. Rossi. 2008. "Regulatory Agencies: Impact on Firm Performance and Social Welfare." Policy Research Working Paper 4509, World Bank, Washington, DC.

Keefer, Philip, and David Stasavage. 2003. "The Limits of Delegation: Veto Players, Central Bank Independence, and the Credibility of Monetary Policy." *American Political Science Review* 97 (August): 407–23.

Kessides, Ioannis. 2004. *Reforming Infrastructure: Privatization, Regulation, and Competition*. Washington, DC: World Bank.

Levy, Brian, and Pablo T. Spiller, eds. 1996. *Regulations, Institutions, and Commitment*. Cambridge, U.K.: Cambridge University Press.

Mariscal, Judith. 2002. *Unfinished Business: Telecommunications Reform in Mexico*. Westport, CT: Praeger Publishing.

McCubbins, Mathew D., Roger G. Noll, and Barry R. Weingast. 1989. "Structure and Process, Politics and Policy: Administrative Arrangements and the Political Control of Agencies." *Virginia Law Review* 75 (2): 431–82.

Noll, Roger G. 2000. "Telecommunications Reform in Developing Countries." In *Economic Policy Reform: The Second Stage*, ed. Anne O. Krueger, 183–242. Chicago: University of Chicago Press.

Noll, Roger G., and Fernando Salas. 1990. "Restructuración y privatización de telefonos de Mexico." Unpublished report for the Government of Mexico, Ministry of Commercial and Industrial Development.

Ramamurti, Rava, ed. 1996. *Privatizing Monopolies: Lessons from the Telecommunications and Transport Sectors in Latin America*. Baltimore, MD: Johns Hopkins University Press.

Wallsten, Scott. 2004. "Privatizing Monopolies in Developing Countries: The Real Effects of Exclusivity Periods in Telecommunications." *Journal of Regulatory Economics* 26 (November): 303–20.

Wellenius, Bjorn, and Peter A. Stern, eds. 1994. *Implementing Reforms in the Telecommunications Sector: Lessons from Experience*. Washington, DC: World Bank.

World Bank. 1995. *Bureaucrats in Business*. New York: Oxford University Press.

11

The Governance of Mexico's Oil Industry

Adrián Lajous

Mexico's oil industry is at a critical juncture: its policies, its strategies, its business plans, and, most important, its governance structure and processes need to be revised. The most pressing challenge, however, is a complete overhaul of the industry's governance. Petróleos Mexicanos (PEMEX) will only succeed in improving its performance and expanding its activities at a sustainable pace, and the country will only be able to take advantage of its oil resources more rationally, if higher-quality institutions are in place.

These objectives can only be achieved by means of pragmatic alternatives that articulate vigorous development of oil and gas markets through more precise and effective state intervention. To accomplish this, Mexico needs to build a new regulatory regime based on a modern legal framework and autonomous, technically competent institutions whose scope ranges from upstream activities to final product markets. Government authorities must regain control of the direction that the oil industry is to follow; the pace of resource extraction; and the social, economic, and environmental impacts of these activities. In addition, they will have to redefine, structure, and

This chapter was written in May 2007. It has not been updated. At the end of November 2008, changes in the governance of the oil industry were passed after a long congressional debate. They do not modify the basic diagnosis that is offered here. These changes will be implemented in the coming months, and more time is needed before they can be adequately appraised.

circumscribe the role of government entities that currently intervene in the sector's operations. They must also accelerate the transition from a monopoly structure to regulated domestic competition and international competition. Potential changes to exclusive state property rights in relation to hydrocarbons and to the state oil company can only be considered after a new regulatory regime is in place and the institutions that promote market development have been consolidated. The process will necessarily be gradual. Its success depends on the adoption of clear objectives and on resolute execution. However, building a basic political consensus is an essential prerequisite for reform of the oil industry.

Structural Continuity

The structural continuity of the Mexican oil industry is the result of a rigid industrial architecture and an important set of binding constraints that have obstructed its modernization. The analysis of recent PEMEX performance, as well as long-term trends, provides the context for the discussion of the potential for change. The conclusions offered are not encouraging.

Industrial Architecture

The architecture of Mexico's oil industry rests on four pillars: exclusive state ownership, de jure state monopoly, extensive vertical integration, and direct administrative control by the federal government. Its origins are inextricably linked to expropriation and to nationalization of the oil industry in 1938. Nationalization responded to the prevailing economic and political circumstances of the time and was preceded by a strong nationalist mandate incorporated into the 1917 constitution. Although oil nationalism is present today in many countries, it originated in Mexico. From the beginning, it was linked to strong government economic intervention and to an organized workers' movement that was subordinated to the state. Later, the import substitution development strategy helped strengthen these three features of the authoritarian corporate state. It was in this context that special treatment was given to the industry, a unique institutional arrangement was established, and distinct forms of control and governance of PEMEX were adopted. These features evolved gradually, were codified in the constitution, and became part of the legal and regulatory frameworks.

State ownership of the oil industry and the limits of its exclusivity are defined in three articles of the constitution and in the bylaws of article 27. The constitution establishes that the nation has sole and direct ownership of all solid, liquid, and gaseous hydrocarbons. No concessions or production-sharing contracts may be granted in relation to these resources. The nation will extract them under the terms established in the relevant bylaws. Petroleum, all other hydrocarbons, and basic petrochemical products are considered strategic areas that only the state can manage by means of state entities, whose ownership and control will be in the hands of the federal government.

The bylaw of article 27 of the constitution establishes that the oil industry will undertake the following activities: exploration, production, refining, transport, storage, distribution, and first-hand sales of petroleum and the products obtained from refining; exploration, extraction, processing, and the first-hand sales of natural gas, as well as the necessary transport and storage prior to processing; and production, transportation, storage, distribution, and sale of oil and gas derivatives that can be used as basic raw materials for industry and are classified as basic petrochemical products. The bylaw of article 27 allows PEMEX to enter into service and public works contracts, although payment must be made in cash and under no circumstance can percentages in the volume or the value of production be paid out, nor can profits be shared. However, this bylaw permits private sector participation in natural gas transportation, storage, and distribution and itemizes only seven products as basic petrochemicals, but it explicitly prohibits any form of production and risk-sharing agreements. This last provision dates back to 1958, while changes to the limits of state intervention in natural gas and petrochemicals were made in the 1990s.

The basic architecture of the oil industry reached its final form in 1970, when existing production and risk-sharing contracts were terminated. The legislative and regulatory history prior to this date had a clear sense of direction: its main objectives were to strengthen the state monopoly and to expand its scope. The 1970s and early 1980s were dominated by the large oil and gas discoveries in southeastern Mexico, and the rapid expansion of productive capacity. The development of these resources was the exclusive responsibility of PEMEX; however, it was strongly supported by engineering, construction, and oil service industries, both domestic and foreign, as well as by international financial institutions. PEMEX was able to maintain its exclusivity given the abundance of low-risk, low-cost resources. It was not until the price collapse of 1986 when possible changes to the industry's structure and private participation in its development were seriously discussed.

The scope of the state monopoly was recently tested, and this may happen again in the near future. In September 2005, President

Vicente Fox sent an ambitious set of initiatives to Congress that proposed opening nonassociated natural gas exploration and production to private investment, as well as transport, storage, and distribution infrastructure for crude oil, oil products, and basic petrochemicals. These initiatives were proposed late in the Fox administration's term, their analytical support was weak, and they were accompanied by a frail lobbying effort. Their intention was basically of a testimonial nature. Although the initiatives required constitutional reform, they generated little interest in Congress, because they were never considered viable.

President Felipe Calderón is highly likely to propose changes to oil industry regulations that would allow private investment in oil industry infrastructure. He will concentrate on modifying the bylaws of article 27, but he will not attempt any constitutional changes, as he does not have the required support in Congress. The current administration needs to act as soon as possible, given the urgent need to maintain and expand the transport, pipeline, and storage infrastructure. Inadequate maintenance, its vulnerability to catastrophic risk, the high costs of supply interruptions, and the logistical problems created by insufficient capacity underline the need to restructure and allocate significant resources for these purposes. The government might also consider opening refining activities to private investment. This, however, requires a constitutional amendment and also assumes the introduction of competition in oil product markets and the establishment of modern economic regulation.

Integrated oil firms perform a series of diverse activities. Exploration and production generate significant economic rents. By contrast, midstream and downstream activities are margin businesses that seek to cover capital costs and achieve a reasonable return, and profits of pipeline networks that constitute a natural monopoly tend to be highly regulated. The complexity of each one of the business lines in their portfolio is further increased by the diversity of their asset management requirements. Vertical integration has been fostered by the long value chains of these firms, as well as by the need to manage the supply and price risks of successive stages that are naturally hedged. Under these conditions, firms try to economize on the transaction costs that they would have to incur in the absence of integration. Given the size of the market, even in countries like Mexico, the optimal scale of processing plants in the oil industry is relatively large. In these circumstances, only regulation and external competition can moderate the market power of large, integrated firms.

The nature and degree of vertical integration in PEMEX are unique in the international oil industry. The diversity and the volume of services that PEMEX provides to itself make it the world's most integrated oil company. Over the years, it extended its activities beyond the scope of the de jure monopoly to areas that, for various reasons, the private sector had not developed. The company was compelled to provide goods and services to guarantee a reliable supply. In other instances, when private companies were able to provide them, PEMEX curtailed their development because of its distrust of market mechanisms. In still others, the industry's monopoly structure prevented the establishment of new suppliers.

Inside the firm, PEMEX managers saw in vertical integration opportunities to grow, reduce supply risks, and improve the terms at which it acquired goods and services. The industrial policy associated with import substitution further promoted vertical integration. Elsewhere, the oil industry moved in the opposite direction, divesting itself of noncore activities and prompting the development of the oil service industry and the growth of engineering and construction firms. By the 1980s, a process that had started two decades previously, acquired greater dynamism. A new cycle of de-integration stimulated technical change and its diffusion, transferring substantive technological functions to the oil service and engineering companies. PEMEX did not participate in this structural transformation, thereby widening and deepening the technological and industrial practice gaps between PEMEX and its competitors.

A good example of excessive integration may be found in well construction, termination, and workover activities. International oil companies do not carry out these activities with their own rigs, except under exceptional circumstances and for specific reasons. In contrast, PEMEX internally manages a drilling organization similar in size to some of the largest drilling companies in the world. Its costs are high, and the technological lag that characterizes its operations has serious consequences for production, well productivity, and field management. This business group's failure to assimilate the technical change that was taking place in the industry during the 1980s and the early 1990s was unfortunate. Another example that affects the industry as a whole involves maintenance. PEMEX's unusual integration pattern is evident in the size and number of workshops in its own production facilities. Oil companies elsewhere delegate these tasks to specialized service providers. Throughout PEMEX, maintenance is costly and ineffective. In addition, PEMEX carries out tasks that large domestic and international firms outsource. This is particularly the case in health services and telecommunications. However, there are other internally supplied services that may be obtained at lower cost in well-developed markets. PEMEX operates a health service for more than 1 million active and retired workers and their families, which employs 11,300 people. It also has 1,700 telecommunications employees. PEMEX personnel also provide a complete range of social services such as schools and daycare centers.

PEMEX's status as a state-owned monopoly, the breadth of its vertical integration, the scale of its operations, and the country's critical need for a secure and reliable supply of its products have encouraged the development of a powerful national workers' union. This pattern is also present in other energy sector firms and in other areas. The Sindicato de Trabajadores Petroleros de la República Mexicana has succeeded in directly appropriating part of the economic rent generated by the oil industry through generous worker compensation and benefits, as well as high levels of overemployment. It has also contributed to the dissipation of economic rent by imposing labor practices that seriously affect PEMEX's operational efficiency.

The federal government, for its part, has relied on direct administrative intervention as its main control mechanism over PEMEX. It has not resorted to economic regulation, as the industry's nationalization internalized the ownership, control, and regulation roles of the industry. This comprehensive framework allowed the use of archaic control instruments that have had negative effects on performance and limited PEMEX's growth. This form of intervention also facilitated the granting of generalized subsidies as part of distribution and industrial development policies, though these were later limited by the requirements of macroeconomic stabilization.

The historical development of Mexico's oil industry and its economic roles, abundant resources, monopoly structure, and governance patterns have isolated it from market forces and secluded PEMEX from the dynamics of a business environment. Under these circumstances, the absence of a comparative perspective that would allow the identification of differences in structure, behavior, and performance with regard to other Mexican firms and to PEMEX's peers should come as no surprise. Comparisons and detailed benchmarking could offer important lessons. So would the sharing of experiences with international firms as well as with state-owned companies in other oil producing and exporting countries. A broader horizon would help to better understand PEMEX and to evaluate alternative governance patterns. It would also contribute to the identification of exceptional factors that effectively determine key aspects of its current industrial structure. The absence of close, regular contact with competitors and the lack of active participation in competitive markets limit PEMEX's industrial experience and business opportunities. Performance and operational gaps are very wide vis-a-vis international comparators. While lags in technology and industrial practices vary by business lines, they are significant in all of them. They are further exacerbated by poor managerial skills. PEMEX has commissioned a series of detailed benchmarking exercises. One, for instance, shows that its Mexican refineries are among the most inefficient in the world.

Industry Performance

Mexico's oil industry continues to be a key strategic sector within a relatively diversified economic structure.[1] For the past 25 years, its contribution to gross domestic product (GDP) has hovered around 6 percent. No other large oil-producing and -exporting developing country has an economy as diversified as that of Mexico. The prominence of the oil industry is assured as it is the source of nearly 90 percent of the primary energy consumed in the country. In addition, it plays a preeminent role in public finances and, to a lesser extent, in the trade balance. Since the 1980s, the oil industry has provided timely and valuable support during the country's recurrent economic and financial crises, though such intervention has not been required during the past 12 years of macroeconomic stability. However, a generalized view prevails that sees the oil industry as a potential lever of economic growth, a key factor of industrial development, and a source of economic sovereignty. Although it continues to be an important sector of the economy, more may be being asked of it than it can possibly deliver given the current structure of the Mexican economy and the prospects of its oil industry.

At various times in the 20th century, Mexico has been one of the largest oil producers in the world. In 2004, production peaked at 3.8 million barrels per day, making it the fifth-largest oil producer. The history of Mexico's oil industry—more than 100 years—has been marked by production and investment cycles led by the discovery and development of giant and supergiant oil fields located offshore and on the coastal plains of the Gulf of Mexico. Nevertheless, production has begun to decline, and in the absence of significant discoveries, this decline will accelerate toward the end of this decade. This trend is determined mainly by the path followed by the Cantarell field, which, at its peak, accounted for 62 percent of total production. By 2010, the cumulative fall in total production is expected to be greater than half a million barrels per day. Parallel to this, investment requirements are growing rapidly, given the increasing cost of developing reserves of producing assets and of exploration in frontier areas. In this context, the fall in proven reserves gains relevance. In 2003–05, the reserve replacement ratio was only 30 percent, and in 2006 the reserves-to-production ratio fell below the 10-year threshold. The maturity of the oil and gas reserve endowment—three-fourths of the original proven reserves have been produced—forces PEMEX to develop new exploration and production strategies. Natural gas provides a successful example of what can be achieved. Production has been increasing, and in the second quarter of 2007 it exceeded 6 billion cubic feet per day given the expansion of nonassociated gas extraction. Although this is a substantial volume, Mexico is not one of the world's large producers. Its entire production goes to satisfy domestic requirements, as the country is a net importer of natural gas.

In 2006, Mexico exported 1.8 million barrels per day of crude oil, worth US$35 billion, of which more than 80 percent went to the United States. Mexican crude oil imports to the United States were exceeded only by those from Canada, with Saudi Arabia coming in third place. PEMEX concentrated its sales on U.S. Gulf coast refineries that have the capacity process heavy crude oils, such as Maya. This explains why Mexico was able to provide more than 15 percent of total U.S. crude oil imports.

The expansion of crude oil exports took place in the context of a deep structural change in the external sector of the Mexican economy. The contribution of oil exports to the balance of trade fell dramatically, despite recent volumetric and price increases. Their share decreased from 11 percent of GDP in 1983 to 5 percent in 2006. During this period, nonoil exports, mainly from manufacturing, increased from 5 percent to 15 percent of GDP. It is noteworthy that oil exports currently represent 25 percent of total merchandise exports, whereas in 1982 they accounted for 75 percent. However, there is growing concern regarding the increase in oil product and natural gas imports. In 2006, their value was US$11 billion, representing 29 percent of total oil exports.

The contribution of the oil industry to public finances has evolved quite differently. In 2006, PEMEX paid the Treasury US$54 billion in taxes and royalties. This figure is equivalent to 35 percent of the federal government's total budgetary revenues. PEMEX's contribution was substantially greater than the total corporate income tax paid by all other firms in Mexico. That same year, PEMEX paid the federal government 2.2 times more in taxes and royalties than the total income tax paid by every individual and corporation receiving nonwage income. Such reliance on oil revenues is explained by Mexico's exceptionally low tax burden and the exceedingly high—and unsustainable—tax rate imposed on the oil industry.

PEMEX is Mexico's largest firm and is the largest industrial company in Latin America. In 2006, its sales reached US$98 billion and its assets were valued at US$111 billion. The latter figure does not include the value of underground hydrocarbon reserves. Nevertheless, it faces serious financial problems because of excessive tax liabilities. Perceptions of crisis and feelings of frustration permeate the oil industry. Despite its abundant hydrocarbon reserves, Mexico cannot satisfy its own fuel requirements. The current operating conditions of the transport and storage infrastructure and its multiple bottlenecks pose serious supply risks. Secular underinvestment in refining and midstream facilities contrasts sharply with the amount of resources allocated to the development of oil and gas fields. However, upstream investments are not producing the expected results and exploration expenditures are clearly insufficient. This is reflected in the continuous decrease in proven hydrocarbon reserves. Nevertheless, investment in the oil industry is not only restricted by financial factors. At the current level of capital expenditures, the binding constraints are of an institutional nature. Government control mechanisms have a negative effect on the design, planning, and execution of investment projects. Also the shortage of high-level technical personnel and experienced managers restricts PEMEX's capacity to absorb capital efficiently. From a macroeconomic perspective, concerns are growing about the dependence of public finances on the flow of oil revenues, as well as the lack of appropriate institutional mechanisms that could help transform the hydrocarbon endowment into reproducible wealth.

Over the past 25 years, oil price shocks have triggered, but were not the cause of, the economic and financial crises Mexico has faced. Foreign exchange flows generated by oil exports have, at times, contributed to the appreciation of the real exchange rate, thereby affecting the international competitiveness of other sectors. In a more basic sense, the higher economic growth and welfare levels that large oil discoveries promised did not materialize. On the contrary, these discoveries raised many of the issues associated with the resource curse syndrome. Perhaps, the most relevant problem posed by large oil revenue flows was that they allowed policy makers to defer key structural reforms that were required to sustain long-term growth. The recurrent failure to implement tax reform and increase Mexico's tax burden to reasonable levels was emblematic of this state of affairs. From this perspective, it must be recognized that the efficient use of hydrocarbon resources depends, in the last instance, on the quality of the institutions that promote economic development. Unfortunately, some of these institutions were debilitated by the magnitude, the pattern, and the nature of oil revenue flows.

Continuity and Constraints

During the past 35 years, Mexico's oil industry has been characterized by the dynamism of its growth and the continuity of its governance structures and processes. Except for a few limited adjustments to the legal framework of this industry, no major changes have been made since 1958, when the state oil monopoly was finally configured. A complex web of restrictions has effectively impeded the modernization of the Mexican oil industry. Its persistence limits the possibility of change and adds complexity to the identification of acceptable solutions to well-known problems. These restrictions reflect a long-standing political belief system, traditional interpretations of specific historical experiences, weak institutions, and vested interests. They prevent granting greater flexibility to a rigid institutional structure and reduce its capacity to adjust to changing circumstances. Given the importance of the industry, a better understanding of the origins and the nature of these constraints is required. To relax them, clear priorities must be set and sequences must be established.

Successive administrations have failed to inform and educate public opinion on the nature of these restrictions, the alternative modes of organization of the oil industry, and the costs associated with rigid governance. They have also been unable to propose safeguards that would reduce some of the understandable concerns and fears regarding change and would protect national interests. A necessary first step is to improve the quality of public discussion on these matters. The government must put forward better and more sophisticated arguments to explain and justify the change that it desires and offer a clear sense of direction. Acknowledging that some of the solutions that in the past promoted the expansion of the industry are now dysfunctional and constitute an obstacle to its development would be convenient. The government must also address the economic and technological changes that make institutional innovation imperative. Information available in the media is insufficient and biased. This is reflected in public opinion polls that reveal contradictory attitudes and growing political polarization. Political parties and their representatives in Congress can make an important contribution: they can raise the quality of the debate about oil policy issues and protect it from partisan political passions. This is needed if oil industry reform is to move forward.

Strategic initiatives involve complex technical preparation, intense political bargaining, and a considerable legislative load; however, the government can do much on its own. It must begin by developing consistent, comprehensive, and detailed proposals on which the necessary consensus could be built. This exercise would force the government to specify changes that it believes are necessary more precisely and to explore potential areas of agreement with different interest groups. Initial proposals can later be adjusted and improved, their justification can be enriched by debate, and basic disagreements can be identified. Explicit proposals could also help moderate the deep distrust that prevails among political groups regarding all energy policy initiatives. The lack of confidence among political actors is the main obstacle to reforming an oil industry that is in crisis.

Dynamics of Change

Institutional transformation is usually undertaken in response to exceptional challenges or to external shocks. It may also be the outcome of fundamental change in the international environment. Relevant examples can be found in the oil industries of Argentina, the Russian Federation, and Spain. Argentina and Russia both radically restructured their state-owned oil companies, as well as the oil industry as a whole, in response to institutional collapse, though Russia had to deal with a more extensive systemic collapse. Spain, however, responding to the challenge posed by its entry into the European Economic Community, reorganized its state-owned oil and gas assets, was able to form an integrated oil company, and launched a well-planned process of liberalization and privatization that was concluded more than a decade later. From this perspective, a better understanding is needed of the factors that have prevented Mexico from transforming and modernizing PEMEX and opening its state oil monopoly to greater competition. Identifying possible events and issues that might unleash basic change in Mexico's oil industry is also necessary, along with better explanations of its structural continuity and of the possible triggers of change.

Notwithstanding its significant performance gaps, PEMEX is far from experiencing institutional collapse. It is one of the world's four largest oil producing companies. In 2006, it produced 3.5 million barrels per day of hydrocarbon liquids and its crude oil exports increased to US$35 billion. PEMEX is an extraordinary cash generating machine. In that same year, its earnings before interest, taxes, depreciation, and amortization exceeded US$72 billion. This flow was only second to Exxon's, but 24 percent higher than that of Royal Dutch Shell and 60 percent larger than that of BP. In recent years, Mexico's confiscatory oil tax regime systematically extracted more than 110 percent of PEMEX profits before taxes, decapitalizing the company. Nevertheless, it succeeded in investing US$13.8 billion in 2006 and proposed a capital expenditure budget of US$14.5 billion for 2007. Under these circumstances, it is not surprising that PEMEX's net debt rose to US$35 billion by late 2006, contrasting with the high liquidity accumulated in recent years by major international oil companies. PEMEX has been a loyal financial agent of the Mexican state, increasing its debt not only to finance its own capital expenses, but also to pay royalties and taxes.

The growing concern about the security of supply of oil and gas in consuming countries poses important dilemmas for exporting countries. The increasing dependence on oil imports from the Persian Gulf concentrates the attention of U.S. foreign policy. To the extent that Mexican oil exports are declining and that this trend is attributed to current institutional arrangements, Mexico may face greater pressures to change the legal and constitutional restrictions that exclude private investment in this sector. In addition, the uncertainty that prevails in the República Boliviariana de Venezuela will focus U.S. interest on Mexico. U.S. Gulf coast refiners are worried by the reduction in the availability of heavy and extra-heavy crude oils, given that some of their capital-intensive processing units were specifically designed to run Maya crude or close surrogates.

The Mexican oil industry is at a crossroads. The expansion phase of the production cycle that began in 1996 is now over. The last 20 years have witnessed few significant discoveries, and none of these were in the giant class. Proven hydrocarbon reserves have declined rapidly in the last 10 years and the reserve replacement ratio is particularly low. The costs of finding and developing reserves are higher, on average, than those reported by large international oil companies. Lifting costs and the capital intensity of production have increased substantially. Expanding the exploration frontier to high-risk structures in deep and ultra-deep waters in the Gulf of Mexico is going to be costly, and assessing and realizing their potential will take many years. For now, Mexico has few strategic options available that can address these trends.

Coming to terms with this critical situation has not been easy or timely, and the authorities do not fully grasp the implications of managing a mature reserve endowment. The manner in which key actors in industry and the government manage these challenges is critically important. They can remain hostages of the illusion of abundance and of a false optimism that is based on questionable assumptions, but under current circumstances, the recurrent denial of new realities entails serious risks. PEMEX will have to channel additional capital expenditures to oil and gas exploration and production. It needs to urgently allocate more resources to exploration and reserve replacement, while at the same time protecting current production levels. It will have to do so at a time when it must also invest significant funds in refining and in infrastructure maintenance.

Mexico's growing reliance on natural gas, liquefied petroleum gas, and gasoline imports, as well as the short life expectancy of its proven oil and gas reserves, pose complex energy security issues. Moreover, chronic underinvestment in refineries and infrastructure, particularly pipelines and terminals, increases costs and affects supply reliability. Aging facilities and deficient maintenance practices are a source of increasing safety and security concerns. A greater availability of investment resources is a necessary, but insufficient, condition for coping successfully with these challenges. Major changes within PEMEX are needed to increase its capacity to effectively execute larger capital expenditure budgets.

Absent other factors, in a context of favorable international oil prices and a gradual decline in production, the Mexican oil industry could find itself in a manageable situation, despite its poor performance. It could remain trapped in a low level equilibrium, further lagging behind international oil industry standards. A history of missed opportunities would continue its course. Minor secondary adjustments would allow deferral of the changes in governance that PEMEX requires. The most important stakeholders—the federal and state governments, consumer groups, the trade union, PEMEX management, and local communities in producing areas—derive considerable advantages from the status quo. This helps explain PEMEX's strength and stability. None of the stakeholders is fully satisfied with the existing order of things, but they are all aware of the main risks that change entails. Breaking the inertia of these interests is one of the major challenges the Mexican state faces.

The risks of a significant fall in oil prices, a higher than expected decline rate of oil production, and a substantial increase in PEMEX's capital requirements add to the vulnerability of public finances and would put the financial health of this state company in jeopardy, especially in a situation in which both prices and volumes fall simultaneously. Under these conditions, financing PEMEX's investment programs becomes more difficult. Recent company estimates of annual capital requirements of US$22 billion are a somewhat surprising. This figure exceeds the capital expenditures of Exxon, the largest international oil company, which invested less than US$20 billion in 2006. The lack of significant oil discoveries, the delays in the development of the Chicontepec fields in Veracruz, the low reserve replacement ratios, and a continuing fall in the reserve to production ratio give rise to a scenario that could eventually trigger impulsive reactions to long-standing problems and overdue solutions. The strength of these endogenous factors should not be underestimated nor should their fiscal implications be overlooked. To cope with these contingencies the government would have to implement tax reform that would allow it to increase nonoil revenues. It would also have to restructure the oil industry.

Role of the State

PEMEX's disappointing performance can be directly linked to its governance structure and processes. The main problem that it currently faces, as well as its central challenge, has to do with the industry's architecture. Its redesign has high priority. Gaps in operating efficiency, inadequate allocation of resources, deficient project execution, implicit price subsidies, trade union privileges, and noncompetitive compensation patterns contribute to the dissipation and capture of economic rent by stakeholders. The use of this rent to finance current government expenditures is symptomatic of fundamental flaws in public policy. The implied costs gain relevance as production and reserves decline and PEMEX's financial situation deteriorates.

The state performs four basic functions with regard to the governance of the oil industry: the design and implementation of energy policy, the regulation of the industry and its markets, the exercise of property rights over hydrocarbon resources, and management of state-owned companies in the energy sector. Regulation includes standards and procedures that apply generally to public sector and private firms as well as those that are specific to the oil industry. It refers both to the regulatory framework and to regulatory institutions. The interactions between the four functions are multiple and should be mutually reinforcing. This is why consistency is essential. The exceptionalism of the Mexican oil industry poses complex challenges in terms of the design of sectoral policies and in relation to their congruence with the rest of the economy. Current conditions require an overhaul of the institutions that govern the oil industry and of the organizations and rules that control its resources.

Energy Policy

The federal government is responsible for designing and implementing energy policy. While economic policy focuses on the nature and forms of government intervention that will improve economic performance, energy policy is an important part of economic policy that influences the exploration, production, distribution, and consumption of energy. Its importance in Mexico is enhanced by the size of the hydrocarbon resource endowment, the level of current production, and the growing consumption of energy inputs. The state plays a crucial role in this sector: almost all primary energy is produced by state-owned enterprises, as well as most of its transformation into secondary energy products. In these circumstances, the direction, pace, and coordination of the investment decisions of these firms; the design of oil product price structures and electricity tariffs; the contribution of the oil industry to public finances; and the balance of trade have been central issues of energy policy for the last 30 years.

Now, however, energy policy will have to address new areas such as the nature of competition that should prevail in the energy sector, the design and implementation of price mechanisms, the nature of regulation in energy markets, the security and reliability of supply, and the reform of the oil tax regime. Energy policy is necessarily long-term, given that the sector is characterized by its capital intensity, the long gestation and execution periods of its investment projects, and the long life cycle of the capital stocks that determine energy consumption patterns. Its implementation requires strong institutions that can develop wide scope, long-term perspectives and can assume responsibility for implementing needed reforms.

The lack of a comprehensive energy policy has created a vacuum that limits the government's ability to formulate viable strategies and consistent proposals. The institutional weakness of the Ministry of Energy is tangible. Many other public entities share responsibility for and authority with regard to the management of state-owned energy companies, but sectoral regulatory bodies have limited independence. Obsolete and unenforceable regulations rule many areas. The Ministry of Energy does not have career personnel with the specialized necessary knowledge and experience, and its high turnover renders training efforts ineffective. The instability of senior and midlevel staff disrupts key tasks that require a minimum of continuity. From 1983 to 2006 the minister of energy averaged 2.3 years in office. During the Fox administration four ministers of energy were appointed. The basic weakness that this pattern reveals is that energy policy decisions are, in practice, taken in other ministries or in the state-owned companies. It also points to the meager autonomy of the state with respect to private interests, given the apparent understanding the Fox administration reached with powerful industrial groups. It is no coincidence that three of the four ministers that served during this period were directly linked to business interests from Monterrey, the home of many energy-intensive industries.

As in other countries, the pertinence of having a sectoral ministry responsible for energy matters has been called into question. The ministry's weakness with respect to the large state-owned companies and to other ministries that effectively control key energy policy instruments is regularly stressed by various analysts of Mexico's energy industry, as is its limited capacity to harmonize the objectives and interests of diverse public- and private-sector actors. Asymmetry of information and of resources shapes the relationship between the Ministry of Energy, regulatory bodies, and state enterprises. Granting managerial autonomy to these state enterprises and broadening the scope and independence of regulatory bodies is also perceived as a loss of some of the traditional attributes that have been formally assigned to this ministry. Finally, the fiscal authorities have, in practice, assumed some of the main responsibilities with regard to the exercise of property rights of hydrocarbon resources. From this perspective, the design and implementation of energy policy is seen as a residual function that hardly justifies the existence of a specific ministry.

This line of argument has a static bias that stresses unsatisfactory aspects of the status quo and projects them into the future. Independently of the long-term structure of the energy sector and the specific forms of governance, maintaining a Ministry of Energy that would offer strong leadership in the articulation and adoption of an ambitious structural change agenda and in the institutional development of the energy sector is convenient. It is precisely during the transition to new forms of governance that strong authorities are needed. The ministry must offer a precise diagnosis of key issues and problems and a clear sense of direction and must overcome the multiple obstacles that a complex transformative process would face. Under the current circumstances, eliminating the Ministry of Energy would send a negative signal: it would, in effect, announce a decision to postpone energy reform once again.

Regulation

Mexico's oil industry is both overregulated and badly regulated and operates in a set of regulatory vacuums, some of which PEMEX has filled, merging the tasks of the operator with others that correspond to the authorities. Responsible government agencies do not have the technical and financial resources to perform critical regulatory functions. This has given additional powers to the operating company, fostering self-regulation. Notwithstanding this situation, PEMEX is subject to rules that are similar to those followed by government agencies. This reduces its operational flexibility, weakens its ability to compete, and prevents it from taking advantage of business opportunities. The evolution of the oil industry within a closed state monopoly has not allowed the development of market institutions or of a regulatory framework and the professional talent that are now needed to design, build, and manage a modern regime congruent with the current overall business environment. This monopoly structure has protected PEMEX from the market discipline required to improve operational discipline.

The centralized administrative regulation of PEMEX constitutes an insurmountable obstacle to its performance as a business concern. Laws relating to, among other things, parastatal agencies; administrative responsibilities of civil servants; procurement, leasing, and services; and public works are drowning PEMEX in a bureaucratic morass. By the same token, annual and quarterly line-by-line government budget controls destroy economic value. The manner in which Mexico's state-owned companies are integrated in the country's public finances is unique in the Organisation for Economic Co-operation and Development. It focuses the attention of PEMEX's executives on controlling expenditure to the detriment of maximizing economic value. Primary financial surpluses are not used consistently as a control variable. Extremely short-term financial targets, often quarterly, affect operating programs and investment projects with long planning and execution horizons. A number of measures that have given PEMEX greater flexibility—off balance sheet financing and multi-annual investment programs—have been useful, but costly; do not appear to be sustainable; and offer only limited options for large-scale, high-risk, complex projects. The logic of this regulatory framework privileges the control of processes in relation to a discipline based on economic results. These controls are determined by tradition and by the needs of the government and pay little attention to the requirements of a business entity.

The control, oversight, and audit functions carried out by the Ministry of Public Administration have done little to eradicate endemic irregular practices in the oil industry and to prevent and penalize cases of blatant corruption. Public sector evaluations and audits have done little to improve PEMEX's corporate performance. The excessive formality of procedures adds complexity to decision making, delays execution, is costly, and implies significant personal risks—administrative, legal, and reputational—for PEMEX executives and midlevel management. These conditions have contributed to the development of a corporate culture that is averse to risk, innovation, and entrepreneurship. Decision-making processes are time-consuming and are frequently paralyzed. PEMEX executives and government officials express a well-founded concern with respect to multiple controls, which do not actually constitute effective control systems. Managers allocate a great deal of their time to protecting themselves from personal risks associated with their own performance. This behavior distorts corporate priorities and fosters bias against projects characterized by greater administrative risks, irrespective of their economic merit.

Excessive legal and regulatory formalism also constitutes a barrier to entry for new suppliers of goods and services, as they have to

invest heavily in acquiring the know-how of bid formulation, because
they must comply literally with detailed rules that are unusual in the
international oil industry. The existing regulatory framework intro-
duces contractual rigidities that tend to increase the costs and reduce
the benefits of large-scale projects.

The liberalization of trade and investment that has taken place in
Mexico has not had a tangible, direct effect on the oil industry.
Little progress has been made in the transition from the current
monopoly structure to one of regulated domestic competition and
international competition, and implicit subsidies that affect the
integrity of pricing structures have re-emerged. The 1993 restructuring of PEMEX into four major operating companies, each with its
own profit-and-loss statements, permitted better assessment of their
respective business lines. Given the volume of product flows between
the subsidiaries, a transfer price system based on opportunity costs
was developed. However, price signals by themselves were unable to
establish the desired level of economic discipline within PEMEX,
given that performance measurement and accountability have not
been as rigorous as they should have been, nor have their consequences been duly taken into account. Greater effective competition,
even the risk of competition, would introduce a greater sense of
urgency in PEMEX with respect to its cost management, its competitive position and its business performance.

Mexico's experience with natural gas illustrates some of the principal obstacles faced by market regulation. In 1995, a new regulatory framework for the development of gas markets was established
and the mission and scope of the Comisión Reguladora de Energía
(CRE) was broadened. During the Fox administration, however,
multiple efforts were made to dismantle the regulated price system.
First-hand sales regulation prevents PEMEX from intervening in the
determination of prices and limits the government's discretionary
power through explicit and transparent pricing rules. The basic principle was straightforward: domestic prices of natural gas should
fully reflect opportunity costs in an open economy. In January 2001,
the minister of energy undercut the CRE, arbitrarily fixing the price
of natural gas for a period of three years. Later, the minister suspended the regulated price regime again, for six more months. These
decisions demonstrated the government's lack of commitment to the
regulatory framework and to the regulatory agency. They also recognized the power of interest groups that had captured both the CRE
and the Ministry of Energy.

Once the regulated price mechanism had been reestablished, the
CRE refused to carry out the relevant adjustments made necessary
by the changes in the natural gas demand-and-supply balance.

Regulated price adjustments were partial, unduly delayed, and not always consistent, jeopardizing the integrity of the price formation system. The result was a growing gap between regulated prices and opportunity costs. This lack of flexibility blocked the introduction of competition in the domestic gas market that direct imports by private parties would have brought about; however, maintaining domestic prices below import prices prevented this possibility. The government decided to control prices below market levels and the CRE meekly accepted this priority. Both had mistakenly identified PEMEX as the main obstacle to market liberalization and had not recognized that the regulatory price regime was the only protection it had against implicit price subsidies granted by the government. The CRE's behavior was conditioned by the asymmetry of information and resources in the relationship between the regulator and PEMEX. The lack of commitment to the regulatory regime, the limited independence of the regulator, and the regulator's scarce resources and instruments resulted in a loss of credibility. The government missed the opportunity to introduce competition in the natural gas market offered by growing imports.

Little progress was made with regard to regulating the liquefied petroleum gas market. Attempts to restructure automotive fuels markets have been limited, contradictory, and untimely, and little attention was paid to liquid industrial fuels. Misaligned relative prices have promoted the development of black markets, and secondary markets for fuels illegally taken from PEMEX have appeared. This partial loss of control in the supply of automotive fuels is a source of growing concern.

The experience acquired since the 1990s offers multiple lessons regarding the difficulties in designing and implementing modern regulatory regimes and the development of independent regulatory institutions. It has also shown the limits of their effectiveness, given a legal tradition and practices that were not fully compatible with the objectives and processes of contemporary economic regulation. The abusive recourse to the *amparo* (a legal stay of action) has repeatedly suspended administrative decisions. The privatization of telecommunications and commercial banking in the 1990s demonstrated the risks and long-term costs implied by restructuring key industries without previously establishing the appropriate regulatory frameworks and institutions. Unfortunately, the experience of other sectoral regulators—the Comisión Federal de Telecomunicaciones, the Comisión Nacional del Agua, the Comisión Nacional Bancaria y de Valores, and the Comisión Federal de Competencia—do not offer much optimism regarding the prospects of achieving timely and effective regulatory improvements in the energy sector.

Mexico needs to increase the effectiveness of the economic intervention of the state. In the oil industry, it must substitute and complement the direct intervention through state-owned companies and government agencies with indirect instruments offered by economic regulation. It is not a question of reducing the scope of state intervention, but of strengthening and expanding it through the use of market mechanisms. In modern economies, regulation has become the main form of state intervention. The rules and standards that are adopted, as well as monitoring and compliance, affect and guide the behavior of economic agents. The regulatory framework restricts individual and collective action, but also fosters it through more precise incentives. It complements other government instruments, such as fiscal policy and statuary disclosure and transparency obligations.

The institutional crisis the energy sector faces can only be resolved by tackling this regulatory challenge. The government must improve the operation of hydrocarbon markets and contribute to their development. It will have to redefine, reorder, and limit the role of government agencies that currently intervene in them. The Ministry of Energy should lead this effort. The introduction of competition in the Mexican oil industry is a particularly complex task. Its starting point is a legal monopoly that has been in place for many decades. Its scope and depth has few precedents outside the formerly socialist economies. The sector's monopoly structure fully conditions production, transportation, distribution, and marketing. For this reason the industry's architecture must be fundamentally modified, an undertaking that transcends the scope of conventional regulatory reform. Under these circumstances, state intervention cannot limit itself to the regulation of existing markets, but must be extended to creating new markets and promoting the establishment of new economic agents. In contrast with other more developed countries, the main challenge for Mexico is not deregulation, but the design of a new regulatory regime and the construction of modern regulatory institutions.

The strengthening of indirect, reliable, and predictable mechanisms of state intervention will allow the introduction of competition in final product markets. The emergence of private agents in a market where a dominant state-oil company prevails is made possible by regulated competition. To achieve this, the scope of the CRE must be expanded, it should be given greater independence, and its technical competence should be improved. Developing rules and institutions that will regulate the oil industry will not be an easy task. Regulation requires strong government commitment. The basic objective is gradual transition from monopoly to a regime of regulated competition without privatizing core assets currently owned by PEMEX. The design of a mechanism that will regulate the formation of oil product prices is a central aspect of market liberalization. In Mexico's open economy, competition will not develop without prices that reflect the costs of alternative supplies from relevant external markets. If subsidies persist, they must be explicit and granted directly by the government, not by PEMEX. A regulated price system provides signals to consumers and potential investors so that they can make rational use of scarce oil products and perform the economic calculations required by decisions on investments in long-lasting assets.

No single path from monopoly to regulated competition is available. The transition from one market structure to the other will be determined by the initial conditions, the institutional constraints that restrict potential options, the goals that are set, and the timing of the process. The costs and benefits of alternative strategies must be assessed. The sequence that is selected needs to be sufficiently flexible to accommodate successive adjustments. Unfortunately, a precise mapping of this transition is not available. Public-sector agencies must begin their planning exercises as soon as possible. They must be aware, however, that the fruits of regulatory reform will only be realized in the medium and long term.

Hydrocarbon Ownership

The government has transferred the management of the oil and gas resources for which it is responsible to PEMEX. PEMEX, in turn, has not been able to fully exercise the policy prerogatives that it was granted. In this field, as in others, the state oil company is a self-regulated monopoly. However, budgetary restrictions imposed by the government have limited, indirectly and implicitly, core aspects of its resource management responsibilities. Although PEMEX is potentially a powerful instrument of the state, in practice it has given insufficient attention to central oil policy functions that were delegated to it by the government. This can also be explained by the complexity of resource management, a function that is subject to wide technical, economic, and social considerations, as well as to difficult choices under conditions of uncertainty and risk. Notwithstanding this state of affairs, resource management must also be recognized as a serious case of public policy failure.

The hydrocarbon endowment should be efficiently exploited for the benefit of all Mexicans of current and future generations. To this end, it is necessary to define the directions that this extractive industry should take and the rate at which the resources may be produced and to manage the impact of its activities. This must be done taking into account both market considerations and energy security objectives. An unavoidable function of government is the definition of the terms and conditions of access to subsoil resources. It must also determine the specific tax regime that will apply to upstream activities, as well as their regulatory framework. The regulatory agency must monitor, supervise, and enforce compliance with the terms of access, including the safety of facilities and working conditions, and control discharges and emissions.

Given secular government budget deficits, one of its main objectives has been maximizing oil revenues. The oil tax regime consists of simple rules relating to the distribution of cash flows between PEMEX and the government. Little consideration has been given to the long-run effects of these rules on the efficient generation and allocation of financial resources. Also the perverse incentives of the current tax regime with respect to the management of hydrocarbon resources have not been recognized. The federal government does not collect royalties as payment for the exclusive access to subsoil oil and gas reserves. Rather, its revenues are derived from the revenues obtained from the sale of crude oil, natural gas, and oil products. As hydrocarbons are not valued in the ground, appraising the performance of upstream activities is difficult. The magnitude of economic rent that is generated by these resources conceals the inefficiency of operational and investment activities in exploration and production. This is been well documented in benchmarking exercises commissioned by PEMEX. The extraordinary wealth of the large hydrocarbon discoveries of the 1970s and early 1980s helped sustain this state of affairs for more than three decades.

Fiscal imperatives have been the dominant force in shaping oil policy. Since 1992, PEMEX has paid taxes and royalties equivalent to 62 percent of its gross revenues and more than 110 percent of its gross earnings. The result of this policy has been the decapitalization of this state-owned company. Recent adjustments in the oil tax regime were insufficient and untimely, leaving this regime far from being competitive. They have, nevertheless, provided some relief. So has the government's decision to repay implicit price subsidies on sales of gasoline and diesel that PEMEX had been asked to absorb. However, more basic change to and modernization of the oil tax regime is impossible without a wide-reaching tax reform that would increase the tax burden to more reasonable levels.

In 2006, Mexico's nonoil tax burden was 10.2 percent, one of the lowest in Latin America, a region that is not known for collecting taxes effectively. Total federal revenues reached the equivalent of 17 percent of GDP when oil tax revenues are included. What is equally surprising is the relative stability of this share over the past 25 years. Also the share of oil tax revenues in total public sector revenues—38 percent in 2006—has moved within a narrow range, despite considerable international oil price fluctuations. In countries with a state-owned oil company, financial weakness of the state is normally associated with a financially weak state-owned oil company. In the case of PEMEX, its capacity to generate large cash flows and pay substantial taxes and royalties reflects low production costs, a real gift of nature.

PEMEX's new tax regime is far from competitive. Based on the standardized measure of the discounted future net cash flows related to proven oil and gas reserves, a value can be given to the subsoil production rights held by this company. This estimate applies criteria established by the U.S. Securities and Exchange Commission that are highly restrictive. In the Mexican case, the proven reserves considered by the U.S. Securities and Exchange Commission are based on particularly conservative estimates of recoverable volumes of oil and gas. However, these standardized estimates were designed to permit consistent comparisons. The resulting figure for 2005 establishes a value of US$3.14 per barrel of oil equivalent for PEMEX's in-the-ground reserves. This is an extremely low number in comparison with estimates for the major international oil companies. For instance, the estimate for Exxon is slightly above US$10, and for Shell it is US$15 per barrel of oil equivalent. The atypical PEMEX figure results from extraordinary high tax and royalty rates paid by PEMEX Exploration and Production. Above all, it reveals the excessive rates of the new oil tax regime.

The statutes that regulate exploration and production activities date back to 1974, when the rich southeast basins were discovered. These regulations are based on the 1958 bylaw of article 27 of the constitution, which sets forth conditions for granting PEMEX permission to carry out exploration and production activities and to construct and operate the relevant facilities. Such permission can only be granted to PEMEX. In 297 articles, the regulatory statute details the extensive information requirements regarding exploration, drilling, and production and abandonment of wells and the transport and storage of primary hydrocarbons. It includes technical specifications of facilities that operations must comply with, including land use.

The regulatory statute reflects the technologies and operating practices of the time in which it was drafted and has not been updated to incorporate the technological change that the international oil industry has experienced since that time or the evolution of regulation in many countries. In addition, this statute does not cover many topics that are commonly dealt with by modern oil industry regulations. The department responsible for regulating exploration and production in the Ministry of Energy has limited technical resources, which prevents it from carrying out effective monitoring and inspection tasks. Knowing if it has rejected an application or revoked an authorization would be interesting. With the disclosure of information that is scarcely used by the Ministry of Energy, PEMEX simulates compliance with its formal obligations and the ministry simulates enforcing the regulatory statute. This situation may have persisted since it first came into effect. Current regulatory activities contribute little to the efficient development of hydrocarbon resources and even less to fulfilling the fiduciary obligations of the authorities.

Responsibility for safety and environmental issues is dispersed among various government departments, which do not have the technical and financial resources that are needed to carry out their regulatory obligations. With respect to environmental matters, the statutes have not assimilated current legal and regulatory requirements.

Even if PEMEX continues to be the only operator, changing upstream regulations and reinforcing the regulatory authority have high priority. In addition, if the government intends to open exploration and production to private investment, it must first demonstrate that it is capable of regulating the state-owned oil company and has the ability to give similar treatment to all companies, public and private. Inevitably, it will have to show credible capacity to manage the country's oil resources in a manner that focuses on the costs and benefits of exploration and production and to manage the use of infrastructure. Achieving such credibility demands time and consistent performance.

PEMEX has advanced in the development of its reserve management system and has begun to improve its estimates of the country's resource potential. In the second half of the 1990s, PEMEX carried out new estimates of proven, probable, and possible oil and gas reserves based on internationally accepted criteria. These estimates were audited by specialized international engineering firms and detailed annual reports have been published. The transparency that they manifest is commendable. Over time, reserve quantification has continually improved and conservative criteria have added certainty to the process. The reserve management system is an essential exploration and development tool. Also the perspective that is given by good potential resource estimates is a critical element in designing mid- and long-term exploration strategies. They are particularly important as proven reserves decline and concerns regarding their adequacy increase. In these circumstances, a better understanding of the magnitude of unproven reserves and rigorous studies that improve the quality of resource estimates are valuable. The time and effort invested in these tasks can have important results. Until recently, their usefulness was underestimated, and additional funds should be allocated to them.

As the reserves to production ratio has fallen to less than 10 years, it is understandable that long-term security of supply concerns have intensified. Discussions with respect to the adequacy of reserves needed to sustain current levels of production and guarantee foreseeable domestic consumption for a reasonable period have gained relevance; these discussions have arisen at a time when more than half of production is exported. Precautionary motives advise giving priority to future domestic supply over current export levels. Recently, unease in Congress led it to assume responsibility for determining export levels. Instead of trying to fix levels at a specific point in time, Congress should develop criteria and decision rules that can help regulate and institutionalize this obligation. Regulating the intertemporal distribution of production while reserve endowments change is no easy task, and protecting the distribution of production from short-term political considerations and pressures will be difficult. Subjecting exports to reserve adequacy tests can stimulate exploration and increase reserve replacement ratios. If this potential incentive does not succeed in increasing reserves, export levels will have to be further reduced.

The benefits implicit in designing more intelligent exploration and development strategies can be substantial. The economic value of better reservoir management can be as significant as discoveries of potential new resources. Moderating the environmental impact of exploration and production activities can reduce economic and social costs. The reduction of safety risks at PEMEX's oil and gas facilities is an obligation that must not be further postponed. A new regulatory authority will have to play a greater and more responsible role in the extraction of subsoil resources. Many lessons can be derived from experiences in the North Sea, Brazil, and Canada. The Ministry of Energy must assimilate them so that it can progress more rapidly in designing a new regulatory framework and establishing an independent regulatory commission.

Ownership of the State Oil Company

The federal government and the oil industry trade union, whose representatives serve on PEMEX's board, have not fulfilled their fiduciary role with respect to its ultimate owners, the Mexican nation. The passivity with which they have exercised the property rights of this corporation has jeopardized its capacity to grow and has severely affected its performance. At the same time, the government's dysfunctional administrative interventions and recurrent political interference have been a source of serious distortions. Trade union leaders have been unable to balance their own interests with those of PEMEX, imposing vertical integration to levels that are unprecedented in the international oil industry and extracting special benefits that are inconsistent with prevailing productivity levels. Notwithstanding the progress achieved with respect to its own past, PEMEX's performance is inadequate in relation to its potential and when it is compared with the performance of international oil companies and other state-owned oil firms.

An explicit, contemporary form must be given to the state's ownership role in PEMEX, clearly differentiating its corporate functions from those that it performs as a government agent. Ownership rights cannot continue to be justified exclusively in terms of the industry's history, general references to national sovereignty, or allusions to the difficulty of forming a political consensus. The government must define the objectives of state property in the oil industry, the role of the state in PEMEX's corporate governance, and the manner in which it will exercise ownership rights.

One of the key objectives of the administrative reform of the Mexican state must be the achievement of a sharper distinction between the state and its agents, the roles of the authorities and those of the management of state-owned companies. Historically, PEMEX has operated as an extension of the federal government. Being a state monopoly and operating as a government entity has induced it to assume roles that are normally performed by the authorities and are not those of a firm that maximizes economic value. Under these conditions, that government officials are tempted to intervene directly in the management of PEMEX and that its own executives want to shape public policy formulation is not surprising. The resulting conflict has marked the relationship between the government and the company and has negatively affected their respective performance.

Even though the government should not intervene in the day-to-day management of state firms, granting them managerial autonomy assumes a precise definition of the objectives against which their performance can be appraised and making senior and midlevel management accountable for company results. PEMEX has not concluded what has been a long transition with respect to the definition of its corporate mission, moving from one that pursues multiple, conflicting objectives—such as employment, regional development, industrialization, energy self-sufficiency, and technological change—to one whose central objective is long-term maximization of economic value, subject to public policy and regulatory constraints. Fortunately, value creation has become an increasingly important reference in decision making and the legitimacy of this objective is questioned less frequently. However, PEMEX still has a long way to go in fully implementing this objective and in internalizing it in the corporate culture. Also a number of social groups and political currents prefer to see PEMEX as an organization that contributes directly to the achievement of traditional objectives, regardless of the economic costs that might be incurred. PEMEX management is lagging in its ability to define, allocate, and assume responsibility for results. Given the number and diversity of the administrative and financial constraints PEMEX management faces, finding explanations, if not justifications, for inadequate performance is always possible.

Government authorities, in their capacity as the owner's representatives, have not exercised the needed leadership. Their intervention has focused on fixing budgetary caps, monitoring compliance with the caps, and auditing budgetary controls. Top and midlevel management have responded by avoiding personal risks. This effort absorbs a large part of their energy, lengthens the time needed for decision making, and discourages initiative. Better, more detailed, and more transparent financial, operational, and audit reports provide evidence that inadequate results and failure to achieve targets have limited consequences. PEMEX has made remarkable progress with regard to the availability and timeliness of the reports it submits to regulators, both domestic and international. Paradoxically, establishing more precise objectives and targets and measuring performance has not contributed to a better allocation of responsibility over performance. A key link is missing, namely, incentives—positive and negative, short term and long-term, monetary and other types—that condition managerial and employee behavior are not aligned and structured in ways that improve performance.

Exercising property rights effectively and strengthening corporate governance processes require basic changes in the composition and operation of PEMEX's board of directors and of the boards of its subsidiary operating companies. These have been particularly ineffectual. Important decisions are not taken at their meetings and few of their members consider their participation in them among their main responsibilities. Low attendance records by board members and their formal substitutes are telling. The boards do not have the committees that deal with specific topics in greater depth as is common corporate practice. PEMEX's board does not even have an audit committee. In most instances, differentiating the role of board members from the one they play as government officials is not possible, creating clear conflicts of interest. The large trade union representation on PEMEX's board limits the nature of the topics that are discussed as well as the discussion itself. Under these circumstances board meetings are largely ceremonial. They are not a forum where the owner's representatives give guidance, delegate powers, and hold management accountable. Its main function is of a latent nature: it is at these meetings that potential and effective vetoes relating to specific issues that may affect any of the parties are posed.

The minister of energy chairs PEMEX's board. Its members are the ministers of finance, communications and transport, environment and natural resources, and the economy; one representative from the Office of the President; the comptroller as representative of the Ministry of Public Administration; and five trade union members. Board members can delegate their participation to designated substitutes. PEMEX's operating subsidiaries follow a different pattern. Their boards are headed by PEMEX's chief operating officer, and their board members are the chief operating officers of the four subsidiaries and representatives of the ministries that are on PEMEX's board. Trade union representatives are not included. None of the board members are appointed in their personal capacities, thereby forgoing the possibility of having independent directors.

In recent years, two initiatives to restructure these boards have failed. The first was limited to substituting the four government ministers with eminent Mexican business people. Aside from the legal impediments that this presidential proposal faced, its objective was mainly symbolic in that it left the trade union representation and governance processes intact. The second proposal exclusively addressed corporate questions, but did not consider any changes in the more general issues of the industry's governance and did not resolve basic problems regarding the relationships between the government and the state- owned oil company. It did not cope with the legal and regulatory issues that restrict the autonomy of the board. The boards of the subsidiary companies, which were established in 1992, have fostered a more robust and disaggregated flow of information. In these boards, technical and business questions are more easily discussed. Nevertheless, they have not taken full advantage of the opportunities this offered them.

Among the numerous and uncoordinated agencies that share responsibility for managing PEMEX, none unambiguously holds and exercises the property rights to the company. In these circumstances, distinguishing ownership functions from other state functions becomes more difficult. Although the Ministry of Energy is formally responsible for sectoral coordination, the Ministry of Finance holds the more important and effective instruments of control in the current institutional setting. The Ministry of Public Administration plays a critical role in the auditing and control functions of state-owned companies and in overseeing the behavior of PEMEX's officers and midlevel managers. Other public agencies intervene directly in specific areas, increasing the complexity of interministerial coordination.

The indifference and negligence regarding energy policy, the regulation of the oil industry and its markets, and the exercise of the state's property rights reflect a failure of political will, imagination, and leadership. These critical matters are fundamental aspects of the structural reforms that are required by the oil sector. They have been postponed by the urgency associated with short-term problems. They also reflect conflicts of interests that have not been constructively resolved. The lack of basic understanding with respect to the oil industry's future has fostered the predominance of simplistic views that have trivialized public debate. Some political currents have looked for inspiration in a golden age of the oil industry that never existed. Others are equally frustrated and impatient to dismantle the current industry structure, but they do not have a consistent alternative proposal and are unwilling to assume the costs of privatization and the possible denationalization of the oil industry.

Main Actors' Behavior

The structure of the oil industry and its pattern of governance influence the behavior of its main actors and determine their attitudes with regard to the modernization of PEMEX. Because of their influence and power, three prominent players stand out: the federal government, the energy-intensive industrial firms, and the trade union. Their ambivalence about and opposition to oil industry reform have delayed and canceled proposals for change. Despite the diversity of their points of view and interests, they have done so without necessarily colluding. In some instances they have vetoed initiatives that one of them supported, contributing to the lack of consensus that has prevailed with respect to the future of the oil industry. None of these groups is satisfied with the status quo, but what brings them together is the perception that basic change could eliminate the benefits and privileges they have enjoyed for many years. The behavior of these actors reinforces the powerful inertia associated with the structural continuity that has characterized the oil industry.

The Federal Government

The government's conduct with regard to energy policy, oil industry regulation, and property rights has been discussed. This section considers only the government's relationship with other stakeholders.

The divergence and conflict of interests within the government in relation to PEMEX during the Fox administration were quite evident. These originated in the lack of clarity of the objectives, roles, and responsibilities of the multiple government agents that participate in the oil industry. For instance, as the Ministry of Finance strived to maximize oil revenues and control PEMEX's expenditure, it confronted the Ministry of Energy, which had in turn formed an alliance with energy-intensive firms that were demanding lower prices for energy and basic petrochemicals. Meanwhile PEMEX sought protection from the control mechanisms put in place by the ministries of Public Administration and Finance. It also reached a number of agreements with the trade union, all of which had a detrimental effect on public finances. At the same time, PEMEX strived for a reduction in the implicit price subsidies that it was obliged to grant on behalf of the government.

The Ministry of Energy was not strong enough to coordinate PEMEX and the Comisión Federal de Electricidad in matters pertaining to liquefied natural gas, cogeneration facilities, and fuel policy. As Congress tried to play a more active role in the design and implementation of oil policy, the context in which PEMEX operated became more complex. Under these circumstances, disorderly decision making deeply affected PEMEX and did not allow any changes in corporate governance.

Large Consumers

Consumer groups, political parties, and public opinion have pressured government authorities to exert direct and effective price controls on oil products and natural gas. During the 2006 presidential elections, two of the main candidates supported this aspiration and committed themselves to a general reduction in oil product prices and electricity tariffs. They were further supported by the media. For many years, the government maintained a policy of low fuel prices. It saw this as an industrial policy tool that supported urbanization and social welfare and justified massive subsidies in light of its promotion and redistribution goals. During the 1980s, the final consumer prices of certain types of fuel were substantially lower than their import prices. This situation began to change later in the decade and during the early 1990s, when the government attempted to align domestic prices with the cost of energy from alternative sources. Since that time, vehicle fuel prices have been fixed in relation to expected annual inflation. For industrial fuels, the policy consisted of trying to bring producer prices in line with their opportunity costs in an open economy. The reference market for both was the U.S. coast of the Gulf of Mexico. Final consumer prices for gasoline, diesel fuel, and jet fuel were similar to the average U.S. price for each, though, at times, domestic prices in Mexico were slightly higher than in the United States. At the same time, these prices were by far the lowest of Organisation for Economic Co-operation and Development member countries' prices. Moreover, industrial fuel prices tended to remain below U.S. prices.

Given the dramatic oil price increases that began in 2004, gasoline and diesel prices have lagged behind U.S. references. The domestic price trajectory was fixed by the government at the end of the previous year, excise taxes were adjusted every month, and eventually subsidies were granted. At the beginning, PEMEX had to pay these subsidies, but in 2006 the government finally absorbed them. However, PEMEX had to pay in full for the implicit natural gas and liquefied petroleum gas subsidies. Maintaining subsidies has hindered the introduction of competition in these markets.

The regressive nature of some of these subsidies has not been fully recognized. Sales of natural gas are highly concentrated. In April 2007, the 10 largest buyers accounted for 66 percent of PEMEX's sales, while residential and commercial customers represented less than 10 percent of total natural gas sales. Automotive fuel subsidies are also highly regressive. The largest consumers of gasoline are high-income households and low-income groups that do not own cars. The impact of gasoline prices on the cost of public transport is relatively low. Other cost components—vehicle acquisition, maintenance, and labor—have a much higher incidence.

The demand for subsidies, explicit or implicit, focuses on goods and services supplied by state-owned companies and is based on the notion that government pricing must necessarily pursue distributive and industrial policy objectives. This assumes that the state has discretional power to fix prices below opportunity costs. Yet the same industrial groups that support natural gas subsidies—the so-called Mexico price—would not tolerate price controls in their own products at levels below those of alternative external supplies. Their competitiveness is based on their total cost structure and not on the price of fuel, which is one of many factors. In addition, identifying alternative price formation criteria for tradable goods other than opportunity costs is conceptually difficult. Politically, direct allocation to private individuals of the economic rent generated by oil is even more difficult to justify.

Introducing competition in oil product, natural gas, and basic petrochemical markets, as well as opening the oil industry to private investment, presupposes the establishment of competitive prices. Under current market conditions, this implies an increase in domestic prices. It is not a temporary anomaly. Deferring price adjustments tends to make things worse. However, liberalizing these markets poses complex challenges: a first step is eliminating subsidies and increasing producer prices. In the area of natural gas, the short-term interests of industrial groups are clearly opposed to those of the federal government. The CRE will have to adjust the regulated price regime; otherwise, it will lose credibility. The Ministry of Finance will need to revise its automotive fuel price policy in 2008 and should transfer this function to the CRE. These measures should be implemented in the context of midterm and long-term pricing policy that will give consumers greater certainty and modify false expectations about the domestic price trajectory of oil products and natural gas. These policies must take into account a wider set of objectives that go beyond increasing government revenue, and prices should be determined by well-defined, explicit rules.

The Sindicato de Trabajadores Petroleros

The collective labor contract between PEMEX and the trade union and the behavior of the union's leadership pose serious obstacles to PEMEX's operational efficiency and productivity. Its high staffing levels are explained by systematic overemployment in all areas of activity, the high level of vertical integration, and the internal provision of a wide array of ancillary goods and services that transcend conventional corporate limits. The resulting scale of trade union membership gives it considerable regional and national political influence. The trade union exerts rigid control over the workplace, fills positions that in other companies are normally assigned to nonunionized personnel, and imposes restrictions on hiring nonunion employees. Union members' pay and benefits are above those prevailing in other industries, periodic compensation adjustments are not linked to productivity, and contingent labor liabilities weigh heavily on PEMEX's financial results. The union's behavior and that of its leaders reflect the authoritarian culture that has prevailed despite Mexico's democratization. The labor market structure is a bilateral monopoly in which PEMEX is the only buyer and the trade union is the only seller. The firm also operates a monopoly for its own products and the trade union plays a political role that strengthens its position with respect to management and guarantees greater control over its members.

PEMEX provides multiple, measurable examples of overemployment. The best documented case can be found in its refineries. Periodic benchmarking since 1991 shows that the wage bill Mexican refineries pay is similar to that of equivalent refineries on the U.S. Gulf coast, even though average wages in this sector in the United States are six times higher than in PEMEX refineries. The examples of overemployment refer to high employment levels driven by contractual workforce rigidities: thousands of workers are formally assigned to facilities that were closed many years ago, and high regional employment levels are sustained despite substantial decreases in activity levels. Outsourcing a number of specialized activities would reduce PEMEX's headcount without modifying the scope of the state monopoly. Such restructuring could yield substantial benefits: PEMEX could reduce costs, acquire more advanced technologies, adopt better industrial practices, and enhance its capacity to execute its functions. However, the union opposes such proposals.

The wage and total compensation structure is the outcome of periodic collective bargaining. It does not respond to broader institutional objectives nor is it the result of a consistent compensation policy. Wage negotiations are constrained by the long-term relationship between the parties, as well as by their awareness of the critical importance of security of supply on other industries and on society as a whole, in addition to its public finance implications.

In addition to attractive wages, the terms and conditions of retirement are exceptionally generous. Life cycle compensation promotes lifetime employment. Furthermore, recruitment practices promote the hiring of other family members at or before retirement. The cost of all these benefits is high. By the end of 2005, current benefit liabilities had reached Mex$267 billion and postretirement benefits accounted for another Mex$201 billion. Total labor liabilities of Mex$486 billion are higher than net PEMEX debt and equivalent to 45 percent of total company assets. Given that only a small fraction of labor liabilities are funded and that they may be underestimated, the situation is unsustainable. Pension, health service, and other benefits will have to be modified in the near future.

The trade union has played an important role in the Mexican political system. As has been the case with other large public-sector trade unions, it was organically tied to the Institutional Revolutionary Party and its predecessors. Since the nationalization of the oil industry it has played a significant symbolic function. The economic resources that it has accumulated have allowed the trade union to participate actively in national and regional politics. Some of its members have been elected to Congress, and others have held political appointments in oil-producing regions. The trade union was always prominent in diverse forms of political mobilization that were favored by the corporatist political regime. Since 1988, many union members stopped voting for the Institutional Revolutionary Party, transferring their loyalty to the Party of the Democratic Revolution in the municipalities where the oil industry is located. However, the trade union leadership continued to support the Institutional Revolutionary Party up to the elections in 2000.

As electoral competition increased, the ballot box became the main source of political legitimacy, and mass mobilization, an activity in which the union excelled, lost relevance. This fundamental change of circumstances poses serious challenges for the union's leadership. The trade union's relationship with the government, and with political parties, will necessarily change. However, new patterns of political interaction have not yet come into play. In this political transition, the union has maintained a lower public profile. The governing National Action Party has granted the trade union exceptional benefits and has conceded additional privileges in the workplace. This conduct is puzzling given the National Action Party's traditional perception of large trade unions as the paradigm of corporatist corruption in the authoritarian state that prevailed until 2000.

Other Relevant Actors

Two other stakeholders affect oil industry performance: nonunion employees and local communities in the main oil-producing regions. PEMEX's technical and managerial personnel face serious problems caused by the lack of a clear definition of their objectives and the scope of their activities, the personal legal risks involved in complying with detailed formal administrative controls, and the political cycles that influence career development in PEMEX. The quality of the staff that is recruited is also affected by these problems and by the absence of competitive recruitment patterns, active retention mechanisms for highly qualified personnel, and explicit employment termination rules.

The company has not developed career planning functions for its technical, midlevel, and executive personnel. In-house training programs are limited and inadequate, and graduate-level education opportunities are scarce. The industry's monopolistic structure restricts the possibility of gaining relevant professional experience outside of PEMEX, thus contributing to an insular corporate culture. Furthermore, the average age of professional personnel has increased given long periods of downsizing and of reduced recruitment. Staff retention measures privileged those with long careers and offered few incentives to younger, talented employees. In addition, the various risks—administrative, legal, and reputational—associated with a career in the oil industry have tended to increase more rapidly than total compensation and job satisfaction. This has taken place in a context where professional careers in the public sector have been losing prestige. These trends have eroded the traditional pride associated with being part of the Mexican oil industry, a highly valued institutional asset.

PEMEX has historically been dominated at all levels by a bureaucratic logic, not a corporate one. The perceived mission of professional employees is one of public service, instead of being geared to creating economic value subject to government policies and regulation. This generalized perception is reflected in the scarcity of managerial skills, in a corporate culture that does not value innovation and entrepreneurship, and in the reluctance to allocate and assume responsibility. A strong risk aversion is present at all levels of the corporate hierarchy. For these reasons, management centers its attention on the use and control of instruments and on process, but not on the outcomes of its decisions.

A scarcity of midlevel and top-level managerial skills and the deficient professionalization of such staff is prevalent in the firm. Even executives identify themselves as technical personnel. However, highly specialized technical careers have lacked support, given that promotion and access to well-compensated positions necessarily imply greater managerial responsibility. This pattern has increasing negative consequences as the level of scientific, technical, and engineering knowledge required by the industry continues to grow. The entry of high-level government officials has not contributed much to a more managerial culture within PEMEX, as their expertise lies in the political sphere and in public administration. The hiring of experienced managers from the private sector has been limited and their performance has not been satisfactory. The firm has been unable to develop the managerial capacities it requires in-house. It needs managers capable of submitting themselves to market discipline and competition. It must train high-level technical teams that can cope with a rapidly changing industrial environment. Weak instruments limit managerial performance, subjecting it to the inertia of mechanical routine. The state oil company must introduce an ambitious program to deal with these constraints and must prepare for the generational renewal that will soon take place.

PEMEX and local authorities have been unable to manage adequately the environmental and social impact of the industry's operations in the communities where its production and manufacturing facilities are located. Unfortunately, the improvement in its environmental performance is long overdue and continues to be unsatisfactory. The principle that the polluter must pay for the damage it causes and cover the costs of remediation has been applied erratically.

The social consequences of oil industry activity have varied over time and across regions. Currently, more than 80 percent of oil production comes from offshore fields far from important population centers under conditions that differ significantly from those that prevailed onshore, in Tabasco and Chiapas, in the 1970s and 1980s.

Damage claims in some regions have been the object of direct political action. This, in turn, has encouraged individual and collective rent-seeking behavior. PEMEX is particularly vulnerable to these types of actions. The cost of interrupting production is high, both in terms of deferred production and the potential damage to oil wells and other facilities and of the safety risks involved. As a state-owned company, PEMEX faces additional political constraints in comparison with private firms. This further weakens its position, particularly when it must deal with local political mobilization. One of the outcomes of this pattern of behavior is the steady increase in the number of claims. Local and state authorities and political groups take advantage of this perverse dynamic to further their specific interests. It can only be addressed by improving the environmental performance of PEMEX and its contractors and by social interventions that are more sensitive to the problems of the local communities where they operate.

The challenges are not small given the extreme poverty that prevails next to large, modern industrial facilities with well-paid workers. Special attention must be paid to the owners of lands that are occupied by PEMEX and to the terms and conditions under which PEMEX makes use of land that it occupies temporarily. Positive incentives linked to the continuity of the firm's operations must be put in place. Finally, rigorous application of the law in these land-related conflicts must guide the behavior of the state-owned company and the relevant authorities.

Proposed Initiatives

The complex problems the oil industry faces have no simple solutions. Market forces on their own cannot solve them and neither can exclusive recourse to direct government intervention. Devising creative and pragmatic alternatives that combine and structure vigorous market development with more precise and effective state intervention is the only way these challenges can be met. The required structural change takes time, and it is therefore unlikely to be carried out during a single government administration. Moreover, as these reforms incur considerable and immediate political costs whose benefits will only be reaped by future administrations, a mature and responsible vision and a long-term commitment are needed.

The transformation of the Mexican oil industry involves multidimensional changes. Some of these must be addressed simultaneously, while others require a specific sequence. Improving the performance of state-owned companies requires a fundamental change in their industrial organization and a redefinition of the rules under which they operate. Liberalizing markets and creating a framework that will regulate competition will mold PEMEX's behavior. New forms of corporate governance and reduced vertical integration in the oil industry will facilitate its control and increase its efficiency. Under current circumstances, state intervention will have to be expanded and reinforced while simultaneously promoting the development of oil product and natural gas markets. Government control of the oil industry will strengthen as PEMEX's governance becomes more effective. In addition, as the firm's scope is more clearly and better defined and liberalization advances, a greater competitive discipline will be imposed. From another perspective, change in PEMEX's governance and limits to its scope will improve its organizational structure. In turn, new regulatory mechanisms and market liberalization could renew the institutional framework by redefining and limiting the role of the federal government. In the last instance, reform of the oil industry must be based on decisive modernization of organizations and institutions.

This overall scheme frames changes in corporate governance within the more general context of transformation of the industry's governance. Modernizing corporate governance and granting PEMEX greater managerial autonomy cannot advance without broader regulatory change and new mechanisms that capture the economic rent generated by upstream activities. The composition and structure of PEMEX's board is of limited relevance if its decision-making powers and the nature of its relationship with the government and the trade union are not fundamentally modified. It is possible that competition in final product markets will not discipline the behavior of PEMEX sufficiently. An option that could then be considered is private minority participation in ownership of the company. This could be proposed, together with the opening of the oil industry to private investment, after the reform of its governance has made substantial progress. Restructuring property rights in the oil industry must be preceded by the adoption of a new regulatory framework inspired by long-term public policies and the development of independent institutions that can protect national interests. That is why changes in property rights will have to await a second generation of reforms.

The following six interrelated reform initiatives are proposed:

• The adoption of an energy policy consistent with other long-term public policies that gives a clear sense of strategic direction, proposes a new industrial architecture, offers new forms of governance for the energy sector, and develops the institutions that could guide and implement it.

- An administrative reform that complements and replaces direct intervention by the government with a set of rules that allows the development of hydrocarbon markets. Regulations of a general nature that control state firms, including budgetary controls, must be fundamentally revised, restricting and channeling administrative and political intervention by the government.
- A regulatory reform of the energy sector that will guide the transition from a monopoly structure to one of regulated competition, establishing a competitive price regime and contributing to market development and the promotion of emerging economic agents.
- The strengthening of regulatory institutions in the energy sector, broadening their scope, endowing them with adequate technical and financial resources, and guaranteeing their independence with respect to private and government interests. Their scope would extend along the entire value chain, from upstream activities to final product markets.
- The design and implementation of an oil tax regime capable of capturing the economic rent associated with upstream activities. The midstream and downstream activities are to be taxed according to general rules normally applied to other manufacturing and commercial activities of the Mexican economy.
- A disciplined exercise of property rights pertaining to subsoil resources and to state-owned companies in the energy sector must be ensured by the establishment of precise limits to government responsibilities, clear rules of access to subsoil resources, and new corporate governance structures and processes for state-owned firms.

These initiatives are fully compatible with the preservation of PEMEX as a dominant, integrated oil company, managed commercially and with an unequivocal national identity.

Note

1. All PEMEX data in this section were obtained from publications available on PEMEX's Web site: http://www.PEMEX.com. The most complete PEMEX annual report is the one filed with the U.S. Securities and Exchange Commission, Form 20-F, which is also available on PEMEX's Web site. Public finance and balance-of-trade data are from http://www.shcp.gob.mx.

Index

Figures, notes, and tables are denoted by f, n, and t, following the page numbers.